ARE YOU IN THE HOUSE ALONE?

GROWING UP WITH GARGOYLES, GIANT TURTLES, VALERIE HARPER, THE COLD WAR, STEPHEN KING & CO-ED CALL GIRLS

A TV MOVIE COMPENDIUM

1964-1999

EDITED BY AMANDA REYES

A HEADPRESS BOOK

CONTENTS

ACKNOWLEDGEMENTS...**1**
FOREWORD *by Jeff Burr* **3**

ESSAYS

FROM CLASSY TO TRASHY: An Introduction To The
Made-For-Television Movie *by Amanda Reyes*...**5**

LEATHER & LACE: A List Of The Made For TV Machismo & Small
Screen Scream Queens Of The 1970s That Rocked Our World
by Amanda Reyes **13**

BLESS THE BEASTS & THE NETWORKS: Eco-Horror Hits The
Small Screen *by Lee Gambin*............................. **19**

RAPE-REVENGE & RAPE-RESPONSE: Narratives Of Sexual Violence &
Justice In The TV Movie *by Jennifer Wallis*..... **25**

WES CRAVEN'S SMALL SCREEN HORROR FILMS: A Retrospective
by Amanda Reyes **32**

THE USA WORLD PREMIERE MOVIE: The Forgotten Red-Headed
Stepchild Of Film Noir *by Paul Freitag-Fey*...... **37**

LOCATING SEXUAL ABUSE IN THE TV MOVIE: From Dangerous Dads
To Day Care *by Jennifer Wallis* **43**

TELEMOVIE MASHUPS *by Amanda Reyes*........ **49**

THE COLD WAR TURNS HOT ON TV: World War III In
Television Movies *by David Ray Carter*............. **56**

LIFE MODEL DECOY: The Plight Of The Small Screen
Comic Book Superhero *By David Kerekes*........ **59**

NIGHTMARE IN BADHAM COUNTY & A BRIEF HISTORY OF SMALL
SCREEN EXPLOITATION: Going Down South & Behind Bars
by Amanda Reyes **63**

YOU CAN GO HOME AGAIN: The Popularity Of The Reunion
TV Movie *by Amanda Reyes* **70**

SCRATCHING ON GLASS: An Introduction To Stephen King
On Television *by Lance Vaughan*...................... **75**

REVIEWS

Stephen King TV Movies **78**
The TV Miniseries **92**
1964–1979 .... **107**
1980–1989 .... **225**
1990–1999 .... **283**

APPENDIX

Cable and the 2000s **308**
Select Bibliography... **325**
Contributor Notes **326**
Index... **330**
About this book.. **338**

This book is dedicated to my husband, David Cohen for his unwavering love and support.

And to the memory of my parents, Joan and Armando Reyes. They had no idea what they unleashed when they let me watch *Trilogy of Terror* with them.

ACKNOWLEDGEMENTS

First and foremost, I would like to express my sincerest gratitude to David Kerekes and Headpress for giving me an opportunity to put together the kind of book I have always wanted to read. David is a great cheerleader in all the best ways, offering guidance and giving me space to offer suggestions. Honestly, my appreciation goes beyond words. So I will just say thank you.

I am also extremely grateful to each and every contributor of this book. Thank you for all of your hard work and patience.

I should add that I wouldn't be here writing an acknowledgment page for a finished manuscript on television films if it weren't for the constant support of my husband, David Cohen. He's my best friend, greatest companion and champion. His willingness to sit through *This House Possessed* each and every time I want to watch it proves his dedication to the cause. Thank you. And I love you.

And a special shout out to the late TV movie historian, Alvin H. Marill, whose *Movies Made for Television* is essentially my Bible. His book laid the groundwork for this journey, and for that I am forever grateful. Rest in peace, sir.

Finally, I'd like to thank all of the people who made and still make television films. You have constantly provided me a place of comfort, warmth and joy. Thank you.

—*Amanda Reyes*

FOREWORD
BY JEFF BURR

The network TV movie of the 1960s and seventies is a strange beast, caught between the two poles of "Cinema" and the invasive, pervasive electronic box that Hollywood initially feared but grew to love. Framed at the Academy ratio of 1.33, which fit perfectly in the pre-HD square Magnavoxes, Motorolas and RCAs, critics likened the TV movie as the next generation "B" film. And there is some truth to that, as most of the TV movies trafficked in genre subjects and featured familiar actors. But the TV movies had more promotion and an individual identity. Creating movies, real movies, for a new medium with its own unique pluses and minuses involved some artistic pioneering.

The filmmakers who worked on these movies rarely got any real recognition or critical ink, but many of the films got European theatrical releases and played in syndication for years. Directors like Paul Wendkos, Lamont Johnson, Joseph Sargent, William Graham, William Hale and John Moxey worked under incredibly difficult conditions, shooting these movies in anywhere from twelve to eighteen days, and often with incredibly shortened postproduction schedules. In a very real sense, the networks didn't need it great, they needed it Tuesday.

As a kid growing up in a small town in Georgia in the late 1960s through the seventies, entertainment options were limited at best. Being a precocious cinephile, a weekly ritual for me was looking at the TV Guide for the week and seeing what new movies were going to be showing, carefully noting the day and time. A campaign of anticipation then followed, hyping the movie to reserve that timeslot in a one-TV house. More often than not, my mom and dad would be caught up in my enthusiasm (ANDY GRIFFITH AND CAPTAIN KIRK ON MOTORCYCLES YOU GUYS!! WHAT COULD BE COOLER???), and we would be rewarded by seeing *Pray for the Wildcats*, *A Cold Night's Death*, *Birds of Prey* or *Brian's Song*.

The elementary school version of the "water cooler conversation" was at the monkey bars on the playground. It was there where you learned what you missed, or could tell what you saw. "Did you see that movie last night? Andy Griffith played this asshole and he got killed riding off a cliff!!" You could rate how the movie entered the zeitgeist by the amount of kids who chimed in and the intensity of the discussion.

And in those days, watching these made for television movies, you knew when they were really special. Some of them just stood out, by way of craft, story and acting. *Duel* is probably the best example of that. I saw it on the premiere night, and my whole family was riveted. No one walked out of the room, not even during the commercials. I don't know how Spielberg did it, and he says he doesn't either. But probably the biggest single reaction I can remember at my house was for *Born Innocent*. My dad, my brother and I were watching it, and the infamous (and later cut) scene with "Johnny" played out. Dead silence, then my dad turned to us both and said, "I cannot believe what I just saw."

It is instant nostalgia for me and for many people when you see Doug Trumball's slit-scan intro, hear Burt Bacharach's instrumental Nikki and see the bold titles ABC Movie of the Week. It brings back more than just the movies… it brings back a time, a place and a moment when your television set turned into a bona fide movie theater and anything was possible. This book will go a long way to rectify the lack of recognition of about thirty years of American cinema that happened to unspool over the airwaves, but totally worthy of a much bigger screen.

FROM CLASSY TO TRASHY: AN INTRODUCTION TO THE MADE FOR TELEVISION MOVIE

BY AMANDA REYES

The seventies are considered the heyday of the made for television movie, and serve as an important benchmark in the landscape of our society. Although the first official telefilm, *See How They Run* premiered all the way back in 1964, this new version of the feature film didn't really come into its own until a few years later.[1] While TV movies appear in different shapes and genres, the medium, even in its most generic form, was a hit, and thousands of films were released on network television over the next few decades.

It is important to remember that in the earliest days of the television movie, there were only three major networks (four if you count PBS), and a lot of eyes were glued to the boob tube nightly. Network executives devised the TVM (TV movie) as an "event," which is not an overexaggeration. Designed to air once or twice, or, if you were lucky, maybe a few more times in syndication, this was the world before time shifting devices like the VCR, or DV-R, and On Demand or streaming selections, giving people one shot to catch the program as it aired in real time. Nielson numbers were vastly different as well. If a program catches ten million viewers today, it's considered a success, whereas, almost three times as many people were tuning into television shows in the seventies.

But aside from tailoring the TVM as event programming, it inadvertently served another purpose. For audiences who did not have the luxury of living in a major city, this particular era of the telefilm became a looking glass into

---

1 The first made for television movie was actually slated to be Don Siegel's *The Killers*, but was eventually released theatrically due to its violent content.

the world of genre cinema. Largely considered the bastard stepchild of its silver screen counterparts, the made for television movie shared much with the drive-in and grindhouse theaters: TV movies also wrangled with low budgets, slumming film stars and tight shooting schedules. If not working outside of the rules, the telefilm still found ways around them, often creating stark messages about the changes in the world around us. However, at the time, exploitation cinema was mostly the reserve of urban meccas that could entice a profit-making audience. Those of us left out of this movement of independent genre film instead had three networks competing for our time and attention. In the decadent seventies mass appeal exploitation topics such as hitchhiking, satanic creatures and voyeurism kept audiences glued to their seats. Regardless of whether the networks were eager to cash in on controversial subjects or had a more commendable notion in mind, these movies reflect an era, and serve as a boob-tubed time capsule for a generation who recall many of these telefilms fondly.

The difference between the experiences of viewing a film in the theater as opposed to viewing a movie on television is fairly obvious. The theater is an all-encompassing and strangely community driven act, even though it takes place in the dark and among strangers, whereas the television movie (or even a theatrical film on TV) is seen from the comfort of home, and with the potential for a lot more distraction. The telefilm structure itself is made for commercials, and with an eye on Federal Communications Commission (FCC) regulations. Also, at least in the seventies, television was free, and the idea of diving into a TVM probably seemed like less of a risk than shelling out hard earned cash for a film the viewer might not like. And, did you really have anything better to do Tuesday night?

It is with the idea that mass audiences would eagerly tune into these films that the legendary Movie of the Week was born. In the seventies all three networks were producing television movies but it's the ABC Movie of the Week that is the best remembered. In fact, "[in] 1971–72, eighteen of the twenty-three top-rated films broadcast on television were ABC [television movies]."[2] A good portion of the most memorable films, such as *Crowhaven Farm* (1970), *Killdozer* (1974), *Trilogy of Terror* (1975), and arguably the most famous television movie of all, *Duel* (1971),[3] aired on ABC between 1969–76. The television movie concept proved so popular the network began airing telefilms several nights a week.

In business terms, the profit to be turned from these often-minor potboilers was undeniable. Telefilms regularly cost under $1 million, and

2 Billy Ingram, "A Short History of the Movie of the Week," *TV Party* website.
3 Technically, *Duel* aired as part of an ABC Movie of the Week offshoot: The ABC Movie of the Weekend.

Darren McGavin in *The Night Stalker*, one of the highest rated telefilms of all time.

drew audiences of twenty-four million or more.[4] There was no denying that the networks might not have the complete attention of a mass audience, but they certainly had the ratings. And, this new medium for television quickly arose as *the* form of programming, with genre movies advancing to the forefront. For instance, *The Night Stalker* (1972) remains one of the highest rated telefilms of all time, enjoying a ratings/share of 33.2/48[5] (which in laymen terms simply means that over thirty-three million households tuned in, accounting for forty-eight percent of the viewing audience)! Good numbers indeed. Most films were shot in as little as two or three weeks, and subsequently it became almost necessary for networks to reflect what was going on in exploitation cinema, at least in terms of production, just to keep up with the vast array of looming airdates.

Like its theatrical counterparts, the quickies were often genre films exploiting the audience's love for anything potentially tawdry or exploitive. Dozens and maybe even hundreds of telefilms took its audience to task with varying results. One of the biggest road bumps for genre television films, of course, is working within the restrictions brought upon by the conservative whims of the FCC, which greatly limits the telefilm's ability to use manipulative shocks. One creative method many TVMs still employ to perk up interest can be found in the salacious titles that bring with them a

4 Kerry Segrave, *Movies at Home: How Hollywood Came to Television*, pp.113–114.
5 Cobbett S. Steinberg, *TV Facts*, p.181.

promise of an exciting night of television. TV movies like *Weekend of Terror* (1970), *Shark Kill* (1976), *Mysterious Island of Beautiful Women* (1979), and *Vacation in Hell* (1979), rarely live up to their sensational monikers, but when they do, they become instant and unforgettable classics.

Indeed, when the telefilm knocks it out of the park, it finds enthusiastic fans for life. There are several small screen movies that are widely considered bona fide cult classics. *Don't Be Afraid of the Dark* (1973), *Bad Ronald* (1974), and *Satan's Triangle* (1975) are now part of a familiar lexicon that represents just a small percentage of original films produced in the early years. The classics arguably brought viewers to their knees, but are still like much of the general telefilm output in that these films travel at a much slower pace than a theatrical release, relying heavily on the ability to sustain suspense without the use of visceral shocks. It was here that the art of genre movies made for television began to fall into the hands of a few skillful directors, producers and writers who took the small screen by storm.

Perhaps the most famous producer of television genre films is Dan Curtis who is also noted for his prolific directing career. After running the show at the popular gothic soap opera *Dark Shadows* (1966–71), Curtis moved to the world of the telefilm, unleashing the popular *Night Stalker* in 1972, which introduced Carl Kolchak to the world and spawned a sequel and subsequent short-lived television series. One of the reasons Curtis excelled in the art of small screen horror was his understanding of the medium as one of restrained terror. In an interview from 1973, Curtis remarked, "Some producers don't care about the story. It's just an excuse to get a couple of quarts of blood on the screen. That's not what scares. It's a mood, a feeling, a whole ambience."[6] And while not always wholly successful, Curtis would go on to produce and/or direct a flurry of entertaining television films, including *Scream of the Wolf* (1974), *Melvin Purvis G-MAN* (1974), *Trilogy of Terror* (1975), and the *Supertrain* pilot, *Express to Terror* (1979), eventually helming the epic and breathtaking miniseries *Winds of War* (1983).

Often working with Curtis was famed author Richard Matheson, who tapped into audiences' fears like no other. Perhaps best known for penning the classic *Duel* (directed by a fledgling Steven Spielberg), Matheson created incredibly memorable telefilm fare that was brought to life by Curtis, including the two Kolchak TV movies, as well as *Dracula* (1974), and the Zuni fetish doll segment of *Trilogy of Terror* (1975). Sharing the same horror sensibilities, Matheson "preferred to be called a terror writer rather than a horror writer because he considered horror to be merely blood-and-guts gore."[7]

6 Associated Press, "TV Horror Film Director Ready to Drive the Stake," *Ocala Star-Banner*, May 20, 1973.
7 Jeff Thompson, *The Television Horrors of Dan Curtis*, p.15.

With *The Over the Hill Gang*, the ABC Movie of the Week arrives!

With Curtis and Matheson churning out the more critically regarded genre films, another giant, but not necessarily a recognized face behind television films, is the escapist king himself, Aaron Spelling. In the seventies, Spelling made his own share of classics, and one of his most famous telefilms is the chilling *Home for the Holidays* (1972), which is the closest the older network TVM ever got to a pure slasher.[8] Later, Spelling would grit his teeth over being called the "Cotton Candy King of TV,"[9] but he was indeed fond of a lot of those early outings, stating the appeal of these projects: "They wanted different kinds of characters. Not everybody had to be a Marcus Welby-like hero. They wanted characters with flaws, ones that didn't have to return the following week, and they wanted to attract actors, writers, and directors who didn't want to commit to five years of a series."[10] True to his groundbreaking nature, Spelling's *The Over the Hill Gang* was the first telefilm to go into production under the ABC Movie of the Week moniker, although *Seven in Darkness* would air first.[11] Spelling would produce approximately 140 made for television films in his lifetime.

Throughout its most popular run, several journeymen directors lent a confident, if often workmanlike, hand to the genre telefilm. One of the most prolific is John Llewellyn Moxey. Moxey collaborated with both Curtis (*The Night Stalker*), and Spelling (*Home for the Holidays*), always reigning in the violence but making up for it with atmosphere, as well as pulling wonderful performances out of his stars, who were working on agonizingly short shooting schedules. He is behind dozens of other well-regarded titles,

8 Indeed, *Home for the Holidays* is often noted as a "proto-slasher" because of how accurately it mimics the slasher subgenre before it was even a subgenre.
9 Aaron Spelling. *A Prime Time Life: An Autobiography*, p.115
10 Ibid., p.80.
11 Ibid. Spelling offers an erroneous synopsis for *Seven in Darkness*, stating it is "a drama about people trapped on a subway," although the film is about a plane crash.

such as *The Strange and Deadly Occurrence* (1974), *Smash-Up on Interstate 5* (1976), *No Place to Hide* (1981), and *I, Desire* (1982), among others.

Moxey was also the man who put out a telefilm that came the closest to emulating the exploitation genre. His gritty *Nightmare in Badham County* (1976) took complete advantage of beautiful women in violent situations, and overseas the film was released in a far more explicit theatrical version, brimming with T&A and violence. (See the chapter 'Nightmare in Badham County and a Brief History of Small Screen Exploitation: Going Down South and Behind Bars' for more).

Certainly, Moxey wasn't the only person rolling out one telefilm after another. There are plenty of other television directors of note, and Gordon Hessler, Jerry Jameson, Walter Grauman, Robert Day, and David Lowell Rich are just a few of the names viewers will see time and time again. Some of them, such as Jameson would direct several telefilms per year!

However, most audiences did not tune in because of the behind-the-scenes names; they were interested in who was appearing on-screen. In his book, *Movies Made for Television*, Alvin H. Marill blithely comments, "Ruth Buzzi (or James Arness or Kristy McNichol or Jack Lord or any of *Charlie's Angels*) on television is a star; in movies, she ain't."[12] Marill's humorous but somewhat cynical observation reminds one of the age-old query, "If I can watch it on TV for free, why would I want to pay for it in the theater?" But despite the idea of such pigeonholing, the telefilm provides a space for TV actors to break the mold of a long-running series in which they were so often trapped.

Perhaps one of the most notable of actors to break out of a stereotype is Andy Griffith, who took on various forms of disillusioned characters in the seventies. Following his sinister performance in *A Face in the Crowd* (1957), Griffith continued to wow audiences with shocking portrayals of the cynical "modern" man on television. In *The Strangers in 7A* (1972), he was a poor man who'd given up on life. In *Pray for the Wildcats* (1974), he was an overbearing millionaire who victimized the struggling "suits" of Middle America (while giving us the great quote, "I'm a hippie with money!"). In one of his best roles, Griffith hunted the greatest prey—man—in *Savages* (1974). A far cry from Sheriff Andy on *The Andy Griffith Show*, America's favorite country boy proved you could walk away from typecasting and sink your teeth into something meatier.

Both *Bewitched*'s Elizabeth Montgomery and the patriarch of *The Brady Bunch*, Robert Reed, used the telefilm to exercise some impressive chops.

---

12 Alvin H. Marill, *Movies Made for Television: The Telefeature and the Mini-Series 1964–1979*, p.9.

Montgomery fared a bit better critically (and was nominated for several Emmys for her television movie work), becoming the face of crimes against women with *A Case of Rape* (1974), and *Act of Violence* (1979), or switching gears to commit heinous wrongdoings in telefilms like the classic *Legend of Lizzie Borden* (1975), and *The Black Widow Murders: The Blanche Taylor Moore Story* (1993). Welcomed warmly by fans, Montgomery's prolific television movie work allowed the actress to prove she was more than a button nosed witch.

Likewise, Reed really dug into dark and lost characters: They may have lost faith (*Haunts of the Very Rich*, 1972), lost hope (*Pray for the Wildcats*, 1974), or just lost their mind (*Secret Night Caller*, 1975). Whatever he was tackling, Reed was up to the challenge and truly broke out of the good-natured father role that he feared he'd be adrift in after life as Mr. Brady.

The telefilm was also a welcoming place for classic actors hoping to make a fast buck in a medium that was still calling for them. Although it is a respectable telefilm, much of the press garnered for *The Screaming Woman* (1972) concentrated on actors the media felt had already seen their best days. The promotion for Olivia de Havilland, Joseph Cotton and Walter Pidgeon revolved around "yesterday's matinee idols"[13] and de Havilland was quoted as simply stating, "I need to work."[14] However, the viewer reception of genre films starring classic actors was always a touch kinder, and the telefilm offered a comforting place for both the actor and the audiences who loved them.

Other actors followed suit, many of whom, like de Havilland, were celebrities from a golden age of show business, whose work was drying up. Even Bing Crosby got in the act in *Dr. Cook's Garden* (1971), managing to find a leading role as an older actor, while breaking away from his (then) perceived gentle demeanor. It is also a fine example of the type of strong writing that aging actors could find on the small screen.

Even with a handful of exceptional filmmakers and eager actors working hard to churn out quality product, most television movies resorted to TV-PG related sensationalism to make up for a lack of cash, resources and/or time, and are too often considered throwaway projects. Unfortunately, while several of these small screen films have reached a cult status, few are available. The phenomenon of the television movie, while fairly well-known, still struggles for recognition and remains one of the most overlooked mediums. Why TVMs are relegated to a mere footnote of modern American

---

13 North American News Alliance, "Senior Actors Enjoy Renaissance on TV," *Sarasota Journal*, Jan 7, 1972.
14 Associated Press, "Veteran Glamor Actresses Returning to the Sound Stage," *The Telegraph*, Mar 4, 1972.

culture is anyone's guess. Certainly, the telefilm format may be more in line with factory movie making, but these small screen features crept into our living rooms night after night, and left indelible marks on many a childhood memory. Oh yeah, and that Zuni fetish doll is terrifying.

This book is split up into several sections. The first portion offers a selection of essays exploring a variety of topics ranging from Wes Craven's telefilm outings to a retrospective on the USA Network's original movie history. The next section is dedicated to Stephen King and his small screen films and miniseries, followed by a handful of reviews of some of the more popular standalone genre miniseries. Finally, the bulk of the book is comprised of capsule reviews, covering the 1960s–90s, which are split by decade and alphabetized within each section. These reviews provide director and cast credits, network listings and original airdates. There is also an appendix featuring a variety of reviews for films released after 1999 and/or for cable television.

While it would be a great pleasure to give you a review of every made for television movie produced between 1964–99, it is an impossible task. Even some of the most well-known movies remain at large (why isn't Richard Lynch's *Vampire* on DVD yet?). Therefore, we put together the best guide we could with the resources we had at our fingertips, VCRs and so forth.

This book presents many different schools of thought; there are articles and reviews that dig deep into cultural anxieties, while other submissions are simply about relishing in the fabulous fashions, sideburns and general nostalgia presented in the telefilm. The act of movie watching is an individual and intimate experience, and that is no different with the telefilm. The contributors to this book span the globe, from the United Kingdom to the United States to Australia. Much like the films presented here, their opinions and writing are as varied as the telefilms they discuss—and, in my honest opinion, just as fabulous!

So, please adjust your antenna for the best reception.

LEATHER & LACE: A LIST OF THE MADE FOR TV MACHISMO & SMALL SCREEN SCREAM QUEENS OF THE 1970S THAT ROCKED OUR WORLD

BY AMANDA REYES

There is a reason why the 1970s is the golden age of the made for television movie. While many of the stories, and sometimes the lurid advertising, drew us to the small screen, it was the cast that kept us glued to our La-Z-Boys. Actresses struck a chord as they asserted a new female-friendly strength in the age of feminism. Telefilms attempted to strike a balance between jiggle and enlightenment and many female characters were beginning to challenge men in the workplace and at home, although they still fell victim far too often. For men it was the stoic seventies, and television evoked images of a heavy drinking smoker who was a great adventurer or at least delivered a good knuckle sandwich. Of course, not all of these images were positive or correct, and many spun a myth that no mere mortal could ever hope to realize, but it made for great TV. And isn't that all that matters?

SMALL SCREEN SCREAM QUEENS

Karen Black Karen only starred in two genre TV movies in the seventies, *Trilogy of Terror* (1975) and *The Strange Possession of Mrs. Oliver* (1977), but it was her turn as four different put-upon characters in *Trilogy* that got her on the list. OK, it's really her performance in the segment 'Amelia' that

A remote island...
A silent killer...
and sheer terror for
five beautiful women
as he stalks them,
one by one.

Above: Can you tell which one of these is a Zuni fetish doll? (*Trilogy of Terror*) Right: Original *TV Guide* ad for *Five Desperate Women.*

Five Desperate Women
A World Premiere
Starring Robert Conrad, Bradford Dillman, Stefanie Powers, Anjanette Comer, Joan Hackett, Denise Nicholas and Julie Sommars.
Movie of the Week 8:30 ⑦

left an indelible mark as she is chased around her groovy apartment by a small but scary Zuni fetish doll. And the ending... Oh, *that* ending! So many of us found our way into the world of horror via Black's toothy grin at the conclusion of her excellent foray into small screen terror.

Barbara Eden Barbara sought to change her sexy genie image through several interesting telefilms. She re-teamed with her *I Dream of Jeannie* co-star, Larry Hagman in the eerie mystery *A Howling in the Woods* (1971), but it was her turn as a schizoid mother-to-be in the excellent *The Stranger Within* (1974) where she was allowed to dive into more hearty material that had real impact. Barbara also reminded us that she had more curves than the Pacific Coast Highway in the flawed but ridiculously fun pilot movie *Stonestreet: Who Killed the Centerfold Model* (1977), which was sadly never realized as a series.

Elizabeth Montgomery Liz was another actress who did her best to escape her good girl image, in this instance after *Bewitched* went off the air in 1972. She turned in a string of interesting performances, but it was her depiction as the maybe-murderess in *The Legend of Lizzie Borden* (1975) that got people to take notice (and won her an Emmy nomination).

Afterwards, the honey blonde actress found a home in television movies. Although she garnered nine Emmys during her memorable career (three times for TV movie performances), she unfortunately never took home the award. Beautiful and talented, Liz made TV magic post-*Bewitched* without ever twitching her nose.

Donna Mills While she is best known for playing the venomous Abby Cunningham on *Knots Landing* in the eighties, Donna's seventies TV movie filmography is vast and notable. Starting with the esoteric and confounding (and entertaining) *Haunts of the Very Rich* (1972), the beautiful blonde starred in at least one television movie a year throughout the decade. Her most outrageous appearance was as a ravishing woman on the run from a giant spider in *Curse of the Black Widow* (1977), and it might also be her most memorable. Seriously, how could anyone forget *that*?.

Stefanie Powers Any decent put-upon heroine list needs a lovely redhead, and Stefanie fits the bill. She made a slew of made for TV movies (fifteen to be exact), many of them horror/thrillers, and she always added a touch of class to the proceedings. The characters that Stefanie portrayed weren't always in control, such as the distraught Rachel in *Sweet, Sweet Rachel* (1971), but there is such a sense of independence behind that beautiful smile, that we knew it would all work out by the end credits.

THE 1970S SCREAM QUEEN TELEFILMS

As far as story conventions go, the damsel in distress motif is as old as the hills. Keying into that classic rule, the Small Screen Scream Queen became a prevalent fixture in the 1970s, with a slew of female-friendly thrillers to keep us home at night. However, many times this women-are-victims theme got a fresh spin, and the Scream Queen emerged, with a spatula in one hand and a bag of sass in the other...

Do Not Fold, Spindle or Mutilate (1970) If *The Golden Girls* liked to swill liquor and play pranks, they'd be the women in this enchanting little movie about four older ladies who create a fake beauty for a computer dating service. They unwittingly lure a psychopath into their lives but he'll need more than a menacing presence to scare these feisty ladies off!

Five Desperate Women (1971) Five women find themselves stranded with two men, one of whom is a cold blooded killer. But which one? *Women* is flawed but full of some wonderfully campy moments, such as when Joan Hackett mourns the loss of a stray dog by screaming, "He was a good little doggie and he liked me!" This proto-slasher is a little light on the splat but makes up for it with lots of great acting from the mostly female cast.

Home for the Holidays (1972) Four daughters from a highly dysfunctional family come to their curmudgeon of a father's house at Christmas only to learn he thinks his new wife is trying to kill him. If only these women cared! However, the tables are turned when someone starts impaling the delish siblings on a pitchfork! The twist ending gives an extra dash of TV movie goodness to an already tight thriller.

Trilogy of Terror (1975) A cult favorite. The audience tends to forget the first two stories of the trilogy, concentrating on the outrageous Zuni fetish doll segment, but there is plenty of fun to be had, particularly in the segment titled 'Millicent and Therese'. While the twist is fairly predictable, Karen acts her little heart out (especially as the predatory Therese) and carries this potboiler on her creepy back!

A Vacation in Hell (1979) Four women and a lucky man find themselves stranded on a tropical island. They are pursued by a beefy native guy who, according to the asexual Barbara (Andrea Marcovicci), must be trouble because "He's a man, isn't he?" There's tons of female bonding, but the gorgeous Priscilla Barnes does it in a bikini! Hippie-dippie never looked so good! A great B-movie, *Vacation* is an honest attempt to bring the grindhouse experience into your living room.

MADE FOR TV MACHISMO

David Janssen While most people associate David with *The Fugitive*, he owned the airwaves during the 1970s as the world-weary P.I., *Harry O*. The 1974 pilot movie *Smile Jenny, You're Dead* (which was actually the second pilot, the first didn't sell) set the tone for many a gritty cop show to follow. He appeared in fifteen other made for television films throughout the decade, including *A Sensitive, Passionate Man*, which earned him an Emmy nod in 1977. Despite his brooding appearance, David came across as thoughtful and a complete professional in every film he appeared in. No small feat considering his silly snakes-on-a-submarine telefilm, *Fer-de-Lance* (1974)!

Darren McGavin Darren was an established and seasoned actor by the time the 'Me Decade' arrived. However, It was his role as Kolchak in the incredible telefilm *The Night Stalker* (1972), and the subsequent short-lived series that made him a small screen legend (the sequel TV film *The Night Strangler* from 1973 fell between the first telefilm and the series). His gravelly voiced, sloppily dressed charm didn't create television magic right away (the series was cancelled after only twenty episodes) but rather a legacy that would eventually lead to the creation of *The X-Files*. Long-term hotness? Darren knew how to do it right.

Above: Life is a horrifying highway for Dennis Weaver in *Duel*. Right: Marjoe Gortner, Robert Reed, Andy Griffith and William Shatner hit the road in *Pray for the Wildcats*.

William Shatner It is sometimes easy to forget that William was once a stud among studs, especially in the arena of the TV movie. He holds a long and fascinating résumé that extends well beyond the seventies and into infinity (or at least into the eighties). He played it straight and serious in *Sole Survivor* (1970) and he took it over-the-top as a charming con artist in *Disaster on the Coastliner* (1979). However, his finest TV movie moment might be *Pray for the Wildcats* (1974), which attempts to pull apart the false mythologies behind seventies masculinity through hippie psychobabble (and it's awesome).

Martin Sheen From the sensitive and groundbreaking *That Certain Summer* (1972) to donning James Dean bravado in *The California Kid* (1974) to the cult hit *Sweet Hostage* (1975), Sheen appeared in an astounding sixteen telefilms and was on the fast track to talented small screen hunk. His lean and mean style represented the world outside of constructed norms and it was that rebellious spirit that also made him a big screen hottie during the same decade.

Dennis Weaver Any machismo list needs a good cowboy and Dennis wore that cowboy hat beautifully. If he'd starred in no other telefilm other than *Duel* (1971) he would have cemented his fate as lone wolf stud, but he went on to make several telefilms in the 1970s. While it's tough to even hold a candle to *Duel*, Weaver also flexed his macho in *Rolling Man* (1972) and *Terror on the Beach* (1973). And who could forget his iconic performance as *McCloud*? A cowboy strolling through the streets of New York on a horse? Only Weaver could make it so damn sexy.

THE 1970S MACHISMO TELEFILM

In a homosocial setting, the all-powerful provider flexes his muscles, savoring the danger that may lie ahead. He is uncompromisingly male, and sometimes overwhelmingly burly (Clint Walker, I'm looking at you). When you are in the mood for some macho men in action, these films should whet the old whistle.

Deliver Us From Evil (1973) A disparate group of men go on a camping adventure that leads to robbery and murder. George Kennedy plays a guy named Cowboy, which is the tipoff that the audience is in for some Old West style survival via seventies machismo. Jim Davis and Jan-Michael Vincent are the voices of reason but the theme may well be that when money talks, macho often walks!

Pray for the Wildcats (1974) While Angie Dickinson and Lorraine Gary have their share of screen time, this film is a decidedly male adventure as the the four leads (William Shatner, Robert Reed, Andy Griffith and Marjoe Gortner) take off across the desert on motorcycles, smoking pot and killing hippies. Well, kinda. Andy Griffith plays the rich-man-turned-evil with so much despicable zeal that he makes up for the other three floundering wannabe "cool" guys. When Griffith sneers, "I'm a hippie with money," you know you are in for a lack-of-morals rollercoaster ride.

Killdozer (1974) This preposterous thriller takes place at a remote construction site where no women are to be found. Instead we've got macho mano-a-possessed-bulldozer and only the most testosterone driven will survive. It's essentially a tale of the blue collar stud going up against the man, *if* the man was a fifty-ton construction vehicle. What's not to love?

Melvin Purvis, G-Man (1974) and **The Kansas City Massacre (1975)** If a man is measured by the size of his gun, then these guys are hot stuff. *Purvis* was a pilot movie that was never realized as a full series but was popular enough to spawn the sequel, *Kansas City Massacre*. Dale Robertson plays Purvis, "the toughest FBI Agent." He tracks down gangs, goes on shoot-outs and enjoys a good cigar. He takes down people like Machine Gun Kelly and Pretty Boy Floyd, and he likes it, do you hear that, he likes it! Classic cars, can-cans and what seem like non-stop shoot-outs make these films a feast of testosterone!

BLESS THE BEASTS & THE NETWORKS: ECO-HORROR HITS THE SMALL SCREEN

BY LEE GAMBIN

The ecologically themed horror film or the natural horror film had its busiest period during the decade that thrived on the made for TV film— the seventies. Of course born from 1950s Atomic-Age monster movies such as *Beginning of the End* (1957), *Them!* (1954) and *Tarantula* (1955), plus the countless ape movies which were all descendants of *King Kong* (1933) and then fundamentally established by Alfred Hitchcock's *The Birds* (1963), the eco-horror film went into full throttle by the early seventies as horror sensibilities were changing rapidly and the global consciousness about environmentalism was taking shape. Films such as *Frogs* (1972), *Willard* (1971) and the megahit *Jaws* (1975) truly cemented this kind of horror film and a subgenre was born that was incredibly successful and popular. While theatrically released films such as *Grizzly* (1976), *The Pack* (1977), *Food of the Gods* (1976) and *Night of the Lepus* (1972) saw audiences embrace this subdivision of horror, the small screen took on the trope and delivered some bizarre oddities that would be forever remembered by cult film fans everywhere.

In a sturdy unpretentious style, director and auteur Curtis Harrington delivered a subdued and yet almost-flamboyant nature vs man TV movie with *The Killer Bees*, which lends itself to the "human-help" branch of the eco-horror movie subgenre (where a social misfit or put-upon outsider uses an army of animals to do their bidding). Its premise is geared toward a misanthropic matriarch in the guise of the very seasoned Gloria Swanson (best remembered as the vampiric old guard of the silent era of Hollywood in Billy Wilder's much lauded noir monster show, *Sunset Blvd.* [1950]). Swanson's eccentric harridan has trained swarms of bees that she keeps in hives to attack members of her estranged (and extended) family who get in her way. ABC kept out of his hair during production of the killer bee gem and let him keep his chosen writers, married team Joyce and John Corrington. Their script reads like a melodramatic play only involving very few characters and keeping the boiling tension just under the surface. There is a steady subversive "repression of the true ego" element that permeates the film and themes such as familial trust, domestic unrest and issues concerning alpha-females duking it out head-to-head boil in unison as Swanson chews up the scenery with her busy bees buzzing about. Gloria Swanson, who got along famously with Curtis Harrington, remaining great friends for years to come, is ecstatic in her delivery and as grandiose in every gesture as she is with spewing out some inspired lines. Initially, Bette Davis was approached to take on the role, but was advised by her personal general practitioner not to take the part, because if she was stung by a bee the results would be dire. Davis lovingly sent an apology letter to Harrington expressing her disappointment.

Director Harrington had a lot more fun (and leeway) making *The Killer Bees* than he did four years later with his next venture into the animal-centric horror film subgenre, *Devil Dog: Hound of Hell* (1978). Harrington was very vocal in later years about the stress caused by producer Louie Morheim, who he claimed made far too many questionable demands, which included the look of the satanic pooch and the casting choices. The issue of being made for TV concerned Harrington: the auteur thought that *Devil Dog* would be more interesting and definitely a more scary ride if it was pushed for a cinematic release. Morheim was unmoved, prompting a disgruntled Harrington to leave out any socially aware commentary that he had intended to inject into his film. But this does not mean it is a lost cause: despite the production issues, *Devil Dog* still holds up as satisfying supernatural hokum. It even opens with a garish and prototypical seventies TV movie satanic ritual (headed by a statuesque high priestess played by the epicene Martine Beswick). *Devil Dog: Hound of Hell* may not be the film that Harrington intended to make, but it is so ruthlessly charming and oozing with seventies telemovie sensibilities that it is incredibly hard to shun. It is a surprising combination of three horror subgenres; one of course being the eco-horror division of having a dog as primary "monster," with the other two becoming increasingly popular during the decade. These being the satanic panic trend taking audiences by storm, as well as the evil child subgenre which took its lead primarily from films such as *The Bad Seed* (1956) but was then bought into an even larger public arena with films such as *The Exorcist* (1973) and *The Omen* (1976). The "devil dog" himself (a lovely German

Above: No VHS artwork in the world could save Richard Crenna from *Devil Dog: The Hound of Hell.*
Right: Meredith Baxter casts a deadly spell in *The Cat Creature.*

Shepherd) would influence the family that adopt him, turning wife and kids against a stoic Richard Crenna who does his best Gregory Peck impression from the aforementioned *The Omen.*

In 1973, Curtis Harrington also delivered *The Cat Creature*, which played with the moody and influential horror pictures from producer Val Lewton, such as *The Cat People* (1944). However, in this seventies ABC Movie of the Week, Harrington decided to maneuver his supernatural focus from shapeshifting (as in Lewton's effort) to the evil-doings of a common house cat.

Larger felines would prove more threatening in the made for TV arena with *The Beasts Are On The Streets* (1978). Produced by Joseph Barbera—of Hanna-Barbera fame, that staple of morning cartoon bliss—this bizarre TV movie rings benign on a surface level, but deep down it aggressively chimes with a firm investment in animal liberation and a suggestion that humanity is powerless if animals decide to turn violent. There is something otherworldly in the film's presentation and its depiction of animals attacking the human cast. It is also perversely satisfying to see these attacks unfold as majestic animals take on unsympathetic people—which is something that the eco-horror film does so well. A Kodiak bear lunges at a car, a panther snarls at a windscreen, elephants stampede, and a giant tiger attacks a hapless human. Unlike William Girdler's *Day of the Animals* (1977), which is a frenzied and masterfully executed horror show employing the "Ten Little Indians" motif, *The Beasts Are On The Streets* might be seen as a superficially playful excursion into the animal-attack subgenre. But as mentioned before, this is not to say that the film does not make clear and passionate commentary on the selfishness, stupidity and malice of the human race in regards to their treatment and disregard for animals. For example, a scene where two obnoxious men drive their beat-up car across the plains chasing ostriches is followed by a herd of rhinoceros that charge at the men and cause them to flee for safety. In this made for TV outing, animals put humans in their place and for devotees to the rights of critters, for the most part, it makes for satisfactory viewing. Lions terrorizing a suburban home is something that is oddly compelling, and a few years later would become a truly frightening image courtesy of the controversial motion picture *Roar* (1981). The characters that populate the film are archetypal staples that exist in most ecologically themed horror movies: the sympathetic female specialist, the left over cowboy, the innocent babe, the relentlessly hideous hicks and so forth. This human zoo is just as interesting to watch as the bestial counterparts.

But mammals don't get to have all the fun: made for television eco-horror is also in the service of insects. Ants are a social and community minded species that feature as the number one threat in the 1977 camp fan favorite, *It Happened At Lakewood Manor* (more often known simply as *Ants*). Parallels between human society and ant society are the focal point of the visually stunning big screen outing, *Phase IV* (1974), and also the giant ant extravaganza, *Empire of the Ants* (1977). But in *It Happened At Lakewood Manor*, ants become the enemy of the people for a melting pot cast that could easily populate a busy Irwin Allen disaster movie. Starring horror movie regular Lynda Day George (*Day of the Animals*, *Pieces* [1982], *Mortuary* [1983]) and, as her mother, the fabulous Myrna Loy (no stranger to horror with films such as *Thirteen Women* [1932] and *The Mask of Fu Manchu* [1932] under her belt), the movie sees ants ingest a powerful insecticide which makes them develop a taste for human flesh, causing much chaos at a world-renowned hotel.

Social issues concerning the relationship between South America and the United States are raised in the brightly lit and endearing *The Bees* (1978), which was bought to television screens by Roger Corman's New World Pictures. At the time, Warner Bros. felt that the film might affect the box office of Irwin Allen's big budget showcase, *The Swarm*, and urged New World Pictures to delay the air date, thus opening their film without adverse killer bee competition. Starring John Saxon and horror legend John Carradine, *The Bees* is a low scale variant on *The Swarm*, which has a key focus on African killer bees. Also of note, *The Swarm*, with its incredible cast and budget, came a couple of years after the made for television *The Savage Bees* (1976), which also incorporated a very similar story. Here African killer bees terrorize the annual Mardi Gras celebration; in Irwin Allen's epic, the bees swarm a festival of flowers hosted by the likes of Olivia De Havilland and Fred MacMurray.

Along with bees, spiders featured in TV movies as nasty predators. *Tarantulas: The Deadly Cargo* (1977), once again similar to *The Savage Bees*, has killer critters imported from a foreign land to wreak havoc on unsuspecting Americans. In many ways, this genuinely creepy and highly effective mesmerizing spider infested telemovie looks as though it inspired Steven Spielberg and company to deliver some family-friendly horror with their nineties hit, *Arachnophobia*. The narrative similarities are too obvious to ignore. While *Arachnophobia* is terrific, *Tarantulas: The Deadly Cargo* is a straight-up horror show without the likes of John Goodman providing broad comic relief.

Rosemary's Baby had a belated made for television sequel in 1976, so why not *The Birds*? Why not, indeed… Tippi Hedren, who, as socialite Melanie Daniels, "bought the avian threat to Bodega Bay" in Hitchcock's 1963 masterpiece, returns in *The Birds II: Land's End* (1994). Ms Hedren was horribly embarrassed by the unofficial and silly sequel, an atrocious mess

Original *TV Guide* ad for *The Beasts are on the Streets*.

that pits a grieving family against angry seagulls, ravens and more furious feathered felons. One of its faults is that it comes from the wrong era, with a colorless tone and an oppressive nineties flatness.

By contrast, *The Rats*, which has nothing to do with James Herbert's moody horror novel, was made in 2002 but is decidedly very seventies in its approach and ethos, being largely set in a rat infested department store. However, for the most part, made for TV eco-horror movies post-1970s are uninspired and far too self-aware to have the charm, personality and sincerity that films such as *Devil Dog: Hound of Hell*, *The Killer Bees* and *The Beasts Are On The Streets* proudly possess.

RAPE-REVENGE & RAPE-RESPONSE: NARRATIVES OF SEXUAL VIOLENCE & JUSTICE IN THE TV MOVIE BY JENNIFER WALLIS

"Years ago, girls didn't get murdered like they do today. It's all that women's lib stuff." *The Bait* (1973)

The rape-revenge genre, typified by such films as *I Spit on Your Grave* (1978) and *Ms.45* (1981), is one that has been amply covered by cult film critics in recent years.[1] Usually beginning with a graphic depiction of rape, the films follow their female protagonists as they personally—and violently—wreak their revenge, "[rejecting] the legal process as a means of redress for the victim."[2] Alongside these well-known examples, rape-revenge narratives also occur in a number of TV movies throughout the 1970s and 1980s. As Alexandra Heller-Nicholas has noted, many of these made for TV ventures coincided with their bigger-budget counterparts.[3] The rape-revenge TV movie differed in several respects, however, largely by virtue of its intended audience. Unlike the cinematic rape-revenge film, generally marketed to the young male viewer, the TV movie was from its early days geared toward a predominantly female audience, reflected in its evening scheduling that capitalized upon housewives' free time.[4]

The 1970s are often identified as the golden age of TV movies, as networks invested more heavily in the genre and sought content tied into contemporary issues. Screened as one-off events, TV movies were an arena where social problems were presented with a sense of urgency, and

1 See especially A. Heller-Nicholas, *Rape-Revenge Films: A Critical Study* and J. Read, *The New Avengers*.
2 A. Young, *The Scene of Violence: Cinema, Crime, Affect*, p.50.
3 Heller-Nicholas, *Rape-Revenge Films*, p.65.
4 Though the 1970s saw TV stations seeking to expand their audiences, women remained a central component of the TV movie audience. G. Edgerton, *Journal of Popular Film and Television* 19 (1991).

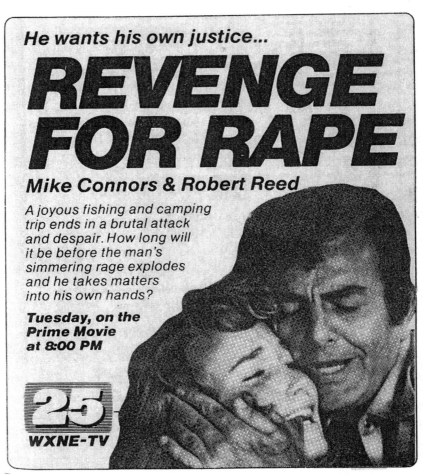

Promotional ad for a rerun of *Revenge for a Rape*.

throughout the 1970s there was a plethora of issues to choose from.[5] A renewed focus on crime during the 1960s and 1970s coincided with second wave feminism; rape was high on the agenda as feminist groups publicly attacked rape myths, and established rape crisis centers. The law came under increasing scrutiny, with individual cases highlighting the inadequacy of rape laws and the pervasiveness of victim-blaming within the legal system. In 1977, the overturning of a man's conviction for raping a hitchhiker prompted protests when the court ruled that any woman accepting a lift in such a way should expect sexual advances.[6] The trial of Inez Garcia in 1974,

5 S. Hilgartner and C.L. Bosk, "The Rise and Fall of Social Problems: A Public Arenas Model", *American Journal of Sociology* 94; L.J. Schulze, "Getting Physical: Text/Context/Reading and the Made-for-Television Movie", *Cinema Journal* 25, p.37.
6 M. Bevacqua, *Rape on the Public Agenda*, p.131.

who shot and killed a man involved in her rape, also attracted protest when her charge of second-degree murder was announced; the dramatization *The People vs. Inez Garcia* aired in 1977, the same year that she was acquitted of all charges. Discussions about rape were readily incorporated into TV programming, with television becoming a campaign space via documentaries such as *The Rape Victims* (1977) and political campaigns that included the testimony of rape survivors (a method used by New York Governor Malcolm Wilson in 1974).[7]

Whilst legal developments and media attention suggested positive changes, the 1970s were nevertheless a period of transition as the courts, police, media, and the public came to grips with new terminology and conceptions surrounding sexual assault. In many TV movies dealing with the issue, the messages about rape that are presented correspond with what Maria Bevacqua terms the 'public agenda' model of rape, in which rape is a matter of law and psychology to be controlled with tougher laws, an act committed by strangers, and something that threatens the safety of "our" women—and thus the American nation as a whole.[8]

The TV movie that comes closest to the typical rape-revenge format is 1976's *Revenge for a Rape*, in which a couple's vacation in the mountains becomes a nightmare when the woman is raped by a group of local hunters and subsequently miscarries the baby she and her husband were expecting. Rather than the victim enacting revenge, the film is told through the eyes of her husband who seeks out the rapists. The plot quickly descends into a generic chase thriller, with the rape an act that is little more than a rationale for the ensuing action. Unbeknownst to the husband is that he's chasing the wrong guys, his wife having identified a different group of men. *Revenge for a Rape* explicitly declares that a woman's identification of a suspect is unreliable, whilst critiquing the vigilantism of her husband. It's notable that this film, as the TV movie closest to the rape-revenge model, places the action in a rural area—hunting season is presented as a frenzy of primitive impulses, with an apathetic sheriff declaring that the period brings "nothing but trouble." Seeking personal revenge is presented in an equally irrational light, with the husband's pursuit of the hunters fuelled by a furious rage at the death of his unborn child (more so than his wife's suffering).

More typical of the genre is what I have termed the "rape-response" TV movie. Jacinda Read identifies such a variant of the rape-revenge film appearing in the 1980s, characterized by a legal focus that emphasized the

7 Ibid., pp.119–20, p.126.
8 Ibid., p.134.

futility of vigilante action.[9] This trend is particularly evident in TV movies of the 1970s and early 1980s. Here, rape occurs in an urban or suburban landscape, where the act of rape is frequently depersonalized and its effects extended to the wider family or community. In *Silent Witness* (1985) for example, the victim's family attempt to bribe her into silence, and the impact of jail sentences upon the rapists' families is emphasized. These TV movies position the city as a threatening space for women, drawing upon contemporary discussions of street harassment and women's use of public space. In *The Bait* (1973), a newsstand attendant seeks out the name of the "nice pretty girl" he's just served, and the heroine of the film—cop Tracey (Donna Mills)—intervenes when a man flashes two young girls on a bus. More often, rape takes place in the home—as in *The Sheriff* (1971) or *A Case of Rape* (1974)—with the act of rape an attack on the sanctity of the American family.

The aftermath of rape in the rape-response movie is concerned less with personal trauma than the use of legal channels to punish the perpetrator. At a time when politicians were putting forward a "tough on crime" line, the rape-response TV movie is sometimes strident in its criticism of legal apparatus and procedures. Both *Cry Rape* (1973) and *A Case of Rape* were explicit in this regard. In the latter, screened on NBC in February 1974, victim Ellen (Elizabeth Montgomery) is subjected to humiliating medical examinations and legal processes are scrutinized. Juries are portrayed as ill-educated, as professionals buy their way out of jury service, and existing rape laws are described as not "mak[ing] much sense anymore." Some films were more specific than others in their exploration of current rape law, especially those based on real cases. In 1978 the Rideout case was widely reported in the media, in which John Rideout had been taken to court by his wife Greta on a rape charge. The case was the first ever marital rape charge—laws surrounding rape between spouses were sketchy and varied between states (it was only in 1993 that marital rape became a crime in all fifty states).[10] The subsequent dramatization, *Rape and Marriage: The Rideout Case* (1980), was notable in its attempt to present the case to viewers in much the same way as a court might present evidence to a jury: events were told from the perspective of both husband and wife, with no concrete conclusion forthcoming (this was a model also followed by 1984's *When She Says No*).

---

9 Read, *The New Avengers*, pp.206–10.
10 Another notable example of a movie based on a real case was *Silent Witness* (1985), which drew upon the 1983 Big Dan's case (also dramatized in 1988 feature film *The Accused*), in which a woman was raped by a group of men in a Massachusetts bar.

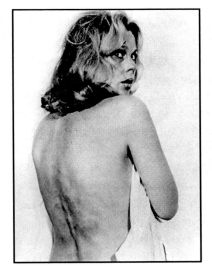

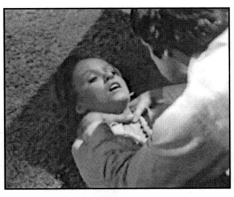

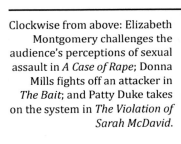

Clockwise from above: Elizabeth Montgomery challenges the audience's perceptions of sexual assault in *A Case of Rape*; Donna Mills fights off an attacker in *The Bait*; and Patty Duke takes on the system in *The Violation of Sarah McDavid*.

In its desire to present different sides of the story, the rape itself becomes almost incidental to *Rape and Marriage* and this is a theme that can be seen elsewhere. In *The Violation of Sarah McDavid* (1981), the act of rape is just one of several examples of "misbehavior" plaguing a high school, with teacher Sarah McDavid's (Patty Duke) final public discussion of the incident used to illustrate the inadequate management of the school rather than her personal suffering. Similarly, *The Sheriff* uses the rape of a young black woman to expose the entrenched racism of a small town, with justice for the victim reliant upon the willingness of white townspeople to speak up against their white neighbors.

The Sheriff, like most of the other films under study here, also addresses popular rape myths and the issue of victim-blaming, with the fact that victim Janet (Brenda Sykes) wasn't a virgin introduced as evidence in court. The idea that women could "invite" rape on account of their dress or actions

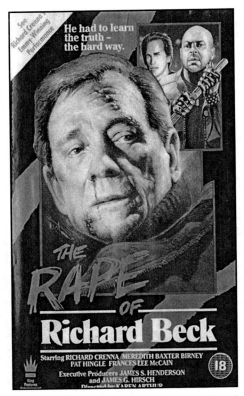

He had to learn the truth – the hard way.

See Richard Crenna's Emmy Winning Performance

THE RAPE OF

Richard Beck

Starring RICHARD CRENNA, MEREDITH BAXTER BIRNEY
PAT HINGLE FRANCES LEE McCAIN

Executive Producers JAMES S. HENDERSON and JAMES G. HIRSCH

Directed by KAREN ARTHUR

18

VHS artwork for the controversial and groundbreaking telefilm *The Rape of Richard Beck*, starring Richard Crenna.

appears repeatedly: in the lingering shots of Candra in *The Awakening of Candra* (1983), the questioning of Sarah McDavid's regard for her personal safety ("What was she doing in there with the door unlocked?"),[11] or Tracey's comments when she fails to be attacked during a police sting in *The Bait* ("Guess I'm not as irresistible as I thought").

The most direct deconstruction of rape myths, however, occurs in two unusual examples that portray male victims, *It Couldn't Happen to a Nicer Guy* (1974) and *The Rape of Richard Beck* (1985). *It Couldn't Happen to a Nicer Guy* employs, staggeringly, comedy to explore the issue at hand: Harry (Paul Sorvino) accepts a lift from a woman who drives him to a secluded spot before forcing him to have sex at gunpoint. The film is an unusual mixture of apparently serious commentary and slapstick humor, as officers roll their eyes in response to his claims of being raped by a woman, accompanied by a jaunty soundtrack. Whatever the film's intentions (and they seem purposefully obtuse throughout), any good is undone by the final scene, in which the rape is incorporated into the couple's role-playing fantasies—his wife, lying in bed, invites him to "get in the car."

The Rape of Richard Beck makes its stance much clearer. This is perhaps unsurprising: director Karen Arthur also directed *A Bunny's Tale* (1985), based on Gloria Steinem's investigation into the working conditions in Playboy clubs. Beck is an officer reassigned from homicide to sex crimes as punishment for making a deal with a prisoner, and is a stereotypical misogynist. Speaking to a terrified rape victim cowering naked inside a phone booth, he barks

11 Many TV movies mirror the 'women in peril' thriller discussed by Peter Hutchings, in which rape victims are either independent women or taking part in activities outside the home. In *A Case of Rape*, the rape takes place inside the home after the victim has returned from an evening class. P. Hutchings, "'I'm the Girl He Wants to Kill': The 'Women in Peril' Thriller in 1970s British Film and Television"', *Visual Culture in Britain* 10.

"You can't stay [here] all day. What if somebody wants to make a call?" and later jokes to his fellow officers about how "hot" he got dragging her to the police car. Beck's rape takes place within the "underground city tour" attraction that he visits as part of his unofficial "safaris" (opportunities for unchecked police brutality), and the rape (carried out by two men) is portrayed as an act of power and control rather than sexual desire. After the incident, numerous rape myths are explicated: he was somewhere he shouldn't have been ("You've been asking for it," says a colleague), and the fact that he gave up his gun to his attackers rather than putting up a fight, fuels rumors that he was in the habit of voluntarily engaging in casual sex. Beck's experience forces a change in him, as he begins to work more sympathetically with sexual assault victims and give lectures to officers in training. Despite the number of TV movies addressing rape at a time when the issue was being publicly discussed by the growing women's movement, it is striking that one of those most effective in its critique of rape myths and official responses has a man at the center of its narrative.

The Rape of Richard Beck is an unusual example, yet illustrative of a central feature of the TV movie in which women are rarely independent instigators of retribution or change. Rape is frequently presented as an act that has as much of an impact, if not more, on husbands and families: Ellen's husband in A Case of Rape says that "It was done to both of us," while 1981's The Other Victim makes the experience of the victim's husband its primary concern. As a crime with an impact beyond the emotional and physical suffering of the victim, rape becomes symbolic of national breakdown (as Sarah McDavid pulls herself up from the classroom floor after her attack, it's no accident that the shot also contains a sorry-looking American flag). As a format with strict time constraints, though, the TV movie's structure also militated against any in-depth analysis of complex issues like rape. Further, it was a genre that tended to reflect conservative right wing ideologies; as a consequence, it rarely gave its female stars center stage as agents in the fight against rape. Instead, it emphasized the legal options for seeking redress. At the same time, these legal avenues were portrayed in an unsatisfactory light: women are frequently seen being "coached" by lawyers or activists, particularly in Rape and Marriage where the influence of a local women's group is akin to brainwashing. If women were not to be encouraged to take matters into their own hands, neither should they place their faith in the courts or other advisors. This seemingly conflicted message, though, well reflected the contemporary climate and active debates about rape that were being played out in the public arena during the 1970s and 1980s.

WES CRAVEN'S SMALL SCREEN HORROR FILMS: A RETROSPECTIVE

BY AMANDA REYES

While the seventies is often noted for its edgy television offerings, it also often projected the strength of the nuclear family and the domestic pleasures of suburbia, a prominent benchmark of Americana. Some programs inverted that motif with images of corruption, sin and death. Just ask the folks living in the infamous cul-de-sac of *Knots Landing*, which premiered in 1979, for instance. Writers consistently destroyed the familial mythos that anchored shows like *Happy Days* and *Eight is Enough*. So, to say that Wes Craven's delicious (if TV-PG) subversions of suburban families were unique to the television landscape might be an exaggeration. However, his frustrated imaginings of a prevalent but antiquated ideology remain fascinating.

By the late seventies, Wes Craven had yet to become a household name. But, he was already a fairly notorious exploitation filmmaker whose *Last House on the Left* and *Hills Have Eyes* were genre films that took no prisoners, immersed in a cynicism that critics often balked at. While many filmmakers may have felt that television was too constrained a medium, it was also a very *popular* medium, and millions of people were tuning in daily. At this point, the telefilm was still young but secure in its reputation, at least with regards to ratings. And, since it more often than not called for workmanlike direction, it seemed an unlikely place for a filmmaker like Wes Craven whose visceral expressions of happy families corrupted by outside forces were marked by extreme violence. His first three TV movies (he made four telefilms in all) aired right as Craven was honing his horror skills, developing into a master of fright. Craven's small screen work feels less substantial, but beneath the veneer of placid landscapes and terrors with happy endings were a trio of interesting, if imperfect, tele-thrillers.

Craven cut his small screen teeth on *Stranger in Our House* (NBC, 10/31/1978), which allowed the director to work with 35mm film, and within the studio system. Based on Lois Duncan's young adult novel *Summer of Fear* (the *Summer* title was used for network re-airings, an overseas theatrical release, and later, home video), this mild supernatural tale pits Rachel, played by a plucky (and tremendously curly headed) Linda Blair against a supposed cousin from the Ozarks named Julia (Lee Purcell), who showcases some devilish powers. After Julia steals Rachel's boyfriend and family, a slight death match ensues. A pleasurable time waster, *Stranger* might well be remembered as harmless holiday fare (it made its auspicious debut on Halloween night), if it weren't for Craven's established preoccupation with the corruption of the family. It is certainly on display here, although missing Craven's then-signature grit and grime. Still, the underlying themes remain intact and are well played, if not presented in any sort of unsettling manner.

The house, where most of *Stranger*'s action takes place, is located in a real gated community near Malibu, propelling a feeling of xenophobia that pervades the telefilm. Most of the exteriors are idyllic but isolated. Even the local mall, which is wonderfully tidy but small, echoes the idea of a community closed off from the rest of the world, a self-made upper class Promised Land. And, like many havens, this safe refuge can't hold off the "sinister" outside world.

Julia, the ominous outsider, appears in the form of the less sophisticated cousin from the Ozarks, imbuing softly played but obvious stereotypes. She intersects with the proper upper class, and immediately desires all of the bells and whistles of a gated suburbia. Early on in *Stranger*, Craven replicates the uncomfortable dinner scene from *Last House on the Left* as a way to express the inherent awkwardness of positioning the lower class outsider within the confines of a more aristocratic space. But Julia cannot properly assimilate into this shiny new world by herself, and needs to employ an aggressive use of black magic (Rachel finds burnt hair and loose teeth located throughout her bedroom). Following through on the happy endings of TV land, it is proven that occultist enchantments are no match for those who truly belong behind the white picket fences.

Craven's next small screen feature is the perpetually goofy but likeable thriller *Invitation to Hell* (ABC, 5/24/1984), which features Susan Lucci (Erica Kane on *All My Children*) in her TV movie debut. Aided by the always-reliable Robert Urich and Joanna Cassidy, *Invitation* embraces the yearning to be immersed in eighties excess... and it will only cost you your soul.

Urich is Matt Winslow, the dependable, hardworking dad who moves his family to a small and posh suburban area resting on the what looks like the outskirts of Silicon Valley, and which also echoes the utopic community in *Stranger*. It is brimming with McMansions, manicured lawns and people enjoying the good life at a club called Steaming Springs (which, as you may

Above: Lee Purcell bewitches 1970s suburbia in *Summer of Fear*.
Left: Promotional artwork.

have guessed, is also a gateway to Hell). Longing for acceptance and hoping to perpetuate a desirable yuppie image, Matt's wife Patricia (Cassidy) is eager, perhaps even desperate, to make a deal with the devil, here in the guise of the tiny and stylish Jessica Jones (Lucci).

Craven was burning the candle on both ends during the production of *Invitation*. He was also working on postproduction for the peculiar sequel to *The Hills Have Eyes*, as well as polishing his soon-to-be-a-classic *Nightmare on Elm Street* script, which may explain the somewhat slapdash feeling of the telefilm. Admittedly, *Invitation* is hardly great cinema (don't misunderstand me, it is entertaining as Hell—pun intended!), but despite the preposterous story, Craven vibrantly captures the greed and self-indulgence of the mid-eighties. Lucci even said in an interview that she felt the film was "realistic." A bit of an off-putting statement considering how outlandish the whole affair is, but indeed, while the story comes across as glossy escapism, the underlying themes of consumerism and greed are also distinctly present.

Like *Stranger*, *Invitation* leaves behind Craven's openly monstrous family intrusions of the seventies, presenting corruption in a more synthetic package. Jessica Jones adopts the sleek high fashion of the era, embraces gadgets and opulence, and most importantly, offers the Winslows acceptance into the upper class. For all intents and purposes, Jessica *is* the eighties American Dream. Patricia is her most obvious target, as she longs for the good life and feels in constant competition for the most expensive furniture, nicest car, sexiest married life, etc. To her, these accouterments lead to security; but to the viewers, it presents an example of how willing some are to exchange personal wellbeing for expensive and attractive things. In fact, the film is awash in high-priced newness, gadgetry, and modernism. The family value fairytales of the past is in conflict with the consumerist desires of a new world. Still, for better or worse, Craven wraps up his TVM with a nice little bow, just as he did with *Summer*, and manages to maintain some of that fifties' conservative ideology.

On his next telefilm, Craven switches the concept of selling one's soul to living a life without a soul. *Chiller* originally aired as part of CBS's Wednesday Night Movies offerings on May 22, 1985, almost exactly one year after *Invitation to Hell* debuted on ABC. Skipping the more overt shiny objects of greed, Craven toned this small screen affair down. And, while the telefilm lacks that oh-so-eighties aesthetic, it comments heavily on the soulless age of corporate greed.

Michael Beck is unnerving as Miles Creighton, a man who was cryogenically frozen by his mother Marion (Beatrice Straight) after his death at a young age. Thanks to a rather devastating blunder at the cryogenics lab, the doctors do their best to revive the long dead man. Luckily, it works, but it would also seem that while his body is back to walk the earth, his soul departed some time ago. Miles resumes life as it should be, and returns to the head of the big corporation that has gone on without him. The company's family atmosphere extends all the way to their acting president, Clarence (Dick O'Neill), who emerges as a kindly uncle figure during Miles' absence. However, Miles doesn't like this warm and happy corporate environment, and literally turns the business into a cold blooded venture.

Craven veers slightly from his usual outside corruption motif, placing the immorality within the peaceful halls of a family run corporation. New too is that the Creighton's are far above upper middle class, and the family unit has changed into something a little less traditional, with Miles' mother a widow with an adopted teenage daughter (Jill Schoelen in a small but good role). The closeness of family also extends to the business world, which Miles sees as ineffective, calling to mind the conservative young lions taking over Wall Street and and seeking other careers offering positions of power. Miles also challenges religion and faith, and is not only cold to the touch, but cold in the heart, and dead to traditional norms of the past. And that's makes him terrifying to the audience.

Compared to Craven's other telefilms, *Chiller* is almost dead silent with quiet and meditative dialog, and it is certainly more brooding, and meticulously paced. It is also wonderfully dark and fairly on target with its conceptions of the stony business world emerging from this era. Screenwriter J.D. Feigelson, who was a fan of Rod Serling, and would go on to pen two stories for the 1980s version of *The Twilight Zone*, brings a discreet psychological terror that pervades throughout *Chiller* (Craven and Feigelson

SOME THINGS WERE
NEVER MEANT TO BE

CHILLER

A new film from WES CRAVEN,
the Director of A Nightmare on Elm Street

Left: Susan Lucci is an irresistible
force of nature and evil in
Invitation to Hell.
Above: DVD artwork.

also directed separate segments of an episode of the new *Twilight Zone* in 1985). The story is further complemented by Craven's unobtrusive direction, which eschews overbearing horror visuals and allows the actors to immerse themselves in the heady material.

Whether Craven, who passed away in August 2015, was aware of it or not, his first three small screen films work along a line of symbiotic allegories that expose the core of the middle class as superficial, greedy and easily corrupted. Capturing the artificial charm of the relics of Americana, Craven also manipulates them, revealing the ugly underbelly of self-indulgence, consumerism and xenophobia. While the stories end predictably with the family rising above the odds, Craven's television films do not veer too far from where his earlier works concluded. However, in those grimy horror flicks, the families were tainted by death, and those who survived were changed forever. The survivors of Craven's telefilms fare much better. But, the themes that repeat throughout his theatrical career are still apparent, and these charming and deceptively intelligent telefilms deserve a look.

THE USA WORLD PREMIERE MOVIE: THE FORGOTTEN RED-HEADED STEPCHILD OF FILM NOIR

BY PAUL FREITAG-FEY

When it comes to genre filmmaking, there are a few names that fans tend to think of that made the movies they love, respect, and over-analyze possible. Roger Corman, Lloyd Kaufman, Charles Band and David Friedman immediately come to mind as being responsible for hundreds of minimally-budgeted epics that could be easily marketed to eager viewers. (The quality of entertainment in the content, in many cases, was a secondary priority.)

The late Tom Piskura is rarely, if ever, among those names. In fact, his name comes up in comparison to those genre film moguls only once that I can find—in a *New York Times* article from 1992, in which he's quoted along with the likes of Corman and Kaufman. But Piskura deserves significantly more praise than he's received: As Vice-President of Programming for the USA Network's West Coast division, he created and shepherded the USA World Premiere Movie.

The USA Network had, since its launch under that moniker in 1980, been friendly to genre fans throughout the eighties, with programming like *Night Flight*, *Commander USA's Groovy Movies*, and *Up All Night*, featuring movies and shorts for the psychotronic mindset. On April 25, 1989, however, the network branched out into creating its own films with the airing of *The Forgotten*, created especially for the network. It proved to be just the tip of the iceberg, as for the next decade, they'd average over twenty new films a year, quickly overshadowing the output of similar basic cable stations like TNT, Lifetime and the Family Channel.

The secret to USA's success was finding their niche, as they couldn't compete with the budgets, promotional powers and epic miniseries of the major networks, nor with the prestige, star power and lack of FCC standards that premium channels like HBO could afford. That niche was film noir.

Clockwise from above: Promotional artwork for the trippy *High Desert Kill*; a newspaper ad for *Murder 101*; and Robert Mitchum brings some class to the USA Original with *Jake Spanner*.

``We`re reinventing the B-movie," Piskura stated in an interview in 1992. "If this were 1940 we'd be doing Paul Muni films and *Petrified Forest*. I think the audience always loved these films, and they were taken away from them. We`ve discovered a sleeping giant."

Piskura wasn't just paying lip-service. By 1992, the network had found its footing when it came to original films. In the first year, the films ran the gamut of genres, from screwball tales like *The Hollywood Detective* or *Jake Spanner, Private Eye* to straightforward horror films like *I'm Dangerous Tonight*, *High Desert Kill* and *The Haunting of Sarah Hardy* to a series of more "prestige" espionage films presented by novelist Frederick Forsyth. A look at production in subsequent years reveals the real ratings winners, however, and while the network continued to produce films in different genres, more than two-thirds of them could be confined to one—the thriller.

The nineties were a big boom time for neo-noir, with films like *The Grifters*, *The Last Seduction* and *One False Move* among the more notable entries. Neo-noir's slutty little brother, the erotic thriller, became commonplace on video store shelves and a staple of Cinemax's Friday After Dark programming. The USA Network offered its audience a downscale, familiar version of the thriller, with tales of falsely-accused murder, reluctant detectives, long cons and sexy serial killers. They were the "B-movies" of their time, much like the film noir of the forties, even to the point of remaking some of the classics in the genre (à la 1991's *This Gun for Hire* or 1989's *Sorry, Wrong Number*) and utilizing plenty of pulp novels as source material.

USA World Premiere Movies, as the opening logo proudly called them, were steeped in the noir tradition not only in content, but in their creation. The films usually starred actors that were known quantities but not A-listers, like Timothy Busfield, Gregory Harrison, Tim Matheson, Madchen Amick, Crystal Bernard and Gregory Hines. They utilized whitebread actors like Richard Thomas and Ted McGinley to play dangerous psychopaths, and the performances show their willingness to break out of their stereotypical roles. The standardized plots resulted in great use of random character actors, and it's virtually impossible to watch a USA World Premiere Movie without thinking some random cop or judge or storekeeper looks awfully familiar, you just don't know from where.

The directors involved were no slouches either. The films employed genre favorites like Fred Walton (*Dead Air*), Tobe Hooper (*I'm Dangerous Tonight*), Larry Cohen (*As Good As Dead*), and Brian Trenchard-Smith (*Atomic Dog*, the second-best film of the nineties inspired by a George Clinton song). There were also soon-to-be-big names like Bill Condon (*Murder 101, White Lie, Dead in the Water, Deadly Relations*) David S. Goyer (writer of *The Substitute*), Frank Darabont (*Buried Alive*) and Gary Fleder (*The Companion*) before making the big budget equivalents of a USA World Premiere Movie in the form of *Kiss the Girls, Don't Say a Word* and *Runaway Jury*. There were also actors making their directorial debut like James Keach (*The Forgotten, Praying Mantis*) and Tim Matheson (*Breach of Conduct, Buried Alive II, Tails You Live Heads You're Dead*)—heck, 1997's *His Bodyguard* was written by *Dynasty*'s Emma Samms!

Most of the people behind the camera, however, came from the trenches of television directing. The roster was filled with TV pros like Thomas J. Wright (*Chrome Soldiers, Snow Kill, Deadly Game*), Arthur Allan Seidelman (*Body Language, Dying to Remember*), Harry Falk (*High Desert Kill*), Sandor Stern (*Jericho Fever, Duplicates, Dangerous Pursuit, Web of Deceit*), and Robert Michael Lewis (*Don't Talk to Strangers, Circumstances Unknown, The Crying Child*), and they were a big part of giving the USA World Premiere Movie the tone that made them so successful.

USA World Premiere Movies took the conceits of classic film noir with their twisting plots and sketchy characters and adapted them to the TV movie format, in which a dangling, tension-filled plot point was necessary every twenty minutes or so in order to keep people from changing the channel while the network exposes them to the joys of "Freedom Rock" and Fabio's inability to believe it's not butter. As a basic cable station, they couldn't show nudity, nor have profane language, nor feature more than a modicum of violence. By design, the USA World Premiere Movies were ruthlessly efficient, having to shoehorn multiple plot threads into a very tightly-controlled package without the benefit of being able to wake up their audience with sadistic violence or a stray boob. From the musical scores of smooth jazz to the brief sex scenes that show just enough beefcake and leg reaching out from under the cover to get the point across, these were thrillers in which the priority was getting the plot from one point to the next in as quick and familiar a way as possible.

The most common criticism of USA World Premiere Movies, that they're well-worn plots that have been done before, and better, completely misses the intended purpose of the films. Nobody is going to argue that 1993's *Voyage* is a better movie than *Dead Calm* even if they share remarkably similar plots—*Voyage* is *Dead Calm* made with one arm tied behind its back and a cast and crew that just want to entertain you with ridiculous plot twists and game talent (in this case, Rutger Hauer, Eric Roberts and Karen Allen) that you may forget by the next day instead of creating a genuinely memorable film. USA World Premiere Movies are designed not to be memorable—they're a tried-and-tested formula, designed for the most ephemeral of experiences.

This isn't to say that USA World Premiere Movies are bad—they're often highly entertaining, and the best of them (like Darabont's *Buried Alive* or Condon's *Murder 101*) rank with some of the better neo-noirs of the era. These standouts aren't notable because they defy some sort of genre convention, they're just memorable because they do what they're intended to do really, really well.

It's no surprise that, unlike a lot of made for television movies, many of the USA World Premiere Movies found their way onto VHS and Laserdisc via Paramount and Universal's home video releases. With a learned eye, you can easily pick out the USA movie from a video store lineup. They've got the stars' names at the top and they're absent-mindedly promoted with some of the blandest covers ever to grace video store shelves—Photoshop the lead actors looking as though they're on the verge of being menaced or menacing, throw in some shadows and part of a publicity photo and call it a day. They're almost always rated PG-13 for such vague reasons as "mature thematic material," "thrilling violence" and "sensuality." (There are a few exceptions, like films that were made for other sources but debuted on USA in a cut form, such as Rutger Hauer in *Past Midnight*, the Pamela Anderson thriller *Snapdragon* and Gary Busey in the *Bad Ronald* copy *Hider in the House*. Purists of the USA World Premiere Movie, of which there may be only myself, consider these actual USA Movies with an asterisk.) Titles were often as efficient as the films themselves, usually having some variation of "Dead," or "Perfect" in them—1991 alone had *Deadly Desire*, *Deadly Game*, *Dead in the Water* and *The Perfect Bride*.

Their prominence on store shelves was short-lived. Few of these films have made the jump to DVD, and some, like 1992's *Drive Like Lightning*, featuring Steven Bauer as an ex-stunt driver hired to drive a stunt car cross-country in a plot that could have been sitting on Roger Corman's desk fifteen years earlier (down to the comic relief small-town sheriff), never made it to video at all, and have been virtually unseen since their original airing. Viewing the films these days mostly involves a random accidental showing on a late-night cable station you forgot you had.

The USA World Premiere Movie is often conflated with the Lifetime Movie, and it's not all that surprising, as many USA productions receive more airplay on the "Network for Women" (and its affiliated movie-only channel) now than they do on their home channel. Certainly, it's easy to confuse titles like *Out of Annie's Past*, *Maternal Instincts* and *My Stepson, My Lover* with Lifetime films, but there is a clear difference. While Lifetime original movies—at least during their prime before moving onto prestige sleaze like *Flowers in the Attic*—tended to concentrate on the melodramatic aspects of the plot with the "thriller" nature secondary to character woes, the USA productions focused on the thriller aspects with character and melodrama secondary. Put simply, Lifetime films are descended from *Stella Dallas*; USA films are descended from *Double Indemnity*. While USA films often did have female protagonists, the stories and situations they fronted weren't exclusively "woman-centric." Only in rare cases (like the addiction recovery tale *The Perfect Daughter* or the later production *Baby Monitor: Sound of Fear*) did the network's films delve into the paranoid motherhood melodrama so often thought of as the heart of the Lifetime Movie.

The nineties boom in USA Network Movies soon petered out, and the thrillers became slowly subservient to varying genres as the network tried to move past its reputation into traditional biopics, like 1999's *Hefner Unauthorized* and more prestige projects starting with 1995's *My Antonia*. Thrillers were still being produced, but with titles that were increasingly odd (1995's *Where's the Money, Noreen?*, 1997's *When Danger Follows You Home*) or simply bland (1997's *Perfect Crime*, 1998's *The Con*) it was clear the golden age was over. The network still makes an occasional original film, but their primetime schedule is now filled with quirky detective shows and quirky crime dramas, their neo-noir heritage left to the wee hours of the night, if noted at all.

Their legacy, however, remains, and in Tom Piskura's hands, the network created over 200 original films, mostly the type of entertaining potboilers with affable casts that film noir fans celebrate with glee. If the USA World Premiere Movie can't make the jump into the cultural canon the way that film noir has, inspiring festivals, conventions and an endless supply of writing on the subject, then the least we can do is justify it as a subgenre. Throughout the nineties, the network carried on the torch of made for television movies with relish and success, taking genre films (mostly noir, but also horror, disaster and science fiction) through the FCC-approved, commercial-scheduled ringer and produced dozens of entertaining little time-passers. Like the films noir of the forties and fifties, the USA World Premiere Movies were efficient, cheaply-made crime thrillers featuring notable performers and journeyman filmmakers going through the paces— even if *Tails You Live, Heads You're Dead* or *Tall, Dark and Deadly* may never rank with *The Postman Always Rings Twice*.

LOCATING SEXUAL ABUSE IN THE TV MOVIE, FROM DANGEROUS DADS TO DAY CARE

BY JENNIFER WALLIS

When locating underage sex in the TV movie, the earliest examples are the slightly salacious "tearaway teen" movies—those productions of the 1970s in which teenage girls become embroiled in drugs, drinking, and prostitution in scenes that often evoke the swinging sixties. *Go Ask Alice* (1973), *Born Innocent* (1974), and *Diary of a Teenage Hitchhiker* (1979), while emphasizing the dangers facing modern teenagers, relied just as much for their appeal on the appearance of their young female stars (Linda Blair is down to a bra within fourteen minutes of *Born Innocent*'s opening credits).[1]

The 1980s, though, saw less of the tearaway teen and more of the much younger abused child. Although the physical abuse of children had come to prominence in the 1960s with the emergence of the "battered child" syndrome, it wasn't until the 1970s that the *sexual* abuse of children gained widespread attention as the American child protection system expanded. If the TV movies of the 1970s showed something of a preoccupation with the rape of adult women (see 'Rape-revenge and rape-response', this volume), those of the 1980s and 1990s showed an increasing interest in the sexual abuse of children. The idea of what constitutes child abuse changes over time (alterations to the age of consent, for example), and TV movies of this period neatly demonstrate late twentieth century developments that situated sexual abuse in two distinct locations: the family and the day care center.[2]

---

1 There are some examples of the tearaway teen movie in the later period, such as 1993's *Why My Daughter?* or 1990's *Daughter of the Streets*, but these are more concerned with the parents' journey to rescue, or seek justice for, their child than with the details of that child's life.
2 I. Hacking, "The Making and Molding of Child Abuse", *Critical Inquiry* 17, p.274.

DANGEROUS DADS & AVENGING MOMS

Coverage of the sexual abuse of children in the 1970s frequently framed the issue as something of a "last taboo"—an aspect of human sexuality that had gone unaddressed in the supposedly liberated discussions of the 1960s. The recognition that threats to children could come not just from the dirty old man in a raincoat, but from individuals much closer to home, began to make its way into the popular press, with *Ms.* magazine running a piece on incest in 1977. The issue was ideally suited to the TV movie, then; a format which relied upon current news stories and events to appeal to viewers.

Many TV movies of the 1980s took the form of "domestic melodramas,"[3] with the juxtaposition of the familiar home environment and sinister or harmful acts transforming the home into a somewhat uncanny site.[4] Helen Wheatley describes "Gothic television" as a genre reliant upon "writing stories of unspeakable family secrets and homely trauma large across the television screen."[5] While her analysis is not concerned with TV movies, many of the characteristics she identifies in Gothic television can be found in the TV movie: family secrets, menace within the home, and the use of flashbacks. Typifying this model is *Child of Rage* (1992), in which a couple adopt a young girl who quickly exhibits some disturbing personality traits. Catherine tortures animals, plans to stab her new parents in their bed, and— in a particularly disturbing scene—offers to give her adopted grandfather "whatever he wants" if he will take her fishing, describing herself as "so hot." As her abuse at the hands of her real parents is divulged in therapy sessions, flashbacks fill in the details of her previous life—her father rasps "You're so hot for Daddy, aren't ya?" Flashbacks are also employed in 1992's *The Boys of St. Vincent*, the use of this method betraying contemporary interest in what was popularly known as "recovered memory."[6] *Child of Rage* goes rather over-the-top, both with its level of detail and its depiction of Catherine's behavior—for the first half of the film she could be read as a genuinely evil rather than troubled child, bringing to mind Patty McCormack's performance in *The Bad Seed* (1956).

Incest in these films invariably occurs between father and daughter— *Something about Amelia* (1984), *Liar, Liar: Between Father and Daughter* (1993), *Stop at Nothing* (1991)—with the revelation of abuse a shock to wives

3 J. Feuer, *Seeing through the Eighties: Television and Reaganism*, p.31.
4 H. Wheatley, *Gothic Television*, p.7.
5 Ibid., p.1.
6 Recovered memory proponents claim that traumatic memories can be buried in the subconscious and retrieved in psychotherapy. The phenomenon was widely discussed during the Satanic Ritual Abuse panic of the 1980s and 1990s, and popularised in the 1980 book *Michelle Remembers*, written by a psychiatrist and his patient (later wife).

and mothers. In some sense, the movies might be viewed as aids to spotting abuse: trademark behaviors such as violent play with soft toys or irrational anger occur repeatedly.[7] As with the "rape-response" film, the legal system is held to account for its inadequate reaction. In contrast to the relative lack of action by women in response to rape, however, the mother of the abuse victim is often given significant agency, and indeed may be presented as heroic in her actions. The figure of the "vigilante mom" appears in *Stop at Nothing* (1991; working with a group of women to kidnap her daughter after her husband is awarded custody), *Don't Touch My Daughter* (1991; she kills her daughter's molester but is not charged), and *While Justice Sleeps* (1994; she shoots her daughter's abuser in court when it becomes clear that his police buddies will get him off). The latter echoes the real-life case of Ellie Nesler, who in 1993 shot the man accused of molesting her son and several other boys. Her arrest and incarceration prompted protest, with "Free Ellie Nesler" bumper stickers sported by some supporters.

Cases like Nesler's were intimately bound up with television coverage. Interviewed by Oprah Winfrey in 1995, Nesler was just one of many individuals who appeared on the talk show circuit of the 1990s to relate personal stories of abuse. Shari Karney, an attorney, appeared on several shows to raise awareness of incest after "recovering" her own memories of childhood abuse during her work on an incest case; her story was dramatized in the 1993 TV movie, *Shattered Trust*. The value of "breaking the silence" had been emphasized since the 1980s, with children as well as adults encouraged to tell their stories—both to raise public awareness of child abuse and as a step toward their own recovery. Indeed, the positioning of the TV movie as a form of "therapy" was made explicit by the broadcasting of helpline numbers after a screening. The tide was turning, however, as exhortations to "believe the children" began to be questioned, and the media circus surrounding child sex abuse claims came under fire from several quarters. Underlying all of this was the specter of Satanic Ritual Abuse, brought to public attention in the high profile McMartin case.

THE DARK SIDE OF DAY CARE

The McMartin preschool scandal is now a byword for moral panic, hysteria, and modern day witch-hunting. The allegations made by a mother in 1983

---

7 The importance of medical examination in confirming or revealing abuse to the mother is also made clear in many films. *Liar, Liar*'s Kelly undergoes a pelvic exam, and in several instances evidence of abuse is uncovered by doctors examining the child for some other reason, such as the cuts and bruises Samantha sustains in a fight in *While Justice Sleeps*.

Left: Ted McGinley exposes the evils of chat rooms in *Every Mother's Worst Fear.*
Above: Pam Dawber asks Brian Bonsall *Do You Know the Muffin Man?*

that her son had been raped by McMartin staff member Ray Buckey sparked a string of similar allegations in preschools across America. The tales of abuse became increasingly bizarre, with children claiming to have been involved in satanic rituals, flown across the country to take part in orgies, and witnessing their teachers flying. The McMartin trials ran for seven years at a cost of $15m, and resulted in no convictions.

The media frenzy surrounding McMartin and other preschools offered an array of outlandish and confusing details. How could so many people be involved with a national underground network of Satanists and be unknown to the authorities? But then how could children make up such fantastic stories if there were no substance to them? This feeling of conflict between children's testimony and commonsense comes across in several TV movies of the late 1980s and early 1990s. *Do You Know the Muffin Man?* (1989) depicts the key features of the trials that were most criticized by contemporary commentators. The tendency of adults to ask leading questions (a mother persistently asks her son if anyone at school has touched him "in a bad way") and the coaching of children by therapists (how else would a young child be familiar with words such as "vagina" or "penis"?) are both covered, as is the public's prurient interest in sex abuse claims. During the trial in *Muffin Man*, the details of a satanic ritual offered by one of the child witnesses leads to an outburst by the defense lawyer, who thunders "Is Geraldo going to rush in here now?!" It's a surprise, then, when the final ten minutes of the film reveal the claims to be true: photographs of children in their underwear are found in the apartment of one of the accused and a Hammer-horror style ritual in a classroom is crashed by investigating officers. This conflict between narratives can also be seen in some of the incest dramas. *Liar, Liar* suggests throughout that the daughter has fabricated her claims of abuse to get back at her father for his frequently violent discipline, with her mother expressing annoyed exasperation: "I don't know what story you're cooking up now, but I don't like it." Like *Muffin Man*, however, the allegations turn out to be true, and a similar narrative arc can be seen in *Stop at Nothing*.

A more straightforward (and damning) depiction of the McMartin trials was the HBO production *Indictment: The McMartin Trial* (1995). Coming after the abandonment of the trial, *Indictment* is confident enough of the viewer's basic knowledge of the case to go straight into the action with no preamble, beginning with the arrest of Ray Buckey and other members of the McMartin family. The main focus of the film is the court case and deliberations of the defense and prosecution, many of whom are uncomfortable with the case being tried at all. The fast pace of the film perfectly conveys the hankering of the press for lurid detail, and the speed with which events developed after the initial allegation had been made. At the end of the film, as the freed McMartin family walk along the seafront with their lawyer, they wonder how people could have been carried away by the allegations rather than "listening to God" for guidance—because, says grandmother Virginia, "they were all too busy watching television."

While day care centers and preschools were the key sites associated with child abuse in the TV movie at this time,[8] the church was also coming under scrutiny as settlements began to be paid to abuse victims from the mid-1980s. *The Boys of St. Vincent*, though emphasizing that it was not a direct portrayal of a single case, took its inspiration from the Newfoundland Mount Cashel Orphanage scandal, where several priests were found to be involved in systematic physical and sexual abuse. Unlike the mythical network of Satanists, the conspiracy of silence surrounding sexual abuse in the church was emphasized as an all too real—and intractable—problem. "Have you ever tried to go above the Catholic Church?" asks one character, and the film's finale is decidedly downbeat as a new group of equally corrupt priests are brought in to replace those recently dismissed.

Partly due to the collapse of the McMartin trial and increasing skepticism about Satanic Ritual Abuse, TV movies in recent years have been less persistent in their pursuit of the child abuse theme. Threats to children still exist, but their location is often more complex than the family/day care dichotomy. The

---

8 Another notable example is *Unspeakable Acts* (1990), based on the Miami Country Walk case of 1985. A few TV movies positioned the high school as a place of threat, the victims in these cases being teenage girls—who might also be used as 'bait' by police to entrap predatory teachers, as in *Hush Little Baby Don't You Cry* (1986) and *Broken Silence* (1998).

Internet is one plot device that allows the threat to children or teenagers to be simultaneously inside the home and out in the wider world, revamping the "stranger danger" for a modern age—as in *Every Mother's Worst Fear* (1998). In many ways, this is a continuance of the Gothic character of the TV movie, with predators' ability to transgress the boundaries of the home possessing something of a supernatural undercurrent. As a "homely" format, then, the TV movie itself brings its fair share of fear, unease, and paranoia into the American home.

TELEMOVIE MASHUPS
BY AMANDA REYES

If there's one thing Hollywood is good at it is repurposing material. The modern world is teeming with remakes, reboots, re-imaginings, and whatever else you can place the letters "re" in front of. While that might be the sort of thing that can make retro lovers throw their hands up in despair (*can they please stop remaking everything?*), it is certainly not a new concept, and television has always made the best of reusing footage in an effort to produce new moneymaking products. Mashups in episodic television is a well-worn concept that includes everything from adding flashbacks from previous installments to editing together full episodes into movie length form. This patchwork creates new formats that work for everything from episodic programming to telefilms to theatrical re-releases.

CLIFFHANGERS

Hoping to capitalize on the nostalgia of the melodramatic serials of yesteryear, in 1979 NBC used the cliffhanger serial structure to promote programs that had the potential to be turned into their own series. The one-hour format allowed for three serials to air each week—*Stop Susan Williams*, which riffed on *The Perils of Pauline*; *The Secret Empire*, which capitalized on *The Phantom Empire*; and *The Curse of Dracula*, which featured the world's most familiar bloodsucker. Divided into short segments, each tale premiered as a story already in progress, as if several chapters had previously aired. This mid-season replacement ran against *Happy Days* and *Laverne and Shirley*, and, as might be expected, flopped. The only serial that got to run its full course was *Curse*, starring Michael Nouri. This Dracula tale was eventually edited into the TV movie format and released under several titles including *Dracula '79*, *The Loves of Dracula* and *World of Dracula*, and enjoys a small cult following.

THE DAN AUGUST COMPILATION MOVIES

In 1970, Quinn-Martin produced the telefilm *House on Greenapple Road*, which is based on the Harold Daniels novel of the same name. Starring Christopher George as Dan August (the character's name in the novel was Dan Nalon), the TVM was successful enough to warrant a series, but George turned down a chance to reprise his role on a weekly basis. He recommended a then-unknown Burt Reynolds to take on the action packed cop show. The short-lived series hardly caught the attention of viewers, but Reynolds' star was just beginning to shine and his prominent role in *Deliverance* (1972) and subsequent fame encouraged CBS to rerun the series during the summers of 1973 and '75. In 1980, Quinn-Martin cobbled twelve episodes together, turning them into six feature-length telefilms. This economical mashup only involved editing the end of one episode with the beginning of another one.

Titles:

Double Jeopardy (aka *Once is Not Enough*)
compiled from *Death Chain* and *Prognosis Homicide*
The Killing Affairs
compiled from *The Assassin* and *The Manufactured Man*
The Trouble with Women
compiled from *Epitaph for a Swinger* (aka *A Climate for Murder*) and *The Titan*
The Lady Killers
compiled from *When the Shouting Dies* and *The Worst Crime*
The Jealousy Factor
compiled from *The Jealousy Factor* and *Murder By Proxy*
The Relative Solution
compiled from *Dead Witness to a Killing* and *Days of Rage*

EXPERIMENT IN TERRA

Hoping to coast on the success of *Star Wars*, *Battlestar Galactica* was a gorgeous—and expensive—adventure into a new universe where man battled robots in their search for the planet Earth. With only twenty-one episodes under its belt when it was cancelled, *Galactica* seemed destined for obscurity. But, subsequent reruns, a disastrous spinoff (*Galactica 1980*) and a wildly popular and well-respected reboot in 2004 have kept Apollo, Starbuck and crew in our collective memory. *Galactica's* legacy was also aided by several telefilms that were cobbled together from the series. The

Clockwise from above: Michael Nouri calls out to his children of the night in *Curse of Dracula*; Ben Murphy, Patricia Stich and Lorne Greene solve crimes in *Griff*; and Timothy Van Patten gets an education in ninja-ing from Lee Van Cleef, *The Master*.

most interesting of the bunch uses the original title from the *Battlestar Galactica* episode *Experiment in Terra*, but combines that episode's footage with several others, including *Galactica 1980*'s *The Return of Starbuck*. *Terra* begins with a co-narration from Patrick McNee and Lorne Greene, as they explain how Earth came to know about the Cylons and their war on humans. Using footage from the pilot movie, and beautiful illustrations showcasing the Cylons as "serpents" (as Greene refers to them), the bulk of the film re-used and expanded footage from *Terra*, and cut down footage from other episodes. The combination of *Galactica* and its 1980 successor has made this TVM a highly sought out curio for sci-fi nuts.

Other titles in the series:

Mission Galactica: The Cylon Attack
compiled from *Living Legends* Part One and Two and *Fire in Space*
Murder in Space
compiled from *Murder on the Rising Star* and *The Young Lords*
Phantom From Space
compiled from *The Lost Warrior* and *The Hand of God*
Space Prison
compiled from *Man with Nine Lives* and *Baltar's Escape*
Space Casanova
compiled from *Take the Celestra* and *The Long Patrol*

Curse of the Cylons
> compiled from *Fire in Space* and *The Magnificent Warriors*

Conquest the Earth
> compiled from two episodes of *Galactica 1980—Galactica Discovers Earth* and *The Cylons Landed*

THE GODFATHER: A NOVEL FOR TELEVISION

Newspaper promotions heralded the re-edited *Godfather* saga as something that has "a sense of continuity and scope that simply could not be achieved in a theatrical presentation." Put together in chronological order by Francis Ford Coppola, *The Godfather: A Novel for Television*, is a four-part miniseries that boasts over seventy extra minutes of footage, although it also tones down the language and violence. Considered a curiosity at the time of its original November 1977 airing, it was met with unexpectedly mild ratings, but is held by many Mafia movie fans as an enjoyable, and even superior, alteration on the first two cherished films. This miniseries is also known as *The Godfather: The Complete Novel for Television*, *The Godfather Saga*, and *The Godfather Novella*, and should not be confused with the 1981 video release *The Godfather 1902–1959: The Complete Epic* or the *Godfather Trilogy: 1901–1980*.

GRIFF

Griff ran on ABC during the 1973 season and only produced thirteen episodes. Lorne Greene played a cop turned P.I. and Ben Murphy was Mike, his beefcake sidekick. Despite its short run, two telemovies were compiled out of four episodes. The telefilm *The Case of the Baltimore Girls* was assembled by stringing together the episodes *The Last Ballad* and *All the Lonely People*. *Death Follows a Psycho* was clumsily patched together from the episodes *Countdown to Terror* and *Elephant in the Room*. For *Psycho*, the editor attempted to make the two episodes seem as though they were occurring simultaneously by adding extra footage with voiceovers. For instance, in one shot there is a radio with an announcer talking about one of Griff's cases while the audience sees him investigating the other one. Despite the awkward inserts, *Death* is worth visiting for Ricardo Monatalban's harrowing turn as a man determined to avenge his son's death.

THE MASTER

In 1984 NBC was hoping their two Friday night mid-season replacement shows would help the fledgling network out of their low rated bind. *Legmen* and *The Master* targeted a young male audience by featuring lots of cool eighties action. *Legmen* was about bail bondsmen and it quickly faded into obscurity after a mere eight episodes. *The Master*, which one journalist reviewed simply as "Master a disaster," seemed destined to the same fate when it was cancelled after only thirteen episodes. However, the pilot caught a young Demi Moore somewhere between *General Hospital* and *St. Elmo's Fire*. To capitalize on the newfound popularity of some of the show's guest stars, *The Master* was redubbed *The Master Ninja*, and re-edited into a series of telefilms, featuring two episodes loosely strung together (essentially the end credits of the first episode and the opening titles of the second episode were omitted). These quasi-TVMs were then released on VHS in at least six volumes, making most of the series available on the home video market. Again, *Master* was headed for relative obscurity, when in 1992 *Mystery Science Theater 3000* saw fit to air two of the TV movies. The goofiness of the premise and the witty commentary by the *MST3K* crew introduced the series to a new audience, and it has properly claimed its cult status.

Titles:

Master Ninja
compiled from *Max* and *Out of Time*
Master Ninja II
compiled from *State of the Union* and *Hostages*
Master Ninja 3
compiled from *Fat Tuesday* and *Juggernaut*
Master Ninja 4
compiled from *High Rollers* and *The Good, the Bad and the Priceless*
Master Ninja 5
compiled from *Kunoichi* and *The Java Tiger*
Master Ninja 6
compiled from *A Place to Call Home* and *Failure to Communicate*

ROMANCE THEATRE

Telenovelas have a long and prosperous history in Latin America, dating back to the 1950s. Like the American soap opera, the genre concentrates on many of the same romantic fundamentals but, unlike those counterparts, the telenovela is most noted for featuring stories that have a distinct ending, as compared to the soap opera's infinite universe. Now the genre is better understood and more accessible to the American public, although that was not the case in 1982 when the series *Romance Theatre* appeared in syndication throughout the country. *Romance Theatre* was an anthology series that featured five thirty-minute episodes, which culminated in one weeklong standalone tale. It was high Harlequin, indeed, and the original host Louis Jourdan only whispered musings of love through his irrepressible French accent. The episodes were shot on video and looked every bit the soap opera format they were aping. The series lasted two seasons, and many of the stories were edited together and released as feature films on home video in 1986. This market proved to be beneficial to the melodramatic romance series, and the original six-film release sold over 100,000 units. Still, *Romance Theatre* remains rare, with scant information available.

Some of the titles in the series:

Isle of Secret Passion
The Awakening of Cassie
Lights, Camera, Action, Love
Love in the Present Tense
Bayou Romance
Gamble on Love

TALES OF THE HAUNTED

It can be hard to remember a time when horror anthology series were all the rage. Shows like *Thriller*, *The Twilight Zone* and *Alfred Hitchcock Presents* began a legacy of small screen terror that eventually morphed into *Tales from the Darkside* and *Monsters*, while Hitch and Serling got their own remakes. In between many of these well-loved shows, are the ones that didn't fare as well. *Darkroom* was an excellent early eighties anthology that ran for six short episodes, and *Tales of the Haunted* only got one story told before moving into horror oblivion. *Tales* was a Canadian series that ran in syndication for thirty minutes every weeknight, and like *Romance Theatre*, told one story throughout those five days. Christopher Lee was the narrator. Their lone tale was titled *Evil Stalks This House*, and features Jack Palance as a menacing interloper who terrorizes a pair of elderly women located in a remote and appropriately creepy house. However, the tables are turned as Palance goes from terrorizer to terrorized. This intended shot on video series ran in July of 1981 on various independent channels and didn't seem to cause too much of a stir (although Lee's involvement generated some press). *Evil* was eventually edited together, cutting out much of the footage (including any existence of Lee's involvement), and squeezed into a one-hour format, which aired on CBS's late night schedule in 1987.

TURNABOUT

This gender-bending 1979 sitcom based on Thorne Smith's popular 1931 novel tells the tale of a successful and happy couple that find themselves in a pickle when they wake up in the other's body after making a wish. *Turnabout* attempts to bring the story into the world of second wave feminism, and has a lot of charm going for it, but little in the way of genuine laughs. The quirky but short-lived series got a new life in an early eighties re-edit, when four episodes of the series appeared as a TV movie. The pilot episode was combined with *Penny's Old Boyfriend*, *Statutory Theft* and *Till Dad Do Us Part*. The new ending, which shows the couple switching back to their original bodies appears to be reversed footage from their switch in the pilot.

MASHOUT? SHOGUN

As a twelve-hour miniseries event, *Shogun* was hard to beat. The finale drew close to 100 million viewers and one liquor store in Burbank reported a 700% rise in the sale of Saki thanks to *Shogun's* popularity. That's what we call a success! However, the running length made it an unlikely European theatrical release, and the 547-minute blockbuster was condensed down to a two-hour version that incorporated some extra violence and nudity while excising the heart of the story. This version debuted on network television in July 1984 and was later turned into a failed Broadway musical!

THE COLD WAR TURNS HOT ON TV: WORLD WAR III IN TELEVISION MOVIES

BY DAVID RAY CARTER

In the closing weeks of 1989, American President George H.W. Bush and Soviet leader Mikhail Gorbachev declared the Cold War over at the Malta Summit. The agreement put an end to the over fifty years of mutual hostility between the nations that began at the end of World War II. More importantly, it was a peaceful end to a particularly "hot" decade for the Cold War, one that saw the initiation of the Reagan Doctrine, the downing of KAL Flight 007, and the Soviet war in Afghanistan.

The tension of the 1980s was, of course, due in no small part to the strident anti-Communism of President Ronald Reagan. Reagan's patriotism infectiously swept across the nation, even taking root in his former stomping grounds of Hollywood. Nineteen eighties' cinemas were home to a new "red scare," with a number of films reinforcing Reagan's belief of communism as an imminent threat to the American way of life. Nineteen eighty four's *Red Dawn* and 1985's *Invasion U.S.A.* both posited communist invasions of America, with the US firmly the victor in both conflicts. Even outside the realm of communist invasions, the Soviet Union was portrayed as the villain in a number of box office blockbusters of the decade. Films like *Rocky IV, Rambo III, Top Gun*, and even the comedy *Spies Like Us* all featured microcosmic Cold Wars with the United States emerging on top each time.

The patriotism—perhaps even jingoism—of American cinema of this period is sharply contrasted with the much more measured portrayal of the Cold War on television. Where films reduced the conflict to good versus evil, television recognized that the reality of the Cold War was more nuanced and understanding and that both parties would be culpable for the outcome. That presumed outcome, a nuclear World War III, was most often presented as a welcome event in American films; a *fait accompli* that would be won quickly and painlessly by the US. TV movies of the period approached the idea of a World War III with far greater hesitation and, in

Catastrophe awaits in
By Dawn's Early Light
and *Threads*.

perhaps a bigger departure from their silver screen companions, without a clear winner or loser.

There are enough World War III TV movies to consider them to be a unique subgenre of the medium. They take on a variety of forms but structurally they fall into two camps: those that deal with the prelude to nuclear war, and those that deal with the aftermath. It is important to make the distinction between these forms and their cinematic equivalents to better illustrate the break between WWIII TV and film. WWIII TV movies, with few exceptions, are all structured around a nuclear war occurring, and in this regard those prelude films are not too dissimilar to their big screen brethren. However, the divergence comes when depicting the results of that prelude. Films like *WarGames, Octopussy,* and *Spies Like Us* each feature varying takes on averting nuclear war—"happy endings," so to speak. WWIII TV movies have no such happy endings and conclude with nuclear war shown or implied, as evidenced in the ending to the aptly named *World War III*, one of the first entries into this subgenre.

Those films that deal with the aftermath of nuclear war are, conceptually speaking, the most similar to cinema, as the post-apocalyptic genre of film was well-established by the eighties when WWIII TV movies first began to appear. There is, however, an even greater distance between television and cinema than is seen in the prelude films. Like Cold War cinema, post-apocalyptic cinema has a tendency to distill the concept into a simplistic good versus evil narrative. Aftermath TV movies dispense entirely with questions of morality and instead focus on the realities of life after nuclear war. Consider that *The Road Warrior* and the 1984 BBC movie *Threads* ostensibly have the same plot—survival after nuclear war—and the distinctions between how the two mediums approach the topic becomes clearer.

It should be noted that while WWIII TV movies deviate from their mainstream cinematic counterparts, they do have something of an analog in cinema. Many of these films have much in common with a strain of pessimistic science fiction films from the sixties and seventies. Titles like *No*

Blade of Grass, *Z.P.G.*, and the speculative documentary *The Late, Great Planet Earth* all offered similar, cynical views of the future.

Though related to this pessimistic science fiction, to refer to these films as pessimistic is an understatement, as the philosophies on display in these works are more akin to nihilism or fatalism. Just as the trope of averting nuclear war at the last second from Hollywood films is subverted, so is the idea that society would quickly pull together and rebuild. WWIII TV movies are deeply cynical about society's chance for survival after a nuclear war, both in regard to the practical aspects of living and to maintaining some type of societal cohesion.

To highlight the breakdown of society through microcosm, these films tend to eschew depicting large groups in favor of focusing on individuals and family units. The genre varies widely on how it treats its subjects, however. Films like *Special Bulletin* and *Threads* focus on small groups of characters but treat them with an almost clinical detachment that is akin to Frederick Wiseman's 1987 film *Missile*. Interestingly given that Wiseman's film deals with the military, military-centric films like *Countdown to Looking Glass* and *By Dawn's Early Light* tend to feature larger ensemble casts and approach the subject more melodramatically, with soap opera style performances.

These films are geographically diverse but tend to share the common temporal setting of immediately before or immediately after the nuclear disaster. Time is of extreme importance in all of the films of this subgenre. Large portions of the narratives are used to orientate the viewer in time and several entries feature on-screen dates or a literal countdown to emphasize the impending doom. With no exceptions, all of the movies take place in the current day relative to their production. It's an important distinction from cinematic portrayals of World War III, which typically take place in the relative future or under conditions different than the then-current state of the world.

This emphasis on time and the constant reiteration of being set in the present day is, essentially, a scare tactic. This shouldn't be that surprising— these are horror movies, after all. WWIII TV movies are horror movies that ultimately had a very short shelf life but were extremely effective in the period in which they were made. Revisiting them in the post-Cold War, post-Soviet Union world is an interesting experience. One gets the sense that these films weren't made out of any antiwar or antinuclear moralizing, but out of genuine fear on the part of the filmmakers that the events they were depicting could someday be a reality. The fact that these films span less than a decade is a sobering reminder for us how quickly the world could change and we could find ourselves back in a similar situation.

LIFE MODEL DECOY: THE PLIGHT OF THE SMALL SCREEN COMIC BOOK SUPERHERO

BY DAVID KEREKES

The popularity of the comic book superhero movie shows no sign of waning. A superhero movie is an event movie—certainly now that digital technology has caught up with the kinetic energy of the comic books themselves, and clued-in individuals are hired to translate these characters and stories for the screen. Superheroes are also a big deal for TV, for much the same reasons, with numerous ongoing shows and several more on the horizon as of this writing—*Luke Cage, The Flash, Iron Fist, The Defenders* among them—their hard-hitting trailers promising impressive special effects and some above average acting. It wasn't always like this. Superheroes were once kids' stuff, but not in a good way; they were flat and awkward and self-conscious in a bad TV movies way.

Many small screen superhero adaptations have been attempted over the years, but likely only the Spider-Man and the Hulk will spring immediately to mind. In any case, the results are far less amazing and incredible than the Marvel comic books that inspired them, grounded by modest TV budgets and technology. I would guess that the real reason these two particular heroes caught on with viewers when a number of others did not was the presence of a catchy theme song and a snappy catchphrase. Viewers of a certain age can easily reel off the (animated) Spider-Man main theme, so too David Banner's plaintive warning, "Don't make me angry... you wouldn't like me when I'm angry".

I haven't forgotten about *Batman*. The 1960s live action series based on the DC Comics character is also fondly remembered, but perhaps for reasons of kitsch and great guest stars and by people who haven't actually watched a single episode in its entirety, rather than as a serious comic book contender. Adam West's Batman—more Vegemite than vigilante—along with the show's high camp silliness, arguably did more to hinder superheroes on-screen than it served to benefit them.

Yet, at least the zany *Batman* kept things rolling. As we see time and again throughout this book, exposition can hide a multitude of sins; less so when it comes to superhero action narratives. Comic books race along apace, with Captain Smashing zipping from this panel to the next for a bad guy to smash. His TV counterparts on the other hand don't even attempt to leave the house without first having a good chat about it.

Few live action TV superheroes share the success of Batman and Spider-Man and the Hulk. Who remembers what The Spirit got up to or what he even looked like on the small screen, much less can hum his theme tune? The same goes for the small screen Captain Americas, all three of them.

Which brings us to Dr. Strange and Nick Fury. These two A-list Marvel characters appeared in feature length TV pilots of their own, but don't be ashamed for not knowing it. *Dr. Strange* (1978) and *Nick Fury: Agent of SHIELD* (1998) are sorely bereft of pulse-pounding action, and while each movie concludes on a note to suggest our hero will be back again very soon, they never came back.

Philip DeGuere's *Dr. Strange* opens with a portentous warning about the battleground that lies beyond the threshold of known and unknown, where the forces of good and evil are in eternal conflict and the fate of mankind hangs in the balance. Enter Stephen Strange (Peter Hooten), a psychiatric doctor with an eye for the ladies. He cares a lot, however, as someone points out early on, more so than some other doctors. Presently, Strange forgoes his chronic womanizing to become a master of the mystic arts for no good reason I can recall, other than his dad was a friend of The Master (John Mills), now too old and decrepit for the job.

Strange must battle Morgana LeFay (Jessica Walter) in the Netherworld, a "Dark Queen" for whom failure means the loss of her beautiful looks. A glowing eyed monster gives her this ultimatum. Unfortunately for LeFay, she finds Strange too damn attractive, and hence she fails. Yes, it's true: womanizing can be a virtue. It evidently was in the late seventies, when *Dr. Strange* was made. But who could know of its usefulness in the eternal fight against evil? A lesson for us all.

Rod Hardy's *Nick Fury: Agent of SHIELD* is a more terrestrial enterprise. David Hasselhoff plays the titular Fury, a macho cigar-chomping agent for the covert law enforcement organization known as SHIELD. He is introduced cracking rocks in semi-retirement in the Yukon, returning to SHIELD soon after when his old nemesis, Nazi Baron von Strucker, is freed from a cryogenics holding cell. Enemy of the free world, HYDRA, is behind it all, hatching

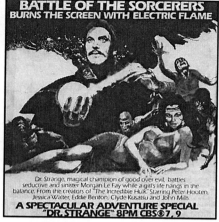

Clockwise from left, above: An evocative *TV Guide* ad for the not so evocative *Dr. Strange*; David Hasselhoff as Nick Fury puts the chokehold of love on Lisa Rinna; and Spidey looks out for Nicholas Hammond in a promo for the live action 1970s *Spider-man*.

new plans with an international cabal of terrorists and Hitler's doomsday weapon, the Death's Head virus, which is part of von Strucker's DNA.

Quite an enticing idea. But that's not accounting for the pratfalls the plot makes to avoid the idea, with ho-hum details of Fury's past, the frayed working relationship he maintains with his superiors, and the seductive allure of the Baron's daughter, Viper—eye candy with a bad German accent, lest we forget she's evil.

Fury is more entertaining than *Dr. Strange* and Hasselhoff is surprisingly okay in the lead role. He plays it straight and is a decent simulacrum of the iconic comic art of Jim Steranko. But the film's failing, which is effectively the failing of all small screen superhero adaptations, is that Fury has no grand stage on which to perform, nothing much by way of thrills beyond popgun shootouts in confined spaces.

To be fair, both *Nick Fury* and *Dr. Strange* take a swing at SFX. The former has a semi-decent animated SHIELD headquarters floating in the sky, and draws on the LMD (Life Model Decoy) of the comics, here an automaton that resembles Fury for use in a firefight. *Dr. Strange* is more adventurous with a stop motion monster in the Netherworld (it wobbles well) and a laser effect that mimics the star tunnel in *2001: A Space Odyssey*. As humble as these effects are, they undoubtedly proved a huge drain on budget, and watching the prototype LMD and the wobbling monster is like watching money falling out of a window. But that's not all. Despite two decades standing between them, *Dr. Strange* and *Nick Fury: Agent of SHIELD* are films that could easily have been made the same week. Not a lot appears to have happened nor improved in the years from one to the other: they are both clumsy in terms of concept and presentation; neither fish nor fowl, not exactly for kids but not wholly deserving of adults either.

I like superhero movies. But I like them more now than I did back then. Most things of a fantastical nature were essential to this kid, yet the screen approach to superheroes remained desperate and disappointing. Jump to a screening of *The Avengers* in a theater in 2012 and the revelation that *Wow! They've finally figured it out!* The journey here, to today's megabuck superhero franchise, has taken many years, but conversely it's also relatively sudden. The spandex outfit, ridiculous last Tuesday, looks pretty cool now, and the latest incarnations of our comic book myths are, on the whole, far more spectacular and better balanced; they are more *believable* than the TV shows and movies that have gone before. Yet, while high fiving the new freaks and mutants, let us not forget Hasselhoff's Fury, Peter Hooten's Dr. Strange and all those others who got left on the bus: the world might not salute you, I-Man, Exo-Man, M.A.N.T.I.S., unaired pilots for *Justice League of America* (1997) and *Birds of Prey* (2002), but it would be no less a place without you.

NIGHTMARE IN BADHAM COUNTY & A BRIEF HISTORY OF SMALL SCREEN EXPLOITATION: GOING DOWN SOUTH & BEHIND BARS

BY AMANDA REYES

Television films of the seventies and eighties often recalled their theatrical B film counterparts, relying on salacious titles and taglines to lure viewers into their clutches (the full page 1974 *TV Guide* ad for the premiere of the Andy Griffin potboiler *Savages* screamed, "He's found the perfect prey... A young, defenseless human"). However, because the FCC monitors television content, the small screen versions often fell back on the more classical elements of genre storytelling. Overt violence, foul language and nudity were a strict no-no for networks and the made for TV movie is frequently viewed as less sophisticated, hamfisted and sadly, disappointing. While television's "adult-content" might not implement the same poetic license devices, many TV genre films did their best to mirror those 42nd Street gems, and for kids like me—who couldn't even get into an R rated film if we wanted to—the small screen offerings were the next best thing. And, while it would seem unlikely that the notorious Women in Prison (WiP) or hixploitation genres could find a home for themselves on television, the networks found different ways to inject common exploitation traits into their restrained offerings.

The WiP subgenre got its start in the 1930s with films like *Ladies of the Big House* (1931), and *Ladies They Talk About* (1933), but gained more traction in the fifties and sixties. While those entries could be rather sleazy, if reserved, it wasn't until the seventies that WiP films entered more notorious territory, with titles such as *The Big Doll House* (1971), and *Caged Heat*

From left: VHS artwork vamps up an already gritty *Nightmare in Badham County*, starring Lynne Moody and Deborah Raffin, seen here in a promotional still.

(1974). Inevitably, early telefilms leaned toward the softer, earlier WiP films but peppered in a bit of the rougher modern fare, and the results were often mixed.

Following the subgenre rather faithfully, one of the grittiest telefilms is *Nightmare in Badham County* (ABC, 11/5/1976). In this tale, Cathy (Deborah Raffin) and Diane (Lynne Moody) are two pretty college girls driving across America during their summer break. Unfortunately, they enter Badham County, which is run by the ruthless Sheriff Danen (a menacing Chuck Connors), and he don't cotton to their liberated ways. He arrests them on trumped up charges, and proceeds to rape Diane in her jail cell. After a shady court hearing, the girls are sent to a work farm run by Superintendent Dancer (Robert Reed!), but while Dancer might be the head honcho, he prefers to let the more sadistic prisoners run the show (such as Greer, played by Tina Louise). The farm is racially segregated, and Cathy and Diane are instantly separated. They are desperate to get help, and intend to contact a family member any way possible, but the people who run the farm are hip to just about every trick Cathy and Diane pull.

Watching the injustices occurring in *Nightmare* is a frustrating experience. The bad guys are always one step ahead of the protagonists and our girls never find an easy out. The leads are tremendously sympathetic and their ordeal is suspenseful, and ultimately, heartbreaking. This is a pull-no-punches kind of flick, encased in heavy dirt and grit. Lacking any glamorization, everyone is a sweaty mess—even Tina Louise, and her fab cheekbones, looks downright grungy. The only semi-likeable baddie is Dulcie (Fionnuala Flannigan) who is another trustee with a soft spot for Cathy. But, even she hardly bends, making it feel like the whole world (or at least Badham County) is against our girls.

Ironically, when *Nightmare* was released theatrically overseas there was some fairly gratuitous nudity included. This format led some audiences to believe it was a true grindhouse effort, and *Nightmare* has certainly

Above: Ida Lupino, Belinda Montgomery, Jessica Walter and Lois Nettleton learn about lockup in the campy *Women in Chains*.
Right: Arlene Farber and John Savage go backwoods in *All the Kind Strangers*.

transcended its more modest small screen beginnings to become known as a fairly notorious B grade sleazefest.

But *Nightmare* wasn't the first telefilm that tried to cash in on the WiP genre. Susan Dey took a similar misguided journey when her character heads across California in *Cage Without a Key* (CBS, 3/14/1975). Her car also breaks down and she becomes an unsuspecting accomplice in a robbery that leads to murder, landing her in a girl's reformatory. And while not as politically motivated, this prison is also segregated, this time by the "good" clique and the "bad" girls, whom Dey inevitably runs afoul of. Using actual detention inmates as extras, *Cage* was presumably conceived as a teen-drama-bordering-on-propaganda telefilm. Yet, it foreshadows the upcoming *Nightmare* through the nuanced lesbian subtext that would become far more overt in *Nightmare*'s flagrantly added footage.

Nightmare's nihilistic tone also brings to mind the 1974 juvie jail shocker *Born Innocent* (NBC, 9/10/1974), where Linda Blair faces an uphill battle against the physical and mental atrocities of a screwed up system. *Innocent* pulls no punches in its grim presentation of teenage reformatories. Blair's character, a runaway who is thrown into a detention center to teach her a lesson, gets lost in the system, and quite literally loses her innocence when she is infamously assaulted with a broom handle, leading her to become just as embittered as her cynical and hardened contemporaries. And while the film does serve to present a more accurate, and pessimistic, view of life as a ward of the state, the notorious rape scene—presented without warning—was met with outrage. The scandal resulted in a congressional hearing, which led to the implementation of the "Family Viewing Hour," as well as a strong suggestion that networks present a parental advisory at the

Left: Susan Dey and Sam Bottoms live life in a *Cage Without a Key*. Above: Jaclyn Smith tries to *Escape from Bogen County.*

beginning of any television production featuring objectionable content.[1]

On the other side of the misanthropic prison bars, *Women in Chains* (ABC, 1/25/1972) is an unintentional parody of the genre (and I adore it). The casting of Ida Lupino as a nasty prison warden is a nod to the actress' appearance in *Women's Prison* (1955), where she played a similar character. In *Chains*, parole officer Sandra Parker (Lois Nettleton) goes undercover in a female correctional facility to expose Lupino, who may be behind the death of one of Parker's charges. Admittedly, *Chains* lacks a lot of grit that these types of films are famous for, but ups its camp factor with silly scenarios: one of the biggest acts of inmate rebellion is putting powder footprints on the cell walls (gee, that will *never* come off!), as well as including a "solitary" confinement chamber that houses two prisoners at a time, which probably defeats its purpose. And, even in its toned down, straight-faced presentation, it manages to be a rather amiable entry into the notorious genre.

Several other films have been produced through the years, including *Inmates: A Love Story* (ABC, 2/13/1981), which looks at what life might be like in a co-ed prison system (answer: it's apparently romantic). In 1994, a female writing and directing team took on corruption behind the walls of a women's prison in the ABC movie *Against Their Will: Women in Prison*

1 The Family Viewing Hour was a policy established in 1975 by the Federal Communications Commission, which declared the primetime hours of 8–9 P.M. as family friendly, meaning networks should be even more wary of violent or sexual content. Although this code was overturned in 1977 the general concept remained and became a staple of primetime television programming.

(10/20/1994). However, with a few exceptions in the realm of made for cable telefilms, the WiP subgenre lost its edge of exploitation, and faded quietly into the small screen sunset.

While *Nightmare in Badham County* stands as one of the most memorable of these small screen WiP entries, it also falls into another popular seventies exploitation subgenre, Hillbilly Horror, also known as hixploitation. Conjuring up many diverse images, from sultry weather and gothic plantations to barefoot children living in lean-to housing, the South, as sometimes depicted in the telefilm, is regarded as a place of conservative domination, where traditional ethics overshadow all other beliefs and values. Although sitcoms of the sixties often presented the South as a place of goofy and simple people (see The *Beverly Hillbillies, Green Acres* and *Petticoat Junction* for examples), the telefilms of the seventies embraced the darker stereotypes, for better or worse, and the product was uniformly interesting.

In *Nightmare* the hillbilly is expressed through its corrupt and racist southern "work farm" system that seeks to oppress, and/or destroy the ethos of strong young liberated women. Strangely, although the men take more of a backseat, they are the dominant force behind the protagonists' torture, and, for one, ultimate demise.

Like the WiP film, hixploitation flicks could be found early in cinema history with titles like *King of the Pack* (1926), and *Mountain Justice* (1930). They remain early markers of poverty stricken white rural Americana that would develop into the debased inbred, and sexually dysfunctional rednecks that filled up drive-ins throughout the seventies. And, again like the WiP on television, the hick mold was toned down, although many nasty undertones come across clearly, especially that of the backward, violent hillbilly man.

All the Kind Strangers (ABC, 11/12/1974) explores these hixploitation conventions with a group of seven clodhopping kids so eager for a whooping, they kidnap unwitting strangers and force them into the role of disciplinary parents. Stacy Keach is the sophisticated Northerner who picks up a precocious child walking down a long stretch of nothing highway. Once at the house, Keach is introduced to his siblings—ranging in age from five to eighteen, and, strangely enough, their British "Ma," even though it has been established that Ma (and Pa) died sometime back. These kids are desperate for a strong authority figure, and pick up random strangers whenever they present themselves. Unfortunately, if the newly and forcibly adopted parental units don't express love with vicious castigation, they are killed off.

Strangers presents Keach as materialistic but enlightened, and the bevvy of uneducated rugrats speak with hillbilly overtones and look like they could use a new pair of shoes. The mute sister (Arlene Farber) defines a backward backwoods sexuality, even going as far as putting a snake in her nuMa's bed in an effort to win Keach's hand. As the eldest sibling, John Savage is pure menace, but, although he's old enough, and stern enough to take over the empty patriarchal spot at the table, he clings to a lower hierarchal space in lieu of recreating the idealized family unit, emphasizing the stereotyped conservative South's desire to maintain an unwavering version of family.

Enforcing conventional family ideals through violent means was also the theme of *Escape from Bogen County* (CBS, 11/7/1977), which features a young Jaclyn Smith (working through her first *Charlie's Angels* hiatus) as a woman who is only seen as property. Her husband is a rough and powerful abuser, who treats his wife like a terrified possession. And, much like Connors in *Nightmare*, he also runs his town on the same fear factor, backed by a stupid and corrupt police force. Michael Parks is the new cop on the block and he'd rather be a country singer than an officer of the law. He is, as you might have guessed, assigned as Smith's love interest. Embodying the perfect Southern Gentlemen, he even serenades Smith as she rots in a holding cell. The film, meant to carry over mainstream feminist underpinnings, loses its message in its hixploitation haze, but the music is nice.

Whereas *Nightmare* was released as a telefilm, and then found itself as a notorious exploitation theatrical release, in a serendipitous move, on December 2, 1978, CBS premiered *Outside Chance*, which sort of follows the same blueprint in reverse. This half remake/half reimagining of *Jackson County Jail*, which had been released the previous year, features Yvette Mimieux reprising her role in the somewhat notorious hixploitation/WiP mashup. Yvette is Dinah Hunter, an advertising executive who runs afoul of a corrupt small town when her car is stolen on a road trip. In *Jackson*, Mimieux kills the guard who rapes her in her holding cell and then flees with a young Tommy Lee Jones. In the "remake," she stands trial for the murder of the officer and is sent to the pokey, where she escapes with the girlfriend of the man who stole her car! Definitely not as gritty as the original, the director of both films injects approximately thirty minutes of footage from *Jackson* into *Chance*, and also has the good sense to cast Betty Thomas as a callous fur poacher, which makes it worth a view just for that!

And again, much like the WiP telefilms, hixploitation never truly took off as a much sought after TVM subgenre, but did enjoy a few more interesting releases. Wes Craven's *Stranger in Our House* (aka *Summer of Fear*, NBC, 10/31/1978) places the hillbilly as an interloper into the more "sophisticated" suburban community, forcing her to resort to black magic and mayhem to fit in. The generally well-received ABC Movie of the Week, *Moon of the Wolf*

(9/27/1972) uses the Louisiana Bayou as the setting for a werewolf horror picture, while also exposing the underbelly of the rich South. Even Roger Corman got into the mix in the 1980 pilot movie *The Georgia Peaches* (CBS), which is a good ol' boy comedy attempting to latch onto the success of *The Dukes of Hazzard*.

Nightmare in Badham County's mixture of the two subgenres helps the telefilm stand out in a way very few other TVMs have, making it a fascinating curio that indicates ABC's awareness of then-popular B-movie fare. Despite its flaws and the unnecessary addition of nudity, *Nightmare* aptly, even if somewhat softly, reflects the drive-in culture of the era, bringing some of its more lovably outrageous features directly into our living rooms.

YOU CAN GO HOME AGAIN: THE POPULARITY OF THE REUNION TV MOVIE
BY AMANDA REYES

The 1985/86 TV movie season was a prolific one, featuring several interesting releases ranging from sophisticated dramas (*An Early Frost*) to lighthearted fluff (*Beverly Hills Madam*), but the season may be best remembered as the year we all welcomed Andy Griffith and Mayberry back into our living rooms. Airing on April 13, 1986, *Return to Mayberry* was seen in over twenty-eight million homes, making it the seventh highest rated telefilm ever at the time of its debut. But Andy and his loyal sidekick Barney weren't the only fondly remembered characters reuniting on the small screen that year. Raymond Burr resurrected *Perry Mason*, recapturing its audience (while establishing a devoted new fanbase), spawning over two dozen more telefilms that featured Perry and his dutiful assistant Della Street (all hail Barbara Hale) bringing justice to mostly high-class citizens caught up in intricate webs of deceit. In fact, the movie series was so popular four more TVMs were shot with different actors stepping in as Mason's upright buddies after Burr's passing in 1993.

This, of course, was not the birth of the reunion movie; it enjoyed previous success in such nostalgic fare as reuniting the cast of *Father Knows Best*, not once but *twice* in 1977, and revisiting the Cleavers in Springfield in 1983's *Still the Beaver* (leading to a new made for cable television series). But it was the one-two punch of *Mayberry* and *Mason* in the 1985/86 season that legitimized collecting the surviving members of well-loved television series.

The reunion TV movie actually has a long history, starting with *Dragnet* in 1969.[1] What's curious about this entry is that it was produced three years earlier, in 1966, before the revived series aired. Apparently Jack Webb, who oversaw and starred in both versions of the show, wanted a different approach for the sixties remake, and held back on the TVM until he found the

1 Richard B. Armstrong & Mary W. Armstrong, *Encyclopedia of Film Themes, Settings & Series*, 201–202.

right balance. Yet, while this telefilm is darker in tone (Friday and company pursue a serial killer), it is quite fondly remembered, and often cited as one of the best entries into *Dragnet*'s long and illustrious career.

Following on the heels of the *Dragnet* TVM, the late seventies saw a small surge in reunion telefilms, bringing back old favorites such as *Maverick* (1978), in an attempt to drum up interest in a potential new series, or simply to get the gang back together, as with *Gilligan's Island* (1978), which was successful enough to stretch that three-hour tour into two more reunion sequels! But, reunion movies aren't without their misfires, interesting though they may be. Nineteen seventy-seven's oddball *Murder in Peyton Place* attempts to reignite the hotbed of sex and betrayal that was so popular during *Peyton Place*'s original run from 1964–69, although it only confused and alienated viewers. The series was also responsible for launching the careers of Mia Farrow and Ryan O'Neal, and consequently, *Murder in Peyton Place*'s producers assumed that neither actor was interested in returning to their small screen roots, and decided to brutally kill off the characters, building a mystery around the murders. While many great *Peyton Place* faces reprise their roles in the telefilm, including Ed Nelson and Dorothy Malone, there were mixed feelings from certain cast members. Christopher Connelly who played Norman Harrington lamented, "It was like going back while everyone else was moving on. Like Ryan and Mia and Lee [Grant]. It was like going back and doing your first job all over again."[2]

Connelly wasn't the only actor who wanted to move forward instead of looking back. In 1981 Max Baer Jr. turned down *Return of the Beverly Hillbillies* (which would prove to be the right decision), and James Brolin declined to rejoin Robert Young in *The Return of Marcus Welby M.D.* (1984). Of course, Baer, a successful producer, and Brolin, a well-known actor, did not have to return to the familiar to pay the bills. Still, while typecasting was a concern, audiences tended to be more forgiving with favorite characters, and actors seemed only too happy to revisit their old series haunts. And then there were the in-name only reunions, such as *Gidget's Summer Reunion* (1985), and *Bonanza: The Next Generation* (1988), which hoped that the idea of those shows were strong enough to withstand new faces.

Whether bringing back original actors or recasting from scratch, many telefilms rely on the familiar as a method to lure in audiences immediately, and underneath the reunion TV movie rests a deeply rooted sense of nostalgia and a yearning to return to traditional ideologies. During the eighties the popularity of revived television series' originally produced in

2 Associated Press, "Remember Rodney, Allison? They've been murdered," *Eugene Register-Guard*, Oct 1, 1977.

Right: The gang—Ken Osmond, Tony Dow, Barbara Billingsley and Jerry Mathers—get back to together in the sweet and well-received *Still the Beaver*.
Below: Warm and fuzzy makes its way back to the small screen in the #1 movie of the 1985–86 season, *Return to Mayberry*.

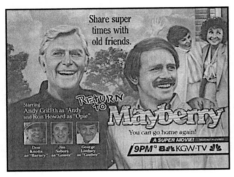

a "better time" was prevalent and offered a conservative nod toward idealized family units, nine-to-five jobs, and life issues that could be resolved before the end credits rolled. It is in this way that television plays the very important role of memory making. Viewers become so attached to characters, places and happy endings that it becomes a part of how audiences remember collective (and sometimes even individual) pasts, real or imagined.

Even in the seventies, when television was still fairly young, viewers were already embracing a desire to return to the comfortable, recognizable faces of yesteryear, foreshadowing the heavy traction these TVMs would gain throughout the eighties. By 1984, the reunion telefilm was in full swing, and the Associated Press wrote about the numerous revival TVMs on the horizon. Reunion movies that were currently in production toward the end of that year include *I Dream of Jeannie*, *Kojak*, *Route 66*, and *Dobie Gillis*.[3] The popularity of these telefilms proved that you could stretch credulity (Steve Austin's son goes bionic in the *Return of the Six Million Dollar Man and the Bionic Woman* for example; and, even more unlikely, Jeannie and Major Nelson are separated in *I Dream of Jeannie: Fifteen Years Later*!). As long as filmmakers kept it friendly and safe, audiences were more than happy to spend a night with their favorite characters in just about any situation.

Brian Levant, co-executive producer of *Still the Beaver*'s spinoff series, *The New Leave it To Beaver* cited the audience's "strong bond" with classic

3 Associated Press, "Lots of old favorites being revived in new TV movies," *Eugene Register-Guard*, Sep 8, 1984.

television characters,[4] while CBS's David Poltrack took a more cynical view, citing reunion movies as a "more efficient product in terms of promotional resources."[5] Poltrack's transparency reveals that the real bottom line of networks was cultivating reliable systems that ensured viewers tuned into their program. In this case, cultivation simply meant leaving the formulas unchanged, because with the popularity of reunion movies, networks also found a form of critic proof television. Not to mention saving writers and producers the extra sweat and tears, pressure, and money needed to invest in successful original programs. It proves that familiarity does not necessarily breed contempt. It's a bit more like contentment. Still, innovation be damned, many of these reunion movies are quite good.

One of the best, as it turns out, is *Return to Mayberry*. Bringing back over a dozen original cast members, *Mayberry* capitalizes heavily on the feel good aesthetic of the reunion movie. Griffith, well aware of the pressure to please his diehard fanbase originally rejected the idea of making a reunion movie until he met up with his old co-stars Don Knotts and Ron Howard on an Emmys show. Even then, he turned down the first script and brought in writers he felt had a better understanding of the characters and setting.[6] The end product was no groundbreaking effort, and critics were largely indifferent about the telefilm at the time of its original airing. But, its adherence to old school ideologies pleased the masses and frankly, this lack of edge and an overwhelming need to remain honest to the characters makes *Mayberry* one of the warmest and most watchable reunion films of the era.

Often, this fashionable new trend in television film led to serial reunions, such as the aforementioned *Perry Mason* series. Other well-loved shows returned again and again (and again), such as *Eight is Enough*, *Hart to Hart* and *The Waltons*. The TVM follow ups were met with varying levels of success, but somehow kept bringing in returning viewers, sometimes for over a decade or so with sequel after sequel. *The Waltons* in particular remains one of the most beloved families in television, and even after the run of their telefilms, surviving cast members still reunite for screenings and other types of meet and greets, much to the pleasure of their devoted fanbase.

Still, as the years wore on, TVM reunions such as *Knight Rider 2000* (1991) and *CHiPs '99* (1998) became less of an event and more of a joke. Journalist Ron Miller aptly wrote, "Even pay dirt turns to mud if you water it down enough and keep stirring it up."[7]

4 Ibid.
5 Newsday, "TV gives lesson in 3 Rs: reunion, revival, remake," *Eugene Register-Guard*, Nov 8, 1994.
6 Alan W. Petrucelli, "Original Cast to Reprise Their Roles in 'Return to Mayberry,'" *Herald-Journal*, Apr 6, 1986.
7 Ron Miller, "Nominations made for 10 worst TV 'reunion' programs," *Bangor Daily News*, Apr 11, 1991.

The unintentional death knell of the reunion TVM may have hit in 2000, when *The Mary Tyler Moore Show* attempted to reclaim their network success with a reboot telefilm *Mary and Rhoda*, which was intended to launch a new series. The only actors to return were Moore and Valerie Harper, who originally played Mary's BFF Rhoda. Moore hoped that the movie would walk the line between old and new, and that the other legacy characters could be brought back in subsequent episodes or movies. Although the TVM was a runaway ratings success, attracting over seventeen million viewers, audiences missed the old gang, and critics and fans alike received the film poorly. It would be one of the last gasps of the reunion telefilm, proving that too much tinkering only estranges faithful fans. And the curtain was mostly drawn on this type of television movie.

Later on, reunion programming developed in interesting ways. As the nineties wore on and television movies became less attractive to the networks, reunions morphed into nonfiction clip shows. Casts from beloved shows like *Laverne and Shirley* and *One Day at a Time* sat in front of pleased audiences recounting their memories of working on a hit series. And it wasn't only the sitcoms taking on this format—the drama series' *Knots Landing* and *Beverly Hills, 90210* also joined this new casual talk show approach.[8] While obviously done on the cheap, when the casts were open to revealing insider moments, or just genuinely interested in sharing the stage once again with their co-stars, the results were charming. *The Andy Griffith Show* was brought back yet again, not once but twice, in this format with surviving members reliving the good old days in 1993's *The Andy Griffith Show Reunion*, and then one decade later in 2003's *Andy Griffith Show Reunion: Back to Mayberry*.

Then, the reunion movie underwent yet another metamorphosis, opting for a docudrama behind-the-scenes approach. These TV movies were not nearly as enchanting, and often more interested in inflated melodrama among horrible period recreations. However, 2005's *Dynasty: The Making of a Guilty Pleasure* (ABC) manages to be self-aware and daring enough to dive into the camp without pretending that wasn't what they weren't aiming for.

After all of these years, the television reunion is still going strong. In 2016 Netflix revived *Full House* with *Fuller House*, and *The X-Files* resumed its journey toward the truth in a limited six-part series. Nostalgia will always be a selling point for those who have immersed themselves in favorite shows, and as long as networks and studios can entice actors back to the set, we can always go home again. Even if for only a couple of hours and in between commercial breaks.

---

8 The popular Knots Landing also enjoyed a reunion miniseries in 1997 titled *Knots Landing: Back to the Cul-de-Sac*.

SCRATCHING ON GLASS: AN INTRODUCTION TO STEPHEN KING ON TELEVISION
BY LANCE VAUGHAN

On the night of November 17, 1979, I did not sleep well. Earlier in the evening CBS aired the first part of a miniseries based on the Stephen King novel *Salem's Lot* and it had quite the effect on me. I would later learn I was hardly alone in my disquiet. One scene in particular refused to loosen its grip, and anyone who has witnessed director Tobe Hooper's uncanny take on the material will instantly know of what scene I speak. It involves the nocturnal visit of a ghoulish sibling to his older brother's bedroom window. Sporting fangs and a pumpkin grimace the child floats among swirling mists while coaxing his brother to allow him entrance with an unearthly scratch upon the glass. If you were a child watching in the late seventies, this haunting scenario had a particularly sadistic sting in its tail, for when it was over many of us poor kids were rushed to bedrooms that looked no different from the one we were so relieved to leave behind on the small screen. Then again, I just watched the nightmare encounter once more to refresh my memory and, some thirty-five years later, it hasn't lost any of its power to chill.

Even though *Salem's Lot* was a huge success on all fronts, King's work (with the exception of various episodes of both *Tales from the Darkside* and *The Twilight Zone* series revamp) was in such high demand throughout the 1980s that it was more likely to be snatched up for cinemas rather than produced for television. Happily the drought would transform into a crimson downpour at the start of the new decade with the 1990 miniseries *IT*. Based on what is arguably the ultimate King novel, *IT* concerns a group of lifelong friends who must confront an evil that exploits their every fear and usually presents itself as a malicious, mocking clown named Pennywise. The grand tome was split into two parts and aired on two (not consecutive) nights, with the first part focusing on the gang of outcasts as naïve children and the second part as

This iconic image from *Salem's Lot* caused many a sleepless night.

world-weary adults. For many viewers, the introductory segment is the stand-out; the concluding segment attempts to up-the-scares provided by Tim Curry as Pennywise in the first half, and it simply can't be done. In fact, one could throw any critique they pleased at this miniseries but there's no denying that Curry delivers one of the all-time great horror performances.

The mid-nineties welcomed a four-part adaptation of what many consider King's masterpiece, *The Stand*, as well as a two-part adaptation of *The Tommyknockers*, a book King himself has described as "awful." Neither lands on their feet but there's no question which one falls from a greater height. Few would expect *The Tommyknockers* to be anything besides diverting entertainment, and in this respect it reaches its modest goal with an exceptionally likeable cast. On the other hand, the mind reels at the possibilities for greatness in *The Stand* adaptation, but most of them are squandered away. The disappointment is all the more bitter given that the epic miniseries starts out with a bang. There are some great moments, but the overall lack of vision (or budget) collide with a few clunky performances for something altogether less than satisfactory.

Next up was 1995's *The Langoliers*, directed by genre regular Tom Holland (of *Fright Night* fame) and based on a novella featured in King's anthology *Four Past Midnight*. The story combines familiar airplane disaster movie tropes with eerie interdimensional *Twilight Zone*-worthy time travel elements. It's a thought provoking albeit long-winded affair further hindered by the instantly dated computer effects, which attempt to visualize what would have been better left to the imagination.

Speaking of visuals, the craft of computer generated effects had developed enough by 1997 to tackle the overzealous topiary hedge animals of *The Shining*. It's well known that King was never a huge fan of director Stanley Kubrick's earlier interpretation of the novel, possibly his most personal creation; nearly two decades later the author would have the last word.

Publicly King often voiced his dissatisfaction with Jack Nicholson's performance, notably the lack of transformation/deterioration in his role of the alcoholic Jack Torrance. But if King's teleplay of *The Shining* is anything to go by, his qualms go deeper. It's safe to say that the three-part telefilm reconstruction doesn't risk eclipsing Kubrick's masterwork, but it's not without its charm. The performances by the two leads, Steven Weber (as Jack Torrance) and Rebecca De Mornay (as wife Wendy), are top notch and although the scares are not quite icicle sharp, there's still something fascinating in spending time in the location (Colorado's The Stanley Hotel) that inspired the novel.

The close of the decade delivered the miniseries King himself lists as one of his favorite adaptations, *Storm of the Century* (1999). I'm of the mind to agree. *Storm of the Century* is a rare beast in that it's not based on an existing work of King's but was created specifically for television. Well aware of the format by this point, King avoids the usual pitfalls and concessions for a straightforward, well-oiled effort that avoids ostentation without ending up drab. Place and setting are utilized to the utmost, and the characters are as relatable as they are memorable. Colm Feore delivers a true stand out performance as the strikingly villainous Andre Linoge.

Storm of the Century was a collaborative effort by King and stunt man turned director Craig R. Baxley. Its success inspired them to team up again for another original miniseries, a love letter to Shirley Jackson's *The Haunting of Hill House* entitled *Rose Red* in 2002.[1]

The symbiotic relationship between television and the works of Stephen King continues. His tales may find splashier glory on the big screen, but the small screen, which inspired much of King's love for fantasy and horror in the first place, allows some of his heftier tales more room to breathe in adaptation. Whether it's cable ready TV movies based on short stories like *Trucks* (2000) and *Big Driver* (2014); popular novels like *Desperation* (2006); miniseries' like the remake of *Salem's Lot* (2004) and *Bag of Bones* (2011); King's multiple stabs at a series' like *Golden Years* (1991), *Kingdom Hospital* (2004), *Nightmares and Dreamscapes* (2006); or the multiple seasoned *Under the Dome* (2013), King's constant influence on television is just as strong as his powerful foothold on cinema and writing in general, which is to say unprecedented and—not unlike my memory of a certain vampire boy floating on air and scratching on glass—everlasting.

---

1 Baxley would helm a *Rose Red* prequel the following year, based on King's characters but written by Ridley Pearson.

GOLDEN YEARS

Director: Kenneth Fink (ep.1), Allen Coulter (eps. 2,4,6), Michael Gornick (eps. 3,7), Stephen Tolkin (ep.5)
Starring: Keith Szarabajka, Felicity Huffman, Ed Lauter, Frances Sternhagen
Airdates: July 16–August 22, 1991   Network: CBS

An elderly janitor, caught in a top secret laboratory explosion, begins aging in reverse, and is pursued by a mysterious government agency.

Beginning life as the outline for a novel that sat gestating in Stephen King's notebook for years, *Golden Years* would ultimately materialize as an original television production, with King himself writing the screenplay for the first five episodes, and providing a detailed outline for the final two episodes. Initially, the idea was for *Golden Years* to be a continuing series, but when CBS decided not to go ahead, the original cliffhanger ending to the seventh episode was edited for subsequent broadcasts and home video releases, to give it a more concrete and optimistic conclusion.

At the time of its original broadcast, King described *Golden Years* as "like *Twin Peaks* without the delirium."[2] Unfortunately, it also lacked the wit, characters, dialog, ambience and beautiful production design of David Lynch's cult television series. There's barely enough story, let alone characters, to keep it interesting and engaging for the seven episodes, let alone try to see where they could have possibly taken it had the show in fact continued as originally planned.

The set-up of *Golden Years* is certainly promising enough, even if it is established in pure 1950s sci-fi B-movie simplicity. Reversing the aging process is something we all probably think about at certain points as we get older, and the best and most emotionally impacting moments of *Golden Years* explore the relationship between the main character, elderly Harlan Williams (Keith Szarabajka), who is growing younger and more virile by the day, and his beloved wife and lifelong partner Gina (Frances Sternhagen) who will continue to age as normal. There are some great moments between the two, particularly as Gina starts to worry that Harlan will stop finding her physically attractive as he grows younger, yet the screenplay doesn't really explore the layers of the relationship as much as it could, instead getting derailed with a lot of political and espionage subplots involving The Shop, the fictional top secret government agency that King has featured in several of his stories, which has been established to investigate paranormal and strange activity, but are evil and malicious in their methods and intent.

Produced by Richard P. Rubenstein and his Laurel Productions (whose long

2 *New York Times*, July 14, 1991.

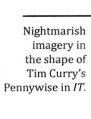

Nightmarish imagery in the shape of Tim Curry's Pennywise in *IT*.

association with King began with the 1982 horror anthology *Creepshow*), *Golden Years* has a very cheap and bare bones look to it, and the makeup used to age Keith Szarabajka is unconvincing and obvious from the start, which is a pity as Szarabajka's performance, along with that of Sternhagen's, provides one of the few real highlights of this moderately entertaining but ultimately disengaging tale. As he often does, King shows up in a cameo role, playing a bus driver in the fifth episode. Of course, hearing the classic 1975 David Bowie song Golden Years on the soundtrack certainly brings a brief sense of cool to the show whenever it pops up. It should have used it more often. [John Harrison]

IT

Director: Tommy Lee Wallace
Starring: Richard Thomas, John Ritter, Annette O'Toole and Tim Curry
Airdates: November 18 & 20, 1990   Network: ABC

Seven young friends forge a bond when they confront and supposedly defeat a mysterious figure of evil in the midst of their otherwise quiet town. Three decades later, their supernatural nemesis returns.

Probably the most viewed small screen adaptation of any of Stephen King's works, and almost certainly the most successful, this epic coming-of-age horror story (originally screened as a two-part miniseries) rightfully takes its place as a true classic of its kind.

The highly respected source novel—a huge tome and one of King's longest works—was ripe for TV audiences whose patience for the master's scares was perhaps better satiated over a couple of nights rather than months. Indeed, it was a hugely successful exercise that paved the way for a spree of highly anticipated small screen adaptations in the immediate years that followed— some good, others less so—but none ever came close to matching this one for sheer fun, scares and excitement; the three key elements that King fans line up for.

The film is of course best remembered for introducing us to the horror genre's most famous killer clown. So much has been made of Tim Curry's scene stealing performance as the shapeshifting antagonist Pennywise (a casting decision that even detractors of the film unanimously praise) that it's easy to forget the contributions of the rest of the cast. Both the young and adult ensembles are instantly likeable and share a genuine chemistry that is never less than engaging. However, it is the teleplay by Laurence Cohen and director Tommy Lee Wallace that deserves the most recognition, being more concerned to depict real people in an unreal situation—the essence of which marks King's best work—rather than simply concentrating on the narrative's purely fantastical elements; the latter approach most often opted for by filmmakers with inevitably dismal results.

Since its original release, *IT* has a garnered a cult following among genre fans, appealing primarily to the nostalgia crowd as a kind of "gateway" horror title, being that it contains just the right mixture of thrills, chills and undeniably cheesy melodramatics that are the stock and trade of all beloved TV movies. As with any adaptation from a popular work, the film has its vocal critics, too; the chief consensus being that far too much has been omitted from the book's narrative pertaining to the relationships among the characters and the very nature of IT itself. But these arguments, as ever, are rather churlish; readers have already been appropriately serviced by the novel, whereas television audiences have an altogether different palate, and this one plays perfectly to the taste of the armchair horror junkie.

IT is both landmark television and a landmark horror title. Admittedly, aspects of the production have dated somewhat, but the majority of it still works well enough and its merits far outweigh the snobbish criticism it has attracted in some quarters. This is not a hatchet job of an adaptation. The epic size of the source novel has been skillfully pared down to a lean, mean three hours of horror that has characters you actually care about and a truly iconic villain that you'll never forget. [Kevin Hilton]

THE LANGOLIERS

Director: Tom Holland
Starring: Patricia Wettig, Dean Stockwell, David Morse, Mark Lindsay Chapman & Bronson Pinchot
Airdates: May 14–May 15, 1995   Network: ABC

 When a red-eye commercial flight passes through an aurora borealis, ten passengers discover that everyone else onboard has vanished.

Despite the almost grade school nature of the computer effects used to visualize the title creatures, *The Langoliers* is one of the more effective Stephen King projects to have been adapted for the small screen.

Based on a novella that first appeared in King's 1990 collection *Four Past Midnight*, *The Langoliers* works so well not so much because of its characters or performances, but in its central themes, the effective build-up of tension, and its clever twist on time travel tropes.

The set-up is pure *Twilight Zone*: a passenger flight passes through an aurora borealis, sending it back only fifteen minutes in time, but to a world that is completely deserted save for the ten people who were sleeping onboard the plane at the time. As the survivors, who manage to land the plane at an airport, try to work out what has happened to them and the people around them, an ominous noise grows slowly louder from over the other side of a mountain range. Described invariably as like "milk being poured on Rice Krispies" and an army of "coked-up termites," it's when the source of this noise finally makes itself known that *The Langoliers* really delivers its sting. In King's take on time travel, the past doesn't exist, and there is no going back to correct mistakes, as the past is literally eaten by the Langoliers, large flying/bouncing balls with nothing but a giant mouth filled with rows of huge, shining and sharp metal teeth that continually rotate like a deadly chainsaw. The Langoliers follow just behind us in time, mercilessly and unstoppably devouring the past, including anyone and anything trapped in it.

A big part of the success of *The Langoliers* lies in the choice of Tom Holland as writer and director. Having written the screenplay for *Psycho 2* (1983), as well as writing and directing two great eighties cult horror films in *Fright Night* (1985) and *Child's Play* (1988), Holland brought to the table a handful of strong genre credentials, and had previously honed his skills in fantasy television by directing episodes of *Amazing Stories* (1985–87) and *Tales from the Crypt* (1989–86).

Holland's screenplay is able to take what is essentially a short film or one-hour television episode at most, and stretch it out to two ninety-minute installments without stretching the viewer's patience. While his direction is solid and he gets some nice performances out of several of the cast members, in particular Dean Stockwell (as a mystery writer trying to apply the logic and deduction found in his books to what is happening to him) and Mark Lindsay Chapman as a British secret service hitman who is questioning his career choice. The most over-the-top performance belongs hands-down to Bronson Pinchot, co-star of the popular sitcom *Perfect Strangers* (1986–93), who chews almost as much scenery as the Langoliers themselves. Pinchot plays an arrogant and failed broker driven to the point of psychological collapse by his domineering father, who always scared him with tales of the Langoliers, and how they would come and gobble him up if he ever wasted time or got lazy with his schoolwork (Stephen King cameos as his boss during a hallucinatory fantasy sequence).

Filmed primarily on location at the Bangor International Airport in King's hometown of Bangor, Maine—where much of the story also takes place—*The Langoliers* has the same fairly bland and flat low budget look of many telemovies and miniseries' from that period, but its intriguing plot and an effective, pervading sense of mystery more than helps to cover its visual and technical shortfalls. [John Harrison]

SALEM'S LOT

Director: Tobe Hooper
Starring David Soul, James Mason, Bonnie Bedelia, Reggie Nalder, Lance Kerwin
Airdates: November 17 & 24, 1979   Network: CBS

 A novelist returns to his hometown to find that sinister changes in his idyllic community might be the work of a vampire infestation.

I was only a youngster when I first saw "prodigal son" and writer Ben Mears (David Soul) swiftly turn two popsicle sticks into a makeshift crucifix to protect himself from an undead Marjorie Glick (Clarissa Kaye). And my heart skipped a beat when I heard Mike Ryerson (Geoffrey Lewis) hiss "Look at me teacher..." while his yellow eyes glared with disturbing burning intelligence, all the while baring his twisted fangs in front of a shaky Matt Burke (Lew Ayres).

From the first viewing of Tobe Hooper's *Salem's Lot* on TV, I was hooked. Addicted. Obsessed by the idea that an entire town would fall victim to darkness; and that one by one, these all-American characters (that looked as though they had popped out of Thornton Wilder's play *Our Town*) would become bloodthirsty, predatory and genuinely terrifying vampires.

This two-part miniseries hit a nerve for me and one of the core reasons it did was that it presented a narrative structure that I have always been insanely attracted to—the *Ten Little Indians* motif. This concept of "the next one is gonna be me" has always appealed to me, and *Salem's Lot*, with its fundamental core essence as a story about townsfolk being birthed into vampirism, served this story-type hunger.

Tobe Hooper's adaptation of Stephen King's sweeping novel about small-town America being devoured by something ancient and very evil is incredibly moody, beautifully structured, happily unsentimental and intelligent with its handling of the terror and its thrills. The pacing is also

The ultimate in terror!

SALEM'S LOT

"SALEM'S LOT" DAVID SOUL JAMES MASON
LANCE KERWIN BONNIE BEDELIA LEW AYRES
RICHARD KOBRITZ STIRLING SILLIPHANT
PAUL MONASH STEPHEN KING TOBE HOOPER

Above: Promotional artwork.
Right: Reggie Nalder proves
to Lance Kerwin that he takes
no prisoners in *Salem's Lot*.

a major highlight, as, given its two-part structure, we are allowed to spend necessary time with these characters. The townsfolk of Salem's Lot are so well written, nicely developed and always interesting to watch that when they turn into parasitic feral monsters it is both creepy and heartbreaking. The film boasts legendary character actors, such as Marie Windsor as boarding house owner Eva Miller and Elisha Cook Jr. as town drunk Ed "Weasel" Craig, as well as newcomers of the time, Fred Willard as realtor Larry Crockett and Lance Kerwin as the brave and intuitive boy Mark Petrie, who survives the vampire holocaust.

Besides the inspired casting and slickness of the piece, three major narrative elements of *Salem's Lot* inspired me from the get-go. Firstly, this was the first time I remembered seeing working class vampires. Replacing the oft-used characteristic of aristocracy (the multiple times I had seen Dracula or fellow counts, princes, countesses and so forth) with school teachers, waitresses and truck drivers gives *Salem's Lot* a very grounded realism that even at a young age I responded to. Instead of a devilishly decedent European gothic terrain where horse-drawn carriages lead hapless victims to opulent but oppressive castles, we had stretches of countryside where a young art teacher like Susan Norton (Bonnie Bedelia) could happily sketch among the grassy surroundings and pristine white picket fences framed the neatly manicured lawns of small-town America. This was Peyton Place—a halcyon serene Norman Rockwell painting conceived in mundane normalcy, but much like Grace Metalious' novel (and sequential filmic adaptation from director Mark Robson in 1957) this town had secrets—secrets that would be rendered meaningless once introduced to the town's most recent residents: the urbane Renfield-stand-in Richard Straker (James Mason) and the elusive Kurt Barlow (Reggie Nalder).

The characterization of Barlow would be the second major highlight for me in regards to how Tobe Hooper altered Stephen King's original vision. Having read the novel after seeing the miniseries, I was so glad Hooper went with the blue-skinned, feral Nosferatu-like towering menace instead of King's sophisticated Mephistopheles. The introduction of Barlow is forever etched in my memory: In a quiet scene where local handyman Ned Tibbets (Barney McFadden) is lying on a bunker in a jail cell, the door gently glides open as if by some unholy magic, and we are greeted by stabbing shock as the horrific image of Barlow's monstrous face snarls head on in full close-up. And later, when Barlow appears in the disheveled Petrie kitchen only to smash June (Barbara Babcock) and Ted Petrie (Joshua Bryant) into each other was a childhood trauma.

Thirdly, and possibly most profoundly, is the fact that *Salem's Lot* would be the first vampire outing to introduce a generation of horror fans to child bloodsuckers. Sure there would be more to come as seen in *Near Dark*, *The Lost Boys* (both 1987) and *Interview with the Vampire* (1994), but here in *Salem's Lot*, the iconic imagery of vampire children Ralphie Glick (Ronnie Scribner) and Danny Glick (Brad Savage) tapping at the window and floating in midair—eyes piercing the darkness and pearly white teeth exposed, with skin deathly pale—is a thing of nightmares. A dark play on the Peter Pan mythology where you will never grow up and therefore never face responsibility—something spookily endearing for second wave monster kids growing up in the late seventies and early eighties.

Salem's Lot is a perfect summary of "small-town disease"—the perpetual darkness, the endless quiet and the inability to connect. Vampirism consumes the New England residence, but it is truly emptiness that suffocates its townsfolk—transforming them into soulless leeches lost in post-McCarthyism America. [Lee Gambin]

THE SHINING

Director: Mick Garris
Starring: Rebecca De Mornay, Steven Weber, Will Horneff, Melvin Van Peebles & Courtland Mead
Airdates: April 27–May 1, 1997   Network: ABC

 A recovering alcoholic, trying to make his mark as a writer, descends into violent madness when he takes his wife and young son to look

after the isolated Overlook Hotel.
Although widely considered not only
one of the better film adaptations of
his works, but a cinematic horror classic
in its own right, it is well known that
Stephen King never particularly liked
Stanley Kubrick's 1980 adaptation
of his 1977 novel *The Shining*. King
reportedly was unhappy with the
way Kubrick handled the story's
themes, and the suggestion that the
lead character, Jack Torrence (Jack
Nicholson) was well on the road to
craziness long before he even reached
the Overlook Hotel.

As a result of King's dissatisfaction
with Kubrick's film, the author was
always keen to re-imagine his book
for the screen, taking advantage of
the string of television adaptations of
his work that were being produced

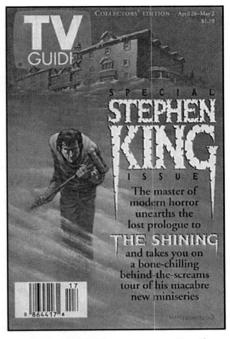

Creepy *TV Guide* cover promoting the
small screen adaptation of *The Shining*.

throughout the 1990s. Curiously, despite *The Shining* being King's story,
Kubrick obviously still retained some control of its cinematic rights, as the
remake was only given the green light after King agreed not to speak publicly
about his dissatisfaction with Kubrick's film.

Bringing back the director of *The Stand*, Mick Garris, was a smart idea,
and King as sole scriptwriter was able to adapt his novel the way he always
envisioned it. Even though he disliked Kubrick's version, there can be little
doubt that King would have felt pressure to try to deliver something that
could live up to the lofty expectations set by it. And while it doesn't have
anywhere near the level of cinematic craft or engaging performances
captured in Kubrick's film, it is a surprisingly effective retelling of a classic
ghost tale. For people who have loved the 1980 movie but never read the
original source novel, the most interesting aspect of watching the miniseries
is to spot all the changes that were made by Kubrick (who clearly wanted
to make a "Kubrick film" first and foremost, rather than a Stephen King
adaptation). King devotees, meanwhile, will enjoy the miniseries for giving
them a more faithful version of the story they are familiar with (an advance
in computer effects also allowed the miniseries to depict, albeit not very
convincingly, some elements of the novel which at the time Kubrick would

not have been able to include even if he had wanted to—such as the animated and shapeshifting hedge animals).

Anyone stepping into the role of Jack Torrence after Jack Nicholson was going to have their work cut out for them, but Steven Weber carries the weight fairly well, and his performance and the screenplay is much more successful in portraying Torrence's madness as something brought on by the presence in the Overlook Hotel, rather than something that was already boiling inside of him prior to his arrival. As his wife Wendy, Rebecca De Mornay does not have the same haunting and lost features of Shelley Duvall, but she is always terrific to watch in any of her roles from around this period, and the rest of the show's limited cast, including Courtland Mead as young Danny Torrence, Melvin Van Peebles, Elliott Gould and Pat Hingle, all earn their paychecks for their respective roles.

The Shining slowly but effectively builds a palpable and mounting sense of horror and dread throughout its nearly five-hour running time, and King buffs will appreciate that a lot of the miniseries was filmed at the Stanley Hotel in Estes Park, Colorado... the hotel that King used as the inspiration for the Overlook in his original novel. [John Harrison]

SOMETIMES THEY COME BACK

Director: Tom McLoughlin
Starring: Tim Matheson, Brooke Adams, Robert Rusler and William Sanderson
Airdate: May 7, 1991   Network: CBS

Jim Norman was a boy when he witnessed the murder of his older brother by a trio of punks. Decades later, back from the dead, the killers are hell-bent on revenge.

Adapted from a short story from Stephen King's *Night Shift* collection, though not quite as dark as the prose piece that inspired it, this made for TV movie is nevertheless a gutsy, tightly paced treat that goes full throttle all the way, successfully belying its limited budget and small screen trappings.

Favorably benefitting from a small but recognizable cast of talents and assuredly directed by genre journeyman Tom McLoughlin (*One Dark Night*, *Friday the 13th Part VI*), the emphasis here is on gore and cheap thrills rather than touchy-feely melodramatics, although an awkward smattering of the latter forgivably remains.

For fans of such fare, the most refreshing thing about this production is that it is a "straight-up" ghost story—the first King adaptation to properly deal in this subgenre since *The Shining*—but whereas Stanley Kubrick's movie set out its stall (some might argue, rather clunkily) on the psychological aspects of a family's haunting, this one takes the opposite approach, exploiting the subject matter with all the visceral, ghoulish joy of an old EC Comics strip, and in fact, the project was originally intended for inclusion in the theatrical horror anthology, *Cat's Eye*, an earlier Dino De Laurentiis production based on the writer's works.

Tim Matheson as the terrorized Jim Norman strikes the correct balance of fear and resolve, while Brooke Adams as his suffering wife sensibly plays it straight, her performance appropriately anchoring the narrative in a vague sense of reality before proceedings becomes too awash with comic book silliness. However, as in any good horror movie, the villains steal the show, with cult fan favorite Robert Rusler being particularly impressive, clearly relishing the opportunity to ham it up as the leader of the gang.

Sometimes They Come Back is not without its faults; the noticeably threadbare plot makes little attempt to refine itself with any logic, and as such, suspension of disbelief is an essential viewing requirement, but for those willing to give themselves over to the carny theatrics, there's much to enjoy. It was ultimately successful enough to be followed by two direct-to-video sequels. [Kevin Hilton]

THE STAND

Director: Mick Garris
Starring: Gary Sinise, Molly Ringwald, Rob Lowe, Laura San Giacomo
Airdates: May 8–12, 1994   Network: ABC

After a deadly weaponized strain of influenza kills off ninety-nine percent of the Earth's population, a small band of immune survivors across the US prepare for humankind's final stand between good and evil.

First published in 1978, *The Stand* was one of Stephen King's most epic and ambitious novels, certainly to that point in his writing career, and any filmic adaptation would need to be similarly grand in order to do the book justice. Fortunately, those involved with the production, including once again Richard P. Rubenstein and his Laurel Entertainment Company, realized this, investing a then rather sizeable amount of $28 million into making sure the vision and scope of the novel was successfully translated to the small screen. The result is impressive and makes for one of the better live-action interpretations of a Stephen King work, certainly of those produced for the television medium.

With solid direction from Mick Garris (*Psycho IV: The Beginning, Sleepwalkers*) and King providing the screenplay, *The Stand* contains a lot of the elements, tropes and character traits that are well familiar within the writer's horror *oeuvre*—including the accident at a government facility that triggers the whole disaster, and ordinary people experiencing psychic

Right: Ominous main titles for *The Stand*.
Above: Turbulent terror arrives during the *Storm of the Century*.

visions—but mixes them all in with just the right doses to make the story appear fresher and stronger than perhaps it really is. The prospect of germ warfare or a killer virus let loose into the atmosphere is a real and very terrifying one, and invokes a sense of paranoia as well as feelings of helplessness against an attack. King makes the situation more relatable and palpable by populating his apocalyptic story with a roster of primary characters that are nicely realized and fleshed-out.

Another reason why *The Stand* miniseries works so well is because of the outstanding cast assembled for it, most of them turning in terrific performances. Gary Sinise in particular shines in the lead role, as a Texas everyman trying to comprehend why everyone but him is dying of the flu, but he is ably supported by the likes of the exotic Laura San Giacomo, Miguel Ferrer, Ray Walston, Shawnee Smith and Jamey Sheridan as the demonic Randall Flagg, a character who would re-appear in a number of King's subsequent works. And it's fun to see two former members of the infamous 1980s "Brat Pack," Molly Ringwald and Rob Lowe, not only together in a project but really digging deep and creating an impact with their roles. Stephen King puts in his usual cameo, but also popping up on-screen are such faces as film directors Sam Raimi, Tom Holland and John Landis, along with noted drive-in movie critic Joe Bob Briggs (credited under his given name, John Bloom) and uncredited appearances by Kathy Bates and Ed Harris.

Complementing the production values and fine performances is the rather excellent soundtrack, which brilliantly uses Blue Öyster Cult's 1974 rock classic (Don't Fear) The Reaper over its opening sequence of bodies dropping dead at the weapons facility, along with other pop hits like Don't Dream It's Over from Crowded House and Boogie Fever by The Sylvers, to go with the instrumental score composed by W. G. Snuffy Walden. [John Harrison]

STORM OF THE CENTURY

Director: Craig R. Baxley
Starring: Timothy Daly, Colm Feore, Casey Seimaszko and Jeffrey DeMunn
Airdates: February 14– 18, 1999   Network: ABC

 The close-knit community of Little Tall Island is preparing for a blizzard, but discovers it has bigger problems when a stranger with dark powers arrives.

By the end of the nineties, Stephen King's popularity—having originally migrated from novels to cinema—was now firmly bankable on the small screen, as well. After a run of notable successes, the ABC network offered him carte blanche in selecting which of his works he might favor to adapt next. Admirably, he decided to try something a little different, creating what he referred to as "a novel for television"; which was essentially a teleplay based on an original idea that he hadn't published.

Storm of the Century begins promisingly, and arguably boasts Stephen King's best writing for television. Fans of his fiction will certainly be pleased that the diverse palette of small-town characters that color his novels have made the transition to the screen perfectly. But the premise itself, delightfully chilling as it may be, simply does not contain enough elements to truly justify its running time. However, the production quality for the most part is high enough to distract from the lost opportunity of its concept.

In regards to the cast, Colm Feore is particularly impressive as the villain, bringing to the proceedings an air of menace and evil in reserve, while character actor Jeffrey DeMunn is his reliable self as the irascible town leader. Timothy Daly as the Sheriff, protagonist and everyman, suitably embodies the typical Stephen King "hero," despite being given little to do but make grandstanding speeches and look puzzled at the supernatural events happening around him.

The film's narrative thrust essentially derives from a moral dilemma presented to the Sheriff: provide an unspeakable sacrifice or risk damning the town's population to an even worse fate. But, like the movie's villain itself, the film takes a ridiculously long time laying out its intention, leading to a thematically satisfying, but fairly predictable ending.

Whether they love 'em or hate 'em, King fans enjoy comparing the adaptations to the novels, and while this "adaptation" without a source story is an interesting experiment, it's not a wholly successful one. There are too many elements of the narrative that feel as if they aren't properly realized, or perhaps, which is more likely, King's remarkable gifts at suspending our disbelief for hokey goings-on is best realized in prose.

Fairly ambitious and passably entertaining, *Storm of the Century* is a slow burn that's chief flaw may be that it demands a little too much from the casual TV viewer, or, on the contrary, the audience may prefer to dedicate the considerable attention required of it to one of the master's novels instead. [Kevin Hilton]

THE TOMMYKNOCKERS

Director: John Power
Starring: Marg Helgenberger, Jimmy Smits, Joanna Cassidy, Traci Lords
Air dates: May 9–10, 1993   Network: ABC

 The inhabitants of a quiet American town undergo subtle but sinister changes after a writer discovers an unusual structure in the woods near to her house.

The TV adaptations of Stephen King's novels are almost as prolific as the writing of the man himself, and not always for the better. Having caught a screening of *Bag of Bones* (2011) on TV a week before sitting down to watch *The Tommyknockers*, let's just say my expectations weren't especially high. I was pleasantly surprised, then, that *The Tommyknockers* turned out to be quite an entertaining, well-paced two-parter.

Committed fans will find many King hallmarks to make them happy here: tales of an ancient and mysterious force in the depths of the woods recalling *Pet Sematary*'s Indian burial ground, and the obligatory reference to the town of Derry (appearing here as a refuge from the Tommyknockers' power). There are also more than a few unsubtle echoes of 1980s horror movies: *Nightmare on Elm Street* (1984), and *Dolls* (1987), but most notably *Poltergeist* (1982), as young Hilly (Leon Brown) talks, enraptured, to an unseen force and later hears the voice of his brother—who has mysteriously disappeared—calling for help somewhere in the house.

Fittingly, the series takes on the tongue-in-cheek approach of many eighties horrors, with slightly silly comic book elements that make it more *Creepshow* than *Children of the Corn*. One of the less disturbing of the Tommyknockers' traits is their desire to help the residents of Haven Falls with various inventions, all powered by an unearthly luminous green light (though it's never quite clear why such an all-powerful force is also heavily reliant on common-or-garden batteries). Consequently, café owner Bryant constructs a device that will automatically make BLTs, writer Bobbi a "telepathic typewriter," and postmistress Nancy—played by Traci Lords—a mail-sorting machine. It's hard to take Lords seriously as she gushes about her "invention," but then we're not supposed to—her casting as the slightly cartoonish bombshell postmistress is inspired, and elsewhere in the film she puts in a genuinely creepy performance as she too falls under the spell of the Tommyknockers.

The success of *The Tommyknockers* lies in the fact that, by the end of part one, the viewer is none the wiser as to what or who the Tommyknockers actually are. Sure, we know there's something not quite wholesome about them, but the various goings-on in this first part cleverly build a sense of unease without offering any clear pointers. (And if you're reading this without having yet watched *The Tommyknockers*, I suggest you turn the page now.) Midway through part two things get more interesting, as Hilly's grandfather begins to investigate the strange incidents

JIMMY SMITS   MARG HELGENBERGER

Something wonderful is happening in Haven.

Pray it doesn't happen to you.

STEPHEN KING'S
THE TOMMYKNOCKERS

Artwork promoting *The Tommyknockers*.

that have taken place in the woods over the years: murders, accidents, and hints of an ancient curse. Personally, I was slightly disappointed when the reveal finally came—not ghostly or demonic forces, but aliens... As Bobbi (Helgenberger) and husband Jim (Smits) explore the spaceship full of desiccated extraterrestrial bodies that has been hidden in their back yard for who-knows-how-many years, I felt slightly cheated, much as I am by the abominably lazy "It was all a dream!" revelation. While the aliens are certainly grotesque vampiric creatures, the sudden switch from subtly creepy to full-on, sometimes slightly cheap, monster effects (very similar, in fact, to the *IT* miniseries) is a shame considering the effective build-up, but—I have to admit—entirely in keeping with the comic book horror aesthetic that *The Tommyknockers* seeks to (successfully) evoke. [Jennifer Wallis]

REVIEWS:
THE TV MINISERIES

According to Alvin Marrill's *Movies Made for Television*, the debut of the miniseries was *The Blue Knight*, which premiered in November 1973 (although *Vanished* from 1971 is noted as the first "long form" TV movie, airing over two nights). While it looked a tad different than the way we tend to envision the miniseries (this layered and complex four-part series was composed of only one-hour episodes, and lacks a lot of the glamorous location and period piece details of some of the more famous entries), it proved that audiences were willing to involve themselves in a limited series. Much like the TV movie, the miniseries took a little time building steam, but by the mid-seventies, this format was generating critically acclaimed productions that varied in themes and topic, covering everything from slavery to vampires.

The miniseries is different than a telefilm in several ways, including its multi-episodic but limited nature, and its larger, overreaching story arc (something that became predominate in long running series in later years). It was also often backed by the kind of money most television filmmakers would have bent over backward for, and its epic, sweeping cinematic quality set it apart critically from its telefilm and even TV series counterparts. Still, there are plenty of genre offerings to be had, and while one tends to think of *The Thorn Birds* (1983) or *North and South* (1985), true crime, horror and sci-fi were all given the royal treatment in this format. Like the telefilm, the miniseries still relies on restrained storytelling devices, focusing on mood and characterizations. But the miniseries has the time and money to immerse its audience in adventures that are just not feasible in a shorter TV movie format, and are also too limited to warrant a full television series run. Inevitably, the miniseries helped to legitimize genre films for television.

THE DARK SECRET OF HARVEST HOME
Director: Leo Penn
Starring: Bette Davis, David Ackroyd, Rosanna Arquette, Joanna Miles
Airdates: January 23 & 24, 1978   Network: NBC

 As a relocated urban family comes to grips with an idyllic village's local traditions, there is a suspicion that paradise isn't what it seems.

Screened on NBC in 1978, the miniseries *The Dark Secret of Harvest Home* is an unusual entry in the seventies folk horror canon, but one that certainly deserves a place within it. Following on the heels of the cult classic *The Wicker Man* (1973), the tale of an urban family moving to an unsettlingly perfect rural village owes more than a little to atmospheric Hammer offerings such as *The Witches* (1966).

Bette Davis provides a direct link with this Hammer lineage. As the matriarch of Cornwall Coombe village, she bears a striking resemblance to her character in *The Nanny* (1965): in a black high-necked dress, white cap, and owlish glasses, she perfectly embodies Widow Fortune, outwardly kindly with a hint of something malicious beneath the surface. Widow Fortune presides over Cornwall Coombe as doctor, wise-woman, and counselor, and it is this insular standpoint that appeals to the Constantines, who are the archetypal neurotic city family. Nick (David Ackroyd) drinks while Beth (Joanna Miles) attends regular appointments with her psychiatrist to get over Nick's carrying-on with another woman; their daughter Kate (Rosanna Arquette) suffers from stress-induced asthma attacks—hardly surprising considering that she is paying a street gang not to harass her on her way to and from piano class. Moving to the Coombe, and beneath the wing of Widow Fortune, appears to remedy all their ills: Kate's asthma disappears,

Original *TV Guide* ad.

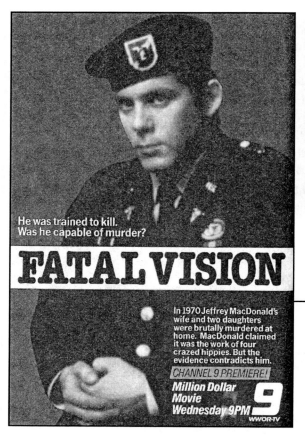

He was trained to kill.
Was he capable of murder?

FATAL VISION

In 1970 Jeffrey MacDonald's wife and two daughters were brutally murdered at home. MacDonald claimed it was the work of four crazed hippies. But the evidence contradicts him.

CHANNEL 9 PREMIERE!
Million Dollar Movie
Wednesday 9PM **9**
WWOR-TV

Left: Gary Cole impresses in the miniseries *Fatal Vision*.
Above: Monsters are afoot in *House of Frankenstein*.

Nick applies himself to his work as an artist, and the Widow seamlessly takes the place of Beth's shrink.

Things slowly unravel as Nick detects subtle hints of something rotten beneath the nauseatingly twee façade of their new home. *The Dark Secret of Harvest Home* uses an awful lot of its five-hour running time to repeatedly signal to the viewer that something is amiss in the Coombe. The residents are quite sickening in their enthusiastic vaunting of "tradition," continually harping on about the wonders of self-sufficiency and emphasizing—rather ominously—that no one need ever leave the village. The rural idyll motif is overdone at times—as Nick crosses a street we see a succession of horses and carts, while the sound of sheep bleating in the background is so frequent as to be almost comedic. There is shock among the onlookers of a ploughing contest when the village rebel uses a tractor rather than a horse and cart, leading to loud cries of "It's against the ways!" "The ways" are tediously present throughout, the villagers using them as both badge of honor and threat, and one begins to wonder why Nick and Beth found Cornwall

Coombe so attractive in the first place (particularly bearing in mind that Nick's photographs of it on their first visit revealed the figure of Widow Fortune lurking, reaper-like, in the background of every shot).

The slow pacing of *Dark Secret*, though, does allow the more sinister manifestations of "the ways" to build gradually without the whole becoming too schlocky. A hallucinatory elixir is given to the couple by Widow Fortune in a nod to *Rosemary's Baby* (1968), corn dollies are found strewn in the fields, and an erotically-charged harvest dance leads up to the obligatory ritual-in-the-woods scene. This final scene, revealing "the ways" in all their bloody glory, is a rewarding end to what is a sometimes slightly plodding, convoluted narrative (a subplot about villager Grace Everdeen, buried outside the cemetery gates in disgrace, for example, never feels properly resolved). Perhaps the most tantalizingly underused element is the appearance of Donald Pleasance, in voice only, reading *Great Expectations* on an audio cassette continually played by the Constantine's blind neighbor—I'd have paid good money to see Donald in the flesh, playing a bumbling police investigator alongside Bette's formidable materfamilias. [Jennifer Wallis]

FATAL VISION

Director: David Greene
Starring: Gary Cole, Karl Malden, Eva Marie Saint, Barry Newman
Airdates: November 18 & 19, 1984   Network: NBC

 Based on the true crime case of Jeffrey MacDonald who was convicted of killing his wife and two small children.

Although time would bring a little gray into the black and white world of the murder of Dr. Jeffery McDonald's family, at the time NBC adapted Joe McGuiness' bestselling true crime book of the same name the real-life justice system and the court of public opinion had already convicted the doctor of the heinous crime. Prolific television screenwriter Joe Gay's adaptation follows the book fairly closely, and director David Greene creates a harrowing and heartbreaking film broken up into two very specific parts, as a way to represent the alleged dual nature of the convicted husband.

The first section of *Fatal Vision* sets up McDonald as the innocent and loving, if a tad eccentric, family man who woke up to a group of hippies terrorizing his home, à la the Manson Family. Brutally, but superficially, stabbed across his abdomen, McDonald finds himself helpless to save his wife and two daughters, aged two and five. Attempting to leave the past behind, McDonald's in-laws stand by his side as accusations fly. However, his father-in-law (the exquisite Karl Malden in an Emmy winning turn) slowly begins to see cracks in McDonald's story and soon embarks on an almost decade-long crusade to see his daughter and granddaughters' murders brought to justice.

The second half of *Fatal Vision* shows a different side of McDonald. One who is cloying, manipulative and sociopathic. A man who had affairs and one who seems to truly enjoy the attention he's been getting from the press. But which side is really McDonald, a man who is still serving his sentence and still claiming his innocence? Probably both.

It's easy to see how audiences could have been swayed by this story. The claim of a marauding hippie group had caused much anxiety at the time, but it is still frankly ludicrous. However, McGuiness, who was hired by McDonald before his trial began, openly admitted that once he got into the convict's good graces he became sure of his guilt and wrote the book with that slant. McDonald later sued McGuiness, and the case was settled out of court. Subsequently, several publications have refuted his book.

At the time, however, America was convinced, and the film does nothing to sway viewers any other way. Even with these ethical issues in mind, *Fatal Vision* is a fascinating watch. It is engrossing, uncomfortable, and full of top notch performances. While Malden is the clear standout, Gary Cole, who had yet to find fame in *Office Space*, or as Mike Brady in the big screen *Brady Bunch* adaptations, is magnificent as the man with two faces. While his character attempts to portray shades of innocence throughout the film, there is a continual glimmer of guilt, as well as one of subdued glee for getting away with it. It's an early marker of the brilliance that was to come from Cole and his prolific career.

While true crime has never been an anomaly in the made for television movie genre, at this point in the mid-eighties, there were still a few years to go before crime really began paying for the networks. Grabbing audiences' attention with a headline, several strong early miniseries', such as *The Atlanta Child Murders*, and *Out of Darkness* set the stage for the true crime films that flooded the networks less than a decade later. *Fatal Visions* is one of the best. [Amanda Reyes]

GOLIATH AWAITS

Director: Kevin Connor
Starring: Mark Harmon, Christopher Lee, Frank Gorshin, Emma Samms
Airdates: Circa November 16 & 17, 1981   Network: Syndicated

During an impromptu underwater salvage mission, a crew finds the Goliath, which sank forty years earlier. Also discovered are the surviving passengers and their offspring.

Back in the 1970s when made for television movies were all the rage and the smaller independent stations didn't have the access to quality first-run syndicated programming, several stations banded together and formed what they would call Operation Prime Time (OPT). These indies teamed up with larger studios, such as Universal's MCA TV, and Columbia, who would foot a certain amount of production costs, with the smaller stations shelling out the majority of the bill. The goal was not to create a fourth network; rather, it was simply an option for smaller stations that wanted to provide unique programming fare from time to time.

OPT was a rather short-lived, but influential, venture, lasting a little over a decade, and their mostly memorable output was typically lush and epic. While they threw a few contemporary romances or comedies into the mix, period pieces and historical dramas were often the name of OPT's game. *Goliath Awaits* is a mixture of the big and small OPT projects, merging grand scale storytelling in the modern day.

Shot on the Queen Mary in Long Beach, California, *Goliath Awaits* was an idea that took years to reach its fullest potential in production. To add some believability to the over-the-top premise, the producers called in experts and the US Navy for consultation. The results manage to make the somewhat hinky science fiction that was so prevalent in film during this era seem far more palpable. Phosphorescent algae lighting up a submerged luxury liner? Sure, why not?

Workmanlike direction from TV stalwart Kevin Connor doesn't offer much in the way of flourish, but is capable, and the director inserts a touch of realism to the some of the technical sequences (some of which were apparently culled clips from other films). Connor was quite at home with fantastical adventure, having previously helmed *At the Earth's Core* (1976), and *Warlords of the Deep* (1978), among others.

But, what makes *Goliath Awaits* so substantial and worth a look is the knockout performances from Christopher Lee, Frank Gorshin and many of the other cast members who ranged from seasoned (Eddie Albert, and John Carradine in a warm and thoughtful supporting role) to relatively new faces such as Emma Samms and Mark Harmon. Other cast members include a pre-*Cheers* John Ratzenberger who goes on and on about the tasty delicacy of octopus eyes, real-life married couple John McIntire and Jeanette Nolan, and the prim and proper Jean Marsh who plays the lovelorn medic who sets her eyes on one of the landlocked cuties. Only Alex Cord seems out of place with a southern accent that goes in and out like the tide.

But even with all of those friendly faces, it is Lee's compelling portrayal of a maybe-benevolent leader who has developed an intense God complex that will keep you glued to your seat. As his right hand (hit)man, Frank Gorshin walks a line that could easily have set him into indulgent bombast but he's uniformly terrifying, providing the right amount of underwater menace.

Goliath Awaits was met with mixed reviews and its VHS release further truncated the sprawling and complex tale, leaving out some of the meatier and more interesting subplots, such as the top secret letter Eddie Albert has asked Robert Forster to intercept. But those who first saw this fantastical yarn upon its original voyage, er, airing, tend to look back on it fondly. [Amanda Reyes]

GUYANA TRAGEDY: THE STORY OF JIM JONES

Director: William A Graham
Starring: Powers Boothe, Ned Beatty, James Earl Jones, Randy Quaid
Airdates: April 15 & 16, 1980   Network: CBS

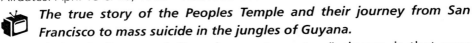 ***The true story of the Peoples Temple and their journey from San Francisco to mass suicide in the jungles of Guyana.***

One of the challenges of "based on a true story" cinema is that your audience knows where the story is going as soon as it begins. William A. Graham acknowledges this fact, and thus begins his *Guyana Tragedy: the Story of Jim Jones* at the end, in the blackness of the Guyanese jungle. Sirens blare, sending the pajama-clad residents of Jonestown rushing to Jim Jones' makeshift amphitheater for a "white alert"—a planned mass suicide to occur as mercenaries approach Jonestown. The throngs eagerly gulp down a liquid of unknown origin, some feeling relief, others disappointment, when Jones announces that this was merely a drill.

"Why" and "how" were the two nagging questions left in the public's mind in the wake of the tragedy at Jonestown. Specifically, "why had they killed themselves" and "how had Jones convinced them to do it?" These questions are at the heart of *Guyana Tragedy*, which was actually the second film on Jonestown. The first was *Guyana: Crime of the Century* from Mexican B-movie king René Cardona Jr.; a quickie, "names have been changed" exploiter that nevertheless was largely factually accurate. *Guyana Tragedy* is decidedly more upmarket in terms of production values and presentation, however it is no less exploitive—teasing the audience with an opening scene that hints at the symphony of death they are going to have to wait over three hours to see. *Guyana Tragedy* presents itself as a biography/psychological case study of Jones but much of it ultimately feels like it is only there to delay the inevitable. Graham appears to be working under the (incorrect) theory that the longer the film makes you wait for the final "white alert," the less exploitive it is, but the longer it is delayed the more the concept of it overpowers the narrative.

Guyana Tragedy falls short of answering the questions in viewers' minds but this is less a fault of the film than simply due to the many inexplicable aspects of Jones' life. We follow Jones from child minister to a segregation-defying crusader for social justice, the latter of which he supported by being a door-to-door pet monkey salesman. *Guyana Tragedy*'s structure is its strength, often presenting the many inconsistencies in Jones' life more ably than the narrative does. One particularly masterfully done scene has the still mild-mannered Jones lamenting to his wife about how exhausting his charity work is. She suggests amphetamines, and as soon as the word is spoken the film abruptly cuts to Jones bathed in light, wearing a solid white robe and his trademark sunglasses indoors. Drugs take the blame for Jones' transformation from an idealistic young preacher to a faith-healing, sex-crazed megalomaniac but the personality shift is so dramatic that this explanation won't be accepted by most viewers.

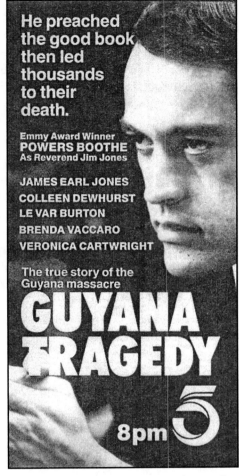

He preached the good book then led thousands to their death.

Emmy Award Winner
POWERS BOOTHE
As Reverend Jim Jones

JAMES EARL JONES
COLLEEN DEWHURST
LE VAR BURTON
BRENDA VACCARO
VERONICA CARTWRIGHT

The true story of the Guyana massacre

GUYANA TRAGEDY

8pm 5

The charismatic Powers Boothe terrifies as Jim Jones in *Guyana Tragedy*.

Guyana Tragedy is a deeply engaging document of a compelling figure. The film offers few satisfactory answers, but the strength of the material is such that few will mind. It features a truly star-making performance by Powers Boothe as Jones. Boothe's charisma rivals that of the real Jones and it is doubtful that a lesser actor could have adequately portrayed the enigmatic leader without overacting. Like Jones, Boothe alternates between benevolence and menace with terrifying ease and his performance alone makes *Guyana Tragedy* rank among the best the genre has to offer.

[David Ray Carter]

HELTER SKELTER

Director: Tom Gries
Starring: George DiCenzo, Steve Railsback, Nancy Wolfe, Marilyn Burns
Airdates: April 1 & 2, 1976   Network: CBS

 The true story of the investigation of the Tate-LaBianca murders and the arrest and trial of Charles Manson and his "Family."

Of the numerous judicial sideshows that have been dubbed the "trial of the century" over the years, only one of them has been so omnipresent that the American President himself has weighed in with his thoughts on the matter. That distinction goes to *The State of California vs Charles Manson, et al.*—the Manson Family trial—and Richard Nixon's widely publicized declaration of Manson's guilt during a critical phase of the trial. Manson held up a copy of the *Los Angeles Times* bearing a "Manson Guilty" headline in an unsuccessful attempt to have a mistrial declared. This incident and the several others like it make up the most memorable scenes in 1976's *Helter Skelter*, based on Manson prosecutor Vincent Bugliosi's book of the same name.

The Tate-LaBianca murders have served as the inspiration for countless films and documentaries since 1969. Most, however, end where *Helter Skelter* chooses to begin—the morning after the Tate murders. The movie accurately depicts the key aspects of the investigation and that of the subsequent LaBianca murders, including the LAPD's initial insistence that the two crimes were unrelated. *Helter Skelter* never hesitates to chastise the LAPD, making much out of their inability to finger Manson and company for the crimes and their mishandling of one of the murder weapons, which, unbeknownst to them, had been in their possession since immediately after the crime.

The time spent on the Manson/Nixon incident and the foibles of the LAPD investigation all serve the same narrative purpose in *Helter Skelter*: the glorification of Vincent Bugliosi. Bugliosi places himself as the true star of the Manson trial, overcoming an inept police department, Manson's tricks, and the inference of the President to secure a conviction. He frames himself as a dedicated but unknown Assistant DA, but the fact of the matter is that before the trial began a fictionalized version of Bugliosi appeared in NBC's *The DA: Murder One* (1969), on which he had served as a technical consultant. It's an interesting bit of trivia that *Helter Skelter* fails to include, instead presenting Bugliosi as a tireless crusader for justice with no interest in the limelight. Bugliosi's self-aggrandizement becomes most transparent in *Helter Skelter*'s obviously fictional conclusion, which sees a remorseful Manson congratulating Bugliosi for defeating him.

Bugliosi's grandstanding aside; *Helter Skelter* is an invaluable document of the Manson trial that makes a valiant effort to provide an objective view of events. It's an unusual take on the now familiar story that places the lawyers and police officers at the center of the narrative instead of the famous victims and their infamous killers. *Helter Skelter*'s focus on the crime's aftermath was unique for the time but would go on to become the standard of police procedural television; *Law and Order* being just one example of a series structured in a similar fashion. Keeping with the theme of objectivity and historical accuracy, George DiCenzo (Bugliosi) and Steve Railsback (Manson) attempt to outdo one another's scenery chewing in much the same way one imagines their real-life counterparts must have. However, the film's true overachiever is Nancy Wolfe's scene stealing portrayal of Susan Atkins. DiCenzo and Railsback come off as simply overly theatrical—Wolfe appears to actually be criminally insane. [David Ray Carter]

HOUSE OF FRANKENSTEIN

Director: Peter Werner
Starring: Adrian Pasdar, Teri Polo, Greg Wise, CCH Pounder and Peter Crombie
Airdate: November 2 & 3, 1997   Network: NBC

Detective Vernon Coyle heads a murder investigation in New York City that unearths a vampire, a werewolf and Frankenstein's creature.
High concept, but strictly low-grade sci-fi horror hokum; this two-part movie (or is it a miniseries?—either way, it's ninety minutes too long) plays like an epic pilot for a TV show, that thankfully, never was.

It begins with promise, boasting fairly impressive production values—albeit, of the mid-nineties direct-to-video kind—but quickly loses its way, struggling to commit to essential creative decisions such as genre, pacing and… well… plot.

The tone veers wildly between the very broadest camp to straight face thriller and back again, which is fun for a while, but the lengthy running time ultimately serves only to allow the writers to buck the viewers' investment so often, until finally, interest in any kind of narrative is lost altogether.

The real victims of the movie are the cast. The leads are all very credible talents, most of whom would find success in various small screen shows a decade later: Pasdar in *Heroes*, Jorja Fox in *CSI* and CCH Pounder in *The Shield*. But this is not anybody's finest work, although Pasdar's performance is arguably on the money, as a detective with perpetually furrowed brows baffled as hell and trying to make sense of the absolutely nonsensical happenings all around.

Perhaps some credit should be given for trying to resurrect the treasured Universal horror movie archetypes Dracula, Frankenstein and The Wolf

Man. But merely a year after the stagnant horror genre had been revived by the very postmodern *Scream* (1996) and its countless clones that quickly followed, it should have been clear to any producer that this was not the time to be revisiting the old school. Even this sin would be forgiven were it not for the fact that the attempt had already been done ten years earlier, in the modestly popular but still quite underrated, *The Monster Squad* (1987), of which this feels very reminiscent, but not in a good way.

Fans of bad television, bad movies, bad anything may well rejoice in its anarchic plotting and madcap goings-on, but really, there are far more entertaining examples of supernatural silliness for TV fans to explore, without having to resort to this overindulgent monstrous mess. [Kevin Hilton]

THE INVADERS

Director: Paul Shapiro
Starring: Scott Bakula, Elizabeth Peña, Richard Thomas, DeLane Matthews
Airdates: November 12 & 14, 1995   Network: FOX

Based on the classic sixties series, an ex-con under alien mind control is fighting to save the Earth.

A complaint offered to plenty of movies is that they have nothing to say. They exist solely for entertainment, and that the creators of the film are just going through the motions of making something to kill an hour-and-a-half without any thought to the world at large. "Where's the social context?" critics ask. "What's the deep meaning behind all of this?"

This is not a complaint that can be leveled at 1995's *The Invaders*, and not just because the two-part miniseries clocks in at just under three hours. No, *The Invaders* has a lot to say—about environmental concerns, about illegal immigration, about the media making us angry. Heck, the film even throws off a bit of dialog about disproportionate racial incarceration so casually that you could be forgiven if you thought they brought back Larry Cohen, the writer of the original sixties television series upon which it was based.

They didn't, however, and that may have been a mistake. The original *Invaders* was a fondly remembered but little seen sci-fi series about one man against an alien invasion which creator Cohen acknowledged was in part a reaction to the Hollywood blacklist of the previous decade. It was only natural that a potential revival for the series as a two-part pilot would have some political context as well, but *The Invaders* tries to throw so much context into the concept that it often forgets the main reason for its existence—to be entertaining enough to make someone want to watch the characters' further adventures.

The catalyst at the center of *The Invaders* is Nolan Wood (Bakula), a former pilot recently released from prison on a manslaughter charge of beating an environmentalist to death. This happened, he states, due to the voices in his head that he can occasionally overcome, though mostly he tends to go along with their wishes in a mopey manner. He wants to get back in touch with his ex-wife and son, but she's since remarried (to Richard Thomas) and the two of them now operate a diner consisting solely of patrons that smoke and order exclusively steak and eggs.

Little does Wood realize that these voices are actually part of a secret alien invasion force dedicated to manipulating the environment of the Earth so that the alien life form can completely take over. To be fair, he realizes it eventually over the course of the two-part *Invaders*, but it also requires the assistance of Dr Ellen Garza (Peña), whose husband the police believes Wood murdered, Wood's estranged son Kyle (Mario Yedidia), who counts flies on a tour bus, and Mexican immigrant Carlos (Raoul Trujillo), who seems to exist mostly as a way to get characters to meet up with each other. Roy Thinnes, the star of the original *Invaders* shows up briefly to advise Wood before vanishing off to parts unknown for reasons never adequately explained.

There's a good idea buried in *The Invaders*, and the idea of an alien invasion put together in order to deliberately destroy the environment of Earth via terrorism and getting rid of environmental regulations is one that could certainly have been explored in a compelling fashion. The problem is that it's fairly obvious why the pilot wasn't picked up as a series—while it sets up a number of curious ideas, the characters in the midst of them aren't well-developed enough that you'd want to see how this ragtag batch of misfits prevents the planet from going to smog. Most of the leads barely share any screen time with each other, and the miniseries hobbles Bakula the most, turning one of the most affable leads in sci-fi television into a mumbling, uncharismatic flatline of a character due to his alien-driven mental disorder.

The Invaders isn't a terrible miniseries by any means, and it offers a heck of a lot more depth in terms of ideas than plenty of similar outings. It's also got a very welcome sense of humor, best shown by the occasional appearances of a right wing (though curiously pro-union) talk show host played by Richard Belzer, who never leaves his chair and makes a reference to how he "respects Law & Order." The problem is that none of this depth or sense of humor go to the characters we'd potentially be following on a weekly basis, so the fact that we never get to find out what happened to them after the admirably conclusive finale isn't particularly disappointing.
[Paul Freitag-Fey]

V

Director: Kenneth Johnson
Starring: Marc Singer, Faye Grant, Diana Jane Badler, Richard Lawson, Andrew Prine
Airdates: May 1–2, 1983   Network: NBC

 Supposedly bringing a message of peace, these extraterrestrials have a different visit in mind.

When Kenneth Johnson originally pitched the idea for *V*, the bad guys were a Nazi-esque fascist group. The network wasn't interested. So, Johnson made the bad guys extraterrestrial lizards. The miniseries was picked up and put into production almost immediately. Presumably, it was the epic sci-fi angle that grabbed the network's attention, rather than the metaphors regarding war, freedom, fascism, Nazis and so forth that Johnson layered into his script. At the start of May 1983, an epic four-hour miniseries aired on NBC to huge ratings. It was a pop culture phenomenon, followed by a second miniseries and a weekly series. Even after all the hype and all the passing years, *V* remains an intelligent, if simplistic, big budget epic TV miniseries with alien lizards.

One day, a series of large UFOs appear, hovering above the major cities of Earth. A very humanoid-looking fellow named John (Richard Herd) introduces himself. John says that his planet needs a chemical compound that they can only find on Earth. If the humans help them get what they need, the Visitors will help us out in assorted technological ways. It all seems very straightforward and nice. But, things aren't always as they seem. Slowly, methodically, the Visitors gain more and more control over the Earth. The Visitors are perfectly willing to make people vanish, impart martial law, set curfews and be as awful as the Nazis or the Stalin Soviets to get what they want. But, what do they want exactly? Will any people stand up to them? Or is it already too late for the human race?

Kenneth Johnson has crafted a wonderfully entertaining epic. He skillfully weaves in scads of characters, including several different levels of Visitors. From the head Visitor, Diana (Jane Badler), who has stepped out of a 1980s primetime soap opera, to the quasi-religious spokesman John, to Willie, played by Robert Englund, who is the goofy Visitor. The humans are a mix of all races, all types of people. Marc Singer's reporter leads the pack. There is the Taylor family, consisting of Dad working down at the refinery and his two sons, Dr. Caleb (Jason Bernard) and Elias (Michael Wright) who is a petty thief. There are the Bernsteins who have a son that is becoming part of the Visitor Friends (aka Hitler Youth) and a Granddad who was in a concentration camp in Germany. There is the young doctor, Juliet Parrish (Faye Grant), who, semi-against her will, becomes the leader of the resistance. And many, many

From left: George DiCenzo and Steve Railsback in *Helter Skelter*; Roy Thinnes and Scott Bakula take on *The Invaders*; and Marc Singer works the uniform in *V*.

more. Most of them are 1980s updates of resistance fighters from movies of the past.

Throughout its 200 minutes, *V* keeps the pace at a steady level. Sometimes it picks up for wild and crazy action scenes. Sometimes everything is much calmer and more human. In general, the government response is omitted. So, the viewer sees the Visitors and the Rebels with no Middle Man. The removal of red tape adds to the pace immeasurably. The parallels between past conflicts that have plagued Earth and the Visitors resemblance to these is strong throughout. *V* simply has the addition of lizard aliens devouring guinea pigs in one big gulp. Plus, several laser battles and spaceship dogfights. Who is going to argue with that? The follow-up miniseries may have lost its way a bit and the TV series might not be anything to go crazy for but this original miniseries is still a strong viewing experience. *V*! [Daniel R. Budnik]

WORLD WAR III

Director: David Greene, Boris Sagal
Starring: David Soul, Brian Keith, Cathy Lee Crosby, Rock Hudson
Airdate: January 31–February 1, 1982   Network: NBC

 The United States and the Soviet Union turn the Cold War hot with a skirmish in Alaska.

Set in "the future" (1987!), *World War III*—the film and the event—begins with Soviet paratroopers dropping into the frozen wastelands of Alaska. They are there to seize a piece of the Trans-Alaska Pipeline; retaliation for an ongoing grain embargo lead by the United States. Standing in their way is David Soul's Colonel Caffey and a handful of National Guardsmen determined to hold the Soviets back. President McKenna (Hudson) searches for a diplomatic solution with Soviet Premier Gorny (Brian Keith), but the situation in Alaska threatens to spiral out of control and engulf the world in war.

World War III came early on in the Reagan era and thus lacks the jingoistic zeal that would later come to typify action cinema. Despite Hudson appearing very Reagan-esque, his President McKenna isn't the hardline anti-Communist that the Gipper was, preferring reconciliation and negotiation to all-out war. *World War III* itself is "soft" on Communism by 1980s standards. The Soviet invasion is the work of a rogue military group and not an official action of the USSR, and the Soviet Premier is depicted as both intelligent and reasonable. The film's militaries are made up of men— and surprisingly, women—and not the superhumans that would come to dominate depictions of the military by the close of the decade.

Although similar in premise to the later *Red Dawn*, *World War III* is first and foremost a political thriller. After an action-heavy opening sequence, the film takes an hour-long diversion for character development before the next gunshot is fired. Viewers tuning in to see victorious American soldiers repelling a vicious Soviet attack were instead treated to diplomatic negotiations and cabinet meetings; more "war room" than actual war. The end result is something far more realistic than is the norm for the Armageddon genre but decidedly less entertaining as well, thus explaining *World War III*'s status as one of the lesser known apocalyptic thrillers.

The film's lack of success or acclaim makes one hesitant to call it influential, but *World War III* does prefigure those films dealing with the start of World War III. The idea of an "accidental" war would become a signature in Cold War cinema appearing in a variety of films from *WarGames* to the comedy *Spies Like Us*. The idea that a rogue element within the Soviet establishment would be the cause of the war reappeared in HBO's *By Dawn's Early Light* and several James Bond films including *Octopussy*.

World War III can also lay claim to being the first in a series of made for television films on nuclear war in the eighties; a rich subgenre that includes 1983's *Special Bulletin*, *Testament*, and *The Day After* and 1984's *Threads*. Each of the latter films wisely takes a more human approach to the subject matter, shifting the focus away from the prewar period and politicians to the post-apocalypse and common citizens. For its part, *World War III* ends with stock footage of various countries while the sounds of nuclear bombers fill the soundtrack. It's a surprisingly powerful and effective ending but unfortunately does little to redeem the film. [David Ray Carter]

REVIEWS
1964–1979

Arguably the greatest era for the telefilm, the birth of the made for television genre spawned a new medium, and filmmakers churned out projects by the dozen. From the ABC Movie of the Week to NBC's Mystery Wheel (which presented revolving feature-length series' such as *Columbo* and *McMillan and Wife*) back to ABC's late night Wide World: Mystery series, the telefilm was never more prominent on network TV than during this glorious fifteen year cycle.

It all began on the night of October 7, 1964, when NBC aired *See How They Run*, a mild actioner that featured three kids on the run from the mob. Although the rest of the sixties did not see a huge investment in small screen films (only a few dozen films were produced, which is nothing compared to the seventies when the ABC Movie of the Week was releasing over forty films a season!), filmmakers tested the waters with various genres. Everything from westerns to dramas to supernatural horror all took a shot at ratings gold, before the swinging seventies got the telefilm truly underway.

Seventies television was just as varied as the sixties, but with a heavier emphasis on horror and thrillers. There's also topical fare, some of which is groundbreaking (*That Certain Summer* [1972] tackles homosexuality and *A Case of Rape* [1974] takes on the sexist sexual assault system), and some of which is not-so revolutionary (1971's *The Feminist and the Fuzz* is cute but pure fluff). Ultimately, however, it was the B-movie-like nature of TVMs with titles such as *Satan's School for Girls* (1973) and *Dawn: Portrait of a Teenage Runaway* (1976) that catapulted some telefilms into cult success. Many of these TVMs are still sought out by collectors and nostalgia buffs.

It is because of the rampant enthusiasm for the seventies telefilm and the sheer volume of output that the bulk of the reviews in this book focus on this era. This section also includes a handful of TVMs from the sixties because it was the obvious starting point for the next decade's incredible output.

Reviews are listed in alphabetical order.

ARE YOU IN THE HOUSE ALONE?

Director: Walter Grauman
Starring: Kathleen Beller, Scott Colomby, Blythe Danner, Dennis Quaid
Airdate: September 20, 1978   Network: CBS

 After a brutal sexual assault, a high school girl pulls her life together and sets out to expose her attacker.

The message TV movie is not an anomaly. Topical issues such as teenage sex (*Young Love, First Love*, 1979), suicide (*Surviving*, 1985), and even the perils of hitchhiking (*Diary of a Teenage Hitchhiker*, 1979) were all brought to the table to various levels of success. The two most propagandistic teenage driven telefilms of this era came about in the early eighties with the antidrug hogwash (entertaining though it may be) *Desperate Lives*, and the compelling but absolutely outrageous "exposé" on the dangers of role-playing games in *Mazes and Monsters* (both from 1982). Another oft-filmed issue was sexual assault, although the victims in those telefilms tended to be adult women. *Are You in the House Alone?* wasn't the first TVM to open up the subject of teenage rape, but it might have been the first to position it in a movie marketed as a horror film.

House tends to get a bad rap because of the advertising link to the horror film genre. Part of the tagline of the original ad reads, "An empty house. A mysterious phone call. Then the most terrifying words a seventeen-year-old girl can hear... Are you in the house alone?" Subsequent reruns were marketed with "A lonely teenager. A crazed youth. A night of terror." In an attempt to tie *House* somewhat loosely to the then growing stalk and slash subgenre, there is indeed some decent suspense, but this telefilm based on the Richard Peck young adult novel of the same name, is, at its heart, a grittier version of the *Afterschool Special*.

While *House* is about Kathleen Beller's character's journey to find strength after a brutal attack, the film ends shockingly with her assailant escaping punishment, because, Beller reminds the audience, "the system is wrong." It is a strangely powerful ending for such a film, and, in this respect, walks well among telefilms such as *A Case of Rape* (1974) where the viewer is forced to the realization that we are living in a victim-blaming society.

That's not to say that *House* isn't problematic. For the sake of creating a red herring, the photography teacher is portrayed as a lecherous authority figure. And, honestly, most of the men in the film are given the short end of the stick, and are either depicted as rapists or sleazebags, or are shown as emasculated by their inabilities to provide for their family. Only the boyfriend character played by Scott Colomby is drawn with any real dimension. But *House* doesn't necessarily veer into man-hating territory; it just prefers to concentrate on the female characters, some of which aren't shown in a great light either.

Far more family drama than horror, *Are You in the House Alone?* tackles contemporary (and somewhat timeless) issues such as loss of innocence, sexual assault and personal empowerment. So, be warned, we're not exactly in Michael Myers territory. But *House* is definitely worth a watch. [Amanda Reyes]

ASSAULT ON THE WAYNE

Director: Marvin J. Chomsky
Starring: Joseph Cotten, Leonard Nimoy, Lloyd Haynes, Dewey Martin
Airdate: January 12, 1971   Network: ABC

 On a covert underwater mission, a perplexed submarine commander fights tropical disease, foreign spies and the threat of mutiny.

Cut-price, splashy underwater spy intrigue from Paramount Television all about an American submarine called *The Wayne*, which is set to sea with a full hold of nukes, scientists, radioactive crap, talky seamen and enemy double agent/sailor Gordon Hoban (*The Born Losers*), who sneaks aboard to activate sleeper agents and steal electronics for the nasty Russians. Commanding the sub on its top secret journey is Leonard Nimoy, a skinny, pill-filled captain suffering from the effects of an unknown virus that warps his mind and causes him to hassle his crew à la Humphrey Bogart in *The Caine Mutiny* (1954).

On the way to melting down, Nimoy misses his freshly divorced wife and makes crazy demands on his men, ordering them to dismantle torpedoes, count bread rolls and polish dials in a manic bid to "cleanse" the vessel of a lax attitude—until an unexpected SOS signal forces him to park the sub at a remote island where he rescues a mysterious "injured" scientist who, once aboard, plans to aid Hoban in his dastardly mission.

Not quite action packed, there's still murder, an explosion, some solid dialog, a Cold War twist and a few tense scenes featuring the fantastic Nimoy who's obviously glad of the chance to forgo his Spock persona and stretch out his terrestrial acting pants.

Directed by TV series legend Chomsky (*Dr. Franken*) and padded out with grainy stock footage of periscopes, diving and waves, it co-stars Joseph Cotten (*Frankenstein's Daughter*), Keenan Wynn (*The Glove*), Dewey Martin (*The Desperate Hours*) and a young, shaved, near unrecognizable Sam Elliott (*Ghost Rider*) who falls off a ladder. [DF Dresden]

BAD RONALD

Director: Buzz Kulik
Starring: Scott Jacoby, Kim Hunter, Dabney Coleman, Pippa Scott
Airdate: October 23, 1974   Network: ABC

 After Ronald accidentally kills a young girl, his mother hides him in a walled up room located in the center of the house.

ABC was known for its primetime genre outings in the 1970s, and *Bad Ronald* is one of the best—and most disturbing. Scott Jacoby stars as the title character, a socially awkward teen who is constantly tormented by the in-crowd. When he accidentally kills one of the popular girls, his mother (Kim Hunter of *A Streetcar Named Desire* and the *Planet of the Apes* films) devises a plan to hide him in the walls of the house and tells the police he has run away. But when his mother goes to the hospital for surgery and doesn't make it home, the house is presumed vacant and sold to another family with three daughters (two of them the ubiquitous seventies TV stars, the Eilbacher sisters). Little do they know that Ronald is still lurking in the walls.

Increasingly ensconced in his own imagination, Ronald creates a fantasy world called "Atranta," and fills his tiny crawlspace with fantastical drawings of its rulers—idealized versions of himself and the princess he hopes to rescue, whom he associates with the new family's youngest daughter Babs (Cindy Fisher). Needing food and his obsession growing, he starts to get sloppy and the girls sense a presence in the house. He takes to spying on the family through tiny peepholes and concocting a delusional plan to take Babs away to Atranta, to rule the kingdom with him.

Based on the 1971 book of the same name by sci-fi writer Jack Vance (one of his few horror outings), the telefilm attempts to humanize Ronald to a certain extent, presenting him as a misunderstood teen driven mad by social starvation and an overbearing mother. In the book, he's a sociopath from the beginning, and his original crime is not an accident; he's an overt child rapist. Actor Scott Jacoby excelled at playing these disturbed youth roles, and this film, combined with his roles in *Rivals* (1972), *Baxter* (1973) and *The Little Girl Who Lives Down the Lane* (1976) cemented his rep as the top teenage creep of the seventies.

Director Buzz Kulik had been working in television for decades (Kim Hunter had worked with him on episodes of *Climax!* in the 1950s), and was an old hand at the TV movie format by the time *Bad Ronald* came his way. Interestingly, Kulik had been replaced by John Newland (of *One Step Beyond* and *Don't Be Afraid of the Dark*) on the earlier telefilm *Crawlspace* (1972), which shares some of the same motifs as *Bad Ronald*—most notably the idea of a young man discovered living in a crawlspace. Still, *Crawlspace* has not enjoyed the lingering acclaim of *Bad Ronald*, the latter of which has gone on to be an influence on countless horror directors working today. [Kier-La Janisse]

BAFFLED!

Director: Philip Leacock
Starring: Leonard Nimoy, Susan Hampshire, Rachel Roberts, Vera Miles
Airdate: January 30, 1973   Network: NBC

 After surviving a terrible car crash, racer Leonard Nimoy has the gift of premonition and is soon investigating a mystery.

Probably tired of loud American *Star Trek* fans shouting "Live Long And Prosper!" at him in the street, Leonard Nimoy traveled all the way to Pinewood Studios in England to shoot this logic defying pilot movie (from ITC and Arena Productions) that failed to inspire a follow-up series.

Cheap, tardy, quite daft but goofy enough to endure and giggle at, watch in dismay as hotshot race car driver Tom Kovack (Nimoy) steers his little car around a bumpy track courtesy of stock footage and absolutely awful, grade Z back projection. Without warning, his head melts mid-race and he suffers a vision that makes him spin out of control and crash through a wall. Fortunately, the wall is made of Styrofoam and he survives, but the collision has somehow opened his third eye and he now possesses the paranormal gift of remote viewing and transportation—a talent he's soon pestered for by blonde ghost hunter Susan Hampshire (*Malpertius*), a supernatural fan who wants to discuss the house and people Nimoy saw while in a trance.

Within minutes, the pair are investigating a spooky mansion hotel in Devon where jumpy Vera Miles (*The Hanged Man*), sneaky Rachel Roberts (*O Lucky Man*), barely sober Valerie Taylor (*What A Carve Up!*) and Ray Brookes (voice of TV classic *Mr. Ben*) all stagger about dropping mysterious clues to a wandering, inoffensive, semi-supernatural murder plot that will leave you, much like the cast, baffled!

Graced with a killer theme tune by Richard Hill (*To Kill a Clown*), nice locations, rancid fashions, lots of slow motion and a hammy, hoity-toity script by Theodore Apstein (*Blood Link*), Nimoy does his best to not be Spock while flashing backward, forward and sideways "across the spectral planes" and there's some stupefying bouts of heartfelt jibber-jabber that explains little, as well as flakey evil, high tea, country bitching, a haunted necklace and a car called Girly.

If you must watch it, be sure to stay tuned for the sequence where Nimoy batters a granny in a wheelchair. [DF Dresden]

From left: Scott Jacoby invites viewers into his creepy world of Atranta in *Bad Ronald*; and Leonard Nimoy looks into the future with Susan Hampshire in *Baffled!*

THE BAIT

Director: Leonard J. Horn
Starring: Donna Mills, Michael Constantine, William Devane, June Lockhart
Airdate: March 13, 1973   Network: ABC

 A female undercover cop acts as sexy girl-bait to entrap a mad killer that hunts and murders young, beautiful women.

Based on the novel *The Bait* by Dorothy Uhnak, Aaron Spelling co-produced this ABC Movie Of The Week which stars Donna Mills (*The Stepford Husbands*) as a blonde, spunky mother-of-one/plain-clothes cop who holds her own in a police force full of smelly, sexist, wide-tied males resentful and envious of her street smarts and arrest record.

As "The Best Legs On The Force," Mills readily threatens a random pervert on a bus, and shuts down a major heroin ring with little effort, and is soon assigned the shocking case of a killer rapist who defiles and murders young women, leaving behind a single baffling clue in the form of a small bottle of Misty Night perfume. Six bodies down, and unable to crack the case, Mills' grouchy desk sergeant, Michael Constantine (*Voyage of the Damned*), caves in to her persistent, mousy peer pressure and begrudgingly allows her to become bait and go undercover posing as a vox pop researcher who strolls the city streets in search of men to question.

Endowed with some dark, late night stalking action, great L.A. street locations, effective drama, dialog and tension, the best things about it remains the blinding pant-suits and the gigantic flares, the chunky sideburns and an excellent cast that includes Noam Pitlik (*Howie And Rose*), Thalmus Rasulala (*Cool Breeze*), Gianni Russo (*Striptease*) and the outstandingly insane and creepy William Devane (who would later appear alongside Mills on *Knots Landing*). Keep watch for a very brief glimpse of Tim Carey (*Speed Trap*) as Big Mike the doorman. [DF Dresden]

THE BERMUDA DEPTHS

Director: Tom Kotani
Starring: Leigh McCloskey, Connie Sellecca, Burl Ives, Carl Weathers
Airdate: January 27, 1978   Network: ABC

 A young man returns to Bermuda only to be haunted by the doomed girl he once loved... and a prehistoric sea creature.

The name "Rankin-Bass" may be synonymous with the world of animated television specials, as Arthur Rankin Jr. and Jules Bass were responsible for family-friendly holiday specials that are just as enjoyable today as they were a half-century ago, including *Rudolph, the Red-Nosed Reindeer*, *Frosty the Snowman* and *The Hobbit*. They may, however, not be the first name you think of when it comes to made for TV spectacles geared for adults—heck, it's unlikely that they'd even rank within the top hundred.

Their reputation is what makes their name on 1978's *The Bermuda Depths* so surprising. A strange genre-bender of a film that never quite figures out exactly where it's headed, *Depths* is all the more compelling due to its enigmatic nature, no doubt in part to the work of director Tsugunobu Kotani (billed as "Tom Kotani"), who also helmed the previous year's Rankin-Bass production *The Last Dinosaur*. Primarily a romantic drama, *Depths* often becomes an adventure film in the *Jaws* mold, with both genres featuring supernatural overtones that may or may not be imagined by the lead character, making for a distinctly unique experience that no doubt became sketched permanently into the memories of the viewers who tuned in expecting a made for TV variation on *The Deep*.

Future soap opera regular Leigh McClosky stars as the improbably named Magnus Dens, whom we first meet in the opening sequence hanging around a beach. He's approached by a mysterious woman (Sellecca) and dreams of his past as a young boy, when he met a similarly mysterious girl named Jennie on a similar beach. He and the girl became friends, to the point where they carve their initials into a wandering giant turtle's shell (which sounds terrible, but is actually quite sweet.). However, this potential for blossoming love is squashed when the girl and the turtle wander into the ocean, never to be seen again.

Cut to years later, after several years of psychiatric therapy and the death of his father from an unseen critter at the family beach house, and Magnus hooks up with an old friend (Weathers) working on a small vessel while he finishes his masters in marine biology. Magnus begins working with his friend under the guidance of grizzled scientist Dr. Paulis (Ives) and everything would be hunky-dorky—if it weren't for the strange warnings of Paulis' spiritual servant Delia (Ruth Attaway).

Soon, the mysterious woman re-appears and introduces herself as Jennie—but due to her name being the same as an old superstition, nobody believes Magnus when he tells them of her existence. But Jennie isn't the only eerie critter showing up, as the aforementioned turtle makes a return as well, and in a much more chaotic form than the one who allowed his shell to be used as a romantic plot device.

The Bermuda Depths doesn't always work, as the acting is a bit on the stilted side probably due to the inconsistent tone, but it's still an admirable, entertaining film with some impressively haunting moments. Part mythical sea romance, part adventure yarn and part monster flick, The Bermuda Depths is the Night-Tide-meets-Gamera spectacle you never realized you needed. [Paul Freitag-Fey]

BLACK NOON

Director: Bernard L. Kowalski
Starring: Roy Thinnes, Yvette Mimieux, Ray Milland, Lyn Loring
Airdate: November 5, 1971   Network: CBS

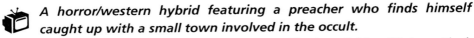 *A horror/western hybrid featuring a preacher who finds himself caught up with a small town involved in the occult.*

Not unlike the TV movies Crowhaven Farm or The Last Bride of Salem, Black Noon attempts to set its occult underpinnings apart through an Old West backdrop. Unfortunately, despite the interesting milieu, Black Noon is just a bit too precious to elicit much in the way of real terror. Regardless, the intoxicating, and downbeat ending almost makes it worth the trip.

Black Noon is one of those films that take its time getting to the sucker punch, and therefore risks losing its audience along the way. Certainly, it's visually compelling (even though the paltry special effects are clunky) with its inimical Old West locale, and hostile cowboys donned in black (and named Moon!), but it lacks the brisk pacing of other TVMs, and the imagery doesn't quite pop in the ways it should. Also, the "twist" is spoon fed to the audience, beginning from very early on. (If you can't figure out what San Males stands for, don't worry; it will be spelled out for you in no uncertain terms.)

Producer Andrew J. Fenady had worked on several westerns, including Chisum and the TV series Hondo, as well as horror films, such as Terror at the Wax Museum and Arnold (both of which his brother Georg directed), and he brought film screen legend Gloria Grahame into Black Noon to fill in the thankless role of Bethia, a housekeeper whose sole purpose seems to be to look judgmental. He had previously worked with her on the western Ride Beyond Vengeance and was helping her kick start her later-life career. She's a perfect example of the restrictive but prosperous venue that television provided aging actors. She's also just one of several prominent and welcoming faces who round out the seasoned cast, including Ray Milland and Henry Silva (who is particularly menacing as the unkillable cowboy).

Preying on several cultural threats—xenophobia and religious corruption to name two—the most interesting menace in *Black Noon* lies in that of the female body, which is presented as either desirous (Mimieux) or disease-ridden (Loring). The beautiful woman is a mute, and her sexuality is derived from her childlike and untouched presence. The "diseased" woman is older, married, but perhaps barren (also reminiscent of *Crowhaven Farm*) and is driven to hysterics when she thinks her preacher husband (Thinnes) has developed a lust for Mimieux (of course he's helpless under the guise of voodoo, mind you). These would be serious issues, if not treated so nonchalantly, and a fantastically frenzied performance from Loring embodying all of the tropes of a woman with a major case of the vapors is inappropriately (and yet still appropriately) over-the-top. When she goes crazy on Thinnes, he totally deserves it. [Amanda Reyes]

BORN INNOCENT

Director: Donald Wrye
Starring: Linda Blair, Joanna Miles, Kim Hunter, Richard Jaeckel
Airdate: September 10, 1974   Network: NBC

A fourteen-year-old runaway is made a ward of the courts and placed in a reform school, where she must confront verbal and physical abuse. In the early 1970s, the women in prison genre became a popular staple in drive-ins and grindhouse cinemas, with films like Jack Hill's *The Big Doll House* (1971) and Jonathan Demme's *Caged Heat* (1974), entertaining audiences with a heady combination of action, violence and sex behind bars. Fresh off her success in *The Exorcist* (1973), Linda Blair was too young to be a fully-fledged (and fully unclothed) WiP performer in 1974 (she would have to wait until her notorious 1983 film *Chained Heat* to accomplish that). But the NBC network managed to achieve the next best thing, casting the hot young star in *Born Innocent*, a telemovie about reform school girls which became the highest rated television movie to air that year, thanks in no small part to the well-placed publicity generated by the film's theme and some of its more controversial elements.

A rather involving and surprisingly downbeat teen drama, the bulk of *Born Innocent*'s notoriety revolved around one scene: the infamous moment when Christine Parker (Blair) is confronted by several of the inmates in the shower stall and raped with a broom handle. Its impact is not overstated—it is an intense, brutal and disturbing sequence, especially considering it was

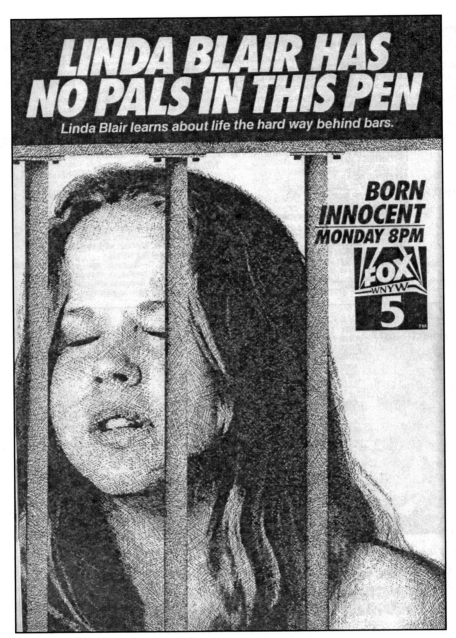

LINDA BLAIR HAS
NO PALS IN THIS PEN

Linda Blair learns about life the hard way behind bars.

BORN
INNOCENT
MONDAY 8PM

FOX
WNYW
5

Enticingly tawdry *TV Guide* ad for a re-run of *Born Innocent*.

filmed for network television. After it was blamed for inciting the rape of a nine-year-old girl (who was attacked with a glass soda pop bottle by several of her peers), the rape scene was subsequently cut from later re-airings of the movie in the USA, although it was reinstated for its home video release in the eighties, and the sequence was intact whenever I caught it on Australian television (including some airings in the midday movie slot).

In many respects, Blair's performance is even more impressive here than it was in *The Exorcist*, as she does not have the crutch of Dick Smith's prosthetic makeup or the vocal dynamics of veteran radio actress Mercedes McCambridge (who provided Blair's demonically possessed voice). Strong support is given by Joanna Miles (as the one truly caring counselor), Richard Jaeckel as Christine's highly strung, borderline incestuous father (the leering way he talks about his daughter's tight jeans is quite creepy), and Kim Hunter (Zira in the *Planet of the Apes* films) as the mother and wife who has drunk herself into ignorance. The reformatory girls are all played by unknowns whom you may recognize from the odd episode of *Mannix* or *Harry O*, but they all have interesting faces and handle themselves quite well under the guidance of director Donald Wyre (1978's *Ice Castles*).

Born Innocent is that rare telemovie that succeeds both as an affecting drama and a piece of grimy exploitation. It all depends on which set of eyes you watch it through. Released on VHS by several labels during the 1980s, it has since been made available on DVD. A paperback tie-in novelization, authored by Bernhardt J. Hurwood, was published in the US by Ace Books in 1975. [John Harrison]

THE BROTHERHOOD OF THE BELL

Director: Paul Wendkos
Starring: Glenn Ford, Rosemary Forsyth, Dean Jagger, Maurice Evans
Airdate: September 17, 1970   Network: CBS

 Many years after joining a secret society, a successful professor is forced into blackmailing a friend.

The questions being posed by the 1960s counterculture were addressed candidly in *Brotherhood of the Bell*, and Paul Wendkos, who had made the first real TV horror film with *Fear No Evil*, turned in one of the best of the bunch with this paranoid conspiracy telethriller, starring Glenn Ford as a defected member of a powerful secret society.

Andy Patterson (Ford) has it all: a cushy academic job, a beautiful (and much younger) wife, and ivy-league connections to movers and shakers all over the world thanks to his old college fraternity, "The Bell." Twenty years earlier, Andy pledged loyalty to that selective enclave, with a promise to pay the bill for his subsequent successes in whatever manner The Bell required. At the start of the film, Andy's number has come up. His assignment: to blackmail one of his best friends, Professor Konstantin Horvathy (Eduard Franz), as a means of stopping him from accepting a prominent university position. As a result, Horvathy commits suicide, and Andy's guilt drives him to speak out about the secret society—only to have his credibility shattered virtually overnight.

His sanity is not far behind, as illustrated through the exaggerated camerawork that hints at the decade of conspiracy thrillers to come: *The Parallax View*, *The Conversation*, *Marathon Man*, and *Capricorn One*. Jerry Goldsmith's jazz/orchestral hybrid score punctuates the building intensity as Andy's life spins out of control, the height of which is his appearance on a nasty tabloid talk show inspired by the confrontational *Joe Pyne Show* of the 1960s (and predating the incendiary mania of later trash TV staples Geraldo, Jerry Springer and Morton Downey, Jr.), which ends in fisticuffs.

David Karp produced and adapted the teleplay from his own 1952 pulp novel *The Brotherhood of Velvet*, which was also the source of a 1958 *Studio One* episode. The 1970 telefilm tones down the sleazier elements of the book (in the book the Horvathy character—under another name—is blackmailed as a closet homosexual, whereas the film threatens him with his political affiliations in the USSR), but the primary theme remains the same—that there are one-percenters who benefit greatly from maintaining the status quo, and they don't like their boat to be rocked. What's brilliant about the film is that its "horror" is completely real, openly known and complacently accepted. Except we don't call it a conspiracy—we just call it capitalism!

With supporting roles by elderly character faces Will Geer, Maurice Evans (Dr. Zaius!) and Dean Jagger (who gives a chilling performance here) as well as future *CHiPs* sergeant Robert Pine as a new initiate to the organization, *The Brotherhood of the Bell* is a classy political chiller that remains as relevant today as when it was made. [Kier-La Janisse]

CALL TO DANGER

Director: Tom Gries
Starring: Peter Graves, Diana Muldaur, John Anderson, Clu Gulager
Airdate: February 27, 1973   Network: CBS

Government spy Peter Graves enlists the "ordinary" skills of "ordinary" civilians to help him win the war on crime.

After CBS Television failed to initiate a series with 1968's pilot movie *Call To Danger*, the always gray and grandiose Peter Graves *(The Clonus Horror)* returns in this second attempt by Paramount Television, which again, went no further.

Following the formula of the original outing, Graves plays secret agent Doug Warfield, a by-the-numbers government operative who handles cases other departments of law enforcement fail to comprehend or solve. With

Clockwise from left: Ronny Cox and Elizabeth Montgomery get serious in *A Case of Rape*; Diana Muldaur and Peter Graves are far less grim in *Call to Danger*; and Roy Thinnes is somewhere in between in *Black Noon*.

his higher spy budget, he's allowed to use a supercomputer (the size of an office block) to select ordinary members of the public to be enlisted in the hope that their particular, obtuse skill-sets will help take down the bad guys.

Director Gries (*Helter Skelter*) doesn't hang about, so, after sparse titles we learn that a Mafia informer (in split pants) has been kidnapped by a homicidal gangster and imprisoned in a fancy, heavily fortified compound to stop him testifying at a grand jury hearing. In response, and after some high tech flashing lights and much paper has been noisily printed out, Graves recruits archer/stock-car driver/bee keeper Clu Gulager (*Feast*) and model/ whore Tina Louise (*The Wrecking Crew*) to assist him in closing the case.

As unrealistic as it all sounds, the stylish hijinks actually work, and it's a shame the show never materialized and further explored the ordinary hero angle (which was filmed while Graves was collar deep in the *Mission: Impossible* series).

Worth at least one spin, watch it for the nice suits, sleek muscle cars, tepid intrigue and cut-price action, and be sure to enjoy the rest of the cast, which includes Michael Ansara (*The Doll Squad*), Stephen McNally (*Black Gunn*) and Diana Muldaur (*Hog Wild*). [DF Dresden]

A CASE OF RAPE

Director: Boris Sagal
Starring: Elizabeth Montgomery, William Daniels, Cliff Potts, Ronny Cox
Airdate: February 20, 1974   Network: NBC

After a housewife is raped a second time, she becomes again a victim to the unforgiving sexual assault laws and antiquated court system.

"This woman is about to become a statistic," an off-screen voice announces as the camera comes to rest on the image of actress Elizabeth Montgomery. "This woman is going to be raped."

Thus begins one of the most depressing explorations of rape aftermath ever to grace the screen—big or small—courtesy of *Omega Man* director Boris Sagal. While not overtly graphic (television's concepts at that time tended to be more subversive than its visual imagery), the treatment Montgomery's character endures from friends, the police, the court, her husband—not to mention the groping paws of the rapist himself—is shockingly frank for the primetime tube of the seventies.

Montgomery plays Ellen Harrod, a housewife who takes night school classes while her husband (Ronny Cox) is away on frequent business trips. One night after class, her classmate and downstairs neighbor introduces her to a handsome young man who offers to give them a lift home. After he drops them off, Montgomery relieves the babysitter, checks in on her sleeping child, and then hears a knock at the door. Assuming it's the babysitter having forgotten something, she opens the door, and the friendly stranger shows his true face.

Like the rapist in Tony Garnett's *Handgun* (1984), the rapist is someone Montgomery is introduced to socially. He rapes her in her own home, and what makes the film much harder to watch is how much time passes before she actually tells anyone about the incident, which causes others to see it as a fabrication meant to hide an infidelity. She reports it only after her attacker rapes her a second time (a scene that was almost cut until Montgomery threatened to walk from the project), this time in her parking garage with a witness who is led by the defense to question what he saw as consensual rough sex (1976's *Lipstick* would also use this argument in its harrowing court scenes). All the doctors and police officers are male, and she passively accepts their condescension as they accuse her of enjoying the rape—of having "safe sex" by denying her own lust for the attacker.

With its deliberately upsetting gender politics, the film works extremely well as an emotional instigator, making it an important contribution to the ongoing discussion on sexual predation. Airing a year before the release of Susan Brownmiller's groundbreaking book *Against Our Will: Men, Women* and *Rape*, it remains in the highest rankings of all theatrical or telefilms ever aired on TV. [Kier-La Janisse]

THE CLONING OF CLIFFORD SWIMMER
Director: Lela Swift
Starring: Peter Haskell, Sheree North, Lance Kerwin
Airdate: November 1, 1974   Network: ABC

A bored executive allows a clone to live out his dull existence.

As in Rock Hudson's *Seconds* (1966), there's a life lesson for all of us in this quaint, confined and dreamy looking teleplay about a smart, successful man called Clifford Swimmer. A man cursed by his daily executive grind, his daft, alcoholic wife Sheree North (*Maniac Cop*), his lumpy son Lance Kerwin (*Salem's Lot*), his rotten highly paid job and his giant house. A man who, thanks to insane lighting and a knotty coating of pancake batter makeup, gives off the impression he's been made entirely out of plywood and blusher.

Wrapped in a demented jumper and determined to escape his own life, Clifford (Peter Haskell) goes to see a "psycho-genetic" doctor played by the great Keene Curtis (*Blade*), who tells him he can clone him an exact replica Clifford that will live out his mundane life at home while he'll be left free to sex it up and pound booze with his mistress Sharon Farrell (*Night of the Comet*) on a variety of tiny, adjacent sets. Clifford readily agrees and undergoes the (mostly off screen) transformation. Then, he pisses straight off on holiday and sends his clone home where it acts all chilled out and loving, much to the delight of his unknowing wife and child.

Shortly after, there's a murder, and bored of the international playboy lifestyle, the real Clifford predictably wants his old, safe life back, only to find he's been replaced by his double, just like Roger Moore was in *The Man Who Haunted Himself* (1970). Conflict ensues.

Produced by ABC Television as part of their Wide World: Mystery series (1973–78), if you can ignore the ugly over-lit studio look of it and forgive the absence of any real SFX, you'll find the hokey science and bitter exchanges by all concerned, North's boozy ramblings, crazy interior design, nightmarish hairstyles, John Karlan (*Hostage Flight*) and the bizarre, threatening behavior of violent loan shark William Basset (*Black Dynamite*,) make it worth at least one spin. [DF Dresden]

A COLD NIGHT'S DEATH
Director: Jerrold Freedman
Starring: Robert Culp, Eli Wallach   Network: ABC
Airdate: January 30, 1973

Something strange is happening in the isolated Tower Mountain research laboratory.

This is a movie with plenty of snow. Snow and isolation. When the cast eventually do arrive, it is comprised of three men, diminishing in an instant to only two: scientists Robert Jones and Frank Enrari (Robert Culp and Eli Wallach). The third man, Adams the helicopter pilot (Michael C. Gwynne), departs before the storm cuts them off.

Jones and Enrari are deposited in a freezing settlement located 14,126 feet above sea level. It is here, in the Tower Mountain summit laboratory, that altitude and stress experiments on primates are taking place for the space program. (The location of the lab is not divulged.) The first thing the team does on arrival is locate their predecessor, Dr. Vogel, whose radio transmissions had become irrational before stopping altogether five days ago. He is discovered frozen to death in front of the radio in the electronics room. Mysteriously, the door is unlocked and the window is wide open.

Things get stranger and the relationship between the two men increasingly frayed as the days wear on. Soon enough, the unwitting Jones and Enrari are headed in the exact same direction as Vogel before them. Too late Jones discovers that their lives are a mirror of the experiments they are conducting on the monkeys and chimps. It's a dark and twisted premise, one that is carried extraordinarily well by Culp and Wallach. (Wallach, an international film star who favored the stage, may well have been attracted to the 'staginess' of *A Cold Night's Death*.)

In TV movies, where exposition is king, it's refreshing to find room given over to atmosphere. The panicked disembodied radio transmission at the start of *A Cold Night's Death* gets the ball rolling. The soundtrack is also worth noting. Having created the innovative electronic soundtrack for *The Andromeda Strain* (1971), composer Gil Mellé goes much the same way here, his blips and beeps complementing shots of cheerless corridors and, in one scene, a half-frozen Jones staggering through them. The ending of the movie may not come as a surprise, nor likely to stand much scrutiny, but this is barely relevant. As a mood piece, Jerrold Freedman's *A Cold Night's Death* works perfectly.

Similarities between Freedman's movie and John Carpenter's *The Thing* (1982), another picture set in a remote research station, have not gone unnoticed. It seems a fair bet that Carpenter drew inspiration from the look of Freedman's movie, from the sweeping snow-covered opening shots, through to an icy protagonist locked outside the base in crippling subzero weather. Add to this the fractious relationship between Jones and Enrari, falling prey to paranoia, and we have everything in Carpenter's movie but

Clockwise from above: Charles Martin Smith rocks out in *Cotton Candy*; Sheree North wonders if two Peter Haskells are a good or bad thing in *The Cloning of Clifford Swimmer*; and Robert Culp and Eli Wallach are at loggerheads in the chilling *A Cold Night's Death*.

the shapeshifting monster. "You're not a man to be trusted!" Enrari accuses Jones in the final act, before shooting him dead.

A Cold Night's Death was reshown on television under the name, *The Chill Factor*. Some of today's audience may find the use of caged animals, in states of agitation, uncomfortable viewing. [David Kerekes]

COTTON CANDY

Director: Ron Howard
Starring: Charles Martin Smith, Clint Howard, Leslie King, Kevin Lee Miller
Airdate: October 26, 1978   Network: NBC

 Unpopular high school students George and Corky form a rock group, and must face-off against archrivals in a Battle of the Bands contest.
The sophomore directorial effort from then-popular TV star Ron Howard (*Grand Theft Auto* was his debut the previous year), *Cotton Candy* is a groovy piece of seventies nostalgia that pays tribute to that great institution of the high school rock band—a rite of passage for many teenagers, regardless of how much talent they possess or how far they get with it. In the years before instant (and usually fleeting) superstardom via the likes of *American Idol*,

getting to play in a Battle of the Bands contest at the local mall was often the highlight of school life (and beyond), and was usually the one sure-fire way for even the geekiest of kids to land a hot date for the prom.

Filmed in Dallas, Texas (at the Lake Highlands High School and Town East Mall), *Cotton Candy* wallows in a sense of innocence and apple pie Americana that could so easily be off-putting and overbearing, but is endearing thanks primarily to fine performances from Charles Martin Smith (Toad in *American Graffiti*) as George Smalley, Leslie King (as the female drummer George falls for), and Ron Howard's remarkably oddball younger brother Clint as Corky Macpherson, George's best buddy and the perfect person to manage the fledgling supergroup this bunch put together in their garage. Mark Wheeler is also great to watch as Torbin Bequette, the cocksure leader of Cotton Candy's rival band, Rapid Fire (a clearly KISS-inspired outfit, with a lot of flash but little substance and an audience of screaming girls at their feet). Wheeler would go on to work with Ron Howard in several of the director's big projects, including playing Neil Armstrong in 1995's *Apollo 13*. But it's definitely Clint Howard who owns the film, giving not only a great performance but also a co-screenwriter credit with his brother. Howard gives himself some great lines of dialog, and he clearly used his character here as the template for his more well-known role as Eaglebaur in the following year's *Rock 'n' Roll High School*.

Mark Ridlen, who played one of the members of Rapid Fire, recalled in an online interview a few years back: "Before it aired on October 26, 1978, all the parents of Rapid Fire purchased VCRs to record it. Home video recordings was then a new and wondrous thing".[1]

Initially conceived as a pilot for an unrealized series, *Cotton Candy* has unfortunately never appeared legitimately on video or disc (Disney apparently own the rights and have it locked away), though some public domain sellers have offered it up over the years (usually dubbed from television transmissions of varying quality). Despite (or perhaps because of) its rarity, *Cotton Candy* has developed a cult following and has even inspired a few indie bands (such as the Suite Sixteen, who recorded a song titled Hot Rash—named after one of the potential band names suggested by Eaglebaur—which features snippets of dialog from the film). An illustrated paperback tie-in authored by the Howard brothers was published by Signet in 1979. [John Harrison]

---

1 Ridlen (now a deejay) screened one of these recordings—replete with the original commercials aired during its first broadcast—at the Tradewinds Social Club in Dallas in 2010. Clint Howard also attended a screening of the film at the Silent Movie Theatre in Los Angeles in 2011.

CROWHAVEN FARM

Director: Walter Grauman

Starring: Hope Lange, Paul Burke, Lloyd Bochner, John Carradine, Cindy Eilbacher

Airdate: November 24, 1970   Network: ABC

 An on-the-rocks married couple move into a seemingly idyllic farmhouse only to be confronted by the occult.

Broadcast just in time for the 1970 Thanksgiving Holiday, this American gothic tale of puritans and witch hunts stars Hope Lange (fresh off the haunted house sitcom *The Ghost and Mrs. Muir*) as Maggie Porter, a middle aged woman who inherits—along with her explosively jealous artist husband Ben (Paul Burke of *Naked City*)—the isolated New England property of Crowhaven Farm, when its original beneficiary dies in a sudden "accident."

Maggie immediately takes a dislike to the place, disturbed by her ability to predict what will be around every corner in a house she's supposedly never been to before. Not to mention she notices that the local handyman is John Carradine, which is never a good sign. But Ben is thrilled with the vast expanse of their new estate, feeling that it will refuel his failing art career, and possibly his marriage. You see, Ben and Maggie are childless; a fact Ben takes very much to heart and which—combined with his inability to provide for Maggie financially—leaves him feeling emasculated and short-tempered. But when a terminally ill neighbor proposes that they adopt her ten-year-old niece Jennifer (Cindy Eilbacher of *Bad Ronald* and *The Death of Richie*), the couple is ecstatic. That is, until the little girl starts to act threatening in that obliging, smiling kind of way characteristic of seventies pedophobia films.

After being visited by a local historian who tells her of Crowhaven Farm's background as an early pilgrim settlement complete with witches and witch trials, Maggie's visions of Crowhaven's dark past become clearer and more frequent; she is convinced that in another life in the seventeenth century, she was accused of witchcraft and killed by the townsfolk, buried alive under

Hope Lange in a newspaper promotion for *Crowhaven Farm*.

TORMENTING DREAM — Hope Lange is tormented by a strange dream — a vision of people in Puritan clothes huddled around a screaming woman, herself—in "Crowhaven Farm," a tale of witchcraft and suspense on the ABC "Movie of the Week" tonight at 7:30.

the weight of giant rocks. When she suddenly becomes pregnant, after being told for years that they can't have children, it seems that some terrible history is repeating itself...

Director Walter Grauman had been working in television since the fifties, but it was really in the seventies that he hit his stride, with not only a handful of TV movies under his belt but also a good run with *Streets of San Francisco* and *Barnaby Jones* (and later *Murder, She Wrote* in the eighties). TV mainstay John McGreevey provides the original script, which manages to be a dense psychological examination of repression and guilt in the face of changing gender roles that were allowing women more independence. [Kier-La Janisse]

CRUISE INTO TERROR

Director: Bruce Kessler
Starring: Frank Converse, John Forsythe, Hugh O'Brian, Ray Milland
Airdate: February 3, 1978   Network: ABC

 After salvaging a cursed coffin from an underwater tomb, a ship's passengers and crew battle the son of Satan.

Aka *Voyage Into Evil*, writer Michael Braverman (*M.A.D.D: Mothers Against Drunk Driving*) packs this enjoyable supernatural clunker with chunks of Irwin Allen-esque disaster lore, an Egyptian curse, a haunted coffin and even a spot of arcane history that involves Mexican pyramids and Mayan hexes and sends it all off on a trip to the gulf of Mexico aboard a small, scruffy cruise ship ominously named after an obscure church of African voodoo—Obeah.

Oblivious and also aboard are tired captain Hugh O'Brian (*The Shootist*), mechanic/valet Dirk Benedict (*Ruckus*), sexed up divorcee Stella Stevens (*Hell to Pay*) and archaeologist Ray Milland (*The Uncanny*) who all end up calling on the help of deranged priest John Forsythe (*Cry Panic*) to do battle with a hellish demon after something goes splat on the poop deck, a cat meows and they all realize that the cursed, haunted looking baby coffin they just plundered from the sea and placed in the hold... is haunted.

Thanks to its low budget, most of the shenanigans are filmed at the dock or on threadbare sets that seldom resemble the location they cut to, and padded out with fog, flashing lights, hammy dialog, mismatched stock footage of lagoons, sharks, wavy horizons and a coral reef—all of which do nothing but add silly charm to the laughably plotted goings-on.

Co-produced by Aaron Spelling, press PLAY to see O'Brian "fight" a shark, Stevens in a bikini, a haunted engine room, bubbles, thunder, the son of Satan, mild terror, a little cruising, a small fire, a cheese-filled explosion, decent chanting and Christopher George (*Graduation Day*) and Linda Day

George (*Panic on the 5:22*) as the real-life smoochy love-sick couple who get possessed and turn bad.

Responsible for episodes of *The Monkees, Ironside, Get Christie Love!, Diagnosis Murder, The Commish* and *Baywatch,* Bruce Kessler began life directing the grindhouse favorites *Killer's Three* (1968), *Angels From Hell* (1968), *The Gay Deceivers* (1969) and *Simon, King of the Witches* (1971). [DF Dresden]

DAUGHTER OF THE MIND

Director: Walter Grauman
Starring: Don Murray, Ray Milland, Gene Tierney, Ed Asner
Airdate: December 12, 1969   Network: ABC

After his deceased daughter makes a ghostly appearance, a respected professor seeks the help of a paranormal expert.

Based on Paul Gallico's 1964 novel *The Hand of Mary Constable*, two "other sides" are unraveled in *Daughter of the Mind*. The first speaks to the supernatural otherworld where apparitions are triggered by a tragic loss, and the *other* other side is that of Communist Russia! The combination may sound strange, but the result is gripping, and often thoughtful, thanks to Ray Milland and (in her TV movie debut) Gene Tierney's heart wrenching turn as grieving parents. This 1969 ABC Movie of the Week marks an early foray into the supernatural, and while the paranormal would go on to become a staple of both the big and small screen throughout the seventies, *Daughter* provides an interesting mix of Cold War paranoia and personal grief.

Regarding this era of the made for TV movie, *Daughter* ventures into what was then mostly uncharted terrain. It doesn't seem all that farfetched that the filmmakers would attempt to mix genres, as a way to test the audience's taste for small screen horror movies while still keeping them on established ground. And, *Daughter* does its best to work both the espionage angle and the common tropes of a supernatural thriller. Sure, audiences love things that go bump in the night, and much of what is seen in *Daughter* is signature to the genre now: séances, creepy kid apparitions (who say eerie things like "Daddy, I hate being dead"), ESP and, of course, the debunker (here portrayed, ironically enough, by a paranormal expert). The cloak and dagger angle isn't quite as fleshed-out, and it is a bit difficult at times to remember which character is doing what, but the effort to combine real-life paranoia with a fear of the unnatural is appreciated.

Luther Davis' teleplay adaptation won an Edgar Award in 1970 (it was nominated alongside episodes from *Night Gallery, Mod Squad* and *Mannix*). And, directed by Walter Grauman in one of his earliest TVM works,

Daughter's story and direction rely heavily on clichés, but to great success, with much credit going to both the filmmakers and the incredible cast of familiar and soon-to-be familiar faces.

Don Murray is the lead actor in this thriller, but he's really part of a much larger, and frankly incredible, ensemble that features a few great faces from classic films, including Tierney and Milland, as well as soon-to-be household names like Ed Asner and Murray himself, who would become a fixture in the telefilm genre in the 1970s and beyond. Pamelyn Ferdin is especially creepy as the ghostly Mary, and petite Barbara Dana puts in an off-kilter turn as Tina.

Daughter doesn't break into new terrain, even by late sixties standards. But it does its best to take the formulas into moody and wondrous places, and is definitely worth a look. [Amanda Reyes]

DAWN: PORTRAIT OF A TEENAGE RUNAWAY

Director: Randal Kleiser
Starring: Eve Plumb, Leigh J. McCloskey, Bo Hopkins, Georg Stanford Brown
Airdate: September 27, 1976   Network: NBC

A fifteen-year-old girl escapes her dead end life and heads to Los Angeles, where she finds love and heartache as a teenage hooker. In a bold attempt to remove herself from her squeaky clean image as the put-upon tween Jan Brady on *The Brady Bunch*, Eve Plumb took the role of a lost youth turned Hollywood hooker in the gritty drama *Dawn: Portrait of a Teenage Runaway*. While she is never not good, Leigh McCloskey, who plays Alexander, the male hustler with the potential to be Prince Charming, easily outdoes Plumb in every shared scene. His tortured and haunted performance warranted a sequel, which came out the year after *Dawn*'s release (*Alexander: The Other Side of Dawn*), and only featured Plumb in a few pivotal scenes.

Dawn was written by Dalene Young, the screenwriter who brought so much realism to teenaged sex in *Little Darlings*. To round out her main character, Young interviewed several young prostitutes, and despite the protagonist's dire situation, Dawn ultimately longs for love and idealizes her relationship with Alexander. The script does its best to expose the dirty world of juvenile prostitution, while also keeping some sort of handle on the romanticism of adolescence. When Dawn is able to finally get the electricity turned on in the apartment she shares with Alex, she calls the florescent lighting "bottled sunshine." Even in the depths of her narcissistic destruction, Dawn manages to preserve some sense of virtue and secretly hopes that someone will save her.

Made to cash in on the success of the infamous TVM *Born Innocent* which aired two years prior, *Dawn* adapts much of the same nihilistic overtone, but to lesser results. Dawn's irresponsible mother (Lynn Carlin) is obviously an alcoholic, but her overbearing nature doesn't seem to warrant the protagonist's desperation to leave home, and life is easily much worse on Hollywood Boulevard. She seems more stubborn and senseless than sympathetic, although her turn from an innocent fifteen-year-old to streetwise hooker is still a shocker.

Bo Hopkins is particularly good as the menacing pimp named Swan (it is interesting to note that his name rhymes with Dawn, perhaps as a way to express the yin and yang relationship of the agreed upon but destructive relationships of the streets). He shows little mercy, openly beating his "girls" and knifing Alexander. *Dawn* does show restraint in the underage sex scenes (which really don't exist at all in the film) but seemingly trades them in for violence and degradation. All is handled in a very TV-PG fashion of course, but the film still shocks in its subject matter and browbeaten setting.

Directed by Kleiser with a sense of edgy despair, it's hard to believe this same filmmaker would bring the bubble-gum bright *Grease* to the theaters in 1978. [Amanda Reyes]

DEATH CAR ON THE FREEWAY

Director: Hal Needham
Starring: Shelley Hack, George Hamilton, Frank Gorshin, Peter Graves
Airdate: September 25, 1979   Network: CBS

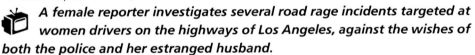 *A female reporter investigates several road rage incidents targeted at women drivers on the highways of Los Angeles, against the wishes of both the police and her estranged husband.*

Death Car on the Freeway must have one of the most ridiculous monikers for a killer in the history of film: how the cast kept a straight face while talking gravely about "The Freeway Fiddler" is a mystery to me. The Fiddler is the sinister driver of a Dodge van who spends his time terrorizing any women of Los Angeles that make the mistake of cutting into the traffic in front of him. On such occasions, he dons his leather gloves, puts on his personal chase music (a horrendous disco/country amalgamation, hence the nickname) and attempts—usually successfully—to run the woman off the road.

Death Car isn't your usual women-in-terror film, however. Up against the Fiddler is KXLA News reporter Jan Clausen (Shelley Hack), who is keen to prove both her independence and her professional worth after separating from her husband, Ray Jeffries (George Hamilton). As reporter for a rival station, Ray is clearly threatened by his wife's developing career, warning her not to make "a crusade" out of her search for the Fiddler and suggesting that she may as well resign, go home, and be a good little girl before she gets fired by her station managers. Jan is having none of it, spurred on by the messages of the Women's Liberation Front—who were gaining ground in the US at the time the film was made, and are directly referenced in a television interview in which a spokeswoman (spoke*sperson*?) aligns increasing car ownership with greater freedom for women.

This is, essentially, a feminist film. Though it may have been advertised on the strength of its spectacular car crashes and the search for a serial killer, it's relatively slow-paced (the opening scene, looking down at a complex freeway system from above, is particularly uninspiring). The real interest lies in the messages the film contains, with the attacks on women's cars seemingly analogous to rape. That the crimes are motivated by sexual frustration is suggested by a psychiatrist (Gloria Stroock) interviewed by Jan, and the blacked-out windows of the Fiddler's van evidently serve a voyeuristic purpose, allowing him to watch without being watched in turn. The incompetence of the police is frequently highlighted—one issues a ticket to a woman caught speeding in her attempt to escape the Fiddler—and the classic defensive responses to rape are adapted accordingly ("Women can help themselves by not making themselves candidates for the Fiddler"). The testimony of a surviving victim is questioned in light of her career as an actress, and local women—Jan included—begin taking "defensive driving" classes. Unfortunately, the cast aren't brilliant (though there is a brief appearance by Sid Haig as a shady biker type); Jan and her newsreader colleagues are at times somber to the point of woodenness. However, it's the idea rather than its execution that provides the film with its originality: at a time when women's rights were frequently being discussed in the press, adapting that discourse into something subtler was a clever way of expanding the debate into homes that might not usually engage with feminist issues. [Jennifer Wallis]

THE DEATH OF ME YET

Director: John Llewellyn Moxey
Starring: Doug McClure, Meg Foster, Richard Basehart, Darren McGavin
Airdate: October 27, 1971   Network: ABC

 When a Russian agent shows signs of switching sides, the KGB call in a hitman to end his life.

First broadcast by ABC during October of 1971, part-time chair Doug McClure (*Tapeheads*) stars in this quirky little spy sham as a Soviet KGB agent sent to the USA to bring about the downfall of the capitalist pig-state from within.

Trained in a replica American town (built in the middle of Mother Russia)

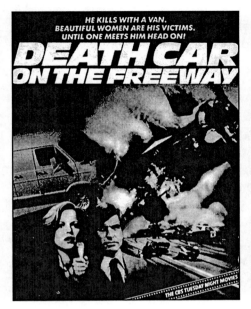

Clockwise from top: Promo art for *Death Car on the Freeway*; Eve Plumb grows up quickly in *Dawn: Portrait of a Teenage Runaway*; and Don Murray and Ray Milland bewitch in the supernatural thriller *Daughter of the Mind*.

and brandishing a .38 and a fine quiff, Doug unexpectedly falls in love when he arrives in the States, and is soon completely assimilated into the Yankee way of life, establishing himself as a successful newspaper owner, complete with a blonde, freshly pregnant wife (Rosemary Forsyth) and a penchant for cherry cola, scuba diving and muscle cars.

After six Cold War years undercover, Doug is offered his target job managing a secret underwater missile project headed up by menacing and homophobic FBI agent Darren McGavin (*Captain America*), who thinks Doug is not what he seems.

Add to the mix hitman Allen Jaffe (*Cutter's Trail*) as a Russian sleeper agent sent to put bullets into Doug's defective head, and you get a more than passable potboiler full of limp intrigue, wood paneling, big sideburns and nice cars—although, sadly not much else.

Based on a thin novel of the same title by Whit Masterson (writer of *Touch*

of Evil), keep watch for the mad eyes of beautiful Meg Foster (*Shrunken Heads*) and the red Russian mustache of bad guy Richard Baseheart (*Flood!*).
[DF Dresden]

THE DEATH OF OCEAN VIEW PARK

Director: E.W Swackhamer
Starring: Mike Connors, Diana Canova, Perry Lang, Caroline McWilliams
Airdate: October 19, 1979   Network: ABC

 Mike Connors tries to save his failing, haunted amusement park business from going under, killing his patrons in the process.

Welcome to Virginia, USA, home of the Ocean View Amusement Park, a place of fun, excitement, popcorn, clowns, joy and huge fucking explosions, fire and collapsing rollercoasters—well, according to "psychic" mother-to-be Diana Canova (*Peking Encounter*), who has scary visions that predict the park's demise, much to the annoyance of park owner Mike "Touch" Connors (*Panic Button*).

Also, there's a hurricane on the way, and it's nearly the fourth of July and Connors' evil, money hungry partner Martin Landau (*Black Gunn*) wants to keep the attractions open to stop the business hemorrhaging cash so he can sell it for profit to a large corporation—but, that's not going to happen because "There's a storm on the way! And my trousers are on fire!" (How's that for dialog?)

Not only is nature forming an orderly queue of rainy disasters to roughly dismantle the park (via stock footage of wind and storms), there also seems to be an unexplained supernatural element of destruction going on, as bumper cars and assorted rides tremble and move by themselves; scaring the bejeezus out of the park patrons, who gasp, choke on candy floss and turn dementedly into director Swackhamer's lens in some hilarious scenes when the cursed (?) park eventually implodes in an extended goofball sequence packed with cracked neon, falling cars, broken rails, unscrewed bolts and popped balloons.

Originally broadcast on ABC and produced by Playboy (!), it's more than enjoyable for all the wrong reasons and crackles along at a colorful, sparkly pace, touching on such wide-ranging subjects as possession, lost love, impotency, precognition and even haunted sandcastles. Toss in some plot points from *Hurricane* (1974), *Jaws* (1974) and *Rollercoaster* (1977) and you have a near classic of minimum proportions you'll watch more than once.
[DF Dresden]

THE DEATH OF RICHIE

Director: Paul Wendkos
Starring: Robby Benson, Ben Gazzara, Eileen Brennan, Lance Kerwin
Airdate: January 10, 1977   Network: NBC

 A teenager turns to drugs and finds himself in a whirlpool of despair and violence, leading to tragic consequences.

The small screen lent itself especially well to adapting tabloid tales and true stories, and when Thomas Thompson wrote an article for the May 5, 1972, edition of *Life* about a father who shot and killed his drug-addicted son, it wasn't long before the article was extended into a novel—*Richie*, also by Thompson—and later adapted into a teleplay for NBC by lifelong television writer John McGreevey. Paul Wendkos, one of the most prolific and reliable directors of the TV movie boom, capably handles the story of a once-supportive father (Ben Gazzara) pushed to the edge by his son's (Robby Benson) unpredictable drug-fuelled outbursts. Eileen Brennan, while not given much to do in the script besides act out the complacent housewife role, is nevertheless fantastic as the increasingly unraveled mother, and even preteen poster boy Lance Kerwin makes an appearance as Richie's younger brother Russell.

As the title implies, it's clear from the outset what the troubled teen's fate will be, and the film reconstructs the events that led up to Richie's tragic demise. After the opening shot of Richie's funeral, we cut to the interior of a car that is careening down the road as a jive-talking Richie and his stoner pals—including a young, mutton-chopped Clint Howard, Harry Gold (William Katt's diminutive friend in *Carrie*) and character actors Charles Fleischer and Barry Miller (*Fame*)—demonstrate the negative effects of barbiturate abuse. Richie's volatile relationship with his father—who is patient but tough, demanding that he drop the deadbeat friends—is fuelled further by Richie's own feelings of guilt and self-doubt about succumbing to peer pressure, which he projects onto his father, enabling him to demonize his father even more. He escapes into a secret strobe-lit room behind a panel in his closet, immersed in the hypnotic effects of the glimmering lights and the wailing guitar solos that blare from his turntable.

When his father files a wayward conduct petition against his own son, to get the support of the system in policing Richie's drug use, Richie has a temporary wake up call. He manages to get clean and get a job at a burger joint. But his recovery is short-lived; when he's rejected by the girl he likes (TV movie staple Cindy Eilbacher of *Crowhaven Farm* and *Bad Ronald*), he responds by O.D.ing on reds (aka Seconal—he takes nine, the same amount that led to Jimi Hendrix's demise). It just goes downhill from there, as Richie never stops using long enough to even hold up appearances. His recreational drug use becomes a fulltime crutch, and for the last quarter of the film he spends a lot of time walking into things and falling down stairs, while the camera adopts his wobbly POV. Eventually dad's patience wears thin and the combination of hatred and pity he feels for this miserable creature who was once an extremely bright young kid, wins out in a controversial final scene that revels in the very right wing morality characteristic of most anti-drug films. The ending of the film was reportedly censored; the sound of Richie screaming following the gunshot was cut out after the initial broadcast, and does not appear in any subsequent version of the film. [Kier-La Janisse]

DEVIL DOG: THE HOUND OF HELL

Director: Curtis Harrington
Starring: Richard Crenna, Yvette Mimieux, Kim Richards, Ike Eisenmann
Airdate: October 31, 1978   Network: CBS

 An oblivious family adopts a cute puppy possessed by the destructive dark spirit of Satan's own bag-rat Barghest.

Sniffing around the same damp tree in the park as *Dracula's Dog* (1978), *Mongrel* (1982), *Cujo* (1983) and *Monster Dog* (1984), here's yet another killer canine movie sure to curl the unwashed hair of any pet lover.

This time, the dog is from the Lakeland Kennels of L.A. The type of place where fuzzy bundles of woof can be purchased by the likes of evil Satanist Martine Beswick (*From Russia With Love*), who, along with her hooded coven and haunted hay barn, plan to infuse an Alsatian bitch with a puppy that'll contain the satanic soul of Satan's mongrel, Barghest. A demon dog that will reign on Earth for 1000 years—neutered or not.

Across town, cheery husband Richard Crenna (*Intruders*) and Tupperware wife Yvette Mimieux (*The Fifth Missile*) discover the tire-marked corpse of their family pooch Skipper on the road home, and on request of their kids, get a new dog from cult member and evil fruit and veg seller R.G Armstrong (*Dick Tracy*). Barely in the house five minutes and now christened Lucky, the evil pooch is scaring people with its face and making its eyes glow green—a hellish display nobody seems to consider an actual threat until, that is, the housekeeper bursts into flames and burns to death.

After concluding "That dog's just not right," Crenna decides to get rid of it and save the day via wonky psychic battles in the backyard and slow zooms to nothing in the house; all of which are accompanied by a fab flute riff that signals satanic danger and/or the onset of yet another pointless red-tinted dolly shot through the garden.

Written by Stephen and Elinor Karpf (*Gargoyles*) and directed by the often great Harrington (*Night Tide*), there's little in the way of graphic violence or action and it's never fully explained why Beswick bothered or why Crenna's family is chosen in the first place—just two of several plot holes riddling the tubby screenplay.

If you have the patience, you'll be rewarded with a fast peek at the (admittedly cool) hellhound when it eventually shows up, some mild terror and brightly colored outrage as the kids become enchanted and evil, mom gets horny, and the house goes mad. [DF Dresden]

DON'T BE AFRAID OF THE DARK
Director: John Newland
Starring: Kim Darby, Jim Hutton, William Demarest, Barbara Anderson
Airdate: October 10, 1973   Network: ABC

 A couple inherits a mansion, only to discover that something else is already living there.

Don't Be Afraid of the Dark (1973) is the quintessential made for TV thriller of a type they just don't make anymore. The best part of seeing movies like this when young is having the bejeezus scared out of us in an innocent and ultimately memorable way. Years later, we can recount where we were and what we were doing when we first saw these films because fear evokes such a strong emotional response.

Kim Darby and Jim Hutton star as Sally and Alex Farnham respectively, a couple who move into a house that Sally has inherited. The house is enormous, sporting an ornate lamppost at the foot of the driveway and really neat architecture. Jim is the typical workaholic and is anxious to become a partner at the firm he works for. He comes off as stern and loud, and never seems to have enough time for Sally, who is meek and tries her best to please him. The manse is too large for them, and the handyman (Demarest) does his best to keep the place in order.

Sally is bored and inspects the bottom of the fireplace, noticing that the opening has been sealed closed. When she questions the handyman about it, he evasively responds that it was necessary... and offers no more than that. This is the part where a red flag goes up as Sally now begins to see multiple pint-size, prune-faced creatures scurrying about when she tries to sleep, as she hosts a party for her husband's boss, and as she takes a shower. As children, we're all afraid of things that go bump in the night, and this film preys on that fear. The handyman knows all about the creatures and is complicit in trying to keep their existence secret.

Alex concludes that the house is somehow responsible for his wife's condition and suggests that she see a doctor. She's the only one who happens to see the creatures and therefore is labeled half nuts. By the end of the film, Sally is a mess and is practically incapacitated due to her mental state. The creatures begin to drag her across the floor and she plays James Stewart to their Raymond Burr, using a flash camera to momentarily blind them. The creatures, however, overpower Sally and pull her away into the depths of the fireplace. Viewing as a young child, this was likely frightening but to adult eyes it seems illogical and silly.

The film benefits from atmospheric cinematography and music from Billy Goldenberg who provided the bone-chilling minimalist score to Steven Spielberg's *Duel* (1971). Screenwriter Nigel McKeand also lends his vocal talents to the creatures, providing some truly creepy voices for them.

Part of the creepiness of this film is attributed to the filmmakers' refusal to explain what these creatures are and what their purpose is. Like Billy and Agnes in Bob Clark's *Black Christmas* (1974), and Michael Myers in John Carpenter's *Halloween* (1978), they are never explained. [Todd Garbarini]

DUEL

Director: Steven Spielberg
Starring: Dennis Weaver
Airdate: November 13, 1971   Network: ABC

 In his car, David Mann accidentally aggravates a truck driver. The driver takes the term "road rage" to epic heights.

It takes one strong talent working at full capacity to place their mark on the world. Louis Armstrong's trumpet playing in the late 1920s changed the face of music. Laurence Sterne's *The Life and Opinions of Tristram Shandy, Gentleman*, published in the 1760s, expanded and altered what a book could do. And, in 1971, Steven Spielberg made Richard Matheson's script for *Duel* into a tense, nerve-wracking TV movie that would raise the bar for all TV movies.

Spielberg brings his entire arsenal of cinematic knowledge and style to *Duel*, including wide-angle lenses, elaborate tracking shots, razor-sharp cutting and the perfect placement of the camera for maximum suspense. Everything Spielberg does well (and when it comes to action and suspense he is one of the best) is in this movie.

David Mann is presented in the barest possible terms. He's a middle aged man in a small red car, driving through the desert to a business meeting. He has a wife and two children. He seems to get a kick out of the talk radio that one can hear in the desert. Then, he encounters a rusty old rig with "FLAMMABLE" painted in big letters across the back. When the truck begins to get in Mann's way, it is initially presented as two people who happen to be going the same way and accidentally bother each other. Unfortunately, the truck driver gets mad. The film becomes a series of ever-escalating encounters that draw David Mann very close to madness.

One of the most intriguing elements of the film is the location used: the desert. The writer and director have chosen a potentially limiting location. Why not choose (budget aside) the heart of a city? More places to hide and more chances for peril. A desert has long stretches of nothing with the occasional hill. The chances for a variety of incidents seem limited. But not when creative minds become involved. *Duel* is filled with endless variations on themes. Trucker in front of Mann. Trucker behind Mann. Trucker sitting ominously still. Trucker going crazy. If he kills Mann, being deep in the desolate desert, Mann would die alone and sweaty.

The fear that *Duel* taps into the strongest is the fear of really profoundly pissing someone off, however accidentally, and having to deal with their unwarranted wrath. This film takes the crazy behavior of a person who feels wronged to its logical conclusion. All Mr. Mann can do is try to keep alive. It is the thought that there are people in the world who act like this that force the horror into reality.

Duel is Richard Matheson at is most stripped-down imaginative. *Duel* is a young Spielberg showing off his bag of tricks and thrilling a nation, then the world. And, *Duel* is poor Mr. Mann. He fights a big rig to the death. May the person you anger be a pillow salesman in a Pinto. [Daniel R. Budnik]

EBONY, IVORY AND JADE
Director: John Llewellyn Moxey
Starring: Bert Convy, Debbie Allen, Martha Smith, Donald Moffat, Lucille Benson
Airdate: August 3, 1979   Network: CBS

 A trio of spies, under the guise of a singing duo and their manager, search for a stolen and volatile explosive.

In an interview in 1979, Debbie Allen claimed that while no airdate had been set for the pilot movie *Ebony, Ivory and Jade*, CBS had ordered four more episodes. However, despite such a promising beginning, if these episodes were actually shot, they never aired and the telefilm was relegated to a mere footnote in the world of "jiggle-TV."

Along with Allen, who plays Ebony, Martha Smith (as Ivory) and Bert Convy (as Mick Jade) round out the cast of bumbling would-be spies. Jade is a rich guy who dabbles in everything from professional tennis to covert snooping. He uses his contacts as a talent manager as a front to get him into hot nightclubs and casinos where he can do his sleuthing in the most glamorous ways possible. Ebony and Ivory provide his cover, and he can usually be found going through things while the two lovely ladies are performing. As you can imagine, this leads the ragtag crew toward all sorts of low-rent adventures.

Honestly, *Ebony, Ivory and Jade* does not make a lick of sense, but it's innocuous, and so silly and fun that it becomes completely watchable. Convy, who dazzles in monochromatic polyester chic, is good as Mick Jade, although it's almost impossible to separate the character from the actor's real-life goofy charm. As one of the more genial but sometimes-awkward game show hosts (he often gave away the clues and answers on *Super Password*) Convy was an absolute comic delight. Mick is far more serious, but he bumbles around almost as much as the real Convy and that makes him perfectly suited to approach the action-hero stereotype with a sense of humor, even if it's mostly unintentional. The girls don't fare quite as well, but look gorgeous in their sexy costumes, and Allen shakes her moneymaker splendidly in the second dance number.

Ebony, Ivory and Jade also features real-life celebs palling around with the prying threesome in an effort to make Mick Jade look like a believable nightclub manager. Both Frankie Valli and David Brenner show up as themselves to tell the girls they are fabulous performers before quickly disappearing from the scene. Among the bubbling pink explosives, the cameos only serve to enforce the surreal feeling. However, the standout here is Lucille Benson as the sexagenarian bad guy. She works as a maid by day, hitman by night!

Slickly directed by the small screen master Moxey, this TV movie should not to be confused with Cirio H. Santiago's 1976 big screen martial arts flick with the same title (aka *She Devils in Chains*). This *Ebony, Ivory and Jade* is probably best thought of as *Charlie's Angels* with one less angel and one that imagines a Charlie/Bosley hybrid as a curly headed tennis bum millionaire. Sold. [Amanda Reyes]

ELVIS

Director: John Carpenter
Starring: Kurt Russell, Shelley Winters, Bing Russell, Pat Hingle, Season Hubley
Airdate: February 11, 1979   Network: ABC

 From childhood to his comeback in 1969, this is a chronicle of the king of rock'n'roll's tumultuous life.

Are you loathsome tonight? Alejandro Jodorowsky has said that the concept of the cage is that when you escape from it, you find you're still trapped in a bigger cage and so forth to infinity. So it was with Elvis Presely, who escaped the Deep South and went from poverty and obscurity to stadia and world domination: a rise and fall that ended in Las Vegas in a purple haze of drugs, fear, loneliness and despair, outlandish costumes, regrets and sideburns; a lonesome, boisterous cowboy, alone with millions of fans.

In 1969, after nine long years away from the stage, Elvis is uncertain about his future, both as man and artist. Still handsome, the king is wild and sexy, but more lost than ever, locked in the International Hotel, reminiscing about his past in postwar Tupelo. Back in those days, young Elvis, traumatized by the death of his twin brother Jesse Garon and worn out by endless money problems, started out from the Sun Studios and imposed his style and music on the ages, from Graceland to Hell.

Whatever you think of Elvis as a singer, the man was never very lucky with his movie career: out of eighteen films, only three or four can be viewed without embarrassment or terminal boredom. But even in his best movies, say *Heartbreak Hotel* and *Love Me Tender*, Elvis, who dreamed of being a "real" actor, looks uneasy in his job of poster child to boss Colonel Parker.

On the other side of the fence, it really takes a special sort of person to play the part of Elvis, he who barely dared to be himself. Future Snake Plissken, Kurt Russell (with Ronnie McDowell singing) seems the only guy for the job (with the peculiar exception of Bruce Campbell years later in Don Coscarelli's *Bubba Ho-Tep*). Like most biopics, Carpenter's *Elvis* (made two years after Elvis' death) tiptoes around its subject when it should grab it firmly by the hips, but it certainly does it justice. Carpenter, then thirty-one-years-old—rising to fame with *Assault on Precinct 13* in 1976 and establishing his reputation as master of horror with *Halloween* in 1978—successfully gives flesh and blood to Elvis. He portrays the rise and fall, the twenty years of sex, drugs, rock'n'roll, the dreams and nightmares of a white man with a black voice and blues spirit, to provide a glimpse of how Elvis became—and still is—Elvis, over the course of this three-hour biopic (the cinema version runs 'only' 120 minutes). But we are left wanting more, with some characters and situations barely touched on.

If you think a 'real' film about Elvis the fiction is still to be made, rewatch the old movies or simply close your eyes and travel back, listening to the records. You'll be all shook up. Generous, egomaniacal, charming, fucked up, paranoid, lunatic, larger than life… tonight, nine years after his last show, Elvis is gonna kick some ass. [Jean-Paul Coillard]

ESCAPE

Director: John Llewellyn Moxey
Starring: Christopher George, Marlyn Mason, William Windom, John Vernon
Airdate: April 6, 1971   Network: ABC

Left: Kurt Russell shakes his moneymaker in John Carpenter's *Elvis*.
Right: Christopher George wants to take you on an *Escape*.

 When criminals kidnap a famous scientist along with his daughter and his formula, a professional escape artist investigates the case.

Endowed with a fantastic opening credit sequence, it's such a shame this pilot movie from Paramount Television and writer Paul Playdon (*Visions*) never kicked off a series, as it has a supercool protagonist who uses kung fu, charm and escapology to solve crimes.

Christopher George (*City of the Living Dead*) is playboy/professional escape artist Cameron Steele, a classy private investigator who lives above a bar used as a watering hole for stage magicians called The Crystal Ball. One day, while out showing off in his fancy car, he is interrupted by the case of missing scientist William Windom (*Raising Dead*), a boffin working on a futuristic GM organism/virus to cure disease, end famine, help breed a master race and clean toilets.

Before the nice professor can gift his discovery to the world for free, he and his daughter Marlyn Mason (*Harpy*) are kidnapped by Windom's "dead" brother, supervillain John Vernon (*Animal House*) and imprisoned in his top secret lab HQ deep below the Happy Land Amusement Park.

Having none of it and out to get the girl, George hankers for the chance to punch the half melted Vernon in the head, and is soon descending elevator shafts and ladders, solving puzzles and escaping from trap after trap as he battles henchmen on his way to the heavily protected lair to save the day.

Low budget, fast paced, a tad 007 and a flaccid joy to view, this has rubber gloves, lab equipment, nice suits, jeopardy, Huntz Hall (*Bowery Blitzkrieg*), a car phone, fist fights and a roller coaster finale. Be sure not to confuse it with the other *Escape* (1980)—a TV movie starring Timothy Bottoms (*Parasomnia*) as real-life drug mule Dwight Worker, a man caught and imprisoned à la *Midnight Express* (1978) for smuggling drugs *into* Mexico. [DF Dresden]

THE FACE OF FEAR

Director: George McCowan
Starring: Ricardo Montalban, Elizabeth Ashley, Jack Warden, Dane Clark
Airdate: October 8, 1971   Network: CBS

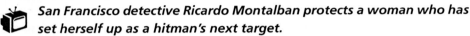 **San Francisco detective Ricardo Montalban protects a woman who has set herself up as a hitman's next target.**

Based on the novel *Sally* by E.V. Cunningham (a pseudonym for Howard Fast), Quinn-Martin produced this CBS Movie of the Week which stars ditzy, paranoid Elizabeth Ashley (*The Cake Eaters*) as Sally Dillman, a ditzy, paranoid school teacher who flees to San Francisco from her Idaho home to further consult with doctors who have informed her she has leukemia and only four months left to live.

Convinced of her oncoming demise, desperate and depressed, she pays $5,000 to a stranger in a random bar and hires an unknown hitman to kill her before the illness puts a full stop to her young life.

After meeting with yet another medical specialist, she's told she's been misdiagnosed and is fitter than most girls her age—news that should delight her, but instead fills her with dread as she has no way of cancelling her own hit.

While literally planking it on a trolley car, she fortunately bumps into the "Doo as I saay!" hairdo of suave police detective Ricardo Montalban (*Joe Panther*), who quickly assumes the role of white knight protector. Believing her odd story and a bit gooey-eyed at all the excitement, he convinces her to retrace her steps in order to identify the acne covered "face of fear" and stop the assassin before he can complete the job.

Nicely shot, well-acted, interesting and peppered with solid dialog, great cars, nice suits, suspicious bit players, a bout or two of cut-price gunfire and a taut plot line, there's some fine SF locations on show; as well as Dane Clark (*Blood Song*), Burr De Benning (*Cruising*) and Jack Warden (*Night and the City*) who can all be seen booking it in several chase scenes scored with bouncy music by Morton Stevens (composer of the *Hawaii Five-O* theme). [DF Dresden]

FEAR NO EVIL

Director: Paul Wendkos
Starring: Louis Jourdan, Lynda Day, Bradford Dillman, Carroll O'Connor
Airdate: March 3, 1969   Network: NBC

After a mystifying mirror brings back a young woman's dead lover, a psychiatrist, specializing in the occult, steps in to unravel the mystery.

Airing as part of the NBC World Premiere Movie series, *Fear No Evil* is a hyperstylized supernatural yarn that was intended to be a pilot movie for a series titled *Bedeviled*. It was to have featured the stunningly handsome and suave Louis Jourdan as Dr. David Sorrell, a psychiatrist whose strange caseload leads him to the bizarre and supernatural on a weekly basis. Unfortunately, the series never materialized, but this telefilm is gorgeously late sixties in design, features much in the way of eerie imagery—and a surprising amount of eroticism—and remains an excellent example of how to bring elegance, charm and terror to small screen horror.

Jourdan is perfectly cast as the reserved, but ultimately compassionate, psychiatrist who attempts to help the lovelorn Barbara (Day), a bride-to-be who lost her fiancé (Dillman) just days before their wedding. The dead lover returns to Barbara at night, through a gothic mirror he had purchased the day before his death. It is here, in the simple but surreal imagery that the film finds its strangest and strongest moments. Underneath the mourning, Barbara is all about *sex, sex, sex*, which include moments of bloodletting! (And, although subtle, probably unlike anything seen on television at this point!) The flashbacks of Dillman during his initiation into the dark side are also compelling and surreal, sometimes recalling images from *Simon, King of the Witches* and *The Last House on Dead End Street* (check out those masks).

Paul Wendkos adds a lot of aesthetic oomph to the proceedings, and tried his hand at a similar version of *Fear No Evil* in another pilot movie in 1979 titled *Good Against Evil*, starring Dack Rambo. The latter failed because by the time 1979 rolled around it had all been done before. The 1969 *Evil* has the benefit of getting there early on, and incorporating a lot of heavy grooviness into the proceedings. Everything from Cubist art (i.e. looking at things from all perspectives) to the softly sexy undertones, helps elevate *Evil*'s admittedly slow pacing.

Making his TV movie debut, the iconic small screen composer, Billy Goldenberg (credited here as William), provides *Fear No Evil* with a creepy and epic soundtrack. The love scenes between Barbara and her ghostly fiancé are made all the more disturbing through Goldenberg's echoed chants and off-kilter strings. The simple mirror imagery only heightens the effects.

While *Fear No Evil* did not become a series, it did spawn a sequel the following year, titled *Ritual of Evil,* that features Jourdan on a similar supernatural journey, as he tries to uncover what was behind the death of one of his young patients. Ah, what could have been! [Amanda Reyes]

FIRE!

Director: Earl Bellamy
Starring: Ernest Borgnine, Vera Miles, Patty Duke, Alex Cord
Airdate: May 8, 1977   Network: NBC

 The lives of the innocent are threatened by a raging fire when a prison convict intentionally sets a verdant mountainside ablaze.

Practically a Xerox of *Flood!* (1976) and produced by Irwin Allen (*The Towering Inferno*) for Warner Bros. Television, an all-star cast of TV movie royalty infests this smoky, plodding and bog-standard disaster epic—all about a forest in Silverton, Oregon, which bursts into flames when malicious chain-gang convict Neville Brand (*Killdozer*) sets fire to his work detail with a carefully aimed cigarette butt.

Thanks to some small scale, but convincing FX by Cliff Wenger, things burn quick here, so it's less than twelve minutes before the flames are sky high and hassling the clouds—which unfortunately gives director Bellamy naught to do but slowly introduce, and then maul, the usual grab-bag of cookie-cut characters. This time they include a retired doctor, a hotshot helicopter pilot, a divorcing professional couple, a missing child, a lovelorn logging boss, a bus packed full of stranded kids, escaped prisoners, countless law enforcement agents and some slightly charred and overwhelmed firemen.

Each character is given a simple treatment and all are either trapped within the woodland inferno, or heading toward its center to rescue a loved one, look at footage of scampering bears, worried frogs and fleeing deer… or to simply fail in their task and slowly roast amid the crackling pines.

Far more enjoyable with many beers and a full room, the main (and possibly only) reason to watch it, is again, the cast, so say "Hi" to Ernest Borgnine, sexy Donna Mills (*Runaway Father*), the great Lloyd Nolan (*Galyon*), punchy Eric Estrada (*Visions*), Patty Duke (*No Child of Mine*), wailing Vera Miles (*Psycho 2*) and moody Alex Cord from *Inn of the Damned.* [DF Dresden]

A FIRE IN THE SKY

Director: Jerry Jameson
Starring: Richard Crenna, Elizabeth Ashley, David Dukes, Joanna Miles
Airdate: November 26, 1978   Network: NBC

 Authority is questioned and panic erupts when Richard Crenna discovers a deadly comet on a collision course with Earth.

A tiny disco ball explosion in outer space unleashes a killer comet that threatens to smush the city of Phoenix, Arizona, in this lethargic, dialog driven disaster clunker directed by the wonderfully hit and miss Jerry Jameson (*Terror on the 40th Floor*).

Originally broadcast in two parts over two nights by NBC, it was made to cash in on the forthcoming release of the much hyped, but equally weak and watery space waster *Meteor* (1979), and so tells the same tale of scientists and observatory staff who discover a comet on a collision course with Earth and their efforts to divert its path—before good manners completely evaporate, society breaks down and everybody panics themselves into the morgue.

Shot mostly in cramped offices and badly decorated home sets, the usual line up of archetypes take their sweet time explaining the who and what in long, wordy belches in the hope that you, the viewer, will connect with one or more, and then root for them and their lousy lives when the comet eventually lands and goes bang.

Hard to like but watchable, bearded astronomer Richard Crenna (*Jade*) labors over dull calculations with assistant Joanna Miles (*Blackout*); cheating husband David Dukes (*Rawhead Rex*) and his porno mustache get laid; young runaways Michael Biehn (*Aliens*) and bubbly Cindy Eilbacher (*Forces of Evil*) coo and kiss; and publicity shy, partially corrupt governor Nicolas Coster (*Golden Girl*) and smug president Andrew Duggan (*It Lives Again*) try to keep the whole situation quiet for fear of causing a human stampede of doom.

Toss in some dozy campers, brat teens, crying wives, a fallout shelter, stock footage of rockets, army recruits, martial law, crappy destruction SFX and a plot premise ignored or possibly re-imagined in the likes of *Deep Impact* (1998), *Armageddon* (1998) and even *Impact* (2008), and you have a long haul, red-eye flight to a ho-hum finale. [DF Dresden]

FLOOD!

Director: Earl Bellamy
Starring: Robert Culp, Martin Milner, Barbara Hershey, Richard Basehart
Airdate: November 24, 1976   Network: NBC

A town mayor risks the lives of many by ignoring calls to open the floodgates of a rapidly crumbling dam.

If you can excuse the barren pun, this here is a dry run for producer Irwin Allen's *Fire!*, which followed a year later in 1977, and it's so similar in premise and intent, you'd be correct in assuming the birth certificate of both featured the word "conjoined."

In this disastrous Warner Bros. Television outing we have the usual cast of TV movie regulars subjected to the damp demands of a mammoth killer puddle when a dam wall cracks open (after an hour!), flooding the scenic countryside and town of Brownsville, Oregon.

For a hero, we have "Irish" helicopter pilot Robert Culp (*Spectre*, 1977), who talks fast and flies low, delivering wealthy fishermen like Roddy McDowall (*It's My Party*) to a fish-bloated lake that supplies and threatens to pop open the dam—a disaster hoping to be averted by the half-assed efforts of dam engineer Cameron Mitchell (*Demon Cop*), who tries to plug the leak, save the day and appear sober.

On the slow way to the eventual torrent of lethal and destructive H$_2$O, you'll find soggy Martin Milner (*Nashville Beat*), Barbara Hershey (*Frogs for Snakes*), Francine York (*The Doll Squad*), Whit Bissel (*Psychic Killer*) and young Leif Garrett (*Skateboard*) playing typical roles in a partially interested fashion, which won't add to your enjoyment, nor stave off the indifference inspired by the ho-hum antics.

Flatly filmed by TV series legend Earl Bellamy (*Speed Trap*), if you have to watch it, be prepared for water. More water. Appalling interior design, sand bagging, lots of dialog, dire miniatures, hardly any large-scale destruction FX, mismatched stock footage and a scene where crazy mayor Richard Basehart (*City Beneath the Sea*) bangs a table. [DF Dresden]

GARGOYLES

Director: Bill L Norton
Starring: Cornel Wilde, Jennifer Salt, Bernie Casey, Grayson Hall, Scott Glenn
Airdate: November 21, 1972   Network: CBS

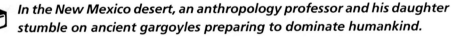 ***In the New Mexico desert, an anthropology professor and his daughter stumble on ancient gargoyles preparing to dominate humankind.***

One of the most beloved genre telemovies of the seventies, *Gargoyles* is perhaps best known today as the first film to feature the work of future Oscar winning makeup and special effects artist Stan Winston (*Aliens*, *Predator*, *Jurassic Park*, the first three *Terminator* films). In fact, Winston would share an Emmy (with Del Armstrong and Ellis Burman) for his work on *Gargoyles*, when the film won the Outstanding Achievement in Make-Up category at the 1973 awards.

Opening with a narrated sequence featuring a collage of gargoyle statues and inspired art, *Gargoyles* has the feel of one of those chintzy but strangely eerie seventies documentaries like *Chariots of the Gods* (1970) and *The Mysterious Monsters* (1975). Though it quickly settles into a routine telemovie structure, it moves along at a cracking pace, introducing us to Dr. Mercer Boley (Cornel Wilde) and his spunky young daughter

Diana (Jennifer Salt from De Palma's *Sisters*), who are heading off on an anthropological expedition across New Mexico as research for the doctor's new book, *Five Thousand Years of Demonology*. A pit stop at a tacky roadside oddity museum soon leads to the discovery of a family of gargoyles living in the mountain caves, who try to stop the pair from exposing them before the thousands of eggs they are incubating have the opportunity to hatch.

While the great makeup and costume designs are the clear highlights of the film, *Gargoyles* has a lot of other positives going for it. Cornel Wilde, a former matinee idol who also directed several interesting films including *The Naked Prey* (1965) and *Beach Red* (1967), has a great screen presence and makes a rugged hero for a man pushing sixty. Also fun to watch is Grayson Hall as the boozy, hysterical motel manager (never without a drink in her hand), and Bernie Casey projects great menace as the lead gargoyle with his creepy, modulated voice and graceful sense of movement (helped by some slow motion cinematography). Scott Glenn also has an early role as the leader of a gang of young mountain bikers whom the local sheriff tries to blame the gargoyles' chaos on.

Filmed on location in the Carlsbad Caverns area of New Mexico, *Gargoyles* conveys a nice haunting atmosphere and effective sense of isolation, and it's a credit to director Bill L. Norton that he was able to do such a good job at short notice and with very little time (he was brought on board at the last minute after the original director balked at the eighteen day shooting schedule). Norton would have a prolific career in television, directing many telemovies and episodes of shows like *Tour of Duty*, *Profiler* and *Buffy the Vampire Slayer*.

Featuring an optional audio commentary by director Norton, *Gargoyles* was released on DVD by Hen's Tooth Video in 2011. [John Harrison]

THE GIRL IN THE EMPTY GRAVE

Director: Lou Antonio
Starring: Andy Griffith, Jonathan Banks, James Cromwell, Mitzi Hoag
Airdate: September 20, 1977   Network: NBC

 Despite being buried by her family months before, a dead girl surprises everyone by turning up in town again.

Claude Earl Jones (*Bride of the Reanimator*) shares screen time with James Cromwell (*L.A. Confidential*) and Andy Griffith (*Go Ask Alice*) in this failed pilot attempt by MGM Television that was supposed to initiate a series that never transpired.

For a plot, we have small-town Chief of Police Andy digging to the bottom of a vaguely mysterious case involving a "dead girl" (Deborah

White) who miraculously shows up driving a car on main street one day—much to everyone's amazement, as she'd been officially pronounced dead and entombed in a grave a few months earlier.

Is it a ghost? An insurance scam? Or is it a collective hallucination induced by the boredom of the town? And just who did they box up, bury and mourn? If anyone can solve the conundrum, it's Andy, and this he does in typical, talky TV movie fashion; casually questioning the town's sleepy and often evasive inhabitants with a low key, cheery manner till the truth slowly emerges.

Devoid of violence or action, director Antonio (*The Chinese Typewriter*) practically ignores the impressive Big Bear, California, locations, choosing instead to fill out the running time with Lane Slate's brisk exchanges of homespun detection, which are as stodgy as an unbaked apple pie. A real shame too, as in spite of being well played and gifted with a great title, it sadly lacks a single memorable scene to separate it from similar seventies fare—deservedly relegating it to near obscurity. [DF Dresden]

THE GIRL MOST LIKELY TO...

Director: Lee Philips
Starring: Stockard Channing, Ed Asner, Jim Backus, Walter Berlinger
Airdate: November 6, 1973   Network: ABC

 After a bullied ugly duckling is transformed into a beautiful swan, she seeks hilarious revenge on those who did her wrong.

Lee Phillips' black comedy is a showcase for the comedic talents of a pre-*Grease* Stockard Channing, who stars as Miriam Knight, a portly, homely girl (achieved by a fat suit, fake eyebrows and a prosthetic nose) who has been through five colleges trying to find anyone who can see past her physical appearance. But every new start leads to more disappointment; as the film opens, she's just enrolled at a new school and despite being outgoing, funny and even bravely flirtatious, she quickly becomes the butt of campus jokes. From college jocks (including *CHiPs'* Larry Wilcox as a dumb football player named Moose) to a cruel junior MD (*The Love Boat's* Fred Grandy) to a conniving cheerleader roommate (the hilariously vacuous Susanne Zenor) who is threatened by Miriam's one success—landing the lead in the school play—the chips are stacked against our heroine and eventually she attempts to kill herself in a reckless driving accident.

Miraculously, she survives, but requires reconstructive surgery, and her figure is slimmed down by a restrictive hospital diet. When the bandages are removed (after a great scene through which Channing emotes her trademark sarcastic humor without the benefit of a face or voice), her doctor revels in his handiwork: she looks like a young Elizabeth Taylor. Sensing her new appeal to men—and to society at large—Miriam decides not to complacently accept her good fortune, but instead to seek vengeance on behalf of all homely girls everywhere, who are never given the opportunities of their better-looking counterparts.

Here is where the film gets really interesting—it could easily have gone with a series of pranks through which its villains get some poignant but restrained comeuppance. Instead, with her little red book/kill list on hand, Miriam dons a series of voluptuous disguises and concocts elaborate schemes to get rid of them all—for good. Meanwhile the cop investigating these bizarre deaths (Asner) is becoming increasingly obsessed with the mastermind behind them; while not quite what she planned on, Miriam may meet her match after all.

Conceived and co-written by the late Joan Rivers (one of very few things she wrote outside of comedy specials), directed by Lee Phillips (who also helmed the Linda Blair/Martin Sheen TV team up *Sweet Hostage*), and featuring familiar faces in many of the bit parts (Annette O'Toole, Reb Brown, Larry Manetti, Dennis Dugan, Jim Backus, Chuck McCann and more), *The Girl Most Likely To...* is an unusual film whose silliness often veils how dark and sad it really is. [Kier-La Janisse]

Newspaper promotion for the controversial adaptation of *Go Ask Alice*.

ABC Wednesday Movie of the Week
8:30 Go Ask Alice

For a lonely girl, drugs provide an easy road to popularity and access to the depths of despair. Startling con temporary drama starring Jamie Smith Jackson Andy Griffith and William Shatner.

GO ASK ALICE

Director: John Korty
Starring: Jamie Smith-Jackson, William Shatner, Ruth Roman, Julie Adams
Airdate: January 24, 1973   Network: ABC

A young woman chronicles her desperate battle with drug addiction.
To fully appreciate *Go Ask Alice* means placing it in its correct cultural context. When the manuscript first hit bookstore shelves in 1971, it was dropped as an "anonymous diary" penned by a drug addict who died a few weeks after her eighteenth birthday. For the next three decades, the book was essential reading for many impressionable tweens and teens, and the telefilm was shown in various health classes throughout the country. Many were haunted by this cautionary tale, even though it was outed as a work a fiction in the late seventies. "Edited" by therapist Beatrice Sparks, it is believed that *Go Ask Alice* is the intertwining of various stories told to Sparks by her patients. Her book is still in print today. Our modern eyes tend to view *Go Ask Alice* with a sense of cynicism, but during the turbulent seventies, it held our attention in a way that few other young adult novels had.

The telefilm aired just two years after the book's publication, and although much of it was played down for television (obviously the infamous line "Another day, another blowjob" was excised from the adaptation), some of the imagery remains disturbing, to say the least. While the protagonist in the novel is never named (the title *Go Ask Alice* refers to a line from the Jefferson Airplane song, White Rabbit), she is called Alice in the film, and is played by Jamie Smith-Jackson in her film debut. Alice's move from alienated youth to casual drug user to addict to pusher to hooker to recovering dopehead is head spinning. Skipping through the novel, the story jumps as though it was itself snorting coke. The overall effect displaces the viewer and, at times, it seems we are a part of Alice's terrifying trips. Where the "diary" analyzed the whys and hows, the telefilm effectively drops you off in the middle of the madness and confusion.

Somehow Smith-Jackson maintains sympathy—no easy feat, especially when she's pushing dope on junior high school kids. But her performance is moving, and after a bad acid trip (not her fault, someone dosed her soda!), where she tries to claw her way out of closet (!) her tormented struggle with sobriety seems almost impossible.

However, the story had two different effects: Some took the moral message to heart and swore themselves to living the straight life, while others felt the protagonist became exponentially cooler after she dropped a tab of acid. The physical change is undeniable. Although the lead actress is obviously attractive, her drug induced softly ironed hair, floppy hats and bell-bottoms look so much cooler on her.

William Shatner and Julie Adams play the parents, and Andy Griffith shows up for one scene (predating his team up with Shatner in 1974's *Pray for the Wildcats*). A young Robert Carradine plays a stoner and Mackenzie Phillips—an actress with her own substance abuse struggles—makes her debut as a shoeless "baby hooker," and starts off one of the most harrowing segments in the film. [Amanda Reyes]

THE GOLDEN GATE MURDERS
Director: Walter Grauman
Starring: David Janssen, Susannah York, Lloyd Bochner, Tim O'Connor
Airdate: October 3, 1979   Network: CBS

When several people plunge to their deaths from a bridge, a policeman and a nun team up to investigate.

According to this Universal Television production, the Golden Gate Bridge in San Francisco claimed the lives of fifteen construction workers before its completion in 1937. One of the dead riveters was the brother of Father John Thomas (Regis Cordic), a priest who visits the structure with his young, attractive, Irish nun/nurse assistant Susannah York (*Yellowbeard*). But only for a minute, as the gloomy father is soon over the rails and assumed to be a drowned suicide in the cold waters below.

Assigned to the case is David Janssen (*Man Trap*) who plays grumpy detective David Silver, an impolite and jaded grouch who mumbles and barks his way through a lot of raspy dialog in pursuit of a psycho who may, or may not have slain old John Thomas. And maybe a few others too, as it soon emerges there's a masked killer in a cape called The Specter pushing random strangers off the bridge.

After several more bodies go splash and sink, the police are left clueless, so it's up to the unlikely pairing of "mad nun" York and "mad cop" Janssen (who has a cat called Dirty Harry) to bring the killer to justice—which they predictably do without much fanfare or excitement. Meaning, you'll need a lot of coffee to help you stay awake to see the end credits—unless you're a massive fan of police procedure, waffly arguments, terrible flirting, sad faces, porn mustaches, justice and discussions about the afterlife, Heaven, suicide and the church.

Well-acted, but slow and soft headed, try to spot Kim Hunter (*The Kindred*), Paul Coufos (*Chopping Mall*) and Alan Fudge (*Bug*) amid the fog and then be amazed to learn this actually played some theater dates as *The Specter On The Bridge*, a title that makes it sound even better than it is.

For an update on how the Golden Gate is doing these days, go watch the morbid tales told in *The Bridge* (2006). [DF Dresden]

GOODNIGHT, MY LOVE

Director: Peter Hyams
Starring: Richard Boone, Michael Dunn, Barbara Bain, Victor Buono
Airdate: October 17, 1972   Network: ABC

 A private eye and his dwarf sidekick tackle a tough case in this seventies homage to film noir.

The 1940s were very big in the 1970s. The cult of Bogart was in full swing and there were numerous attempts at recreating or updating the look and feel of the great forties' detective films, from Roman Polanski's *Chinatown* to Woody Allen's *Play it Again, Sam*. This little known TV movie, clearly a labor of love from writer-director Peter Hyams, is one of the best.

It's Los Angeles in 1946. Down-at-heel detective Frank Hogan (Richard Boone) and his dwarf sidekick Arthur Boyle (Michael Dunn) receive a visit from a glamorous blonde, Susan Lakely (Barbara Bain). Susan hasn't seen her fiancé, Mike Tarlow (Gianni Russo), in five days, and wants Hogan to find out if he has another woman. Hogan and Boyle track Tarlow down to a hotel room, but, on entering it, Hogan is bopped on the head by an assailant who flees. "Thanks for the help," he says, trying to pick himself up off the floor. "Well, what did you want me to do?" asks Boyle. "Punch him in the knee?"

They learn that Tarlow is also being sought by Julius Limeway, the fat man who owns the swank Top Hat Club. Limeway wears a white suit and sits in his club all day, eating clams and being lugubrious (in the 1940s, he would have been played by Sidney Greenstreet, but here the role is nicely handled by Victor Buono, best known for his turn as King Tut in the *Batman* TV series). It becomes clear that Tarlow was the man we saw at the beginning of the film, shooting one of Limeway's couriers dead on a bus and stealing a briefcase full of money.

The plot thickens of course, with double and triple crosses, and Hogan getting bopped on the head some more ("I really hate getting beaten up."). Kept abreast of developments, Susan does a lot of girlish weeping à la Mary Astor in *The Maltese Falcon*, while Hogan is convinced she's lying through her teeth. The action culminates in a Hitchcock-like scene in a cinema, where a gunman synchronizes his shot with one in the movie being screened.

While it takes its cues from *The Maltese Falcon*, this is more than just a pastiche. It's atmospherically shot in soft focus so that light comes through windows in bright foggy bursts (almost the opposite of film noir, really). Boone, who played the black-clad gunslinger Paladin in the existential

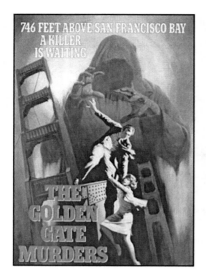

From left: Exceptional promotional artwork for *The Golden Gate Murders*; Richard Boone and Michael Dunn reinvigorate the noir with *Goodnight, My Love.*

TV western *Have Gun—Will Travel*, conveys a wonderful world-weariness as Hogan. The engine that drives the movie, though, is the relationship between Hogan and Boyle. Boyle, who is usually thinking about his next meal, is constantly undercutting the action with wry lines ("Francis, she's crying again," or, after one of Limeway's florid speeches, "Francis, I think I'm going to be ill"). The hulking Boone and diminutive Dunn make a great comedy double act, and if this *had* been made in the forties, they probably would have been in a whole series of films together. Sadly Dunn, a very talented actor, died at the age of thirty-nine just two years after this was made. [Chris Mikul]

HAWAII FIVE-O

Director: Paul Wendkos
Starring: Jack Lord, Leslie Nielsen, Nancy Kwan, James Gregory
Airdate: September 20, 1968   Network: CBS

 Steve McGarrett, the charismatic head of Hawaii Five-O, clashes with US intelligence as he hunts down the Red Chinese agent Wo Fat.

The feature-length pilot of *Hawaii Five-O* introduced audiences to many of the elements that would become familiar during the popular series' long (1968–80) original run. Jack Lord's Steve McGarrett is as tough and stoic as ever, with a bit of a sensitive touch and Morton Stevens' now classic and iconic theme music is there, as is the great and wonderfully-edited opening title montage, though both are in slightly different forms to those in the regular series. There are other differences between the pilot and the ensuing series as well—McGarrett's right hand man, Danny "Dan-O" Williams is played by Tim O'Kelly, perhaps best known for the classic 1968 Peter Bogdanovich film *Targets* (in the series, Dan-O was played by the more familiar James MacArthur). Likewise, the part of Hawaii's Governor is played by Lew Ayres, as opposed to Richard Denning, who portrayed the character throughout the show. There are also some uncomfortable attempts at comedy between two of McGarrett's top agents, Chin-Ho (Kam Fong) and Kono (Zulu), which was thankfully downplayed in the series.

In this pilot, which was later edited into a two-part episode entitled *Cocoon*, McGarrett comes face-to-face for the first time with Wo Fat (Khigh Dhiegh), the Red Chinese agent who would re-appear several times throughout the series' run. He was, effectively, the Blofeld to McGarrett's 007, with the head of Five-O not getting to throw the book at him until the very last episode of the series. When we first meet him in the pilot, he is subjecting a US intelligence agent (and close friend of McGarrett) to an insidious sensory deprivation torture chamber designed to extract information: a large water tank installed in the hull of an old cargo ship, into which the agent, after having his eyes, ears and nose filled in with dental clay and a bizarre breathing apparatus placed over his head, is submerged in water until all mental resistance is broken down. It's a very strange, eerie opening to the show, more reminiscent of an Irwin Allen sci-fi series than a cop drama. Off-kilter camera shots and fish-eye mirror reflections add to the strange, almost experimental feel to the pilot at times. Of course, the viewer suspects all along that McGarrett will end up in the deprivation chamber at some point, though he naturally proves a tougher nut for Wo Fat to try and crack.

Filmed entirely on location, one of the main selling points of *Hawaii Five-O* was its exotic (and then novel) setting, and the pilot certainly does its bit to encourage tourism and highlight the natural beauty and scenic splendor of the Hawaiian Islands. Thankfully though, the filmmakers didn't shy away from also showing some of the sleazier elements which the islands had to offer, and forty-five-plus years later it's great to have a visual record of all the seamy cocktail bars, strip joints and gritty skid-row motels which have sadly since given way to gentrification and "progress."

While there were much tighter and more exciting episodes of *Hawaii Five-O* to come (seasons two and three being particularly strong), the pilot movie remains a highly satisfying introduction to a classic piece of American crime fiction TV. [John Harrison]

HEATWAVE!

Director: Jerry Jameson
Starring: Ben Murphy, Bonnie Bedelia, Lew Ayres, David Huddleson
Airdate: January 26, 1974   Network: ABC

 In the midst of a heatwave, a young couple escapes the city for the mountains. But the mountains pose new problems.

"The weathermen don't seem to know what's going on," says Laura Taylor to her husband Frank. It's the start of the movie, barely five in the morning, but the temperature is already 97°F and creeping steadily up, just like yesterday. And the day before. The overworked air conditioning unit in the young couple's bedroom clatters to a stop. By midday the temperature is 115°F.

Frank (Ben Murphy) heads off to work and Laura (Bonnie Bedelia) heads for the supermarket. Their journeys make *Heatwave!* look for a spell like a pared down version of Goddard's *Weekend*, with its microcosm of a society in disarray. People are collapsed on the sidewalk, tended to by paramedics. Animals scavenge whatever water they can find. Perishable goods are taken off-sale for health reasons, causing little riots in supermarket aisles. And so on. At the Laundromat, the heavily pregnant Laura has a funny turn. When Frank's office is forced to close as part of an energy-saving contingency plan, the couple decide to leave the city for the hills, deducing it'll be safer there.

Heatwave! is a bit of a mess. It's not all bad, and this early section depicting the city grinding to a halt is effective, as is the failing of humanity in a crisis. (When the couple stop to help an old timer, he steals their car.) But then other aspects of the movie are unlikely or just plain bizarre. The ongoing quarrel Frank has with his in-laws, for example, serves no definable purpose. On the other hand, an encounter with a traveling beer salesman (David Huddleston) in a diner provides a *longueur* that is achingly misplaced. Its crude purpose is to enable the final act, when the salesman returns unexpectedly to save the day for Laura and Frank.

But what a final act! Stuck in the mountains, miles from anywhere and without electricity, the couple must build an incubator if their premature baby is to survive. Frank rounds up sympathetic townsfolk, who he then sets to work building the incubator—a complex piece of equipment—from bits and pieces of junk, like a benign A-Team. The salesman provides the gasoline for the generator that powers the incubator, thus forgoing his opportunity to make a mint selling beer to the parched masses from the trunk of his car. Shots of the sun in the sky remind us about the heatwave.

This end sequence is so far removed from everything else in the movie, and goes on for so long, I'm of the opinion the screenwriter left some pages on the bus into the studio that morning and was forced to make-do.

Director Jerry Jameson is another prolific name in television, working on shows and TV movies through to the present. He also directed *Airport '77* (1977) and the drive-in horror favorite, *The Bat People* (1974). [David Kerekes]

HEY, I'M ALIVE

Director: Lawrence Schiller
Starring: Ed Asner, Sally Struthers, Milton Selzer, Hagan Beggs
Airdate: November 7, 1975   Network: ABC

 After a small plane crashes in the wilderness, an estranged couple has their faith and health tested by the elements.

Partially based on a true story (from a 1963 book by Helen Klaben and Beth Day), lumpy Edward Asner (*Fort Apache The Bronx*) runs out of plane fuel on his way to San Francisco and crashes his tiny aircraft into a desolate, snowy Yukon forest—much to the alarm of his wobbly-eyed passenger Sally Struthers (*A Deadly Silence*).

Narrated in flashback by Struthers, she tells the cold, plodding and inspirational story of how she met amateur pilot (and staunch, religious zealot) Asner, and how they took to the air, hit the ground, got injured, built a fire, and, in the spirit of survival, learned how to band together and forage for food while accepting each other's personal quirks and opposing beliefs.

Lost in the barren wilderness for forty-nine days, the duo eat snow, grow beards, wear hats, figure out how to signal for help, slap each other awake and endure Asner's half-assed Australian/Canadian accent, which wanders across many geographical borders in search of a home.

Hardly exciting, and with little to recommend it, the only joy you'll find between the opening and closing titles is Struthers' constant whining, Asner's emotionless, solid turn and the fact that the rescue squad fail to find them each and every fly over. Personally, I was praying for a grizzly bear attack, an avalanche, or a freak hunting accident to bring an end to both of them and the preachy bible-heavy dialog which the pair recite and discuss endlessly as they try to save each other's soul—as well as skin.

Director/producer Schiller is responsible for dozens of TV features, including the morose *Marilyn: The Untold Story* (1980), the memorable *The Executioner's Song* (1982) and the forgettable *Double Jeopardy* (1992). [DF Dresden]

HITCHHIKE!

Director: Gordon Hessler
Starring: Cloris Leachman, Michael Brandon, Cameron Mitchell, Henry Darrow
Airdate: February 23, 1974   Network: ABC

In search of a new life away from an unloving partner, a woman gives a ride to a mysterious man.

Universal Television produced this taut, no-frills road trip thriller starring a practically-on-fire Cloris Leachman (*Herbie Goes Bananas*) as Claire Stevens, a woman on the run from a disintegrating relationship who fills her car trunk with red luggage and heads out on the highway in search of peace, quiet and a chance to rethink her life while she stays at her sister's house, hundreds of miles away in San Francisco.

Barely down the road and looking for adventure, she picks up depressed, toy-boy hitchhiker Michael Brandon (*Rock 'n' Roll Mom*)—who is still wet with sweat after using a lethal hair clip to murder his slutty stepmother (Sherry Jackson) pre-coitus.

Unaware of her passenger's heart-stopping tendencies, and blind to the fact she's now harboring a wanted killer, Leachman smiles as she drives; slowly becoming more and more attracted to her mysterious, near silent traveling companion who encourages her to talk about her feelings, dreams and girly ambitions until she cracks wise and sets herself up as his next victim.

Despite being light on the action, things are kept watchable with some solid dialog, claustrophobic car interiors, a smear of mud, crazy trousers, pregnant pauses and nice, but brief performances from cops Henry Darrow (*Night Games*) and pipe-smoking Cameron Mitchell (*Kill Point*), who play the detectives hoping to find the odd couple before more bodies pile up.

Those interested in the Passenger From Hell genre should check out the classic *The Devil Thumbs A Ride* (1947), *Hitch Hike* (1977) and of course, both versions of *The Hitcher* (1986, 2007). [DF Dresden]

HOME FOR THE HOLIDAYS

Director: John Llewellyn Moxey
Starring: Sally Field, Julie Harris, Jessica Walter, Jill Haworth, Eleanor Parker
Airdate: November 28, 1972   Network: ABC

An ailing man summons his four daughters home for Christmas. He informs them he believes his second wife is trying to kill him. A mysterious figure in a raincoat begins to murder the daughters one by one.
Not that there are many who'd need much convincing that a family Christmas gathering is the perfect breeding ground for horror, but who better to illustrate this point than legendary TV movie director John Llewellyn Moxey (*The House That Would Not Die*, *The Night Stalker*, *No Place to Hide*, et al), celebrated screenwriter Joseph Stefano (*Psycho*) and a wall-to-wall cast of heavy hitters, like Sally Field, Julie Harris and Jessica Walter, to name a few? Tie all that up with an Aaron Spelling/Leonard Goldberg Production bow

and the possibility of failure is scarce.

Walter Brennan plays possibly paranoid patriarch Benjamin Morgan who beckons his four generally estranged daughters to his bedside to plead with them to assist in the disposal of his second wife Elizabeth (Harris) who he believes is slowly poisoning him. Thoughts that dad is delusional are leveled by the knowledge that Elizabeth spent time in an asylum having been accused of dispatching her previous husband in a similar manner. Having gone against public opinion defending Elizabeth's innocence, pride now keeps pop from going to the police.

It's not long before the sisters' assorted dysfunctions surface, Freddie (Jessica Walter) is a boozy pill popper, Joanna "Joe" (Jill Haworth) has had a string of failed relationships, eldest daughter Alex (Eleanor Parker) is an overburdened dumping ground attached to the phrase "emotional prisoner" and Christine "Chris"(Sally Field) is the underestimated "baby" who claims to "have a habit of needing too much." All of the girls live in the shadow of their mother's suicide. On the surface, their mother killed herself suffering from a broken heart when father took up with Elizabeth but it is implied that his desire to leave her was spurred by the fact that she failed to give him a son, leaving all of the siblings liable by birth, at least in their father's eyes. His guilt generating disapproval is inescapable and his longing and dissatisfaction is buried in each of the sisters' very names. The wise thing to do when confronted with such a toxic environment is to simply walk away; unfortunately, in this case, that self-preserving action opens you up to being stabbed with a pitchfork by a shadowy figure in a yellow raincoat. Welcome home.

With its holiday setting, unidentifiable mystery killer and extended late in the game chase sequence giving way to a surprise unveiling complete with confession, *Home For The Holidays* can easily be pegged as a slasher flick forerunner. On the other hand, its anchored cynicism of family bonds, macabre sense of humor and tendency toward lightning flashes of histrionics insure its uniqueness. Due to budgetary and time restraints, the production was forced to forgo an originally scripted snowstorm and rely on rain, a concession that may actually work in its favor. The constant onslaught of dismal dampness outside mirrors the sense of dreary disappointment indoors, making the dank familial discord feel utterly ineludible. [Lance Vaughan]

THE HORROR AT 37,000 FEET

Director: David Lowell Rich
Starring: William Shatner, Chuck Connors, Roy Thinnes, Tammy Grimes
Airdate: February 13, 1973   Network: CBS

The passengers and crew of a 747 on a transatlantic flight discover demonic forces in the cargo.

What happens when seventies era airplane disaster clichés collide midair with the same decade's morbid fascination with the occult? It turns out you get something low in logic yet high in entertainment value, namely, *The Horror at 37,000 Feet*. It doesn't hurt that everyone who bought a ticket on this particular flight is either a television legend or a shameless scene-chewer, or in the case of William Shatner (who portrays a priest who's looking for the faith he's lost at the bottom of a bottle)—both. One would think we'd all be in highly capable hands with *The Rifleman*'s Chuck Connors on board as captain, and *Gilligan's Island*'s "Professor" Russell Johnson as his co-pilot but neither are much of a match against the supernatural forces unleashed by *The Norliss Tapes*' Roy Thinnes as a clueless architect transporting an ancient altar and Tammy Grimes as an undercover demon apologist. *The Beverly Hillbillies*' Buddy Ebsen is along for the ride as well and his priceless befuddled expression speaks volumes. In fact, he can barely keep a straight face.

As ostensibly derivative as *Horror at 37,000 Feet* may sound, it's overall one of a kind. Somehow the everything but the kitchen sink game plan, paired with its over-the-top performances and fearlessness in regards to its profoundly surreal conclusion, ensure that ultimately it's in a class all by itself. There's really no use fighting it, my advice is to put the rational part of your brain in the overhead compartment, securely fasten your seatbelt, and prepare for an onslaught of supernatural mayhem including voodoo baby dolls that spew green ooze, blasts of artic air so cold they freeze a dog mid-bark, killer elevators, human sacrifices, ominous chanting pouring out of earphones and a creepier than you'd expect, late in the flight, appearance from a funky phantom in a hooded robe. If none of the aforementioned sounds like your cup of tea, this journey is still worth taking as a simple eye-opening reminder of how much air travel, haunted or otherwise, has changed over the decades. Non-stop smoking, drinking and chauvinistic asides appear to be highly encouraged in this too groovy to believe shag-carpeted, double decker lounge club in the sky. If this plane is representative of modern life in the States it's no wonder the ancient spirits are less than excited about being relocated.

It's all perhaps silly and even preposterous but there's something about the giddy madness aboard this craft that's highly contagious as well, so don't be surprised if you find yourself inexplicably unnerved before you get your feet back on safe, sane, solid ground. Shatner may always be better remembered for his notorious airplane-set *Twilight Zone* episode 'Nightmare at 20,000 Feet' or for his legendary stint commandeering a spacecraft boldly going where no man has gone before, but for sheer outlandish television excess, in my book, you just can't get any higher than *The Horror at 37,000 Feet*. [Lance Vaughan]

THE HOUND OF THE BASKERVILLES

Director: Barry Crane
Starring: Stewart Granger, Bernard Fox, William Shatner, Anthony erbe
Network: ABC   Airdate: February 12, 1972

 The detective Sherlock Holmes investigates a case that involves the cursed Baskerville family and a spectral animal.

There are very few US TV movies that occupy a period setting, and fewer still set in Edwardian England with non-American lead actors. *The Hound of the Baskervilles* is one such TV movie, an adaptation of the most famous case handled by the fictional detective, Sherlock Holmes. Here the sleuth is played by Stewart Granger, and Bernard Fox is his trusted assistant, Dr. Watson. Both actors (English and Welsh, respectively) are adequate, if failing to bring any real fizz to their roles. Fox shamelessly mimics Nigel Bruce, possibly the defining Watson, and in so doing upstages the grandfatherly Granger. Granger wears a deerstalker, but his keynote powers of deduction are decidedly underwhelming.

It's hard to muster interest in a story that limps along at such a sorry pace. The teleplay, by Robert E. Thompson, truncates Sir Arthur Conan Doyle's long and complex whodunit to chats in bright rooms and the small stage set that represents Dartmoor. There is time for a roaring prologue, however, an unnecessary backstory to the Baskerville curse. Here, William Shatner plays Hugo Baskerville, a badly behaved lord who laughs a lot and throws women around. He comes to a swift and sticky end on the moors in the jaws of the 'orrible hound, in truth a medium sized dog that otherwise doesn't appear often—unlike Shatner. Shatner returns as another character, George Stapleton (named Jack in the original story), the villain of the piece. One might wish that Shatner was still a lord who laughed a lot, because as Stapleton he brings an element to the movie that breaks it. Period setting and British accent are irrelevant. This is Shatner doing Shatner—on the moors with a butterfly net. If he was dressed in his Starfleet uniform he wouldn't look any less out of place.

Conversely, Anthony Zerbe is hypnotic. The Californian actor pulls off a convincing plummy British accent, bringing to the role of Dr. John Mortimer—another red herring—a sly depth that belongs in a better movie. This is England as seen through the backlot of Universal Studios. Apart from stock footage of the Houses of Parliament and a steam train, *The Hound of the Baskervilles* represents a romantic if wayward analogy to the British Isles, one in which no one talks or dresses right, London might easily be a village in Transylvania, and Bobbies have gunfights with convicts on the lam.

Director Robert Crane was a familiar name in television, having produced and directed many top shows, including *Hawaii Five-O* and *Mission: Impossible*. He was also a world-class bridge player. His murder at age fifty-seven in 1985, the week of a regional bridge tournament in Pasadena, remains unsolved. He was bludgeoned and his nude body dragged to the underground garage of his home in Studio City. Crane himself might make for an interesting movie of the week one day. [David Kerekes]

A HOWLING IN THE WOODS

Director: Daniel Petrie
Starring: Barbara Eden, Vera Miles, John Rubinstein, Larry Hagman
Airdate: November 5, 1971   Network: NBC

 An unhappy housewife travels to her remote hometown only to be greeted by secrets and a creepy howling dog.

In a bid to escape her city life for a few days, fashion illustrator Liza Crocker (Barbara Eden) returns to her hometown of Stainesville, Nevada. She has asked her husband for a divorce, and is hoping that the separation will allow the two of them to come to terms with the decision.

As she slowly begins to reacquaint herself with the community, she is disturbed to discover that the inhabitants seem mysteriously affected by a common secret. Some of the locals greet her warmly, but others with hostility and caution. Something is clearly amiss, and the longer she stays, the closer she finds herself to a shocking revelation that even members of her family have tried desperately to hide.

This one's a bit of a head scratcher. First off, the title is unintentionally misleading—the movie has nothing to do with werewolves and, in fact, it's not even a horror movie. Actually, it's very hard to categorize since, for the most part, it really isn't about anything, per se. And yet, it's undeniably compelling, suggesting that the title—evocative as it is—is what keeps the audience in anticipation, as opposed to anything happening on-screen.

Barbara Eden—here in a dramatic role—totally sheds any preconceptions audiences might still retain from her the lighthearted *I Dream of Jeannie* character that made her famous, and which in fact, had only ended the year previously. She would go on to work almost exclusively as an actress in made for TV movies that spanned all genres. Additionally, in a creative move that the producers must have appreciated was as commercially lucrative as it was ballsy, she is reunited with her long time *Jeannie* co-star Larry Hagman, playing her husband, although their relationship here could not be further removed from the high spirited comedy that had endeared them to viewers throughout the latter part of the sixties. One scene in particular, when the estranged couple meet up (Hagman, though second billed, is largely absent throughout much of the picture) to discuss their marriage and its dissolution, serves as an effective reminder of the range of both stars.

As fine as it is to see the leads playing against type and bringing their 'A' game (yet some of the supporting performances are distractingly wooden) and veteran director Daniel Petrie is as reliable as ever, there is one chief problem—the mystery element that the audience has presumably tuned in for is so vaguely addressed that one forgets the crux of the events that are unfolding. In effect, we end up caring deeply about Eden's character, and even some of those around her, but we don't know why. It certainly feels like a creative choice rather than bad filmmaking, but the merits of this narrative technique are questionable, while, admittedly, it was employed to good use in Nicholas Roeg's *Don't Look Now*, which—and perhaps not coincidentally—this film pre-dates.

A rewarding but disappointingly insubstantial curiosity for those that are interested, NBC's *A Howling in the Woods* is all atmosphere and foreboding. But devoid of any genuine suspense and shackled by a wandering narrative that culminates in a predictable, sigh-inducing climax, it's enigmatic to a fault. [Kevin Hilton]

THE INITIATION OF SARAH

Director: Robert Day
Starring: Kay Lenz, Shelley Winters, Morgan Brittany, Morgan Fairchild
Airdate: February 6, 1978   Network: ABC

 The relationship between stepsisters is strained when, at college, one explores social acceptance and the other telekinetic revenge.

Many dismiss *The Initiation of Sarah* for jumping on the revenge of the telekinetic oddball train spearheaded by the success of Brian De Palma's 1976 big screen adaptation of the Stephen King novel *Carrie*. It's a fair enough assessment as several elements and scenes are shamelessly pilfered, but as far as small screen also-rans go, it's better than most and deserves credit for adding more than a few flourishes of its own. For all of its faults, and there are a few including a smudgy, over-edited climax, *The Initiation of Sarah* is rarely less than thoroughly entertaining.

Kay Lenz stars as Sarah Goodwin, a shy introvert who downplays her incredible ability to telekinetically knock people on their derrieres whenever they anger her. Morgan Brittany plays her more gregarious half-sibling Patty

Left: Kay Lenz and Morgan Brittany are part of *The Initiation of Sarah.*
Above: A KOOL newspaper promo for *KISS Meets the Phantom of the Park.*

Goodwin. The two acknowledge their differences while remaining thick as thieves until they enter college and the more outgoing Patty is accepted into a sorority reserved for the snobby elite and Sarah is only welcomed into a rival sorority of outcasts. Although moving in different directions, the Goodwin girls vow to remain tight but their sisterly bond finds a formidable foe in the form of Jennifer Lawrence, the Queen Bee of Patty's sorority played to the bitchiest hilt by Morgan Fairchild. During the course of this production if you find yourself asking, "In exactly what universe would Kay Lenz be considered a frumpy, undesirable underdog?" the simple answer is, "In any universe where Morgan Fairchild declares it so!"

Obviously a great deal of the fun to be had here can be found in the delicious anticipation of Fairchild receiving her exceedingly well-earned comeuppance. The payoff is not quite as satisfying as one might predict but the not too shabby consolation prizes include a sweet turn from Tisa Farrow, as a put-upon waif nicknamed Mouse, Robert Hays playing against type as a bamboozled jock, Tony Bill as the sensitive student teacher who clarifies the flick's modest moral to Sarah by advising, "Hate is the only real evil power—don't give in to it," and best of all, Shelley Winters doing her best Shelley Winters as conniving housemother Mrs. Hunter, who means to harness Sarah's powers, add a little black magic, stir in some ritualistic human sacrifice and destroy the opposing sorority for good.

Admittedly, on more than a few occasions, you get the feeling that several pages of the script must have gotten lost in the shuffle. A strong implication is made that Sarah's birth mother may in fact be Winters' shady Mrs. Hunter and then we never hear a peep of that possibility again. Still, there's something genuinely rousing about witnessing Sarah gain her sea legs and rallying her fellow outcast sorority sisters to take charge of their own self-images and destinies. It's no stretch to say that the entire ride is often teetering toward over-the-top camp territory but the plethora of winning performances insure that the unlikeable characters are just as intriguing as the likeable ones and that viewers are never left out of the fun. [Lance Vaughan]

THE INVASION OF CAROL ENDERS

Director: Burt Brinckerhoff
Starring: Meredith Baxter, Christopher Connelly, Charles Aidman, George DiCenzo
Airdate: March 8, 1974   Network: ABC

Possessed by the reincarnated spirit of a woman who may have been murdered, Carol Enders investigates her own death.

Produced by the great Dan Curtis (*Trilogy of Terror*), here's a strange and strained teleplay about love, life, reincarnation and revenge from beyond the grave, all shot in long takes on interior sets with harsh lighting and slow cameras.

The wooden schmaltz begins when posh brain doctor Charles Aidman (*Deliver Us From Evil*) is at work one day fixing heads. Across town, his sulky, cheating wife Diana (Sally Kemp of *The Glove*) crashes and dies (off screen) in a car "accident." At the moment of her death, her "karmic spirit" is let loose and sent to invade the recently vacated body and empty blonde head of young bride-to-be, Carol Enders (Meredith Baxter), a fatally injured patient in Aidman's hospital, dying after being previously battered into a coma during a late night sex attack.

Reborn—sort of—and confined in the cramped, tiny hospital, the merged Carol/Diana is cheerfully bewildered at first, but soon comes to terms with her new "selves" by crying rivers one minute and talking about the afterlife the next, freaking the fuck out of her befuddled fiancé Christopher Connelly (*Jungle Raiders*), who soon discovers that this new Carol may have been the victim of a murder, or a crime or something.

Who cut Diana's brakes? Is there an afterlife? Will the guilty be punished? Will Carol/Diana learn to love anew? Can't they all just get along? How grumpy will the police get? And just how much of the set remained free of Meredith Baxter's teeth marks by the end of it all?

Low budget, soft and tacky looking, it's tattooed with brittle, non-stop chattering, so even if you love bright, light, supernatural, 4:3 candy floss, you'll still need beer to ease the passing of its paltry running time. If you can find it, keep watch for the excellent Phillip Pine (*Brainstorm*) as a cop and the always drunk and sleazy John Karlen (*Killer's Delight*) as a scruffy alcoholic with a pimp mustache. [DF Dresden]

IRONSIDE

Director: James Goldstone
Starring: Raymond Burr, Geraldine Brooks, Don Mitchell, Barbara Anderson
Airdate: March 28, 1967   Network: NBC

 After Ironside is paralyzed in a botched assassination attempt, he creates a special task force and sets out to find his assailant.

Detective Bob Ironside is probably best remembered as the curmudgeonly aggressive and somewhat cheerless police chief reconciled to a wheelchair, who, along with his motley assortment (by late sixties standards) of do-gooders, solves special crimes for the police force. While much of that synopsis remained consistent throughout *Ironside*'s popular eight-season run, the pilot movie injects the forever-serious cop with a determined (and unexpected) dose of biting humor and pathos.

Fresh off his extremely successful run as Perry Mason, the commanding Raymond Burr opted for a change of pace with Bob Ironside. Much like Mason, Ironside is always in control, but he's a lot more vocal about how he maintains that control, and almost as outspoken about his own personal doubts. As someone who has a sporadic relationship with the series, the depth of the pilot film's character development was an unanticipated treat, and it was nice to see Burr play a less than perfect type of guy.

Also surprising was that Don Galloway's Ed Brown, a character who is so ingrained in the series, is little more than masculine eye candy in the telefilm. He's given very little do (and this was promptly addressed in the series' first episode, which allows Brown more crime solving moments). Ironside's complicated and sometimes abrasive relationship with Mark Sanger (Don Mitchell) is the highlight of the pilot. Their affiliation slowly goes from one of distrust to respect, and this is Mark's starting point from potential lifetime criminal to lawyer. Racial issues are also put on the front burner, adding layers to Ironside's decidedly diversified gang of crime fighters (and there's a bit of feminism too: Barbara Anderson holds her own against Burr, and is one of the telefilm's highlights in a hilarious scene in an art gallery—she's not going to take your crap).

Director James Goldstone's furious cuts and frenetic pace blend beautifully with Quincy Jones' energetic score, making for a fast paced watch. But, the real star of Goldstone's adept eye is the way he captures the growing hippie community of San Francisco. Featuring notable subculture personality Tiny Tim (in a stunning and oddball cameo), and positioning Ironside and his square gang against the easygoing guitar-playing bohemians, the film sees a country in the midst of intense change. Ironside remains the authoritative presence, but it's also obvious that the "bad guy" won't be as identifiable as they were back in his old black and white *Mason* days (note: this goes for Ironside's attempted assassin as well).

Ironside is a fondly remembered series, and the show produced another TV movie titled *Split Second for an Epitaph* during the height of its popularity in 1968 (which features flashbacks from this pilot film), as well as a reunion movie in 1993, filmed shortly before Burr's passing. [Amanda Reyes]

ISN'T IT SHOCKING?

Director: John Badham
Starring: Alan Alda, Louise Lasser, Edmond O'Brien, Ruth Gordon, Lloyd Nolan
Airdate: October 2, 1973   Network: ABC

A sheriff in a sleepy town investigates the suspicious deaths of several elderly residents, and finds himself in a race against time to stop the killer from striking again.

Isn't It Shocking? takes place in the town of Mount Angel (population 1,325), where Sheriff Dan Barnes (Alda) is awaiting his move to a new job at nearby Horse Creek—a move he looks forward to with relish, if only to escape the clutches of local motel owner Ma (Pat Quinn) who has her eye on Dan as potential marriage material. Murphy's Law dictates that it all kicks off just as Dan's getaway is imminent, with a number of Mount Angel's elderly residents dying in their sleep. Dan smells a rat, or more precisely, turpentine, menthol and nutmeg, smeared on each of the victim's chests. Add to that the fact that Mount Angel's pensioners all seem to sleep half-dressed—missing their pajamas tops or nightgowns—and Dan needs no encouragement to throw himself wholeheartedly into solving the mystery.

Assisting him is police secretary Blanche (Lasser), whose bizarre interpretation of office wear (pigtails and *Wizard of Oz*-style gingham dresses with matching head scarves) hides a flair for police work that comes to the fore as she helps Dan prevent the rest of Mount Angel's older residents being wiped out. The on-screen relationship between Lasser and Alda is great to watch—one suspects they're improvising in more than one scene—and their blossoming romance is a central theme throughout the film without the point being labored.

The film becomes a clever take on the traditional teen slasher flick, with Dan racing from house to house to warn everyone over sixty that they may be the next victim, and bends horror conventions even further in adding comedy to the mix. Jesse (Nolan) reads out a list of appointed officers in neighboring Horse Creek, the most galling to him being Moth Superintendent, and Dan quips with store-owner Myron (Liam Dunn) about "fumbling around" with girls. I couldn't decide if the shots of the killer (played by O'Brien) menacingly eating a candy bar after each murder were intended to be comedic, however.

The high point of the comedy-horror weirdness comes in the shape of Ruth Gordon playing 'Crazy' Marge Savage, the obligatory cat lady. "They're dropping like flies," she muses at the funeral of one victim. "Fantastic." Crazy Marge turns out to be the last woman standing, and the final scenes of the film see Dan and Blanche dispatched to her cat-infested house to stand guard, where they joke about eating cat meat sandwiches whilst unbeknownst to them the killer sneaks into Marge's bedroom. ("Crazy Marge drinks beer?" "She's a swinger." "Nobody who's a swinger goes to bed at 7:30.") In what has to rank as one of the more surreal death scenes in a movie, we see Gordon confronting the killer in her nightdress, armed with a gun: "You lose, buckwheat! Get yourself another girl!" [Jennifer Wallis]

KILLDOZER

Director: Jerry London
Starring: Clint Walker, Carl Betz, Neville Brand, James Wainwright
Airdate: February 2, 1974   Network: ABC

 Menace from space infects construction equipment with misanthropic rage; homicidal fun ensues as indie music fans thrill.

Perhaps rightfully overlooked as a low budget TV gag that lives up to writer Theodore Sturgeon's Law that, "Ninety percent of [science fiction] is crud, but then, ninety percent of *everything* is crud," *Killdozer* is still a mildly enjoyable relic of slow seventies Saturday afternoon television.

Witness: From the cold depths of space a great blue hemorrhoid slips toward Earth, crashing to rest on a tiny island "200 miles off the coast of Africa." An island that might as well be a small prison work camp, occupied as it is by a mere six-man crew of roughnecks marooned there by the Warburton Oil Resources Company in order to prepare the place for... something important yet somehow unnamed. 'Tis a small island indeed, for in mere moments crewman Mack (Robert Urich) manages to aggravate the

Clockwise from above: Carl Betz and Clint Walker take on *Killdozer*; *TV Guide* ad for the excellent *Murder By Natural Causes*; and a goofy title for an electrifying serial killer drama, *Isn't It Shocking?*

asteroid by ramming it with his D-9 Bulldozer. Angrily the rock begins to emit a savage industrial hum and electrical glow, a glow that flows right into the bulldozer and blasts Mack with a critical burst of cosmic radiation.

And from there on in things get dicey as the D-Niner, possessed now by malicious alien intent, sets out to wipe the puny humans from the face of its new domain one by one. Humans who somehow simply cannot manage to outmaneuver a slow moving piece of land grading machinery across rugged terrain, and perish for the foolishness of defensive strategies along the lines of, "Hey, if I crawl inside of a flimsy corrugated tin pipe, there's no way a six-ton piece of demonic construction equipment can get me…"

Much absurdity follows, aided and abetted by "Special Guest Star" James Wainwright's (aptly named a "general purpose actor" by IMDb) turn as Dutch, a bargain basement Ernest Borgnine type, a bit of drunkenness, and some latent homosexual references to "night swimming" before the survivors make their last-ditch effort to put an end to the "rogue machinery" with a device from an earlier and far superior sci-fi story.

The minute cast does manage to milk quite a bit of pulp melodrama out of a rather ludicrous plot (Dennis [Carl Betz] to Kelly [Clint Walker]: "What's this with the funny blue light? I'm no piece of candy!" Kelly to Dennis: "You're a sourball!"), and there is a good scene or two (Killdozer's satanic victory salute), but *Killdozer* is still very much the kind of made for TV movie in which the commercials don't seem at all out of place. Altogether it might remind one of that old *Six Million Dollar Man* episode wherein Steve Austin races around against a killer tank. But with an even lower budget and slower pace. Still, it could have been more ridiculous; Batman could have shown up... [Tom Crites]

KILLER ON BOARD

Director: Philip Leacock
Starring: Claude Akins, Patty Duke, Jane Seymour, Frank Converse, William Daniels
Airdate: October 10, 1977   Network: NBC

Trapped at sea aboard an infected ship, the crew and passengers fight among themselves to stay alive.

All aboard the SS Monte Claire, a salty sea tub of doom where sultry tour guide Jane Seymour (*Live and Let Die*) and her wandering British/American accent says "Welcome" to a gaggle of everyman TV movie characters who stroll up the gang plank for a posh thirty-day cruise. A place where they can relax, catch a tan and then get buried at sea all bug-eyed and dehydrated from the effects of a tropical disease, smuggled aboard in the blood and snot of a dying stowaway.

Among the cast of regulars determined not "to try the fish" are a 'Nam vet, a pondering widow, a junkie bass player, a lounge lizard, an unloving husband, a bad jazz singer, some brat kids and worried captain Claude Akins (*The Curse*), doctor Murray Hamilton (*Jaws*) and spray tanned coffin lid George Hamilton (*Pets*).

All are given a few moments each to recite their lines and avoid contagion, but when most fail, the ship is quarantined at sea, panic ensues and the flu-like symptoms begin ridding the decks and thin corridors of seamen, passengers and crew. Which happens... very, very slowly.

Written by Sandor Stern (*Web of Deceit*), the bulk of the running time is cheap-to-shoot bad conversations in cramped quarters, with any action relegated to limp close ups of sweaty jowls, blood shot eyes, gritted teeth, bedside confessions and frequent use of the phrases: "Somebody get me a doctor!" "Everyone just stay calm!" and "He's dead."

Also includes giant sideburns, cold turkey, Thalmus Rasulala (*New Jack City*), Patty Duke (*Prelude to a Kiss*), a salad bar, a foot chase, a really terrible end theme, lots of crying and a sing-a-long. [DF Dresden]

KISS MEETS THE PHANTOM OF THE PARK

Director: Gordon Hessler
Starring: Gene Simmons, Paul Stanley, Peter Criss, Ace Frehley, Anthony Zerbe
Airdate: October 28, 1978   Network: NBC

 Four hard rocking superheroes, collectively known as KISS, battle a mad inventor and his automatons at Magic Mountain amusement park.
Nineteen seventy-eight was the year of KISS. Each band member released a solo album. They were touring around the world, making millions. There was a KISS comic book casting them as mystical superheroes. It was also the year of *Superman: The Movie* and *The Incredible Hulk*. It was only logical that the superhero version of KISS got their own movie. Hanna-Barbara stepped up to the plate. Right before Halloween, NBC aired *KISS Meets the Phantom of the Park*. Nineteen seventy-nine was not the year of KISS. It was the year of KISS re-grouping. History shows that this movie had something to do with it.

The film is camp at its most entertaining. It never winks its eye at the viewer like *Wonder Woman* or the 1960s *Batman.* It just posits four young hard rockers playing a series of concerts at Magic Mountain. These rockers are loved by all, as witnessed by all the people at the park dressed as KISS. (Although a few of the people in KISS makeup may be mimes.) KISS just happens to have super magical powers, along with the ability to rock an audience. Hard.

Abner Devereaux (Zerbe) is the mad inventor. Devereaux makes all the animatronic figures for the park, along with doing much of the design work. He is fired. He blames KISS. Devereaux builds KISS androids and attempts to steal the talisman that brings the boys their powers. This madman is against a hard rock good time. In 1978, this will not stand.

The film spends a lot of time with Devereaux showing his animatronic gorillas and animatronic barbershop quartets. And, all that is fun. However, when KISS takes over the movie, when they begin to rock, when they begin using their powers, this film becomes awesome. Their stage show was the best around. The songs are as bland as ever but that's hardly the point. Can these boys fight? The answer is: they can. There are long fantastic fight scenes between the boys and Devereaux's automatons. These include kung fu guys, giant white apes and, the best scene ever, KISS fighting monsters in the Chamber of Horrors. It was Halloween and, for every youngster watching, this was exactly what they wanted.

KISS Meets The Phantom of The Park gets a bit of a bad rap. Not sure why. What did one expect from a film with a superpowered hard rock band fighting an animatronic Frankenstein monster? To this viewer, only one band could have pulled this off and made it so damn entertaining. It's not

Journey. They may have been fine in a videogame but the Wolfman would have kicked Neal Schon's ass. It's not The Doobie Brothers, who would have been too damn high and laid back. It might have been AC/DC but the songs would have been too good. It simply had to be KISS. (A European Theatrical Version was released as *Attack of the Phantoms*.) [Daniel R. Budnik]

THE LAST DINOSAUR

Director: Alex Grasshoff
Starring: Richard Boone, Joan Van Ark, Luther Rackley, Steven Keats
Airdate: February 11, 1977   Network: ABC

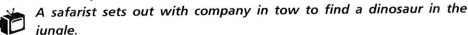 *A safarist sets out with company in tow to find a dinosaur in the jungle.*

The Arthur Rankin, Jr. and Jules Bass production team are best known to millions of television audiences as Rankin and Bass, the men behind the unforgettable holiday-themed, stop-motion animation outings *Rudolph, the Red-Nosed Reindeer* (1964), *Santa Claus is Coming to Town* (1970), *Here Comes Peter Cottontail* (1971), and *The Year Without a Santa Claus* (1974). Christmas and Easter would not be the same without a viewing of these specials on either television or home video. Though the bulk of their work is comprised of television movies and specials, they also collaborated on theatrically released films like *The Daydreamer* (1966), *Mad Monster Party?* (1967), *The Wacky World of Mother Goose* (1967), and *The Last Unicorn* (1982). This prolific producing and directing team assembled a crew of talented sculptors, writers, editors, photographers and musicians to create some of the most memorable family entertainment.

Just prior to the beloved made for TV movie *The Bermuda Depths* (1978), Rankin and Bass made *The Last Dinosaur,* a low budget film that was originally intended for theatrical release, but was shortened by 11 minutes to a 95-minute running time and aired on ABC, which is good because the film has a TV movie feel to it to begin with. Warner Archive has released the full, uncut 106-minute theatrical cut on DVD-R (if you're looking for the original 95-minute cut, good luck finding it).

Written by William Overgard, scored by Maury Laws, and directed by Tsugunobu Kotani (listed in the credits as Tom Kotani), *The Last Dinosaur* is a fun movie for the twelve-year-old set and under, though I am sure that Rankin and Bass completists will find much to enjoy here. Mason Thrust, Jr. (Boone) is a cantankerous and misogynistic safarist who meets the sole survivor of an expedition who witnessed the existence of a Tyrannosaurus Rex. Intrigued, Thrust puts together a team that includes the sole survivor, some experts, and, against his wishes, just because she's a woman, photographer Francesca Banks (Van Ark). They travel to the jungle locale and have a few close encounters with beasts that should have been dead millions of years ago, one of which is the T-Rex who roars a little like Godzilla. Along the way, they encounter some Neanderthal dwellers, one of whom resembles Nova from *Planet of the Apes* (1968); she runs off with Francesca's purse. It's a fairly straightforward tale involving the usual Rankin and Bass special effects, which, at times, look just like that. The cheesiness is part of the film's charm, though it is slow moving by today's standards. The nighttime scenes are all shot day-for-night, and the film begins

Advertisement for *The Last Dinosaur*.

and ends with the Nancy Wilson tune The Last Dinosaur.

The Last Dinosaur cover art boasts the exciting painting that was originally intended for the film's theatrical one-sheet; this image also appeared on the French poster when the film was distributed theatrically as *Le Derniere Dinosaure*. [Todd Garbarini]

LEGEND OF LIZZIE BORDEN

Director: Paul Wendkos
Starring: Elizabeth Montgomery, Fionnuala Flanagan, Ed Flanders, Katherine Helmond
Airdate: February 10, 1975   Network: ABC

 Based on a real-life murder case, this excellent adaptation reconstructs the infamous crime and Lizzie's part in it.

Paul Wendkos' *The Legend of Lizzie Borden* is one of the most dramatic and well executed of the seventies' telefrights. With intertitles demarcating separate segments of Lizzie Borden's trial, the film recreates the still-unsolved crime that has fascinated the public for over a century. Elizabeth Montgomery, eager to escape the typecasting of her most well-known role as perky suburban witch Samantha Stevens on television's *Bewitched*, was nominated for a well-deserved Emmy for her role here as the title character, Lizzie Borden, rumored to have butchered her parents with an axe (Montgomery was also, strangely enough, a distant relative of the real-life Borden).

The film begins in the immediate aftermath of the crime and is retold piecemeal through foggy flashbacks. The community doesn't buy Lizzie as the culprit, and even her sister and housekeeper, who have witnessed her selfish tantrums and threats to father and stepmother, say nothing. Interestingly, while in real-life Borden was ostracized by the community following the events, the film uses the opportunity to examine how the media sensation surrounding the case fuelled the fervor of the growing feminist movement, the first winds of which had just swept into the town of Fall River at the time. The prosecutor's wife is moved by Lizzie's plight: when he scoffs that Lizzie is "hiding behind her skirts," his wife asserts that men themselves are to blame for putting women in that role, adding that, "you have no idea how heavy these skirts can be."

The film also has an unsettling sense of dislocation that fits nicely with Borden's alleged physician-prescribed morphine abuse and the theory that she may have committed the murder while in a fugue state. The film also seizes the chance to explore salacious theories that she may have stripped nude before the murder to avoid leaving traces of evidence, which contributes to the courtroom drama's few moments of overtly sensationalistic imagery. It also stands as a chilling character study; Lizzie is at turns aloof, daddy-obsessed and cruel, her hard-worn sister Emma (Helmond, miles away from her oversexed septuagenarian character on *Who's the Boss*) crumbling emotionally while Lizzie fusses over which gloves to wear to court.

Little has been written about director Paul Wendkos, but the most oft-quoted (and quite apt here) observation comes from Christopher Wicking and Tise Vahimagi's *The American Vein: Directors and Directions in Television*, in which they describe his best work as "having a clinical detachment that prevents any easy transference onto the characters. It's as if we're viewing them as insects under a microscope." Wendkos would later revisit this terrain with the Emmy-nominated TV movie version of *The Bad Seed* (1985), based on the 1954 William March novel about a homicidal child descended from a female serial killer. [Kier-La Janisse]

LIKE NORMAL PEOPLE

Director: Harvey Hart
Starring: Shaun Cassidy, Linda Purl, Hope Lange, James Keach
Airdate: April 13, 1979   Network: ABC

 Based on a true story. Young adults with slight mental disabilities, Roger Meyers and Virginia Rae Hensler meet by chance. Romance blossoms.

At odds with how society perceives them—their courtship scrutinized and frowned upon—this couple resolve to stand defiant against the prejudices of those around them, and, in time, carve a future together that inspires their various critics to reconsider their opinions on love and perseverance.

A class act production from top to bottom, and while writer Joanna Lee and director Harvey Hart each deserve high praise for their efforts behind the lens, it is the leads, Shaun Cassidy and Linda Purl, delivering career best performances that make this one unforgettable.

Admittedly, the plight of people with disabilities has always been a source for compelling drama, and Hollywood (especially in recent years) has shown no reluctance in bringing such stories to the screen, drawn to true-life examples like moths to a flame and churning out a string of formulaic bilge that, in most cases, is more likely to elicit groans of seen-it-all-beforedom from audiences as opposed to anything akin to real empathy.

That said, only the most jaded of viewers would survive this particular triumph-over-adversity story without feeling even the slightest pluck at their heartstrings. And this is because the movie never feels like a production cynically contrived (like many do) for the purposes of being a showreel for its stars and industry awards bait. It may in fact be that rare example of a project that is genuinely heartfelt, and, most commendably, it doesn't strive to pity its characters because of their disabilities, but rather, condemns the limited understanding with which society treats people who have difficulties. It doesn't preach, but rather, sensitively informs.

Amidst the rest of the cast, there's decent supporting turns from some familiar faces, Hope Lange, Zalman King (before soft-core efforts like *9½ Weeks* and *Wild Orchid* would make him more famous as a producer) and James Keach, who, as Roger Meyer's brother (his real-life counterpart wrote the book on which this is based) gives a particularly affecting portrayal; full of love and care for his sibling, fearing the worst yet always hoping for the best.

A pitch perfect TV movie that casually invites your interest with a simple premise, and then holds you entranced for the next ninety minutes, despite the fact that it promises zero twists and delivers exactly what you expect to happen, precisely as it occurs. But none of that matters. This is the king of small screen "love conquers all" dramas.

Never released on DVD, it does still make the odd appearance on TV, but depressingly, this is another example of a forgotten gem that deserves a much wider audience. Definitely worth the hunt for TV treasure hunters.

[Kevin Hilton]

LOOK WHAT HAPPENED TO ROSEMARY'S BABY

Director: Sam O'Steen
Starring: Stephen McHattie, Patty Duke, Broderick Crawford, Ruth Gordon
Airdate: October 29, 1976 Network: ABC

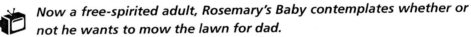 ***Now a free-spirited adult, Rosemary's Baby contemplates whether or not he wants to mow the lawn for dad.***

Divided up into biblical "chapters" and bereft of any bloodshed, terror or harsh words, there's still a lot to moan about and gawk at in this mildly psychedelic Paramount Television Production, which uses half its ass to update the sorry, satanic story of poor Rosemary Woodhouse—a character given a second inning here by novelist Ira Levin (author of Roman Polanski's seminal 1968 feature *Rosemary's Baby*).

Editor of *Cool Hand Luke* (1967), *Day of the Dolphin* (1973) and *Chinatown* (1974), a possibly underwhelmed Sam O'Steen sits the wrong way in the director's chair and curses this cut-price sequel with a far lower class of paranoia and black candle than the original. It may have chanting, attic masses, chalk diagrams and a return outing for Ruth Gordon as nosy neighbor Minnie, it's all to no avail, being far from its namesake in terms of budget, performance, script and plot.

Instead of Mia Farrow, we're stuck briefly with Patty Duke (*Call Me Anna*) as Rosemary, the panicked mother of Satan's child Andrew (Philip Boyer), a pet-killing brat (who eats raw meat) that gets kidnapped and raised by a hooker until he grows up to be a confused, introspective hippie played by Stephen McHattie (*Kaw*).

Little more than a talky, actionless miscarriage, for co-stars we have Satanists Ray Milland (*Aces High*) and Tina Louise (*The Trap*), and crusty cop Broderick Crawford (*Hell's Bloody Devils*), who all chase, question and fight with each other in order to gain control of the reluctant black heart and soul of poor, drug-addled McHattie—a perplexed, AWOL "Lizard King" waster, who at one stage dons the stage makeup of Marcel Marceau.

A suburban grab-bag of simplified satanic lore, plainly shot for the masses, it's not as interesting as it sounds, being most noteworthy for the voiceover commentary supplied by the caped Milland and Gordon, some fine garage tunes and the scene where a jonesing son of Satan hungers for rock 'n' roll. [DF Dresden]

MAYDAY AT 40,000 FEET!

Director: Robert Butler
Starring: David Janssen, Don Meredith, Christopher George, Ray Milland
Airdate: November 12, 1976 Network: CBS

When a plane's hydraulic system is crippled by a gunshot, two brave pilots battle the odds to save the day.

Talking chainsaws David Janssen (*Two-Minute Warning*) and Christopher George (*Enter the Ninja*) lead the thespian roll call for this dopey, memorable chunk of useless seventies cheeze which makes a full fat snack when served with similar TV ham like *Terror in the Sky* (1971), *Horror At 37,000 Feet* (1973) and at a stretch, *Nurses on the Line: the Crash of Flight 7* (1993).

Alongside the *Airport* films—*Airport* (1970) through to *The Concorde... Airport '79* (1979)—this film is one of the main culprits parodied in the classic *Airplane!* (1980), so, if you love that, you'll love this as it serves up the same stable of now iconic characters with straight-faced cheek, a lot of lumpy dialog, rubbish FX and a fantastic cast who all seem blissfully unbothered by the damage they were doing to their chances of ever winning an Emmy.

Before they fly into a snow storm and scream "Mayday at 40,000 feet!" we're confronted with their hastily written lives, so prepare to endure the presence of a reborn romance, a racist criminal, a grumpy doctor, a cowboy navigator, an ailing pilot, a hot stewardess, an angry policeman and a dying passenger, until a game changing stray bullet from a Magnum handgun cripples the plane's hydraulic system, making it impossible to land the bird. Looks like I picked the wrong week to stop sniffing glue.

Classic TV mayhem with a vast array of familiar faces, try to stay awake

Advertisement for the ill-advised *Look What Happened to Rosemary's Baby*.

to see crabby type-cast alcoholic Ray Milland (*Premature Burial*), sexy Linda Day George (*Pieces*), fossilized Broderick Crawford (*The Yin And Yang Of Mr. Go*), Don Meredith (*Terror Among Us*), the brilliant Marjoe Gortner (*Viva Knievel*) and even Al from *Happy Days* (Al Molinaro).

The similarly themed *Turbulence* (1997) was also—oddly enough—directed by Robert Butler. [DF Dresden]

MEN OF THE DRAGON

Director: Harry Falk
Starring: Jared Martin, Katie Saylor, Robert Ito, Joseph Wiseman
Airdate: March 20, 1974   Network: ABC

When his younger sister is kidnapped in Hong Kong, martial artist Jared Martin back fists his way to the rescue.

Brought to you by Wolper Productions and obviously inspired by the global success of Bruce Lee's *Enter The Dragon* (1973), here's a flappy, fist and flare filled crock of soft fu from the director of the equally impoverished *The Death Squad* (1974).

Partially filmed on location in a fab looking Hong Kong, high-kicking brother and sister Jared Martin (*Willow B: Women In Prison*) and statuesque blonde Katie Saylor (*Swinging Barmaids*) fly in to visit judo buddy Robert Ito (*Hollow Point*) so the trio can take in the sights, drink tea and buy jade to bring back to the USA.

Before you can yell "Holy crap lady, them's some tight fitting denim pants!" beautiful Saylor is kidnapped by white slave trader Joseph Wiseman (*Dr. No*) and whisked away to his secret kung fu island where she is forced to take drugs, hang in the chill room and stumble around in a stupor till she's auctioned off to the highest bidder.

In response to the disappearance, Martin and Ito meet and recruit "the men of the dragon" at a dojo, do fake fu, drink tea, sniff about for clues and eventually get smuggled onto Wiseman's island fortress where they axe-kick, punch and martial art everyone till Saylor (and her giant stunt double) are free to leave.

Pretty much a faint Xerox of the *Enter the Dragon* plot, it even uses the same sound FX and features hokey 'Eastern' philosophy, high-waisted pants, stoned ladies, turtle neck sweaters, eye-melting colors, ridiculous, scream-filled combat and shite henchmen who take ages to die in slow motion.

Despite a decent script, mad hairdos, 'bong' music and some likeable, lukewarm characters, ABC had yet another damp squib pilot movie that failed to inspire a follow-up series. [DF Dresden]

MURDER BY NATURAL CAUSES

Director: Robert Day
Starring: Hal Holbrook, Katherine Ross, Barry Bostwick, Richard Anderson
Airdate: February 17, 1979   Network: CBS

 A wealthy wife wishes to become a wealthy widow, and, along with her down-on-his-luck lover, plots her husband's murder.

Whether it was intentional from the beginning or not, *Murder by Natural Causes* was the first in a trilogy of stylish mysteries written by the great Richard Levinson and William Link, the co-creators of *Columbo*. Along with *Rehearsal for Murder* (1982) and *Guilty Conscience* (1985), it rounds out a trio of incredibly adept and engaging contemporary thrillers for the small screen. Arguably, *Natural Causes*, a terrifically pared down little whodunit, is the best of the bunch.

Levinson and Link have been attached to some of television's greatest achievements. From poignant topical issues like homosexuality in *That Certain Summer* or interracial relations in *My Sweet Charlie* to engaging crime stories via *Columbo* and other appealing characters, the dynamic writing/producing duo very seldom miss the spot. A great example of their work can be found in *Natural Causes*, which is a twisty tale of duplicity and deception. Hal Holbrook is a mentalist who uses several underhanded methods to give the appearance that he is an authentic mind reader. As noted by his exquisite digs, he's an extremely successful soothsayer, but his Achilles Heel is that he suffers from heart problems and has to constantly check up on his pacemaker. This gives his wife the idea (ludicrous it may be, but perfect for TV movieland) that he can be scared to death.

Katherine Ross is almost *too* good as the nearly sociopathic "perfect wife" who strings along anyone who can help her get rid of dear old hubby. She, along with Holbrook, are aided by a small but amazing cast, including Barry Bostwick as the sexy but hammy out of work actor who knows he probably shouldn't be a part of plotting someone's death but can't say no to the fortune that lies ahead. The intense twenty or so minute segment featuring a fake interview Bostwick arranges with Holbrook creates several nerve jangling moments of suspense, and there are twists galore as the tale unwinds and unwinds *and unwinds* until its goose bumps-inducing final moments.

This is an elegant and literate work of suspense that makes the most of the less is more theory of filmmaking. Directed with finesse by Robert Day, *Natural Causes* is stylish but holds back on any sort of obvious flair, allowing the actors—Holbrook in particular—to shine. And keeping a lighthearted touch on their production, Levinson and Link even make a nod toward *Prescription: Murder*, which was the name of the play that unleashed

Left: Tie-in novel promoting *The Night Strangler*.
Above: Darren McGavin fends off Barry Atwater in the highly rated and well-loved *The Night Stalker*.

America's favorite disheveled detective, *Columbo*, onto the world (it was also the title of the good lieutenant's 1968 pilot movie). *Natural Causes* is not to be missed. [Amanda Reyes]

THE NIGHT STALKER

Director: John Llewellyn Moxey
Starring: Darren McGavin, Carol Lynley, Simon Oakland, Ralph Meeker
Airdate: January 11, 1972   Network: ABC

 Incorrigible reporter Carl Kolchak hunts down an ancient vampire in modern day Las Vegas, infuriating the city authorities.

When first we meet reporter Carl Kolchak (McGavin), he's putting the finishing touches on his latest story, listening intently to the contents of his tape recorder to ensure he has all the details straight. It's a tale of murder, the saga of a crazed killer stalking the dark streets of Las Vegas and gruesomely dispatching young women. Despite the official police reports, though, which couch the killings as the work of an ordinary maniac, Kolchak knows there's much more to the story. For as he delved deeper and deeper into the twisted tale, Kolchak realizes that the oddities surrounding the case all lead to one inescapable conclusion: the killer is a centuries-old vampire.

As the narrative proper begins, we're invited to experience the story from the beginning, as Kolchak lived it, so that we might see what he saw and better understand how he reached his startling conclusions. Thus, we follow along as Kolchak is first introduced to the case, and proceeds to wend his way through the Las Vegas underworld tracking down the bloodthirsty murderer. We witness Kolchak's frustration as he battles the brass, annoyed at his incessant attempts to sidestep their authority; we meet Kolchak's constellation of inside men and women who keep him up on the latest tips, and ensure he's one step ahead of the men in blue; and we watch as his skeptical investigations into the occult evolve into an unshakable belief in the terrifying truth.

Though the film's lurid vampire particulars certainly have a grisly appeal, the real fun here comes from being so intimately involved in Kolchak's detective work. Richard Matheson's cunning screenplay makes deft use of Kolchak's tape recorder, scattering the reporter's voiceover narration throughout the film. This creative device at once allows explicatory information to be conveyed quickly and efficiently, and ensures we experience the story via Kolchak's eyes. What's more, owing to the magnetic personality of Kolchak the man, as brought wonderfully to life by Darren McGavin, we are also quickly won over to Kolchak's point of view.

As the story progresses, and our understanding of Kolchak intensifies, we realize that the mystery of Carl Kolchak is just as fascinating as the mystery of the vampire. In fact, the entire vampire storyline seems to function, at least in part, as a vehicle to explain Kolchak's life story. Like Janos Skorzeny, the ancient bloodsucker he is tailing, Kolchak seemingly cannot find a home, forcibly removed from town after town once his antics became insufferable. Thus Kolchak spends much of his life roaming around the dark streets of cities, searching desperately for the next scoop, his lifeblood, so to speak. For Kolchak, catching the vampire isn't just a noble act of public assistance, or even the closing paragraph at the end of a great news piece. It's a chance at redemption, to prove to the dimwits in the big cities that covering important stories is where he belongs.

It comes as no surprise, then, that the film doesn't roll credits once the mystery is solved and the city is freed from its curse. Instead, we watch as Kolchak is hauled before the city authorities, and unceremoniously kicked out of town. His tireless efforts have been for naught. His story will not be printed. In so many words, the powers that be tell him he is an undesirable element. There's no place for Kolchak in Las Vegas. Penniless and alone, Kolchak is left to roam the highways, recounting the details of the saga on his tape recorder, and keeping his eyes open for a new town to haunt. It's a bleak ending, to be sure, but this gloriously downbeat denouement is a most fitting conclusion to one of the greatest made for TV fright films ever created. [Thomas Scalzo]

THE NIGHT STRANGLER

Director: Dan Curtis
Starring: Darren McGavin, Jo Ann Pflug, Simon Oakland, John Carradine
Airdate: January 16, 1973   Network: ABC

Intrepid reporter Carl Kolchak is on the hunt for redemption, and a blood-harvesting murderer, in the dark world of underground Seattle.
Kolchak is back—in Seattle this time—soon after being fired and kicked out of Vegas on a trumped up murder charge. Not a man to give up easily, Kolchak has been spending his time trying to convince everyone he meets that the Vegas vampire saga really happened. As our story begins, we find him in a local watering hole, seated across from yet another non-believer. Kolchak's vociferous incredulity reaches the ears of another patron, Carl's old boss, Vincenzo (Oakland). Hearing Kolchak's familiar wail, he groans to himself: even in Seattle, he can't find solace from Carl's insufferable personality. As luck would have it, Vincenzo is managing editor at the *Daily Chronicle*, and, after some haggling, Kolchak once again finds himself on the beat. His first assignment, dig into a baffling murder.

In terms of overall story structure, this enjoyable sequel to *The Night Stalker* follows closely to the pattern established by its predecessor: Kolchak investigates a series of murders and discovers they are connected. As he delves deeper into the story, he realizes there is a supernatural component to the gruesome goings-on. When he attempts to report the tale, he finds himself at loggerheads with the civic authorities. Despite innumerable impediments, Kolchak persists in his work and succeeds in getting to the bottom of the mystery. Instead of *Night Stalker*'s ancient vampire in search of blood, however, here we have a megalomaniacal doctor murdering young woman as part of a decades-old quest to obtain immortality.

Since Kolchak's character was well-established in *Night Stalker*, writer Richard Matheson doesn't spend much time fleshing out the tempestuous newsman's personality in this installment. Instead, he's free to dwell on colorful plot points and delve into the killer's complex backstory. Thus, we are treated to an assortment of engaging details, including an elaborate underground city beneath present day Seattle, a mysterious series of killings that seem to follow a peculiar pattern, and a brilliant but troubled man relentlessly searching for the elusive elixir of life. Despite *Night Strangler*'s overall similarities to its famous forbearer, such memorable touches give the film an appeal all its own.

Matheson's comparatively optimistic handling of Kolchak this time around is also a welcome development. In *Night Stalker*, Kolchak is essentially a man apart, forever struggling against a world that won't cut him a break. Here, although his wild conjectures continue to raise some eyebrows, he's finally able to present hard evidence that proves he's on the right track. In addition, he's afforded the unflagging support of both Mr. Berry, the *Chronicle* historian who helps research the mystery, and a fetching belly dancer named Louise, who goes so far as to serve as bait for the killer. Despite ultimately finding himself booted out of Seattle, and once again out of a job, the future is looking bright: for now he has a plan, a team, and a new story to tell. Watch out New York, Kolchak's coming back. [Thomas Scalzo]

NIGHT TERROR

Director: E.W. Swackhamer
Starring: Valerie Harper, Richard Romanus, Nicholas Pryor, John Quade
Airdate: February 7, 1977   Network: NBC

 A late-night drive to reach her sick son takes a turn for the terrifying as Valerie Harper runs afoul of a relentless murderer.

Our story begins with Valerie Harper receiving the news that her son has been hospitalized in Denver. The fact that she is in Phoenix, and unable to fly to her boy owing to some inclement Colorado weather, compels her to set out on a late-night drive in the family station wagon. Not long into the trip, she happens upon a murder in progress on the side of the highway. As bad luck would have it she makes unwitting eye contact with the murderer. As worse luck would have it, she's running out of gas. Suddenly, reaching her son becomes a secondary concern: first, she needs to outwit a cold blooded killer who cannot abide any living witnesses to his crime.

While owing a clear debt to *Duel* and its enthralling tale of hunter versus hunted on the highway, *Night Terror* manages to set itself apart from Spielberg's legendary film in several ways. By doing away with the questions as to *why* the protagonist is being chased, we're allowed to focus all of our attention on *how* Harper might escape her ordeal. Second, the fact that our hero here is a woman, and arguably handles herself with more pluck and reserve than Dennis Weaver, speaks to the efforts of director E.W. Swackhamer to take the highway horror tale in a unique direction. Finally, while *Duel* takes place primarily during the day, and affords its leading man occasional respite via normal human company, Swackhamer's film takes place almost exclusively at night, in an unpopulated stretch of country, ensuring that Harper is largely alone in her struggles.

This night-scene focus of the film deserves particular attention. Not only does it add substantively to the tension, but also highlights the moviemaking talents involved in the project. For we can only assume that lighting a film like this—one comprised primarily of cars driving on a highway at night—must have been a significant challenge. Instead of allowing such concerns to limit the believability of the picture, however, or plunging us into perpetual darkness, we're treated to an impressive assortment of creative lighting schemes that manage to increase the tension. From the halo of a streetlamp, to the haze of headlights, to the soft glow of dashboard running lights, what we can see in any given scene is severely restricted by whatever light source happens to be available. We're thus constantly kept on edge, always wondering if the killer is lurking just beyond the limits of our vision.

The film's tension is also enhanced by a succession of strategically inserted narrative details. For starters, we have the fact that Harper's character is introduced as a bit of a scatterbrain, incapable of handling complicated situations. As the challenges pile up, we're not sure she's going to be able to pull herself together enough to overcome them. Next, we have the late night drive through a desolate stretch of the Southwest. Were this tale to take place on the populated East Coast, its plausibility would have taken a major hit. As it stands, the fact that not many other cars are on the road is no surprise. Add in details ranging from a fierce rain storm, an avalanche of rocks blocking the road, a paucity of gas stations, and the difficulty in both finding a working payphone and having the correct change, and we're treated to an engrossing tale that grips us more tightly with every new obstacle thrown Harper's way. (Aka *Night Drive*.) [Thomas Scalzo]

THE NORLISS TAPES

Director: Dan Curtis
Starring: Roy Thinnes, Angie Dickinson, Claude Akins, Vonetta McGee
Airdate: February 21, 1973   Network: NBC

 A reporter who seeks to debunk the occult walks into the path of a violent demon.

From people lining up around the block to buy a ticket for *The Exorcist* to the Ouija board, supernatural mumbo jumbo was king during the 1970s. Television latched onto the genre because it provided a great vehicle for a medium (pun intended) that was prisoner to the FCC. Ghost stories offered straightforward, and PG-rated ways to generate suspense through creepy houses and flowing nightgowns, and many a telefilm tried to capture the Nielsen rating with tales of the unexpected. Dan Curtis capitalized on this movement and became an undeniable heavyweight in the realm of spooky television. He generated frenzied chaos with Zuni fetish dolls and he brought a vampire named Barnabas Collins into our living room every afternoon. In retrospect, the monster in *The Norliss Tapes*, which is a combination of a zombie, Frankenstein's Monster and the Incredible Hulk, is both silly and awe inspiring. Watching him wreak havoc throughout Northern California is a giddy pleasure, and the scares remain brutal and morbidly beguiling.

Riding high on the success of *The Night Stalker*, Dan Curtis attempted to achieve ratings gold twice with yet another supernatural pilot, and *The Norliss Tapes* was released within months of *Stalker*'s sequel, *The Night Strangler*. This was William F. Nolan's (*Logan's Run*) first teleplay, loosely adapted from a story by Fred Mustard Stewart. Nolan may have penned this scary film with the idea that the Kolchak mythos could use some opposition. It featured an author named David Norliss (Thinnes), who was the antithesis of the charmingly disheveled Kolchak. Norliss was sophisticated and an intellectual, but he was also aloof and a lot less relatable, often reviewing how many miles he had driven during the voiceover narration. The creator of *The X-Files*, Chris Carter, has openly admitted the influence *The Night Stalker* had in the formation of his own hit series, and if Mulder

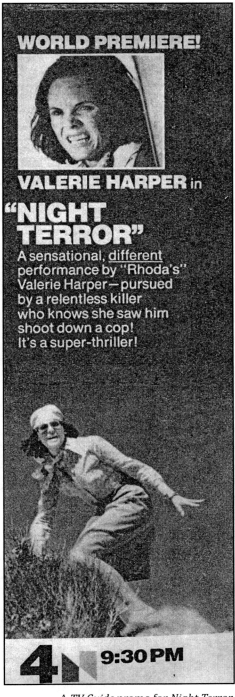

A *TV Guide* promo for *Night Terror*.

is Kolchak then Scully must be Norliss (both Darren McGavin and Thinnes would appear on different episodes of *The X-Files*).

Despite his detached nature, Thinnes brings a sense of melancholy to Norliss, and his unstoppable and sometimes misguided fixations with thwarting the illogical aided the film greatly. Angie Dickinson is fantastic as the damsel in distress, although she seems strangely underwhelmed by the encroaching terror. There are quite a few scenes of pure dread, as her zombie/Frankenstein/demon husband rips doors off of cars and stalks pretty young victims. Unfortunately, *Norliss* could not win over enough viewers to warrant a series and the pilot movie ends in a frustrating cliffhanger. Although a sequel titled *The Return* was planned, it never came to fruition.

The Norliss Tapes has enjoyed a DVD release, and even if the overly serious debunker has one foot inside of humorless artifice, he still manages to bring on the scary in fun, and timeless ways. [Amanda Reyes]

THE POINT

Director: Fred Wolf
Starring: Dustin Hoffman, Mike Lookinland, Paul Frees, Lenny Weinrib
Airdate: February 2, 1971   Network: ABC

 In this animated film, Oblio, the only round-headed boy in a village of points, is made to feel "pointless."

Dustin Hoffman narrates the famed animated feature dreamt up, written and produced by the late songsmith Harry Nilsson, based on his album of the same name. In a land where everyone and everything has a point, the birth of a pointless child throws the kingdom into an existential crisis. Young Oblio (voiced by Mike Lookinland of *The Brady Bunch*) is a pleasant, round-headed child who is beloved by his community despite his freakish appearance. Beloved by everyone, that is, except the Count's son, who lashes out at Oblio after his athletic prowess is challenged in a game of triangle-toss. He pulls in the big guns in the form of the bullying Count, who convinces the kindly old King that Oblio's round-headedness is in fact "against the law," resulting in Oblio's banishment to The Pointless Forest with his pet (and accomplice) Arrow.

On their journey, Oblio and Arrow meet a bizarre stable of characters, no doubt inspired by Nilsson's own colorful real-life extended entourage: A Rock Man, a Leaf-Seller, a trio of bouncing fat ladies and the anarchic Pointed Man, who points in every direction, pointing at nothing. Nilsson has admitted that the story idea came from an acid trip, and the lysergic visuals created by animator Fred Wolf (whose animation team here shared members with Frank Zappa's *200 Motels* the same year) certainly reflect that, not to mention the psychedelic songs. While Me And My Arrow was the hit of the bunch, songs like Think About Your Troubles and Lifeline are plaintive and powerful tunes as iconic as anything in the Nilsson canon. As Oblio and Arrow near the end of their journey, they come to the realization that sometimes the most pointless things have the greatest benefit to human existence.

While Nilsson himself acts as the storyteller on the original album, Dustin Hoffman was brought in to voice the narrator for the film. Hoffman was at the height of his fame, about to embark on a spate of films that would include *Straw Dogs, Lenny, All the President's Men, Marathon Man* and more, and as a result, his contract for *The Point* did not allow subsequent airings to use his voice. After the initial telecast, Hoffman's narration was replaced by that of Alan Barzman, and later Nilsson pal Ringo Starr for the video release—and (most strangely of all) Alan Thicke for an eighties telecast. The various characters—who range from histrionic to hilariously understated—are brought to life by a small cast of voiceover giants including Paul Frees, Lennie Weinrib (the voice of Timer from the *Time for Timer* PSAs) and Bill Martin (in his first role—he would later voice Shredder in the *Teenage Mutant Ninja Turtles* cartoon, among other things). A treat for Nilsson aficionados and seventies animation fans alike, *The Point* is one of the greatest animated fables of all time. [Kier-La Janisse]

Creepy *TV Guide* ad for *The Norliss Tapes.*

POOR DEVIL

Director: Robert Scheerer
Starring: Sammy Davis Jr., Jack Klugman, Christopher Lee, Madelyn Rhue, Adam West
Airdate: February 14, 1973   Network: NBC

 A happy-go-lucky, but blundering devil gets one last chance to score a human soul for his boss Lucifer.

Poor Devil has garnered a bit of cult reputation over the years, thanks to Sammy Davis' connection to Anton LeVay and the Church of Satan (around the time this film was produced, Davis was made an honorary member of the Church). It also upturns the angel story in *It's a Wonderful Life*, only now it's a struggling demon named Sammy (Davis) who is desperate to get a promotion (at the beginning of the film, Sammy is saddled with the unenviable task of shoveling coal into Hell's giant furnace to keep it heated), and singles out a disheartened accountant named Burnett J. Emerson (Klugman *sans* toupee). In its own version of *The Odd Couple*, a friendship develops and soul selling ensues.

Despite upside down pentagrams and name-dropping the Church of Satan, *Poor Devil* remains playful, sometimes funny and absolutely innocuous. It's hard to believe that religious groups protested this somewhat sentimental pilot telefilm, although it's doubtful the prospective series would be able to feature everyone leaving an episode with souls intact, which may have presented a problem for certain viewers. But they mustn't worry too much; Sammy's powers were quite limited and it would seem even Lucifer himself (Christopher Lee!) isn't looking to send hellfire to the surface of Earth.

Everyone is in fine form here, and aside from the previously mentioned actors, Adam West is a lot of fun as Emerson's smug boss. You want to see his comeuppance as much as the poor down-on-his-luck accountant!

Poor Devil is also a time capsule, not just for funky monochromatic suits of the seventies, but also for some of its location shots. Filmed in the heart of San Francisco, the legendary (and now partially demolished) City of Paris Department Store can be seen in all its yuletide glory. Yes, although this telefilm aired on Valentine's Day (as part of February sweeps, which I'm sure had NBC proclaiming, "The devil made me do it!"), *Poor Devil* derives some of its humor from placing the act of soul selling during the holiest time of the year.

Poor Devil was sort of a synergistic creation between two separate parties. Both Sammy Davis, and a duo named Earl Barrett and Arne Sultan separately approached NBC with an idea to make a weekly series that revolved around soul selling. NBC saw the potential and brought everyone together. Sammy was anxious to do the project, as his variety show, *NBC Follies*, had just been cancelled, and he loved working in television. Christopher Lee was also excited about the prospect of steady work in the United States, and felt this was his shot at introducing himself to a larger American audience. Unfortunately, it was not to be and the TVM remains an oddball curiosity of the seventies.

Five years later, *Human Feelings* (aka *Miles, the Angel* [1978]) took the soul selling/redemption spin and spun it once more in a tale about an angel looking for six virtuous souls in Las Vegas. [Amanda Reyes]

THE POSSESSED

Director: Jerry Thorpe
Starring: James Farentino, Claudette Nevins, Diana Scarwid, Harrison Ford
Airdate: May 1, 1977   Network: NBC

 Having died in a car accident, an alcoholic priest is returned to the land of the living on the condition that he must seek and destroy evil.

All is not well at a women's school in Salem, Oregon; there are suspicions of sexual promiscuity and improper conduct, but of more concern are the unexplained deaths by spontaneous combustion that is reducing their number—and neither the pupils, nor the members of the faculty, are exempt from the sinister force that moves among them.

An early appearance by Harrison Ford on the brink of *Star Wars* fame is probably the main reason why this little known *Exorcist* rip-off (and a late one at that!) has not faded entirely into obscurity. However, his brief but impressive turn aside (playing a sort of Professor Indiana Jones that indulges in the advances of his female students instead of shunning them), there are several other reasons why this little shocker is well worth revisiting.

It's pretty sleek for a TV movie, boasting high production values and some nice special effects work. Only the fact that the action is all but limited to the girls' school location reminds us that this is entertainment devised and budgeted for the small screen. Two-time Emmy nominee Charles G. Arnold, serving as director of photography, ensures that it remains a visually classy affair throughout, even as the underdeveloped plot threatens to expose everyone's best efforts for the shameless schlock that it evidently is.

Assuming the lead is James Farentino, delivering a phoned-in performance that feels labored and perhaps even dismissive of the material. He holds it together passably enough, but surely there was more depth—or at least fun—that he could have mined from the part of a sinful man of the cloth that dies, goes to Heaven, comes back with a mission and finds himself surrounded in a school of beautiful women. Genre fans would have to wait until 1981's *Dead and Buried* to see the actor at the top of his game, whereas

Joan Hackett is indeed very good, playing the overworked teacher who later becomes the nail-spitting, vomit-spewing (again with *The Exorcist*!) possessed of the movie's title.

As for the supporting cast—assembled primarily of young females—they are given little to do but shuffle around in nightgowns. However, eagle-eyed viewers may delight in spotting a few up and coming fresh faces, P.J. Soles (*Halloween*), Dinah Manoff (*Grease*) and Diana Scarwid (*Mommie Dearest*) among them.

At a hopelessly brief running time, there is perhaps too much unexplored territory for the film to be considered a genuine contender of its kind; almost no information is provided regarding the nature of the demon, and the possession arguably arrives too late, feeling more like a payoff to the audience's patience as opposed to the climax of what should have been an increasingly taut satanic chiller. Nonetheless, it's highly ambitious stuff for the small screen that offers up some risqué themes, a brilliantly game performance by Hackett and a couple of effective set-pieces along the way.

Not too difficult to locate, having been released as part of Warner's Archive Collection, it holds up decently against the slew of underwhelming demonic possession movies that have recently returned for another cycle. Imagine a late night Halloween special of *Highway to Heaven* and you'll know what to expect. [Kevin Hilton]

PRAY FOR THE WILDCATS

Director: Robert Michael Lewis
Starring: Andy Griffith, William Shatner, Robert Reed, Marjoe Gortner
Airdate: January 23, 1974   Network: ABC

Leaving behind spouses to question the validity of their marriage, four businessmen embark on a dusty bike trip to Mexico.

Swanky lounge-beat music by the great Fred Myrow coats this drama-in-the-desert feature from ABC, which stars William Shatner as a disillusioned, disappointed advertising executive cursed with a hollow home life, no money and a nemesis in the shape of business client Andy Griffith (*Gramps*), a loud shit-kicker who invites/challenges Shatner and his work colleagues Marjoe Gortner (*Wild Bill*) and Robert Reed (*Prime Target*) to a motorbike road trip to Baja, Mexico, where he'll sign a contract that will make them all rich.

Cautious of Andy's blaggard behavior and seriously considering a dose of LSD, "Shat" and the boys reluctantly don stylish Wildcats team jackets and nervously rev off through an unforgiving desert toward an uncertain horizon—while back at home, wives Lorraine Gary (*Jaws*) and Angie Dickenson (*Dressed To Kill*) are left with nothing to do but ponder the collective mid-life crisis of the males and examine the crumbling remains of their broken relationships.

Written by Jack Turley (*Empire Of The Ants*) and little more than a mildly psychedelic cattle drive on dirt bikes, all concerned ride for real and undergo reflective flashbacks and contemplative asides in a well-played, convincing and frequently serious outing that can boast one of Andy Griffith's most menacing and deranged performances. "Yeah! I'm a hippie!"

If anything, you should check it out just to see the unexpected finale and the melancholic, near suicidal Shatner, who wanders around wearing bug-eyed spectacles and a fantastic lop-sided wig. [DF Dresden]

PRESCRIPTION: MURDER

Director: Richard Irving
Starring: Peter Falk, Gene Barry, Katherine Justice, Nina Foch.
Airdate: February 20, 1968   Network: NBC

Having constructed an ingenious alibi, esteemed but adulterous psychiatrist Dr. Flemming coolly strangles his wife. But Flemming's criminal planning is no match for the instincts of Lt. Columbo.

Prescription: Murder has an interesting history. It is a pilot for the *Columbo* series as we know and love it only in retrospect; it was conceived and presented as a one-off movie written by Richard Levinson and William Link, based on a stage play they had developed from an episode of *The Chevy Mystery Show* that they wrote back in 1960.

The long gestation between the first glimpse of Columbo (played in *Chevy Mystery* by Bert Freed) and Peter Falk's debut as the character paid off, as this is a smoothly executed take on that old "perfect murder" chestnut that stands up as a superior, early TV movie in its own right. But in establishing the highly robust template for the later *Columbo* series, it now also seems as warmly familiar as a favorite pair of slippers.

The series' best ingredients are in place, more or less: the villain's dark deed (and strong motive for it) opening the film, then the ingenious attempts to cover it up; the non-appearance of the unassuming Columbo until at least half-an-hour into the story, then the delicious war of attrition—"Just one more thing…"—as the 'tec politely but incessantly wears down his arrogant suspect; and, not least, the soon-to-be omnipresent khaki raincoat, although here it looks new and nicely pressed, and Columbo doesn't wear it all the time.

It's a testament to his greatness that Falk offers such a complete performance in what could have remained an ephemeral, one-off TVM. The mischievous twinkle in his (one good) eye may not be quite as pronounced as in later installments; he may have a neater, conservative-era haircut; and he may even lose his temper at one point, but his Columbo is also pretty much the finished product. The idea of pitting Columbo against a psychiatrist is a neat device; the shrink's casual if exasperated, off-the-meter analysis of the detective concisely highlights the traits that make him so enduring and enigmatic a character, just in case we weren't to encounter him again.

As the dastardly Dr. Flemming, that velvet-voiced staple of general purpose sophistication, Gene Barry, sets the benchmark for the high profile guest stars to follow; watching his temper slowly fray and his slick façade gently crack over ninety minutes remains highly entertaining, even though we've since seen similar deflations in scores of *Columbo* villains.

Prescription: Murder was well received, but it still took three more years for NBC to make an official *Columbo* pilot (1971's *Ransom for a Dead Man*), before going on to commission the series proper. [Julian Upton]

REVENGE FOR A RAPE

Director: Timothy Galfas
Starring: Mike Connors, Robert Reed, Tracy Brooks Swope, Deanna Lund
Airdate: November 19, 1976   Network: ABC

 After his pregnant wife is attacked and raped in a tent, a husband ventures into the savage wilderness seeking justice.

Decked out in wide collared shirts and sporting a fine, over-dyed Elvis quiff, TV movie fence post Mike Connors *(Too Scared to Scream)* is Travis Green, a questionably more mature husband who fawns over his freshly pregnant young wife Tracy Brooks Swope *(Terror on the 40th Floor)*.

Both are enjoying a quiet camping trip in a San Bernardino, California forest until they go get supplies at a redneck supermarket—a place where the overprotective Mike is immediately thrown into a huff when Tracy is drooled over by a group of scruffy hillbilly hunters.

Back at camp minutes later, and while Mike is out emptying his indignant bladder behind a tree, Tracy is set upon and raped (off screen) by a filthy trio of mouth breathers and is soon rushed to a redneck hospital where she has a miscarriage—a turn of events that sends the already fuming Mike into an even greater rage. In need of assistance, he goes to see disinterested local sheriff Robert Reed *(Nurse)* but is told it's the middle of hunting season, the deputies are all busy and the attackers could be from out of town and may never be caught.

Upset at the news, and probably tired of listening to Jerrold Immel's soppy background music, Mike despairs at first, but then takes it upon himself to hunt down and kill the rapists by any means necessary, so off he goes into the hinterland, armed with only a stick and some flashbacks.

Possibly not an inspiration for Meir Zarchi's *I Spit on Your Grave* (1978), those used to Connors' "softer" roles in the likes of TV fare such as *Mannix, Diagnosis Murder* and *The Love Boat* will probably be surprised at the brutal subject matter and savage edge on display here, as he's quite a decent and believable revenge machine once the lights go red and he's allowed to rant, run, and kill.

Capped off with a nice twist finale and deftly written by Yabo Yablonsky, fans of ugly faces and leafy revenge in a forest should double-bill it with the faintly related and far, far nastier *The Beasts* (1980). [DF Dresden]

SARAH T.--- PORTRAIT OF A TEENAGE ALCOHOLIC
Director: Richard Donner
Starring: Linda Blair, Verna Bloom, William Daniels, Larry Hagman
Airdate: February 11, 1975   Network: NBC

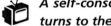 ***A self-conscious teenager who needs help coping with her problems turns to the bottle.***

After a square up containing statistics on teenage alcoholism, this early Richard Donner film (*The Omen, The Goonies*, etc.) is a study in intergenerational hypocrisy as much as a call for concern about the rising number of teen lushes in seventies North America. Donner already had over a decade of TV work behind him (including episodes of *The Banana Splits*!) when he cast sixteen-year-old Linda Blair as the eponymous Sarah Travis, who we first meet during one of her parents' swinging parties—after which she proceeds to down all the leftover tumblers of booze in secret.

The next day at school, we see one reason she has turned to alcohol— she is painfully shy. She tries out for Glee Club, nervously fumbling her way through an off-key rendition of Carole King's It's Too Late, and the committee heartlessly ejects her mid-song. Her absentee dad (Hagman) cheers her up with some swanky denim duds, which she wears when neighbor boy Ken (Mark Hamill) gets roped into taking her out. They end up at a house party with the Glee Club gang, with Sarah once again assuming the role of social outcast. When offered a drink, she coyly accepts, and then raids the bar for a heavy dose of liquid courage. One of the snobby teens attempts to embarrass her by asking her to sing, but the thoroughly oiled Sarah knocks it out of the park, impressing everyone. She loosens up, has a good time, feels involved, and most importantly, throws a pie at the girl who mocked her. But when Ken has to practically carry her home drunk, her parents suspect he's to blame. Still, he is intrigued by the girl, and the two start dating.

Sarah's drinking intensifies with any added stressor—her parents fighting, the discovery that Ken is seeing other girls—and their kindly housekeeper takes the hit when the parents notice their scotch has been watered. Sarah's alcoholism only comes out in the open when she gets blind drunk while babysitting and endangers a child. She goes to a tough counselor (Michael Lerner) who susses the situation immediately and refers her to AA, which is too much for her mother (*Medium Cool*'s Bloom) to bear, seeing as she cares more about saving face than she does her daughter's wellbeing. In AA Sarah meets other kids her age and even younger—the youngest being a diminutive eleven-year-old (Eric Olson, a regular on *Apple's Way* at the time) who is a real cut-up. Seeing such a young kid confess to his alcoholism strikes a chord with Sarah but she has much further down to go before she will admit to her own problem.

Through Lerner's character, the film is critical of the parents' double standards concerning both drinking and socialization, and the scenes where he calls them out are both potent and funny. *Sarah T* was a ratings hit at the time, and compared to similar TV movie *The Boy Who Drank Too Much*, it offers a more believable portrayal of what would drive a teen to alcoholism in the first place—a need to overcome social awkwardness—as well as what it does to keep them there. Still unavailable officially on any form of home video, the last circulating 16mm educational print of the film in North America was destroyed by Swank Motion Pictures circa 2010. [Kier-La Janisse]

SATAN'S SCHOOL FOR GIRLS

Director: David Lowell Rich
Starring: Pamela Franklin, Kate Jackson, Jo Van Fleet, Lloyd Bochner, Roy Thinnes, Cheryl Ladd (as Cheryl Stoppelmoor), Jamie Smith-Jackson
Airdate: September 19, 1973   Network: ABC

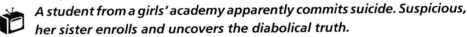 ***A student from a girls' academy apparently commits suicide. Suspicious, her sister enrolls and uncovers the diabolical truth.***

Given the film's title, the big reveal at the climax doesn't come as much of a surprise. The seventy-odd minutes preceding it, however, are a cavalcade of seventies center-partings, moody lighting, mildly terrifying suspense, two-thirds of *Charlie's Angels* and Luciferian evil.

After an arresting opener, featuring a pretty girl being chased and some grade A screaming, we're plunged straight into the strange goings-on at the not-at-all-suspiciously-named Salem Academy for Women. Pamela Franklin stars as Elizabeth, a young woman trying to find out the truth about her sister's apparent suicide. The academy is seemingly attended solely by pretty orphans and odd teachers. *Dynasty*'s Lloyd Bochner is in fine form as the decidedly odd psychology professor, Delacroix. He twitches and sweats in the way that only a middle aged man confronted by a class full of leggy teenage girls can. His teaching on the breaking of the will not only makes him look like a refugee from Operation Paperclip, but also a superb *Scooby Doo*-style red herring.

The Invaders' Roy Thinnes is the girls' favorite. With his wing collars, hip teaching techniques and intense stare, surely he can't be behind the string of suicides? Either way, he's the type of teacher you read about in the papers when they run off with one of their pupils. Director Rich puts the whole thing together with a good deal of craft. The handy power cuts give him a great excuse to utilize some attractive camerawork as Elizabeth creeps around the requisite spooky basement. The setting may be a little hackneyed, but he manages to draw out a fair amount of suspense from the material he has to work with.

Okay, some of the performances are a touch weak—producer Aaron Spelling must have seen beyond Kate Jackson's and Cheryl Ladd's shortcomings to cast them in *Charlie's Angels*, and Jo Van Fleet veers into Bette Davis-style melodrama whenever she's onscreen. Aside from these small missteps, this is a typical example of the TV movie: solid, professional and entertaining. Franklin, all cropped hair and doe-like eyes, does well in a very similar role to Jessica Harper's in Dario Argento's vaguely similar (and marginally better) *Suspiria*. Having cut her horror teeth in 1973's *The Legend of Hell House*, she obviously understood the genre, and easily outshines the rest of the young cast.

About half way through, a fleeting mention of the Salem witch trials telegraphs where the plot is going, but, even so, the fiery climax is effectively done. The sight of a group of girls happily facing immolation and, in one of the genre's most memorable images—Satan casually walking into an inferno—do go a good way to outweigh a slightly ludicrous chase scene which ends with a poor guy being hit with a stick by Cheryl Ladd. The film's best moment, however, comes at the very end. As the academy is ablaze, with people trapped inside, the local sheriff is spectacularly unconcerned. Perhaps evil finishing schools burn down all the time in his neck of the woods. [Rich Flannagan]

SATAN'S TRIANGLE

Director: Sutton Roley
Starring: Doug McClure, Kim Novak, Alejandro Rey, Jim Davis
Airdate: January 14, 1975   Network: ABC

 A coast guard helicopter pilot investigates a derelict boat in the Bermuda Triangle and appears to find evidence of the supernatural.

This mischievous TV movie opens with crawling text explaining that "thousands of men, women and children have vanished off of the face of the Earth just off the East Coast of the United States," and that what we are about to witness is "one explanation." In fact, the film's earliest scenes have a grounded, near-documentary quality that plants a deceptive seed in the viewer's head that will be exploited before the film's end. *Satan's Triangle* is all about pushing away the cobwebs of superstition, presenting you with cold hard facts, and then, just as you've eased into the hammock of comforting rationality, deviously slicing the ropes that secure you and chuckling as you fall into a deeper abyss than the one you were originally fearful of. Doesn't that sound like fun?

The coast guard helicopter team of Lt. J. Haig (McClure) and Lt. Cmdr. Pagnolini (Michael Conrad) answer a distress call from a seemingly abandoned boat in the notorious Bermuda Triangle. Onboard Haig discovers one skittish survivor named Eva (Novak) and several dead men; one of whom, appears to be levitating above the floor. A rescue attempt fails and Pagnolini must return to base to tend to the low-on-fuel helicopter, leaving Haig and Eva alone aboard the boat until further assistance can arrive. Soon we are made privy to many a strange occurrence as Eva recalls what befell the doomed ship through flashbacks. It seems all was going well until they came across a priest stranded at sea named Father Martin (Rey). As soon as he was brought onboard, the weather changed for the worse and deadly accidents became the norm as if the presence of the holy man enraged some malign force whose territory they were in. After hearing Eva's incredible story, Haig delivers a logical explanation for everything; even the floating cadaver is revealed to be simply pierced and hanging from the pointy snout of a Marlin. As he told Pagnolini earlier, Haig has no problem believing in God, Santa Claus or the Easter Bunny but he can't quite swallow the devil.

So there you go, time to hit the hay. Eva sure has a spooky way of telling a story and the events depicted were admittedly eerie but Haig has a handle on everything and all's well that ends well, as they say. Eventually Both Eva and Haig find themselves back on Pagnolini's helicopter and ready to fly off into the sunset, except something isn't quite right. Why is Eva suddenly acting weird? I'm not one to give away endings, so I won't, but allow me to advise first time viewers to put rubber bands around their socks to prevent them from being knocked off. With one chilling, indelible smile, everything we've come to understand begins to unravel at a steading pace until a crescendo of horror is reached. For my money it's truly one of the most unnerving moments ever depicted on the small screen or anywhere else. In the end, *Satan's Triangle* is much bigger than the sum of its parts and if there exists a purer representation of the uncanny than its last ten minutes, I don't know, and don't want to know, what it is; some terrors defy rationalization. [Lance Vaughan]

SCREAM, PRETTY PEGGY

Director: Gordon Hessler
Starring: Sian Barbara Allen, Ted Bessell, Bette Davis
Airdate: November 24, 1973   Network: ABC

 A co-ed finds work at a modern gothic mansion, and becomes curious about the mysterious woman in white who lives above the garage.

This breezy tale of gothic horror presents some rather heady family dynamics that come complete with a supposedly insane sister, a haunted, guilt-ridden brother and a drunk mother. Plucky Peggy (Allen) has no idea that she has walked into the housekeeping job from Hell, but even after spying a mysterious woman running around the estate at night, she continues on with her employer, a renowned and enigmatic sculptor named Jeffrey Elliot (Bessell). In the end, although she talks a lot about feminism and the new liberated woman (even negotiating a higher wage for her housekeeping job), Peggy is most interested in attracting the attention of Jeffrey, whose disturbed works should have been the lovely girl's first clue. However, despite having a predilection for romance and the domestic, Peggy turns out to be a decent detective too, and stumbles upon mysteries and secrets almost as often as Jeffery tucks away dead bodies.

Although it feels like the script for *Scream, Pretty Peggy* (co-written by Hammer Studios legend Jimmy Sangster, and Arthur Hoffe, whose sole screen credit is this eccentric tale) is cobbled together from various other stories (most notably *Psycho*), there are a few sharp flashes thrown into the mix. Those wonderfully chilling moments are a testament to Hessler's adept direction, and Bob Prince's unnerving score. Despite the story's limitations they create a tension that lies thick on the contemporary gothic telethriller. (Random TV movie note: But please take those clever references to family skeletons to heart; they are not a metaphor!)

Scream, Pretty Peggy also benefits from a game cast. In a maybe unintentionally hilarious turn, Bette Davis, substituting liquor for tea and giving Peggy a bit of hell in an attempt to get her out of the house, does very well as the overbearing mother (it also looks like her ornate nightgown wardrobe could have been leftovers from *Whatever Happened to Baby Jane?*). And Allen is in fine form here, making Peggy a charming, if slightly pushy, wannabe liberated woman who refuses to take Mrs. Elliot's guff and persists in investigating the lady above the garage.

However, the spookiest things in *Scream, Pretty Peggy* come in the form of Jeffrey's unsettling sculptures. Created by Don Chandler, these figures are either bug-eyed block figures or hulking monsters painted blood red, and hollowed out in the middle (and I'm sure you can guess why). The art direction of Joe Alves is wonderfully consistent with these menacing statues, and almost every work of art in the Elliot's house, whether Jeffery sculpted it or not, is worth looking at. Chandler, who is most famous for sculpting Bruce, the shark used in *Jaws* would work again with Alves on *Jaws 3*, where Alves had moved up the ranks to director. [Amanda Reyes]

THE SECRET NIGHT CALLER

Director: Jerry Jameson
Starring: Robert Reed, Hope Lange, Sylvia Sidney, Robin Mattson
Airdate: February 18, 1975   Network: NBC

Businessman by day, obscene phone caller by night, a disturbed family man finds himself in troubled waters as his life falls apart.

In the days before "star 69" took the phun out of prank phone-calling, an IRS manager could easily procure the phone numbers of subordinates and residents, call them up and whisper vile things to them. Then, technology came along and put the kibosh on the practice. What's shocking about *The Secret Night Caller* (1975) is that the film stars Robert Reed after he hung up his T-square following the demise of *The Brady Bunch*! He plays Freddy Durant, a bored IRS manager and owner of a plant nursery. His teenage daughter (Robin Mattson) frolics in front of him in a bikini, and his wife (Hope Lange) makes small talk during mealtime. Driven to distraction from his unexciting job, he's the consummate professional, failing to give in to bribery by a businessman and politely warding off the advances of an exotic dancer (Elaine Giftos) who probes him for evidence that he's the phone freak who's been harassing her.

The film begins with a creepy apartment dweller who freaks out fellow single tenant Charlotte (Arlene Golonka) with his pronounced and noisy gait. She races to her apartment in time to get an obscene phone call. As she drops the phone, a close-up reveals the bizarre optical effect of a pair of lips moving in the mouthpiece as if the caller is *in* the handset! She tells her co-workers about the call; they all look like they stepped off the pages of *Good Housekeeping* or *McCall's*. Durant, their boss, is professional with them, carefully masking the tortured soul beneath his civilized veneer. All sexual deviance is alluded to, and it's a big kick to see the typewriters, rotary phones and other outdated machinery of the period prior to the widespread office infiltration by the personal computer; smoking was allowed *everywhere*.

A second phone call to Charlotte's apartment sends her fleeing and crashing her car, which lands her in the hospital. The guilt of his actions compels Durant to take care of her hospital bills, and everyone thinks that he's a great guy. Little do they know…

The one person who *does* know is the dancer who discovers his true identity and demands $10,000 in cash to keep quiet. Durant is forced to plead for the money from the businessman whom he previously shooed out of his office, and gets it in exchange for concessions. His confrontation with the dancer leads us to believe that he might kill her, but he races off for reasons that become clearer later when he attacks his wife for her overall complacency.

John Carl Parker wrote the score and his style is typical of the music of the period, though during the phone call sequences it takes on an air that is sinister and creepy, recalling Billy Goldenberg's score for *Duel* (1971).

The one unanswered question is: what exactly *did* Durant say during those phone calls? [Todd Garbarini]

SEVEN IN DARKNESS

Director: Michael Caffey
Starring: Milton Berle, Barry Nelson, Lesley Ann Warren, Dina Merrill
Airdate: September 23, 1969   Network: ABC

 When a plane crash leaves them stranded in the wilderness, seven blind people fight for survival against insurmountable odds.

Leonard Bishop's novel *Against Heaven's Hand* provides the basis for ABC's first official Movie of the Week; a peculiar and quite wonderful feature that serves us up a little model plane (on strings) flying through a massive electrical storm as it makes its way to Seattle.

Aboard the Airfix twin-prop are a group of seven blind people on route to a sight convention where they hope to consult with doctors and schedule treatment for their condition. Unfortunately, before they reach their destination, the storm worsens and the seeing-eye pilot loses control of the craft and slams the bird into an isolated mountainside, killing everyone… except for the blind people.

That's right. Not only are the seven missing the gift of sight, they now have to contend with being marooned in a dangerous, unknown wilderness with no food or guidance and nothing else to do but dodge wolf attacks, tie themselves together with a ball of wool, and stumble about, casually falling down leafy ravines.

On top of all this, one of the group is a heavily pregnant woman, while another is a depressed war hero, and the rest just bicker and spit bile at each other in a dark hornet's nest of past secrets, self-loathing, self-preservation, self-interest and regret. Hurrah.

Filmed cheaply on small, thrift store sets, if you've no sense of humor you'll find it a mildly tasteless, albeit inspirational tale of perseverance against impossible odds. If you're the opposite, you'll still find it just as tasteless, but you'll laugh a lot more as Michael Masters (*Sssss*), the brilliant and cranky Milton Berle (*Evil Roy Slade*), Barry Nelson (*Island Claws*), panicky Alejandro Rey (*Mr. Majestyk*) and confused Dina Merrill (*Caddyshack II*) all frequently fail to maintain the fourth wall.

If you're interested in cinema featuring the visually impaired, go hunt for the low budget Filipino wonder *Blind Rage* (1978), a movie about a blind gang who attempt a complicated and bloody bank heist. [DF Dresden]

SHE'S DRESSED TO KILL

Director: Gus Trikonis
Starring: Eleanor Parker, John Rubinstein, Connie Sellecca, Jessica Walter
Airdate: December 10, 1979   Network: NBC

 A fading fashion designer stages a comeback at her remote mountaintop mansion, unaware that she's also invited a cold blooded killer.

To be a Barton Girl you must be beautiful, ambitious and, apparently, snarky. Irene Barton (Jessica Walter) isn't concerned with playing housemother, she only cares that her models bring in the big bucks and you can worry about your morals later. This makes the girls rather competitive, especially newcomer Alix (Connie Sellecca in a very early role) who will do just about anything to make it to the top. Boozy Regine (Eleanor Parker) needs the Barton Girls to help her regain her status as a fashion designer. Despite her palatial digs, which you have to take an aerial cable car to reach, Regine is running out of both money and ideas and has resorted to stealing concepts from her assistant Tony (Peter Horton before his signature beard). She's staging a very exclusive show at her mansion where the Barton Girls will show off Regine's, er, Tony's haute couture to fancy buyers and the ultra-rich. A spot opens up on the modeling roster when someone poisons another model's lipstick (!), killing her almost instantly. Alix is more than game to play with the big girls but despite the incredible clothes (designed by Travilla, no less), the showstopper occurs when yet another model is murdered.

She's Dressed to Kill is ludicrous. It's almost impossible to not guess who the killer is, yet the motive comes directly out of left field. Nevertheless, despite its faults, the film's style over substance approach seems to be inspired by the Italian giallo genre, making it an interesting watch for Euro-horror fans. Director Gus Trikonis was no stranger to the B-movie world, and worked on several low budget exploitation films, including *Moonshine County Express*

(1977), before easing into the world of television. He brings a strong sense of atmosphere that makes up nicely for some of the script's shortcomings. The film also makes good use of the Palm Springs Aerial Tramway, which was used in several other TV movies, including *Skyway to Death* (1974) and *Hanging by a Thread* (1979).

Played with a completely straight face, *Dressed* misses its potential for camp, although Eleanor Parker's dippy Regine captures a screwy sense of humor. It's as if Parker is in another film altogether and she is the highlight with her purposely overdone performance as the bitchy, washed up fashion designer.

In the early 1980s, *Dressed* was retitled as *Someone's Killing the World's Greatest Models*, most likely to lure viewers who may have already seen the film, along with those who like salacious titles. The ploy worked because the film ranked sixth for the week when it re-ran in 1983 under its new moniker. [Amanda Reyes]

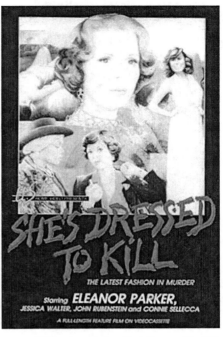

VHS artwork for *She's Dressed to Kill*.

SMILE JENNY, YOU'RE DEAD

Director: Jerry Thorpe
Starring: David Janssen, Andrea Marcovicci, Jodie Foster, Clu Gulager
Airdate: February 3, 1974   Network: ABC

 When a crazed photographer threatens the life of a beautiful model, a detective is hired to protect her.

Considered the second pilot movie for the memorable *Harry O* TV series (the first aired a year earlier and was titled *Such Dust as Dreams are Made Of*), morose David Janssen (*Inchon*) is great as retired San Diego detective Harry Orwell, a solitary firebrand who lives in a run-down beach shack, barely surviving on disability payments. A man with a bullet in his back and a half built sail-boat called *The Answer* on his porch, which once repaired and sea worthy will be his one man ticket to solitude in the middle of the ocean.

To raise cash for mast wax, Harry (who narrates and hates phones) moonlights as a private detective and helps cop buddy Clu Gulager (*Hit Lady*) and a family friend solve a case involving a trail of dead bodies that indicate the next victim may be supermodel Jennifer English (Andrea Macovicci), a woman currently being stalked by peeping tom/non-flyer weirdo Zalman King (*Galaxy Of Terror*).

Well shot, nicely conceived and graced with credible dialog by Howard Rodman (*Coogan's Bluff*), brief gunfire, oversized chess pieces and a surprise appearance by a young Jodie Foster (as a smart-mouth beach waif who "adopts" the endearing Janssen), it's a likeable outing unharmed by its tired, predictable plotting or meager budget.

Co-produced by ABC and Warner Bros Television and divided into two halves for the series reruns, keep watch for co-stars John Anderson (*Scorpion*) and Howard Da Silva (*Nevada Smith*) and don't expect any car chases. Harry O takes the bus. [DF Dresden]

SNOWBEAST

Director: Herb Wallerstein
Starring: Bo Svenson, Yvette Mimieux, Robert Logan, Clint Walker
Airdate: April 28, 1977   Network: NBC

 An aging ski champion helps locals fend off a vicious yeti-like creature that is picking off locals and tourists at a popular Colorado ski resort.
The critical and commercial success of Steven Spielberg's *Jaws* (1975) not only ushered in the era of the modern blockbuster, but also created the "nature strikes back" subgenre which remained popular for the next few years, before the sci-fi craze created by *Star Wars* (1977) moved in on its territory. Unlike the monster movies of the 1950s, these creatures weren't created by atomic radiation, mad scientists or some other calamity[2]. They were just naturally dangerous beasts feeding on anyone stupid enough to invade their territory.

Of course, *Snowbeast* differs from the likes of *Jaws* and William Girdler's *Grizzly* (1976) in that it is based on a mythical creature rather than a factual one, but the formula is exactly the same, just toned down somewhat for television (especially in the boobs and blood departments). The screenplay by Joseph Stefano (who did much better work on Hitchcock's *Psycho* and *The Outer Limits* in the 1960s) apes *Jaws* to such an extent that it even features a scene where a couple of the lead characters discuss cutting open a slain grizzly in order to verify that they have got the right beast that's been eating up all the local residents and tourists! And you've gotta love dialog exchanges like this (delivered with the utmost seriousness, of course):

2 One exception from this period is John Frankenheimer's misfire *Prophecy* (1979), an environmental horror about a grizzly bear deformed from years of toxic waste dumping.

SHERIFF PARADAY: I understand she was a guest at your ski lodge. I was hoping you could help me identify her.

TONY RILL: I must have seen her *somewhere*. Maybe I'll recognize her when I see her face.

SHERIFF PARADAY: She doesn't have one.

While no great shakes as a monster flick (the creature is rarely shown and the killings all fade to a red screen just as the fun is about to begin), *Snowbeast* is still an enjoyable attempt by television to cash in not only on *Jaws* but the whole bigfoot/yeti zeitgeist that was popular during the 1970s. The cast includes a familiar roster of TV faces and former film stars, including Bo Svenson, Yvette Mimieux (*The Time Machine, Jackson County Jail*), Sylvia Sidney, and Clint Walker (who had previously battled killer wildlife in the underrated 1966 adventure/western yarn *Night of the Grizzly*). Director Herb Wallerstein was an assistant director on William Castle's classic *The Tingler* (1959), and spent most of his career directing episodic television shows such as *Star Trek, The Brady Bunch, Happy Days, Petrocelli, Wonder Woman* and *The Six Million Dollar Man*. His own ending at the age of fifty-nine could have made for a good TV movie itself—bludgeoned to death in 1985 by an illegal alien from El Salvador who had been working as Wallerstein's maid at the time.

Released on VHS in the 1980s (as *Bigfoot* in some countries), *Snowbeast* was released as a bare bones DVD in 2008 on the Pro-Active Entertainment label in the US. Alpha Video also issued it on DVD in 2009, paired with the 1976 pseudodocumentary *The Legend of Bigfoot*. [John Harrison]

SOMEONE I TOUCHED

Director: Lou Antonio
Starring: Cloris Leachman, James Olson, Glynnis O'Connor, Andrew Robinson
Airdate: February 26, 1975   Network: ABC

Laura learns that her husband, Sam, has given her syphilis. What's more, Laura has just become pregnant with their first child.

An ABC Movie of the Week about syphilis feels exactly like the sort of thing that network television did in the 1970s: A melodrama that tries, very earnestly, to deal with the issue of casual sex and the dangers of VD. Cloris Leachman plays book editor Laura Hyatt, who has had more than one emotional problem throughout her marriage to Sam, played by James Olson. After many years of trying and one miscarriage, Laura is pregnant. Unfortunately, Sam has had a dalliance with a twenty-year-old named Carrie (Glynnis O'Connor). The Hyatts now have syphilis. There is a theme song, sung by Leachman called Someone I Touched. There is a gentleman from the Board of Health who keeps appearing to talk about VD. There is touching music. Carrie has a very unpleasant mom who belittles her and slaps her a lot in scenes that can't be deemed entertaining by anyone but sadists. And, Laura's boss is played by Kenneth Mars. At this point, the viewer might see a problem with *Someone I Touched*.

The movie itself is well-written, well-acted, well-paced. The TVM places its large moments (and its big twist) at a decent distant apart. Occasionally it's too melodramatic for its own good. Its treatment of Carrie isn't that great. But, the Hyatts have reconciled by the end. And, America has learned a lesson. Within the film, Cloris Leachman and Kenneth Mars are given several scenes together. The first scene, before the troubles begin, involves them discussing the books their office are working on. The scene feels like improvisation between two folks who had recently appeared in Mel Brooks' *Young Frankenstein*. Their following scenes are found deep in the drama and it's tough to look at the two of them together and not expect this to become a send-up of VD films. It is not.

There is something very nostalgic about VD that could be taken care of with a few injections. It must have been a tough time for parents when all they had to warn their kids off of casual sex was "You're going to have to get some shots." Once the 1980s hit, parents could promise their children disease and death if they had casual sex. Everyone took their lives into their hands and men spent a lot of money on condoms. *Someone I Touched* feels almost like a nostalgic *Afterschool Special* that happens to be based around adults rather than a serious journey into the problems of a couple who have neglected one another.

Someone I Touched is from a different time period in America in more ways than one. A well-made TV movie that doesn't become as funny as Leachman and Mars would lead one to believe it's going to be. It has light moments but, in the end, it is as serious as getting touched by Kenneth Mars can be. That will vary by viewer. [Daniel R. Budnik]

SOMEONE'S WATCHING ME!

Director: John Carpenter
Starring: Lauren Hutton, Adrienne Barbeau, David Birney, Charles Cyphers
Airdate: November 29, 1978   Network: NBC

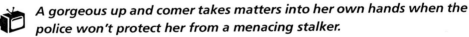 *A gorgeous up and comer takes matters into her own hands when the police won't protect her from a menacing stalker.*

New to Los Angeles, TV director Leigh Michaels rents an apartment in a high rise complex, that unbeknownst to her, has been the location of a series of seemingly unconnected suicides of young women. Soon, she begins receiving strange gifts and threatening phone calls, and all evidence suggests that they are emanating from an unhinged male in the apartment building opposite. He knows her every move. And she knows he is watching. The police are powerless to intervene without substantial proof of her endangerment, so instead, she recruits the help of her boyfriend and one of her colleagues in an effort to stop him… before he stops her.

A lesser seen thriller from genre maestro John Carpenter (and produced in the prime of his career, no less!), this never gets close to reaching the heights of his masterpiece *Halloween* (1978), made the same year, but is certainly cut from the same cloth, and, as such, it packs more entertainment and suspense than most big screen thrillers could ever hope to muster.

Of course, the plot itself is nothing new, instantly drawing comparisons to Hitchcock's *Rear Window* (1954)—of which it arguably rips off wholesale—and in lesser hands this would be cause for concern, but with Carpenter, it's cause for celebration. Interestingly, the similarly themed 1993 thriller *Sliver*, based on a novel by Ira Levin, would feature many of the same ideas that were specific to *Someone's Watching Me!*, and, minus the eroticism, is close to a carbon copy.

Tailoring this kind of adult material to the small screen (though it was conceived as a cinema release) means that—despite much posturing to the contrary—this is very much a soft-core thriller that's low on violence, but high on menace; resulting in a movie that comes on like a sharp toothed animal on a leash, that never really gets the chance to bite. But having said that, it's quite refreshing to see a thriller that executes the fundamentals of the genre so well that there is no need to throw buckets of blood at the camera in an effort to obscure any creative shortcomings—especially considering the gore drenched eighties were just around the corner, all but rendering this kind of low key thriller instantly extinct.

Lauren Hutton is well cast in the lead role, playing both tough and vulnerable when the script demands; and Adrienne Barbeau particularly stands out as her sympathetic co-worker who's eager to help her fight back.

Most notable is the excellent cinematography from Hollywood veteran Robert B. Hauser (*The Odd Couple*, *A Man Called Horse*); every frame impresses, and though made for television, it looks leagues above the average movie of the week.

Unavailable for decades, the movie was finally given a DVD release in 2007. Completists of Carpenter's work should lap it up. And so too, should everybody else. [Kevin Hilton]

SOMETHING EVIL

Director: Steven Spielberg
Starring: Sandy Dennis, Darren McGavin, Jeff Corey, Ralph Bellamy
Airdate: January 21, 1972   Network: CBS

 A young couple move into an idyllic Pennsylvania farmhouse, only to discover the place is a domain of evil.

An old man runs through a barn in slow motion. He's clearly being chased, but his assailant remains tantalizingly off screen. Cornered in the hayloft, the old man turns his back on his pursuer and plunges to his death through the open hayloft door. Time passes, and as the opening credits roll, we witness a wholesome young family picnicking in the verdant fields adjacent to the ill-fated barn. Paul (McGavin), the patriarch of the clan, reclines on a blanket. Young Stevie (Johnny Whitaker) scampers about the fields. Marjorie (Dennis) sketches the details of the nearby farmhouse, paying particular attention to the unassuming For Sale sign in the front yard. Before her drawing is complete, she begins pleading with her husband to purchase the place. Despite his initial reluctance, and annoyance at what will become a lengthy commute to his job in the city, Paul caves and begins discussing details of the sale with the owner.

Clearly, there's something odd about the house, a fact driven home with graphic vividness when Gehrmann (Corey), the previous owner, is spotted spattering chicken blood over the nearby fields in an attempt to ward off evil spirits. But for levelheaded city dwellers the Wordens, such eccentricities are written off as the comical superstitions of uneducated country folk. But then Marjorie hears the baby crying. It is a haunting sound, seemingly emanating from all directions at once, and tinged with what seems to be the faint outlines of speech: an eerie, inarticulate cry for help. At first, Marjorie shrugs it off, assuming it was in her head. After checking on her family, and taking a close look around the barn, she's convinced it was nothing. But as the days pass, the crying continues, louder, more insistent, and most definitely emanating from the barn.

With such an enticing setup, it's a shame that the film never really comes together. Sure, we have some promising moments here and there, including vague hints that this house, and maybe even the entire town, is a dwelling place for sinister spirits. And the palpably eerie atmosphere throughout is a testament to Spielberg's burgeoning talents. But the hoped-for lurid details of the town's dark legacy never materialize, and the haunting-of-Marjorie storyline never becomes the blood-curdling crescendo of horror it was seemingly intended to. Talk of pentacles and other methods of warding off malevolence fill up the runtime, but don't ever have the payoff we might expect.

Clockwise from top left: Andrea Marcovicci and Zalman King in a pilot movie for Harry-O, *Smile Jenny, You're Dead*; excessive ad for the excessive *Star Wars Holiday Special*; and Robert Culp enters the *Spectre*.

In the end, if the nondescript title is any indicator of how this story came together, we can only assume that the filmmakers, including writer Robert Clouse, never really knew what story they wanted to tell, possibly landing on the bewildering tale of demonic possession out of sheer desperation. Without a doubt, *something* is evil in this house and in this town, but it's anybody's guess what that something actually is. [Thomas Scalzo]

SPECTRE

Director: Clive Donner
Starring: Robert Culp, Gig Young, John Hurt, Gordon Jackson
Airdate: May 21, 1977   Network: NBC

 Threatened by evil, a wealthy family enlists the help of a supernatural investigator trained in the black arts.

Penned by Gene Rodenberry and produced by Twentieth Century Fox, a well-cast Robert Culp (*Spy Hard*) is excellent in this spooky detective outing as supernatural investigator William Sebastian—a quirky, paranormal puzzle-solver whose heart has been stolen by a demon and hidden away inside a voodoo doll.

When offered a case involving a rich, gloomy family cursed by bad luck and unexplained deaths, Culp invites bourbon-soaked psychologist friend Gig Young (*Bring Me The Head Of Alfredo Garcia*) to come along and help expose the mysterious truth behind a satanic cult that uses murder, witchcraft, deceit and evil shape-shifters to get their way.

Enticed by the large fee and excited to ride in a private jet, the duo (who bounce brilliantly off each other) travel to the family's exclusive Cyon Estate in England where they encounter some pretty decent black masses and a cadre of "I know his face" British actors hamming it up with pointed sneers, silent stares and suspicious actions—all filmed with devilish, low budget charm and a forked tongue placed in several cheeks.

Shot on damp, creepy English locations and stained with the satanic lore of novelist Dennis Wheatley (*The Devil Rides Out*), there are further tips of the hat to Hammer movies, as well as memorable scenes involving the disco-lit caves of Hell, Culp's hollow chest cavity and a sexy succubus who bursts into flames when a magical tome is placed atop her knockers like a holy bra.

Above average for a TV movie but shy of being classic, it's directed by the genius who made David Niven a playboy Dracula in *Vampira* (1975) and stars the tenacious Gordon Jackson (*The Great Escape*), snooty James Villiers (*Repulsion*), young pilot John Hurt (*Monolith*), sexy Vicki Michele (*Queen Kong*) and Roddenberry's real-life wife Majel Barrett (*The Suicide's Wife*).

Not quite Sherlock Holmes vs. Satan, but close. Keep watch for a few revealing flashes of mammary and some saucy Benny Hill-esque S&M scenes that were considered too hot for TV broadcasts. [DF Dresden]

THE SPELL

Director: Lee Philips
Starring: Susan Myers, Lee Grant, James Olson, Helen Hunt
Airdate: February 20, 1977   Network: NBC

 An unhappy teenage girl discovers supernatural powers within herself. Revenge becomes her evil hobby.

Carrie, the book and the film, turned puberty and sexual awakening in the American teenage female into screaming, bloody fury. As with all popular entertainment, it was imitated. As with all imitations, there are strange variations. *The Spell* is one of these. Fifteen-year-old Rita is tormented by her classmates. Rita is a bit plump. That seems like it might be the reason for torment. But, Rita's really just kind of weird. The film seems like it's going to be about Rita tormented to the point of explosion, like *Carrie*. But, it's not.

Rita lives in a beautiful mansion in San Francisco with her loving mom (Grant), her not-so-loving father (Olson) and much cuter sister (Hunt). The majority of the film revolves around the parents trying to figure out what is going on with Rita. *The Spell* implies early on that the girl has some sort of supernatural power. She causes a classmate to severely injure herself. She makes a woman spontaneously combust. Rita's sister almost drowns and her dad is almost hit by an errant car.

Mom is desperately trying to understand her daughter. Dad seems completely uninterested in Rita and cares more about his younger daughter. The way the movie presents Rita makes the viewer inclined to agree with him. Rita is antisocial and vexatious in the creepiest ways. One would think they'd try to present her in a sympathetic manner. But, it never happens. Rita's ugly sweaters don't help.

The dad is unpleasant. Rita is unpleasant. They constantly clash while mom tries to find some sort of peace. The supernatural events build as the film goes along. The plotline about her classmates becomes very much a secondary part of the film. The viewer learns that Rita feels different from the other girls and she likes it. Then, the twists begin to come. One which isn't expected; one which is. Something resembling witchcraft begins to loom large in the mix.

The Spell is about a girl who is different from the other girls. One of the twists here is that she likes being different. She wants to be different. It's too bad that the way the filmmakers present Rita isn't very pleasant. She's unlikeable. Her sister is nicer than her. It makes for an odd dynamic when the viewer reaches the ending, because there's no real sympathy for Rita. Unlike *Carrie*, whose journey is heartbreaking, Rita is kind of a jerk.

This is a well-made film that probably knows exactly what it's up to. Honestly. The only extremely obvious misstep is the main musical theme. It seems to combine the melody from John Denver's Sunshine On My Shoulder with the main music from the *Shazam* TV series. Not a great combination of music for any day of the week. Maybe they are Rita's favorite songs combined? That sounds like something she'd enjoy. [Daniel R. Budnik]

STAR WARS HOLIDAY SPECIAL

Director: Steve Binder
Starring: Mark Hamill, Harrison Ford, Peter Mayhew, Carrie Fisher
Airdate: November 17, 1978   Network: CBS

It's up to the Star Wars crew to help Chewbacca save his family in time to celebrate Life Day!

Not long enough ago that viewers couldn't bootleg it on their VCRs and in a galaxy that is, sadly, this one, George Lucas approved a TV special based on his 1977 hit movie *Star Wars*. The plot (for lack of a better term) follows rogue pilot Han Solo (Ford) as he struggles to outwit agents of the Empire in order to get his friend and co-pilot Chewbacca (Mayhew) back to his home planet in time to celebrate the Wookie tradition that is Life Day.

Forget about Jar Jar Binks, the Ewoks and even Han shooting first; in terms of atrocities against geekdom's most beloved franchise, they're simply artistic misdemeanors. However, TV producer/director Steve Binder's attempt to bring the movie event of all time to the small screen is a feature-length rampage that would surely be considered a hate crime if only it didn't retain the credibility of involving so much of the creative talent behind the original.

Having been screened only once on US and Canadian television and officially unavailable in any format (even to this day), it was throughout the eighties and most of the nineties, little more than a pop cultural urban legend; much talked about but little seen. However, with the rise of the Internet and YouTube, curious fans of the series were granted the ability to self-inflict this nonsense onto their retinas in the millions, no doubt much to Lucas' dismay and then presumably their own.

Much like the Zapruder footage, watching it is an infinitely more distressing experience than engaging in the wild speculation that it generates: Who was behind this? What was their motive? Most fingers would have to point toward Binder, whose television credits went on to include *Beauty and the Beast: A Concert on Ice* and *The Chevy Chase Show*, of which, alarmingly, in terms of content and zero entertainment factor, this *Holiday Special* would fit snugly in between.

Lucas and *Star Wars* fans all agree that the only element of this TV movie come variety show disaster that even approaches something watchable, is a short animated sequence that introduces the character of bounty hunter Boba Fett. The fact that this film's high point is when no human being is appearing on the screen to embarrass themselves even further, says all that can be said about special appearances from the likes of *Golden Girls*' Bea Arthur, musical group Jefferson Starship and a particularly disturbing exchange between singer Diahann Carroll and a Wookie child, in which her holographic self tries to seduce him by way of an advanced version of Sex-cam 'net porn.

In short, if you're a hardcore *Star Wars* fan and have always wanted to hear Carrie Fisher sing lyrics over John Williams' unforgettable score... No! I still can't recommend you see it. [Kevin Hilton]

THE STRANGE POSSESSION OF MRS. OLIVER

Director: Gordon Hessler
Starring: Karen Black, George Hamilton, Robert F. Lyons, Lucille Benson
Airdate: February 28, 1977   Network: NBC

Mousy Mrs. Oliver seems content with her tidy, colorless existence, but someone or something inside of her has other ideas.

After awaking from a disconcerting dream in which she sees her own lifeless body lying within an opened casket, Mrs. Miriam Oliver (Black) is convinced that she's dying inside. Her life has become a dull ritual with no prospect of anything exciting on the horizon. When we meet Miriam's overbearing husband (Hamilton), who doesn't let her work, study, volunteer, or do much of anything besides stay at home and think about having a baby, it's easy to understand the source of her fears. And when Miriam decides to shed her drab attire for a new, vivacious look, it seems a logical reaction to her circumstances. What doesn't seem quite right is the palpable shift in personality that accompanies her change in wardrobe—a metamorphosis so startling that her husband almost doesn't recognize her. When we realize that Miriam herself seems unsure why she's acting so differently, it becomes clear that someone, or something is attempting to possess Mrs. Oliver.

As is the case with several of Richard Matheson's legendary teleplays—*Duel*, *The Night Stalker*, and *Dying Room Only* among them—*The Strange Possession of Mrs. Oliver* features a protagonist at once isolated from normal society, and tormented by a preternatural foe. For Miriam Oliver, though, the nemesis seems to be coming from inside of her. But who or what is it? An enigmatic opening scene, featuring a burning house and disembodied screams, provides the semblance of a clue, especially as Miriam expresses a clear aversion to fire. But what is her connection to the house? How does her murky past explain her present behavior? The mystery only deepens as Miriam finds herself drawn to things she never considered before: a form-fitting red blouse, a striking blonde wig, brightly colored lipstick, and a penchant for drinking and dancing. When she crosses paths with a man who's certain her name is Sandy, Miriam's sense of herself begins to dissolve.

A testament to Matheson's succinct storytelling and Karen Black's believable portrayal of a woman seemingly losing her mind, this simple, unassuming film engulfs us in a wonderful atmosphere of unease and uncertainty. From the slow, softly lit journey down the eerie hall of the mortuary of Miriam's nightmare, through scene after scene of Miriam wandering aimlessly through a hazy seaside town, the entire film feels like it is taking place within a dream. Miriam's gradual degradation into her new personality adds to the hallucinatory effect—her muddled sense of reality serving as our window into this odd world and constantly keeping us off balance. Though this low key film is unlikely to attract the attention of casual viewers looking for high-octane thrills, *The Strange Possession of Mrs. Oliver* offers a well-paced story, an appealingly creepy atmosphere, and an intriguing mystery, you just need to allow yourself to fall under its spell. [Thomas Scalzo]

THE STRANGER WITHIN

Director: Lee Philips
Starring: Barbara Eden, George Grizzard, Joyce Van Patten, David Doyle
Airdate: October 1, 1974   Network: ABC

A woman becomes pregnant, even though her husband has had a vasectomy, and she begins to exhibit strange behavior as a result.

In the late 1960s and well into the 1970s the devil was big box office. Roman Polanski's *Rosemary's Baby* (1968) and William Friedkin's *The Exorcist* (1973) made enough *moola* to cause other big studios to follow suit (Richard Donner's 1976 outing *The Omen* proved popular with its prestigious cast and it spawned many other *Omen* projects). This method of entertainment also made its way to the small screen, and it's hard to believe that at this time television was considered a form of substandard entertainment, a virtual dumping ground for lesser material while feature films were held in high esteem. The roles seem to be completely reversed now! Ironically, I find the 1970s to have been responsible for some of the most memorable and creepy TV movies ever made. While the devil certainly played a role in a good number of them, some of these flicks had more of a sci-fi slant to them.

An interesting though bizarre little television outing is Lee Philips' 1974 film *The Stranger Within*, which was released on VHS in the 1980s with a very creepy cover. (Be aware that there are at least a handful of other films with this same name.) Barbara Eden trades in her genie outfit for that of a suburban housewife, Ann Collins, who finds herself pregnant despite the fact that husband David (Grizzard) had a vasectomy, a maneuver on his part so that her health would not be harmed by a pregnancy. When it becomes apparent that she is, in fact, pregnant, David reels, knowing that he cannot possibly be the father. Infidelity becomes the prime suspect and it momentarily causes a rift between them. As the pregnancy progresses, Ann manifests strange behavior that includes eating massive amounts of salt and raw meat, and speed-reading through a physics book. It becomes apparent that she was impregnated by something far more sinister than another man…

The Stranger Within began life as many *Twilight Zone* episodes did. It originated in the form of a short story written by the great Richard Matheson: *Trespass* first appeared in the September/October 1953 issue of *Fantastic* magazine. Mr. Matheson penned the teleplay for the film, as he also had adapted several of his own stories into genre favorites, *Trilogy of Terror* (1975) and *Dead of Night* (1977), both directed by Dan Curtis for television. Those films benefitted from a shorter running time, and *The Stranger Within* would have probably done better as a vignette in this format. Despite the somewhat long lulls in between the start and the bizarre conclusion, *The Stranger Within* is an entertaining showcase for Ms. Eden's considerable talents and is definitely worth seeking out. [Todd Garbarini]

STREET KILLING
Director: Harvey Hart
Starring: Andy Griffith, Bradford Dillman, Harry Guardino, Robert Loggia
Airdate: September 12, 1976   Network: ABC

Andy Griffith pursues criminals through the courts in an attempt to bring justice to the streets of New York.

Voraciously typed by TV script machine William Driskill (writer of 1957's *Rockabilly Baby*), here's a slow, solid slab of courtroom drama fat with a platoon of TV movie regulars.

There are rides in elevators, stuffed briefcases, wide ties, stern words, meetings, phone calls, reports in duplicate and the odd perm or two on show as city prosecutor Andy Griffith (*Winter Kill*) tries to catch and convict a school of lawless scallywags via a chain of dull courtroom/office sequences where everyone discusses the plot and slowly figures out that the crimes involved may have links that may go all the way to the mayor.

Plodding along like a pointless, chat-filled episode of *Matlock*, most of the proceedings are set in a courtroom, or an office. Or a hallway attached to an office. It's light on the action too, with only brief flashes of a loaded gun or a dark alley to pass the time and it shamefully wastes the talents of Don Gordon (*The Gamblers*), Anna Berger (*Hebrew Hammer*), Bradford Dillman (*Piranha*) and Robert Loggia (*Jagged Edge*) who just amble about wishing they took that episode of *Kojak* instead.

Hidden under the legal molasses and worth a mention is the fleeting use of Times Square at night, some great afros, nice cars, fat cigars, wild comb-over hairdos, a funky pool hall, Gerrit Graham (Beef in Brian De Palma's *Phantom of the Paradise*) as a junkie doctor and a minimal amount of killing—street or otherwise.

Produced by ABC Circle Films, you'll have to really, really love police procedure and lots of talking to make it through to the closing credits. If not, just watch for the screen debut of Gigi Semone as Kitty. [DF Dresden]

SWEET HOSTAGE

Director: Lee Philips
Starring: Linda Blair, Martin Sheen, Jeanne Cooper, Bert Ramsen   Network: ABC
Airdate: October 10, 1975

 A disturbed man kidnaps a teenaged girl, but she soon develops feelings of respect and love for him.

Between *Badlands* (1973) and *The Little Girl Who Lives Down the Lane* (1977), a young Martin Sheen starred as Leonard Hatch, an asylum inmate who believes himself to be the embodiment of Samuel Taylor Coleridge's Kubla Khan. He lives an exuberant inner life, but is rattled whenever his delusion is threatened. It's not long before he escapes in search of his mythical Xanadu and runs into Doris Mae Withers (Blair), a sassy teenage farmgirl whose potential is constantly derailed by her accusatory father and put-upon mother, both of whom seem threatened by their own daughter's intelligence. When her truck breaks down on the way back from town, Sheen pit stops in a stolen vehicle and offers her a lift. But after she airs her own grievances about being stuck in a dead-end, he decides to whisk her away with him to Xanadu—by force.

Still, the title of the film is enough to alert the viewer that this won't be a harrowing hostage horror as much as the kind of soppy Stockholm syndrome romance that proliferated as the eighties slouched into view (see also *My Kidnapper, My Love*, 1980). The sexual tension is immediately palpable; problematic in today's context for a number of reasons but in line with the general structure of what was deemed "women's entertainment" at the time, be it Harlequin novels, gothic horror or movies of the week (it should be noted that the romantic elements of the film purportedly do not appear in Nathaniel Benchley's 1968 novel, *Welcome to Xanadu*, on which the film is based).

Leonard takes Doris Mae to an isolated cabin he's appropriated, renames her Christabel (after another famous Coleridge poem), and her womanly talents are quickly put to work cleaning the place up. His moods are erratic—one minute he's galloping around the room, over-annunciating in a strained mid-Atlantic accent, and the next he's shoving his pouty hostage in a confused rage. He has some sort of sexual hang-up and likes that Blair also scoffs at the centrality of sex in relationships—but this of course is a means of protecting herself from any embarrassment she might feel about being a virgin. He, on the other hand, is frigid—his fear of sex helping to neutralize the threat of sexual violence that underlies the pulpy romance of Stockholm syndrome stories. Doris Mae quickly learns how to navigate his mood swings, and grows to like him—even love him. He's like no one she's

Left: Andy Griffith pleads his case in *Street Killing*.
Right: James Brolin finds himself *Trapped*.

ever met—he is both teacher and lover, and he comes from *another place*; his worldview is fantastical and unfettered.

Sheen goes overboard (including an amazing scene where he peels down the highway yelling "I'm Betrayed! I'm Betrayed!! Betrayed!!"), and Blair resorts too easily to sulking, but overall turns in an assured performance, offering up one of her most likeable and believably compassionate screen characters. Directed by Lee Philips, a TV lifer whose output included the subversive Stockard Channing revenge-comedy *The Girl Most Likely To...* (1973) from a teleplay by Edward Hume—who had also co-written the hostage docudrama *21 Hours at Munich* (1976)—*Sweet Hostage* may have questionable sexual politics but remains charming all the same, and its central casting can't be beat. [Kier-La Janisse]

THE TENTH LEVEL

Director: Charles S. Dubin
Starring: William Shatner, Lynn Carlin, Ossie Davis, Stephen Macht
Airdate: August 26, 1976   Network: CBS

 A controversial experiment on the subject of obedience, gives participants the false impression that they are torturing a subject.

During the decade between the cancellation of *Star Trek* and the first of its motion picture spin-offs, William Shatner appeared in an array of minor films and TV projects, none more illogical than the CBS movie *The Tenth Level*. Based upon Stanley Milgram's 1960s research, Shatner stars as a psychology professor who conducts underhanded experiments where volunteers are asked to punish subjects who answer questions incorrectly. The volunteers believe that they are administering increasingly severe electric shocks to the subjects, who they can hear pleading and screaming.

Milgram and Shatner were concerned with the propensity in people to do things that they find repugnant or distasteful, when a figure of authority orders them to. Footage of Nazi concentration camps gives a pretty obvious example. Shatner, short of work and not wanting to blow it, does a good job of reigning in his mannerisms, and emotes as only he can in the almost climactic scenes. The rest of the cast go through the motions, with shock-haired Ossie Davis in particular wooden as hell. TV stalwart Stephen Macht, making his debut, is fun in a role that would have suited James Woods if it were a proper film. He twitches and sweats as he launches into a fantastic slow motion rampage, smashing up the superbly retro-looking analog apparatus in the laboratory.

The implications of the research are fascinating and troubling, with a frighteningly high sixty percent of volunteers administering the maximum dose of electricity. The then-recent actions of US soldiers in Vietnam are mentioned as inspiration for the experiments. Davis makes an interesting point accusing the WASP Shatner of not being able to empathize with the subjects because his racial group has not suffered the deprecations of genocide or mass oppression. If these points had been expanded upon a little more, then the film may have been a more interesting one. Unfortunately, all such considerations are lost beneath a sea of terrible production values. The film was shot directly onto videotape, and has a washed out, fourth generation-copy porn film look. Despite exteriors being filmed at Yale, interior scenes have a real bargain basement feel, especially a "crummy bar," which seems to be six feet wide.

An overbearing score from Charles Gross and a completely unnecessary "For Mature Audiences Only" disclaimer give proceedings a 1950s feel, despite the funky CBS jingle at the beginning. Dubin had been active in the fifties, and despite being a regular director of the *M*A*S*H* TV series, his work here harks back twenty years. Shatner fans will find plenty to enjoy here, as will psychology students, but *The Tenth Level* is ultimately a frustrating, almost interesting ninety minutes. [Rich Flannagan]

THEN CAME BRONSON

Director: William A. Graham
Starring: Michael Parks, Bonnie Bedelia, Akim Tamrioff, Martin Sheen
Airdate: March 24, 1969   Network: NBC

After the suicide of a close friend, the impossibly cool Bronson leaves his nine-to-five lifestyle and rides his hog through America.

In 1969, the big three networks were becoming interested in a new age demographic that fell between the ages of ten and thirty-one. Realizing the marketing and viewership potential of the American youth, NBC attempted to speak to the counterculture movement through Bronson

(Parks), an enigmatic lone wolf who rode the highways, and solved people's problems with his own take-life-as-it-comes demeanor. The pilot telefilm is beguiling and, in spots, almost documentary-like, as it follows Bronson and his companion, a gorgeous young woman who refuses to be named (Bonnie Bedelia). Well, at least until the end of the film.

Created by ex-newspaperman Denne Bart Petitclerc, Bronson was loosely based on former Hell's Angels biker and fellow reporter Birney Jarvis, who had traveled across the country on his hog. Reliable character actor Michael Parks filled the role nicely. Parks related well to the character, and also considered himself a bit of nomad, on his own since he was fourteen-years-old. Although he'd been working as an actor for over a decade before *Bronson*, he was still searching for that star-making role; now, some four decades later, he is still often associated with this freewheeling character.

Hoping to ride on the biker craze brought on by *Easy Rider* and the success of hip new shows like *The Mod Squad*, this pilot telefilm proved to be an enormous success for NBC. Critics and audiences loved it, and despite its desire to evade pithy synopsizing, it was nicknamed a "*Route 66* for a new generation." Finally, someone on television was speaking to a generation of those either already on the road, or heading in that direction, and the network invested heavily in the series, which follows Bronson on similar adventures throughout the country. Unfortunately, it was because the fans of the TVM spent more time outdoors and were mostly uninterested in episodic programming that the series failed, and was cancelled after its first season.

Despite the disappointment, the pilot film remains a mesmeric time capsule that encapsulates the feeling of late sixties youth looking for the meaning of life, and it captures the country at its most gorgeous and serene. Bronson's quiet charms provided a tranquil antidote to a nation polarized by Vietnam and proved that sometimes finding yourself was all about getting lost. [Amanda Reyes]

THIEF

Director: William A. Graham
Starring: Richard Crenna, Angie Dickinson, Cameron Mitchell, Hurd Hatfield
Airdate: October 9, 1971   Network: ABC

A suave burglar with gambling debts finds it difficult to give up his crooked life.

About halfway through *Thief*, Neil Wilkinson, the titular thief, finds himself in a casino washroom taking stock of his life. It is not a good day for Wilkinson, having gambled away almost all the money he owes to a dangerous man called Jim, with whom he has an imminent appointment.

Also in the washroom is a jolly man shaving. Neil humors the stranger in order to lift the wallet he spies in the jacket hanging on the wall. But the jolly man is smarter than he looks and tells Neil he may as well give the wallet back because it's empty; the casino has cleaned him out.

Wilkinson (Richard Crenna) is a man with two lives: a pension salesman in the eyes of his new girlfriend, Jeannie (Angie Dickinson), while to others he is a burglar of repute. He dresses like a salesman to cruise affluent neighborhoods for houses to rob. He has a pocketful of dog biscuits to occupy guard dogs, should he encounter them, and an innate ability to smooth-talk his way out of a tight corner, as happens when a homeowner returns unexpectedly to find him in her driveway, departing the scene of the crime. Wilkinson acts like he's lost. Without breaking a sweat, he then helps carry the homeowner's groceries to her door.

Penned by John D. F. Black, who co-wrote *Shaft* the same year, *Thief* effortlessly runs from one gem of a set-piece to another. The washroom scene reveals a character more troubled than he is dashing or daring, as first he appears. It's the movie's turning point. Wilkinson is on parole and wants to do right by his son, yet still he steals jewels. When eventually he arrives for his important meeting, cap in hand, Jim (Robert Webber) accuses him of using his son as emotional leverage. The meeting doesn't go well, and Wilkinson arrogantly puts himself in an even tighter spot, vowing to deliver the outstanding cash in twenty-four hours.

The movie ends in a pinhead instant, with Wilkinson about to make good on his promise. Instead, he is shot dead in his home by a strung-out kid, seen fleetingly only once before in a parole office early in the picture. In resolving its ethical conundrum—that of a criminal who wins out and even gets the girl as a bonus—it's a kick in the nuts. But as unexpected as it is, the death of Wilkinson is as near as dammit a perfect end to the movie.

Thief features a veteran cast at the top of its game, one that also includes Hurd Hatfield, and Cameron Mitchell as Wilkinson's long suffering buddy, Charlie ("You can't offend people who can hurt you!" he advises him). A musical score by Ron Grainger breezily rounds out a wholly satisfying TVM.

No stranger to the format, director William A. Graham is probably best known to sleaze fans for the 1980 miniseries, *Guyana Tragedy*. His *Thief* should not be confused with Michael Mann's 1981 movie of the same name, which was based on the memoirs of real-life jewel thief John Seybold. However, I like to think of Graham's humble TV offering as a quiet influence on Mann. What's more, the idea of the antihero who can't stop gambling, using money he desperately owes, turns up again in another movie, Karel Reisz's *The Gambler* (1974). [David Kerekes]

TRAPPED

Director: Frank De Felitta
Starring: James Brolin, Susan Clark, Earl Holliman, Robert Hooks
Airdate: November 14, 1973   Network: ABC

 James Brolin is trapped in a department store policed by a ravenous pack of Dobermans.

Despite working with a script that feels like it was tossed together in about fifteen minutes, this killer dog thriller by the director of *Dark Night of the Scarecrow* is a heck of a lot of fun. The story centers on James Brolin and his admirable efforts to win back the affections of his daughter, Carrie (Tammy Harrington). You see, Brolin is a drunk, and has made a habit of ditching important family events for the comforts of the local bar. But he's determined to change. He's going to buy Carrie the doll she really wants, and he's going to meet her for dinner. After all, his ex-wife Elaine (Clark) is moving to Mexico City that very night, and bringing Carrie with her. This dinner may be his last chance to see her for quite some time. He's going to be there.

At the department store, biding his time as the sales clerk hunts down the coveted doll, Brolin steps into the hallway for a smoke. What he doesn't realize is that it's almost closing time, and that the clerk will forget him. Nor does he foresee that he'll be knocked unconscious by a pair of department store ruffians and left for dead in the bathroom. Or that the store's security system is a pack of Dobermans. When he wakes up from his beating, the doors are locked and the dogs are roaming free. As the reality of his plight sinks in, and the dogs begin to growl in furious anticipation, Brolin's character morphs from suave charmer to disheveled mess. And then he gets bitten in the leg. As Susan and her new beau grow increasingly miffed at the man's tardiness, Brolin's dinner plans take a backseat to surviving the life-and-death duel in the department store.

Though this set-up is patently ridiculous, director Frank De Felitta keeps the inanity at bay, making canny use of his limited resources to create an atmosphere of terror. For instance, the soundtrack is saturated with barking and snarling. Even when the mongrels aren't on-screen, we know they are there, waiting, ready to pounce at any given moment. This constant threat, coupled with Brolin's increasingly feeble state as he loses blood, establishes and maintains an appreciable level of tension. Some memorable set-pieces also serve to keep the anxiety high and the tale moving. The most engaging of these involves a sweaty, pale-faced Brolin crawling out onto a perilous ledge. His plan: use a fishing rod to snag an archery set propped up on a display floor table. All he needs to do is reel in this catch and then launch arrows into his growling nemeses.

Such action scenes aside, though, Brolin the actor isn't given very much to work with here. Sure, there are ravenous dogs at every turn, but without any humans around to commune with, his emotive opportunities are limited to exaggerated gestures and a bit of yelling. Impressively, Brolin makes the most of what he's given, awkwardly climbing on furniture, yelping at his pursuers, hobbling frantically up a flight of stairs, and, in my favorite moment, delivering a karate kick to a kiosk that gets in his way. Brolin must surely have realized the absurdity of the film, but instead of phoning in his performance, he plays up the role with admirable gusto. *Trapped* may not be a masterpiece, but Brolin's enthusiasm ensures that the audience walks away happy. (Aka *Danger Doberman*; *Doberman Patrol*.) [Thomas Scalzo]

TRIBES

Director: Joseph Sargent
Starring: Darren McGavin, Jan-Michael Vincent, Earl Holliman, John Gruber
Airdate: November 10, 1970   Network: ABC

 A hippie goes up against his drill sergeant in this dramedy about the Vietnam War.

Darren McGavin, better known to telefilm fans as future vampire-fighting ink-slinger Carl Kolchak, plays tough Vietnam-era marine drill sergeant Tom Drake, who zeroes in on reluctant hippie recruit Adrian (Vincent) as the bane of the recent batch. The sun-soaked, free-spirited Adrian shows up in sandals and love beads, and Drake can see trouble brewing, even though he secretly doesn't see eye to eye with his right wing commie-bashing co-workers.

Written by Tracy Keenan Wynn (son of character actor Keenan Wynn), for which he and co-writer Marvin Schwartz won a Primetime Emmy, *Tribes* was a ratings hit and a timely attempt to bridge a volatile intergenerational communication gap. The opening credit sequence fetishizes the head-shaving ceremony of military boot camp, set to the soft sounds of frequent Bobby Sherman songwriter Al Capps and Marty Cooper—the latter the writer of squeaky pop hit Peanut Butter and onetime member of the Shacklefords alongside Lee Hazlewood. A primal drumbeat is set against the repetitive chanting of the military drill to expose a commonality within the friction.

The promotional campaign seized upon this conflict with the tagline, "Wanted by the United States Marines: For AWOL, insubordination... and doing his thing." But in fact, the biggest threat Vincent's character poses is not outright insolence as much as his ability to go through the motions of following orders without having his spirit broken, and to devise coping tactics that also help his fellow soldiers adapt. Throughout boot camp, he tests better, performs more efficiently and acts more responsibly than

A WORLD PREMIERE!
TRIBES TONIGHT

Can a hardnosed Sergeant drill a peace-loving flower child into a fighting Marine? Darren McGavin, Michael Vincent and Earl Holliman star.

8:30 PM
ABC MOVIE OF THE WEEK

Clockwise from top: *TV Guide* promo for *Tribes*; Karen Black fights for survival in one of the best remembered telefilms in history, *Trilogy of Terror*; and Kathleen Quinlan and Peter Graves hope to find other survivors in *Where Have All the People Gone?*

expected, despite lacking the formal schooling and social structure of many of his fellow privates. His comrades can't help but notice this, and one by one, they turn to him for guidance.

At first, Adrian's resolve causes Sergeant Drake start to question his methods of training; Drake's co-workers accuse him of going soft when his troops look content and focused (as opposed to terrified and frustrated) on the field. The accusation derails him. "I will not stand for any more smiling during drill, is that clear?!" But eventually Drake starts to question the purpose of the training, and by extension, the purpose of the war.

The film is full of many familiar TV faces, but McGavin in particular gives a moving performance as the drill instructor in crisis, and despite prefiguring Kubrick's *Full Metal Jacket* in some ways, *Tribes* is that rare war film that celebrates rather than dehumanizes its individuals. [Kier-La Janisse]

TRILOGY OF TERROR
Director: Dan Curtis
Starring: Karen Black
Airdate: March 4, 1975   Network: ABC

 An anthology horror film starring Karen Black. The final segment involves a Zuni fetish doll. It's tough to forget.

In the first half of the 1970s, Dan Curtis became the king of TV horror. His supernatural soap opera *Dark Shadows* had become a cult series. In 1972, Curtis and author Richard Matheson made the telefilm *The Night Stalker*, which became the highest rated TV movie up to that time. One year later, the team followed it up with *The Night Strangler*. In March of 1975, Dan Curtis directed a three-segment anthology film based around Matheson's short stories. Karen Black was the star, appearing in all three segments in four different roles. That film was *Trilogy of Terror*.

Each of the segments is named after the lead female(s) in the tale. The first one is 'Julie,' set on a college campus. It involves lust, sleaze and an interesting twist. The second tale, 'Millicent and Therese,' is about twin sisters living in an old mansion. The third tale is 'Amelia.' A young woman buys her anthropologist boyfriend a Zuni fetish doll.

'Julie' is a decently told tale that never completely takes off. A student decides that he must possess a teacher named Julie. So, he takes her out, drugs her, blackmails her and makes her his sex slave. It's pretty sleazy. There is an implication that the student is prostituting Julie out to his friends. A twist occurs but it happens very quickly and isn't incredibly satisfying. One moment Julie is at her darkest point and then there's the twist. It feels like there's a scene missing.

'Millicent and Therese' is a lot of fun for Karen Black fans. She plays the very repressed Millicent. She also plays the blonde-haired, mini-skirted twin sister Therese. They have a very unpleasant passive-aggressive relationship. The problem with this tale is that the outcome is really obvious. One would think it was probably really obvious in 1975, too.

'Amelia' starts off slow and calm, setting the mood. It gives Karen Black time to talk on the phone with her mom and boyfriend about her life... and about a strange Zuni fetish doll. Suffice it to say, this creepy doll with the huge teeth comes alive. Amelia must fight for her life. The sequence where she does so is sharp, fast and scary. It is a triumph of sustained terror.

Trilogy of Terror starts strong but then loses its way right around the time the 'Julie' twist occurs. The film coasts along a bit, with some very interesting performances within some very obvious storytelling. This is a trick. The middle tale seems to exist to put the viewer into a state of "Oh, this is going to be just OK." Then, the Zuni doll attacks and this becomes classic. It's too bad that all three aren't up to the level of the third. But, this film is very watchable and fun. It's not the best Curtis-Matheson team up but a worthy one. [Daniel R. Budnik]

WHEN MICHAEL CALLS

Director: Philip Leacock
Starring: Ben Gazzara, Elizabeth Ashley, Karen Pearson, Michael Douglas
Airdate: February 5, 1972   Network: ABC

 A woman is distraught when she begins to receive phone calls from a relative who died fifteen years earlier.

Helen Connelly lives a satisfied life; happily settled down with her attorney husband and young daughter, when from out of the blue she begins to receive a series of disturbing phone calls. She hears a child's voice on the other end of the line—but not just any child; it is a voice eerily similar to her nephew, Michael. But Michael was believed to have died young many years ago, lost in a blizzard. And yet, if that is so, how is it that this caller knows how to relate to Helen in familiar ways and with intimate details? Is it merely someone playing a sick game, or is Michael really calling?

A solid, if ever so slightly disappointing thriller from the TV movie's golden age, *When Michael Calls* takes great care in setting up the story and crafting the suspense, but all of the good work is sadly undone as it moves toward the final act, which is of course a bit silly, but worse than that, simply dull.

The premise itself is delightfully chilling and the haunting phone calls are particularly effective. It's easy to understand why it's so often cited as one of those movies that, when seen at a certain age, stays well remembered, if albeit, as something a little scarier than it actually is. But small quibbles aside, this is an otherwise compelling and understated gem with a remarkably decent cast that deserves greater recognition.

Based on the novel of the same name by horror scribe John Farris (a big screen adaptation of another of his novels—*The Fury*—would prove to be a late-career hit for Kirk Douglas) and with a taut screenplay by James Bridges, the material—though still essentially pulp—remains top drawer. Bridges, having cut his teeth penning several episodes of *The Alfred Hitchcock Hour* in the sixties, is obviously in his comfort zone here, and would go on to have a moderately successful career behind the camera, re-teaming with Michael Douglas at the end of the decade with the theatrically released, *The China Syndrome* (1979).

Cult film actor Ben Gazzara is serviceable as the lead, though no more than that, and if there is to be any criticism leveled at the writing, it might be that there is an overemphasis on mood rather than characterization. Mostly remembered for featuring Michael Douglas in one of his earliest appearances, providing what is little more than a supporting role with some genuine substance, it really ends up being more his movie than anyone else's.

When Michael Calls—also popularly known as *Shattered Silence*—just

about ticks all the boxes one would realistically hope for given it's small screen trappings, and for the most part, has aged remarkably well. Widely available on DVD on budget labels, this is one call that's worth picking up.
[Kevin Hilton]

WHERE HAVE ALL THE PEOPLE GONE?

Director: John Llewellyn Moxey
Starring: Peter Graves, Kathleen Quinlan, George O'Hanlon Jr., Verna Bloom
Airdate: October 8, 1974   Network: NBC

 After a series of solar flares turns most people into white powder, a desperate family fights for survival.

Penned for NBC by Lewis John Carlino (*Seconds*) and Sandor Stern (*Pin*), here's a Rapture/UFO tinged sci-fi feature starring the one and only Peter Graves (who outsmarted giant grasshoppers in *Beginning of the End*) as a fossil hunting father who takes his son and daughter on vacation deep into the caverns of an L.A. hillside so they can bond as a family and find ancient stones.

While hacking at granite below ground, an earthquake strikes, forcing them back to the surface where a frightened hillbilly guide tells them they just missed a blinding white light in the sky that seems to have knocked out all the radio and TV stations. Guessing it was a harmless solar flare, the group prepares to head home, but before they can leave, the hillbilly turns pale, takes ill and dies. Shocked, they decide to bury the man but can't—as his body has vanished, leaving nothing behind but an empty pair of dungarees and a mess of white dust.

Officially freaked out, the family struggle down the mountainside toward civilization where instead of finding help and assistance, they discover empty streets, unparked cars, abandoned buildings, open doors, billowing curtains, half eaten meals and household pets gone feral—raising the question "Where have all the people gone?"

If you can forgive the partial exhumation and make-do tweaking of the plot from *Day of the Triffids* (1962), this is a fine, effective, loveable and often creepy feature brimming with low budget desolation, heaps of spilt talc, confused survivors, vacated supermarkets, sun flares, actual flares, gunfire, ridiculous animal attacks and memorable performances from Kathleen Quinlan (*My Giant*), Verna Bloom (*After Hours*), Jay W. McIntosh (*The Healers*) and George O'Hanlon Jr. (son of George Sr., the cartoon voice of Hanna-Barbera's George Jetson).

A big hit broadcast numerous times on both sides of the Atlantic, fans of UK pre-cert video tapes will be first to tell you this saw a release in 1982 on the collectible Iver Film Services label—an outfit responsible for unleashing such rare delights as *Honky* (1971), *Birds of Prey* (1973) and Andy Milligan's *Blood* (1974). [DF Dresden]

WILD WOMEN

Director: Don Taylor
Starring: Hugh O'Brian, Anne Francis, Marilyn Maxwell, Marie Windsor
Airdate: October 20, 1970   Network: ABC

 The year is 1840. With an offer of freedom, five female convicts embark on a dangerous wagon train mission into war-torn Texas.

Any movie—even a TV movie—that opens with a screaming catfight in a women's prison yard is worth more than a casual glance. If you do donate time to this harmless, smartly colored western, you'll be treated to at least three more babe-brawls, a cute, clever and often cracking script (by Richard Carr) and some fine, cut-price period piece performances from a posse of cowgirls who all trade life in the stockade for a dangerous mission into Mexican held Texas of 1840. A place where they'll deliver supplies and engineers to an American army camp in exchange for their freedom.

Led by rock-faced frontier man Hugh O'Brian (*Twins*), the troupe battle bandits, wear gingham, crack wise, load rifles, shoe horses, make pies and get drunk on sour mash and avoid anything too action packed or violent or too expensive to film. But that's okay as the sets, costumes, nifty ghost town location and great turns by Anne Francis (*Mazes and Monsters*), Sherry Jackson (*Stingray*), Marilyn Maxwell (*Rock-A-Bye Baby*), Marie Windsor (*Love Me Deadly*) and Cynthia Hull (*The Eye Creatures*) are more than enough to hold it all together.

Basically the same plot as *The Dirty Dozen* (1967), the premise theft can be forgiven here as the five girls (disguised as the wives of traveling settlers) spit and sass with the best of them in some decidedly standard western set-ups, ambushes, hoedowns and shoot-outs that are far from amazing, but well-handled and a soft goof to watch.

Produced by Aaron Spelling as an ABC Movie Of The Week, it's based on the novel *The Trailmakers* by Vincent Forte—screenwriter of Mario Bava's *Baron Blood* (1972). [DF Dresden]

YOU'LL NEVER SEE ME AGAIN

Director: Jeannot Szwarc
Starring: David Hartman, Jane Wyatt, Ralph Meeker, Jess Walton
Airdate: February 28, 1973   Network: ABC

 After a bitter argument, a troubled husband allows his wife to leave, only to have her vanish into thin air.

Remade with the same title in 1986 and based on a short story by the prolific Cornell Woolrich, David Hartman (*Island at the Top of the World*) and Jess Walton (*Return of the Mod Squad*) star as Ned and Vikki Bliss, a pair of flare wearing, candy bar eating "newlyweds" enjoying their huggy two-year honeymoon until an argument about visiting the in-laws results in a bitten hand, a bitch slap, a slammed door and the line "You'll never see me again!" which leaves grumpy architect Hartman home alone with nothing to do but go back on the smokes, have a long face, ponder regret and miss his angry spouse.

By the next evening, and with no word from his gingham wrapped gal, Hartman becomes increasingly worried about the brunette's absence and begins cold-calling relatives and co-workers. Eventually, he hits the streets with a photo and a description—all to no avail as his wife has simply disappeared into thin air. Distraught, he informs the police, who offer no help and, instead, lecture him about lovers' spats and domestic violence, which only drives him to expand his one-man search to out of state bus routes where he gets to threaten violence on oily gas station attendant Larry Watson (*Gentle Savage*).

After a while (and a weak flashback complete with echoed "You'll never see me again!" audio), the cops receive a tipoff and begin investigating the slowly unraveling Hartman, who then becomes the primary murder suspect and a fugitive from the law.

Devoid of blood and violence, but well scripted and acted, slightly gripping and capped with an odd and rewarding twist finale, the always unsurprising Szwarc (*Jaws 2*) keeps things moving, but sadly fails to make it special enough for anyone to love outright. [DF Dresden]

REVIEWS
1980–1989

Although ABC's popular Movie of the Week series had officially ceased in 1976, the "Movie of the Week" appellation stuck as all three networks continued to furiously pump out one-off telefilms, before cable and the late eighties direct-to-video markets became major competitors. The face of the TV movie hadn't really changed much during this era, but there was an unmistakable shift away from supernatural horror. To be certain, there were still bona fide classics finding their way into living rooms. Movies such as *Dark Night of the Scarecrow* (1980), *This House Possessed* (1981), and *Don't Go to Sleep* (1982) have deservedly grown into cult items, still loved by a loyal audience. But that sense of supernatural discovery that many a wide-eyed kid felt in the previous decade was quickly fading from the screen.

However, there was a short but interesting flux of "slasher wannabes," that held back on the things that made the slasher so much fun (i.e. nudity, violence) but still managed to intrigue and even scare audiences (what was up with the ending of *Hotline*, anyway?). *Deadly Lessons* (1983) is probably one of the most overt examples of this type of programming, but other pleasantly escapist thrillers like *Fantasies* (1982) and the remake of *I Saw What You Did* (1988) were up for the challenge.

Aside from horror, drama, true crime and even reunion movies saw big numbers during the decade of excess. *The Return of Perry Mason* (1985) was only outdone by *A Return to Mayberry* (1986) (although *Mason* was popular enough to spawn a series of made for TV movies that aired until Raymond Burr's death in 1993), and casts from *Gunsmoke* (1987, 1990), *Eight is Enough* (1987, 1989) and even *The Munsters* (1981) all gathered again, while fans reminisced about the good old days. (See 'You Can Go Home Again' for more about the TV reunion telefilm.)

A desire to return to simpler times may have been triggered by some of the headier TV movies and miniseries' that attempted to tackle the horrors of the Cold War. Films like *World War III* (1982), the miniseries *Amerika* (1987), and, most profoundly, *The Day After* (1983), terrified children who wondered what they would like to become *if* they grew up.

In short, the eighties present a wildly mixed bag, but while the output was hard to categorize, the product remains uniformly intriguing.

AMITYVILLE: THE EVIL ESCAPES

Director: Sandor Stern
Starring: Patty Duke, Jane Wyatt, Fredric Lehne, Peggy McCay
Airdate: May 12, 1999   Network: NBC

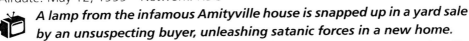 ***A lamp from the infamous Amityville house is snapped up in a yard sale by an unsuspecting buyer, unleashing satanic forces in a new home.***

The Evil Escapes is the fourth film in the seemingly never-ending *Amityville* franchise, and a particularly poor effort too. An exorcism of the original house is declared successful—though not before landing one Father Kibbler (Lehne) in the hospital—and the house contents are sold off in a yard sale. Any horror aficionado knows how the devil loves an electrical appliance, and it transpires (almost instantly) that the evil of Amityville has simply relocated; as one priest declares in an admirably straight-faced manner, "the evil in that house could transmigrate into that lamp!"

One look at the lamp in question would suggest that it might harbor sinister forces, being an elaborate affair of twisted metal in a vaguely human shape (why not "transmigrate" into something less conspicuous, like a toaster?). Nevertheless, it's snapped up by Helen Royce (McCay) for her sister Alice Leacock (Wyatt) in California, its arrival coinciding with that of Alice's daughter and grandchildren who are moving in after the death of her son-in-law.

From then on, all the usual horror tropes are played out: black sludge oozes from the taps; the waste disposal unit switches itself on just in time to shred someone's arm; a family pet dies horribly; all the household electrical equipment develops a fault. The creepy blonde girl is here as well, communing with her dead father through the lamp, *Poltergeist* style. There's perhaps one scene that verges on the genuinely creepy, when a man's arm suddenly embraces mother Nancy (Duke) in bed, but otherwise the whole film is predictable to the point of being mind numbingly boring. Just to remind us of the lamp's malevolence, we see it switching itself on and off at such regular intervals that it becomes quite hilarious (it's not plugged in, obviously); IMDb user thekingofplain suggests using this as the basis for a drinking game, but I'd advise this only if you want to get fantastically wasted.

Most of the action happens in the final five minutes, when Father Kibbler arrives in the nick of time to save the souls of everyone in the house—the creepy blonde kid levitates and stabs him, before Grandma Leacock athletically throws the lamp through the attic window to smash onto the cliffs below. (Why this would end the matter when we've already seen the evil presence move—sorry, transmigrate—from the lamp to the house is a mystery, but I suppose you need as many avenues as possible left open for all those sequels.) The final scene is by far the least scary of the film, as the family's overweight tabby cat meows plaintively at the wreckage of the lamp before turning to the camera, its eyes bright red. Be afraid, be very afraid. [Jennifer Wallis]

THE BAD SEED

Director: Paul Wendkos
Starring: Blair Brown, Lynn Redgrave, David Carradine, Carrie Wells
Airdate: February 7, 1985   Network: ABC

 A remake of the 1956 psychological thriller; a mother realizes that her young daughter may be a murderer.

Paul Wendkos' updated adaptation of William March's 1954 novel has been given an unfair shake in light of its celebrated screen predecessor (directed by Mervyn LeRoy in 1956), but it remains a highly disturbing work in its own right.

Blair Brown stars as Christine Penmark, a single mother (?) who starts to suspect that her picture-perfect nine-year-old daughter Rachel (Wells in one of her few screen roles) is responsible for the "accidental" death of one of her classmates while on a seaside school outing. At first Christine questions whether she's spoiled the girl too much, but when she finally catches her daughter in the act, and can see the child weaving through the subsequent interrogation with expert manipulative tactics, she realizes that Rachel is a sociopath, with no conscience. When it is revealed that Christine's long-term night terrors about being chased through a cornfield by a murderess are in fact memories of her biological mother—famed serial murderer Bessie Denker (based on real-life killer Belle Gunness)—she accepts the blame for her daughter's behavior due to her own tainted genetics.

The update to 1985 brings a wealth of enthusiastic expository dialog about serial killers from David Ogden Stiers (who plays Christine's friend Emory), with Lynn Redgrave starring as his therapy-obsessed wife, the latter in full-on fabulous eighties self-help mode. Unfortunately, the film suffers due to its two lackluster central performances—Carrie Wells in particular is no Patty McCormack. The real prize in the cast is David Carradine as the deviant, drunken maintenance man Leroy, who finds a kindred spirit in the pint-sized killer. While Leroy was a major component of the story in the previous versions, the lecherous pedophilic aspects of the character are really let loose here—he grabs Rachel's tights, comments on being able to see her underpants beneath her dress, teases her about going to the electric chair ("Maybe they have a pink one for little girls"). There is something eerily romantic about their secret interplay, partially because it's the only honest relationship in the film. But ultimately she's an outwardly cherubic little girl and he's a drunk, so she easily maintains the upper hand.

The tale's many layers of challenging subject matter are unfettered by the Hays Code that prevented certain aspects of March's novel from being addressed in the 1956 version. Aside from the restoration of the novel's original controversial ending, another hallmark of the update is that the signs of substance abuse as stress relief are ever-present throughout the story. "It's times like these I wish I were a drinker," says the father of the young boy Rachel murdered for his penmanship medal. Leroy's alcoholism is contrasted with Christine's turn to nicotine and sedatives. Everyone has their means of forgetting.

All versions of *The Bad Seed* pose their own unique take on the "nature versus nurture" debate, but it's somehow fitting that the story's most daring aspects found a welcome platform on the small screen, beamed directly into the living rooms of worried mothers everywhere. [Kier-La Janisse]

BATES MOTEL

Director: Richard Rothstein
Starring: Bud Cort, Lori Petty, Moses Gunn, Gregg Henry
Airdate: July 12, 1987   Network: NBC

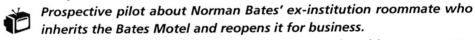 ***Prospective pilot about Norman Bates' ex-institution roommate who inherits the Bates Motel and reopens it for business.***

Now the title of a moderately successful television series, this strange entry in the *Psycho* legacy, little known as it was anyway, has been swept (and rightly so) even further under the carpet of obscure big screen spin-offs.

Originally conceived as the pilot for a potential TV series exploring odd goings-on in the Bates Motel, it's easy to see why this incarnation failed to receive the desired greenlight for a full season and, instead, went on to become much better recognized as that hardly witnessed made for TV movie with its confusing "Is it, or is it not, a genuine *Psycho* film?" VHS cover artwork that could be found (unrented, of course) in most video shops of the eighties. Indeed, it is now quite a rarity.

It begins promisingly enough, with Bud Cort (forever the boy in *Harold and Maude*) as Alex West, a young man who suddenly inherits the infamous Bates property after his friend, father-figure and fellow inmate at the local mental hospital, Norman (not played by Anthony Perkins, but by his stuntman throughout the *Psycho* series—Kurt Paul), passes away. On entering the motel, he runs into Willie (Petty), a homeless woman who has taken up residence there and decides to befriend the new owner in a bid to stay on and to help Alex as he struggles to adjust to life outside of the asylum, which isn't easy, as he begins having disturbing visions, among them—a woman dressed in black that just might be "Mother," returned from the grave to wreak havoc.

It's hard to tell what Richard Rothstein, in his capacity as writer, producer and director, was hoping to achieve with this effort that seems specifically designed to turn off fans of the big screen franchise, only to instead, opt for a kind of one-man Abbott and Costello style of comedy and faux *boo* scares that were charming in the forties, but sort of moronic in the eighties.

The main problem is that it can't decide what it wants to be. It's at once a screwball comedy, and then, during the last thirty minutes, goes off on a wild tangent, as we follow the newly re-opened motel's first guest, a middle aged woman that's intending to commit suicide, being drawn into joining a frat house party full of teenage ghosts (led by a young Jason Bateman) that are connected in that they all killed themselves. This last part, played fairly straight, is an overly long and depressing sequence, and what's more, it totally abandons the main cast, whom we only rejoin as the whole *Scooby Doo* wraparound reaches its predictable climax.

The hero and victim of all this is Bud Cort, who tries in vain to navigate a linear performance throughout all the half-realized nonsense that it seems impossible for one ninety-minute movie to contain. While, surely Lori Petty is the villain, incredibly irritating as the nomadic runaway with a heart of gold who can't help but run off at the mouth given any opportunity to sound like the whining, petulant child her character is. In short, it's just plain annoying. [Kevin Hilton]

THE BEST LITTLE GIRL IN THE WORLD

Director: Sam O'Steen
Starring: Jennifer Jason Leigh, Eva Marie Saint, Charles Durning, Jason Miller
Airdate: May 11, 1981   Network: ABC

 All-American teenager Casey Powell develops an unhealthy obsession with her weight, leading to anorexia and hospitalization.

Based on the 1978 novel of the same name, this ABC Movie of the Week came at a time when eating disorders were increasingly on the agenda in the American media. That year saw the release of Hilde Bruche's *The Golden Cage*, an analysis of anorexia for a general readership, while *The Best Little Girl in the World* was penned by psychologist Steven Levenkron, whose name is indelibly associated with that of Karen Carpenter, arguably his most famous patient.

As a dramatization of a book penned by a specialist in the subject, the film is unusually thoughtful in its portrayal of eating disorders. The reasons for Casey's (Jennifer Jason Leigh) descent into anorexia are various, but at the heart of the matter is a volatile family life. Though presenting an outward image of the all-American family, conversations in the house repeatedly turn into shouted rows—significantly, these often occur around the dining table, with Casey left alone as her mother, father, and older sister storm off to continue their argument elsewhere. Subtle details—such as Casey's arranging of her clothes hangers to leave an equal amount of space between each, or her frantic cracking of her knuckles—point to an underlying obsessive nature without laboring the point.

As the film progresses, subtlety is lost to more graphic illustrations as Casey's weight drops to dangerously low levels. A shot of her from behind disrobing for a doctor's examination reveals a startlingly skeletal frame (this looks like a body double or prosthesis, though the jury's still out on that one), and when admitted to a specialist clinic is subjected to hyperalimentation (the administration of nutrients via injection into a vein), which is presented as an unpleasant and painful process. The clinic doesn't come out in a particularly good light (a fellow patient manages to hoard pills to commit suicide, and

TV Guide ad for *Bates Motel*, an early attempt to bring the success of *Psycho* to the small screen.

Casey easily escapes through a side door when no one's looking). Rather, it is kindly psychologist Clay Orlovsky (Jason Miller) who is the guiding influence, though one has to question the wisdom of a psychiatrist declaring to his young female patient, "I love you."

It is Orlovsky who forces Casey's family to face up to their bad behavior, and indeed throughout the film there is a keen awareness of the outside factors to blame for her condition. Her classmates pore over fashion magazines (one mother has promised her daughter a glamorous dress if she loses weight); her ballet teacher suggests she might make a good dancer if she lost "a couple of pounds here and there." Most explicitly, a doctor pins the blame on fashion magazines with models looking like "cadavers," linking such images to a national obsession with thinness.

It's interesting and well thought-out on the whole, but the film's slow-pace certainly doesn't help the already downbeat subject matter. [Jennifer Wallis]

THE BOY WHO DRANK TOO MUCH

Director: Jerrold Freedman
Starring: Scott Baio, Lance Kerwin, Ed Lauter, Mariclare Costello
Airdate: February 6, 1980   Network: CBS

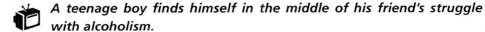 *A teenage boy finds himself in the middle of his friend's struggle with alcoholism.*

Seventies small screen idol Lance Kerwin plays Billy Carpenter, a high school hockey benchwarmer who takes on a handful when he befriends teammate Kenneth "Buff" Saunders (Baio). Buff lives with his widowed father—a former hockey pro turned alcoholic bartender—and he's been in five different high schools and has a rep as a troublemaker despite being highly intelligent and a potential star athlete himself. He's antisocial, and shrugs off Billy's incessant attempts to make friends with him, but the two are stuck together when Buff loses a couple teeth in a hockey game and Billy is charged with taking him to the hospital for stitches. As the two embark on a delicate friendship, Billy notices that Buff dips into the sauce rather freely for his age, seemingly to spite his father.

Coaxed into attending an intimate house party, Buff brings the beer, gets smashed, punches out a classmate (Dan Shor of *TRON* and *Ghoulies III: Ghoulies Go to College*)… and then wets his pants. When he gets enrolled in an AA residential program against his will and his deadbeat dad won't show for the meetings, Billy volunteers to sit in, much to the chagrin of his own parents (perennial screen grouch Ed Lauter, and Mariclare Costello, the pasty hippie from horror classic *Let's Scare Jessica to Death*). A pretty heavy responsibility for a fifteen-year-old kid with an active social life, considering the meetings are five nights a week. Buff and his dad lie to each other about their drinking and the efforts they're going to curtail it, and Billy is stuck in the middle of two alcoholics who won't face the truth.

Baio shrugs and grunts through most of the film, his character acting flamboyantly irresponsible and hostile to everyone barring a few moments of genuine enthusiasm related to his ability to memorize facts and statistics. Despite the title, this is really Kerwin's show and he gives a solid dramatic performance (until the end when the whole thing explodes into overwrought histrionics). That said, while its portrayal of teen alcoholism seems somewhat square at times (see *Sarah T.--- Portrait of a Teenage Alcoholic* for a more believable take on the issue), the Baio/Kerwin dream-team remains a pretty compelling draw for the film. This telefilm was based on a novel of the same name by Shep Greene. [Kier-La Janisse]

BRIDGE ACROSS TIME

Director: E.W. Swackhamer
Starring: David Hasselhoff, Stepfanie Kramer, Randolph Mantooth, Adrienne Barbeau
Airdate: November 22, 1985   Network: NBC

When London Bridge is moved to Lake Havasu, it also brings along the essence of Jack the Ripper, who is reborn and terrorizes the town.
Stranger than fiction: London Bridge was dismantled in the late sixties and shipped off to Lake Havasu, Arizona, where it now serves as an oddball tourist attraction. While several films have used the bridge as part of its background, this telefilm may be the only project to utilize it as an actual plot point. Combining the crazy story behind the bridge with the unsolved Jack the Ripper case is interesting to say the least, and *Bridge Across Time* probably works best if you let go of logic and reasoning (which, honestly, often needs to happen when watching some of these films).

The true-crime story of Jack the Ripper has been mythologized by many an imaginative writer, and having the cold blooded killer travel through time isn't all that original either (both the theatrical film *Time after Time* and the *Fantasy Island* episode 'With Affection, Jack the Ripper' are two wildly varied examples), but despite rehashing the concept, *Bridge* is a captivating, if completely silly, little TVM that uses its straight face to carry across the preposterous premise.

David Hasselhoff and Stepfanie Kramer (*Hunter*) are good in their leading roles (with Hasselhoff giving an earnest turn as a guilt-ridden cop), but it is the seasoned supporting cast that carries this film into more watchable territory. Clu Gulager, Ken Swofford, Randolph Mantooth, Adrienne Barbeau (in some seriously shoulder-padded frocks), Rose Marie (!) and Lane Smith

The time: 1985
The crime: Murder
The suspect: Jack The Ripper!

The only ones who can stop him are his next targets!

BRIDGE ACROSS TIME

Starring
David Hasselhoff
"Knight Rider"
and
Stephanie Kramer
"Hunter"

FRIDAY NIGHT WORLD PREMIERE
MOVIE! 8PM 4, 10

Above: Jennifer Jason Leigh doesn't want to be *The Best Little Girl in the World*. Right: *TV Guide* ad for *Bridge Across Time* aka *Terror at the London Bridge*.

are prepared to do battle with a kooky idea, and they bring it home.

Bridge is just one of four films that stalwart small screen director E.W. Swackhamer helmed in 1985! Known mostly for episodic fare, the confident Swackhamer gives this TVM an impressively slick feel, and while the murder scenes obviously lack much in the way of gore and violence, the by-the-numbers stalk and restrained slash is interesting, if not completely suspenseful.

A late-entry horror TVM, screenwriter William F. Nolan (*Logan's Run*) crams a lot of ideas into his thriller, and for the most part, each subplot reaches its full conclusion—although it's unlikely the audience cares too much about Hasselhoff working through the guilt of killing a young teen by accident while he was a police officer in Chicago. Think about it—who can say no to seeing a *Knight Rider* vs. Jack the Ripper smackdown? *Bridge* is available on DVD under its aka *Terror at London Bridge*. (Another aka is *The Arizona Ripper*.) [Amanda Reyes]

THE BURNING BED

Director: Robert Greenwald
Starring: Farrah Fawcett, Paul LeMat, Richard Masur, Grace Zabriske
Airdate: October 8, 1984   Network: NBC

 An abused wife takes matters into her own hands when she sets the couple's bed on fire while he sleeps.

Based on the Faith McNulty book about battered wife Francine Hughes' murder of her abusive husband, *The Burning Bed* was director Robert Greenwald's second Emmy-nominated television film (he produced the Olympic massacre drama *21 Hours at Munich* in 1976) and a landmark in changing attitudes on the matter of domestic violence.

Charlie's Angels star Farrah Fawcett surprised critics by turning in a powerful performance as Francine Hughes, who reluctantly marries her moody high school sweetheart Mickey (LeMat) and finds herself at the bottom end of a thirteen-year cycle of physical and emotional abuse. The film begins with Francine's arrest and is recounted through flashbacks as she details her dire history to her defense lawyer (TV regular Richard Masur).

It was the former Angel's first such dramatic role, and one that earned her an Emmy nod (she lost out to Joanne Woodward for the CBS movie *Do You*

Lance Kerwin and Scott Baio take on the message movie in *The Boy Who Drank Too Much*.

Remember Love). Paul LeMat is perfectly cast to play the childlike, charismatic lover who relies on his imposing bulk when his ego is threatened, and the frequent scenes of domestic violence are unrelenting and fairly graphic for the time. But it's the complex character drama that makes the film so watchable. The supporting cast includes character actors James Callahan and Grace Zabriskie as the conflicted parents of Francine's abuser, who see what is happening but remain loyal to their son. Francine's own mother encourages her to tough it out, saying, "You make a hard bed, you have to lay in it." Both maternal figures are complicit in Francine's ongoing abuse, possibly because they have been acclimatized to such abuse themselves. Only her best friend Gaby, played by the spunky Penelope Milford (*Coming Home*) urges her to leave, which only results in Francine being further isolated from her one means of emotional support.

Through over a decade of terror she maintains her resolve, despite a monotonous roster of government employees insisting they can't help her. Finally she commits the crime that gives the film its title.

Hughes was acquitted after her lawyer's plea of temporary insanity. It was a monumental decision and case, and the premiere of the film adaptation stirred up a loud response from North American audiences, prompting hundreds of calls to domestic abuse crisis centers (one center in Massachusetts reported 150 calls that night alone), not only by victims of batterers but by batterers themselves.[1] It premiered on October 8, the first day of National Domestic Violence Awareness Week.

It drew fifty-two percent of the television audience when it premiered; making it NBC's highest rated made for TV movie of the season, and the seventeenth most successful to this day. Director Robert Greenwald has since become an outspoken political documentarian (*Outfoxed: Rupert Murdoch's War on Journalism*), but all these accomplishments combined may never equal the lingering reputation of his 1980 film, *Xanadu*. [Kier-La Janisse]

THE CASE OF THE HILLSIDE STRANGLERS

Director: Steven Gethers
Starring: Richard Crenna, Dennis Farina, Billy Zane, Tony Plana
Airdate: April 2, 1989   Network: NBC

> *A Los Angeles police officer deals with his own problems while in a race against time to stop the Hillside Stranglers before they kill again.*

In the brief period between November 1977 and February 1978, forty-three-year-old car upholsterer Angelo Buono and his younger cousin, Kenneth

---

1 Paula Krebs, "Burning Bed Prompts Floods of Calls" in *Off Our Backs*, Vol. 14, No. 10 (Nov 1984), p.8.

Bianchi, held the greater community of Los Angeles in the grip of fear, as they embarked on a violent campaign of abduction, rape, torture and murder that left at least ten women dead, their bodies often dumped on the hills above Hollywood, resulting in the press dubbing the killer "The Hillside Strangler" (the plural being added following the couple's arrest and exposure). While the majority of those killed were streetwalkers, the pair also claimed among their victims a ballet student, two teenaged school kids playing hooky, and an aspiring actress.

Based on a 1985 book by true crime author Darcy O'Brien, *The Case of the Hillside Stranglers* was one of several telemovies based on infamous serial killer cases that were being produced during the 1980s and early-1990s (the best of which were *The Deliberate Stranger* in 1986, with Mark Harmon as Ted Bundy, and 1992's *To Catch a Killer*, starring Brian Dennehy as John Wayne Gacy).

Told from the point of view of the two killers as well as the lead cop investigating the killings, *The Case of the Hillside Stranglers* is driven along by the morbid, yet strong and undeniable, fascination which the story holds, as well as a trio of strong performances in the lead roles. Dennis Farina, a former Chicago policeman, seems an unconventional but interesting and ultimately effective choice to play Buono, the self-absorbed "Italian Stallion" (as he liked his women to refer to him), and he has good support from—and chemistry with—Billy Zane as the younger Bianchi. Zane has a quirkiness to him that suits his character, who, after his arrest, tried (and failed) to claim the oft-used multiple personalities defense. The reliable Richard Crenna also brings some strength and presence to the piece, as the investigating sergeant, Bob Grogan. The real Bob Grogan also makes an appearance in the movie, playing the cop who arrests Bianchi in Washington in 1979 (the arrest ultimately led to the solving of the Hillside Strangler killings, which had suddenly stopped a year earlier after the cousins had a falling out in Los Angeles).

Being a telemovie, the violence and some of the more depraved tortures Buono and Bianchi subjected their unfortunate and terrified victims to have been toned down somewhat, but there is still a nice atmosphere of L.A. sleaze that permeates the movie, and it is overall a better and more effective production than the 2004 film on the same case, *The Hillside Strangler*. There was also a direct-to-DVD movie called *Rampage: The Hillside Strangler Murders* released in 2006, but the definitive film on this terrifying and gripping case is yet to appear. [John Harrison]

Clockwise from top: Patty Duke and Jane Wyatt looking pensive in *Amityville: The Evil Escapes*; a brooding Farrah Fawcett in an ad for *The Burning Bed*; and mob violence is highlighted in a promotional ad for *Dark Night of the Scarecrow*.

CAVE IN!

Director: Georg Fenady
Starring: Dennis Cole, Susan Sullivan, Leslie Nielsen, Julie Sommars
Airdate: June 19, 1983   Network: NBC

 A wanted cop killer hides among a tour group that becomes trapped underground in a cave-in.

Terrible. But recommended. Here's another classic Movie of the Week from Warner Bros. Television and "Mr. D" himself—Irwin Allen. This time it's all about the man-made and natural failings at the beautiful underground passageways of the Five Mile Caverns in Yellowstone Park.

Basically there's only the small matter of a location change separating this feature from Allen's *The Night the Bridge Fell Down* (1983), seeing as it, too, mixes a standard disaster scenario with a deranged gunman situation.

With few scenes actually filmed in picturesque Yellowstone, much of the proceedings are shot on crappy, confined, ever-collapsing interior sets built on the WB backlot, that the cast (and what a cast) can never seem to escape from. Opening titles are brief and cursory, so we're thankfully given a quick character introduction to our players, and then it's straight into the obviously cheap and fake caves, where—shock horror—the group are imprisoned by a cave in.

Trapped and with a killer among them, Dennis Cole (*Fatal Encounter*), Susan Sullivan (*Killer's Delight*), and Julie Sommars (*The Harness*) all act scared, while vacationing cop Leslie Nielsen (*Surf Ninjas*) is soon troubled by laughable flashbacks to a recent shootout that got his partner killed and ancient pebble expert Ray Milland (*Frogs*) is ignored and left alone to piss and moan about stalactites and hateful relationships in a highly acidic display that makes great use of his apparent ill health and spiteful turn of phrase.

In fact, all the cast supply a generous amount of comedic gold via flashbacks to ridiculous skits which add little to the film overall, but that's not the main reason you should hunt this down: You should do that just to see the fantastic turns by the very straight-faced Nielsen and Milland—a pair who seem to be involved in a private cut-throat competition to out-gripe, out-bitch and out-bastard each other till one of them has died from it. [DF Dresden]

CONDOR

Director: Virgil W. Vogel
Starring: Ray Wise, Wendy Kilbourne, Vic Polizos, Craig Stevens
Airdate: August 10, 1986   Network: ABC

In a futuristic L.A., Condor agent Ray Wise and his robot partner hunt a villain intent on destroying the city.

Looking way older than 1986, produced by Orion Television and set in a far off, futuristic L.A. of 1999, Ray Wise (*Dead End*) stars as old school rebel cop Chris Proctor, a dishy, dumb and dozy misanthrope working for an international peace keeping force called Condor—a government department that seems to hire its staff more for their appalling 1980s fashion sense than their criminal detection skills.

Operating from Hampton Towers, wisecracking Ray wears futuristic UGG boots, never buttons his shirt properly and keeps his suit jacket sleeves rolled up as far as they can go. He misses his just-killed partner and moans when his boss, Craig Stevens (*God Is My Co-Pilot*), assigns him a new, talky partner in the guise of Wendy Kilbourne (*Turn Back The Clock*)—a "computer in drag" that wins Ray's acceptance by beating him at arm wrestling.

Before long, the duo are chasing a superterrorist called The Black Widow (Carolyn Seymour), a leather-clad master criminal (with a jet pack) who plans to kill Wise and blow up Hollywood after escaping from jail.

Lazily scripted by Len Janson and Chuck Menville, devoid of any major SFX and little more than a bog-standard cop/buddy movie given a quick wipe with the *Bladerunner* cloth, it'll hardly knock anyone's socks off with its originality, but so what? Much of the fun here is from the off-kilter future society that has robot burger bars, radio watches, laser pistols, mini choppers, in-car computers, exploding models, face punching and a near hysterical Wise who bounces around the set looking for something to stamp on, snort or complain about.

Terrible, but recommended, it's cheezy junk with a stuffed crust that's hard to hate, and another chipped gem from director Vogel—a man responsible for classic episodes of *Honey West*, *Knight Rider*, *Mike Hammer*, *Wagon Train*, *Mission: Impossible*, *Miami Vice* and *Quantum Leap*. [DF Dresden]

DARK NIGHT OF THE SCARECROW

Director: Frank De Felitta
Starring: Charles Durning, Robert F. Lyons, Larry Drake, Jocelyn Brando
Airdate: October 24, 1981   Network: CBS

 After the vigilante execution of a small-town mentally challenged man, <u>something</u> comes back for revenge.

In a small Southern farming community, Bubba Ritter—a kindly adult but with the mental development of a child—shocks the entire town when it appears that his playing in secret with Marylee, a little local girl, has resulted in her bloody death. For Otis P. Hazelrigg—a privately tormented man himself but with a strong influence over others—it's the final straw, and he gathers together a small posse of men to take the law into its own hands.

Chasing Bubba into a field they find him hiding inside the costume of a scarecrow. But the ruse is short-lived and the vigilantes have their justice, shooting him dead. But something is wrong; the girl that Bubba had supposedly killed—is alive—he had in fact been her savior.

Following a brief and unsuccessful trial to lock away those responsible for Bubba's murder, the town begins to revert back to normal, until a sinister presence begins to reveal itself to the guilty ones and they begin to meet their demise in ever more grisly ways. Are these just accidents—or, as some claim to have witnessed, does a scarecrow walk among them?

Originally conceived as a theatrical feature, but then tailored for television, this is particularly macabre material for the small screen. Presumably greenlit on account that it fed into the hugely popular slasher cycle that was then enjoying its zenith. It does, by necessity, stray away from gory visuals but replaces them with genuinely atmospheric chills that are consistently creepy throughout.

Although Hollywood veteran Strother Martin was intended to play the lead role as the vicious Hazelrigg (but sadly passed away before production), Charles Durning excels in the part, giving a multilayered performance that invites the audience at once to despise him, pity him and by the end, almost sympathize for him. Indeed, as bad guy parts go, Hazelrigg—a postman— is an excellent emanation of the dangerously downtrodden blue collar American worker that lives on the fringes and in the shadows of society; a sort of Travis Bickle by way of *Deliverance*. He's frustrated, with no outlet save for violence. In one of the more disturbing elements of the film, it is heavily suggested that his murder of Bubba is motivated less by revenge and more by jealousy, envious of the mentally challenged man's close relationship with the girl.

Larry Drake as Bubba is also well cast. Despite later achieving cult recognition as a villain in genre-fare such as *Darkman* (1990), *Darkman II* (1995) and *Dr. Giggles* (1992), he has rarely been better than in this, where he plays the scared and confused victim to perfection.

Single-handedly responsible for the scarecrow subgenre of horror films and sharing more than a couple of thematic traits with the much later produced and more popular *The Crow* (1994), the movie's influence has a long reach considering it's still widely unknown.

Boasting a compelling lead performance, a pace that rarely slacks and a hauntingly enigmatic ending, it's high time it found the audience it deserves. It's technically efficient, too. Novelist and sometime filmmaker Frank De Felitta brings the goods in what could easily have been forgettable hokum. Of course, that's not to say it isn't hokum—because it is—but it's the very best kind. [Kevin Hilton]

THE DAY AFTER

Director: Nicholas Meyer
Starring: Jason Robards, JoBeth Williams, John Lithgow, Steve Guttenberg
Airdate: November 20, 1983   Network: ABC

The aftermath of nuclear war between the United States and the Soviet Union as experienced by the residents of Kansas and Missouri. The Day After holds several distinctions for the TV movie genre that have yet to be surpassed. It remains the most-watched television movie of all time with over one hundred million viewers. For comparison, that number has only been surpassed by the finale of *M*A*S*H* and airings of the Super Bowl. One of the few households not watching ABC that night was the White House. President Ronald Reagan and the Joint Chiefs of Staff had received private screenings of the film earlier in the month, with the President later remarking that the film left him "greatly depressed." In addition to unprecedented success, *The Day After* is one of the only films—television or theatrical—to have had a major effect on American foreign relations. Reagan would go on to remark in his memoirs that *The Day After* directly lead to the 1987 Intermediate-Range Nuclear Forces Treaty with the Soviet Union, which was a large step toward easing the nuclear tensions of the Cold War.

As implied by the title, *The Day After* is post-apocalyptic cinema albeit of a decidedly different stripe, being neither action nor science fiction but a character-driven drama. This is an *immediate*-post-apocalypse film, and rather than focusing on battle-worn heroes à la *The Road Warrior* or similar works, *The Day After* shows a world of universal victimhood. The film specifically focuses on Lawrence, Kansas, and Kansas City, Missouri, and how the lives of individuals are affected by the onset and aftermath of World War III. *The Day After* spends little time addressing the issues surrounding the conflict, instead only providing the viewer with snippets of information via radio or television broadcasts. The effect is to minimize the emphasis on the US and USSR as nation-states, and to allow the story to be told without the trappings of nationalism typically associated with nuclear war cinema.

The pivotal event occurs at exactly the one-hour mark, bisecting *The Day After* neatly into equal portions pre- and post-apocalypse. The delaying of the incident allows sufficient time for the audience to know the characters well, specifically Jason Robards' Dr. Oakes who emerges as the main focus. Oakes' struggle to treat the wounded in a hospital is one of the three perspectives the film offers; the others being that of an Air Force officer and a rural farmer. Each of the three men's stories is ultimately the same; a tale of ever-increasing tragedy for those unlucky few who survive the initial blasts. The poignant final scene ends with Oakes being comforted by a fellow survivor; a brief moment of hope that is slyly and effectively undercut by the camera pulling back to reveal the desolation that surrounds the two men.

The Day After is strikingly similar to the more-acclaimed BBC television movie *Threads* from 1984, which doubtlessly was influenced by its American cousin. Of the two, *Threads* is distinctly more factually accurate in regards to the effects of nuclear war, but takes a detached, almost clinical approach to its subject matter. *The Day After* therefore emerges as the more effective of the two works, despite *Threads* inarguably being the more viscerally horrifying. *The Day After*'s strength is its moderation; by downplaying the effects of nuclear war, it somehow manages to make the prospect of it all the more terrifying. [David Ray Carter]

DEADLY LESSONS

Director: William Wiard
Starring: Diane Franklin, Donna Reed, Larry Wilcox, Ally Sheedy
Airdate: March 7, 1983   Network: ABC

During a summer session at an all girls' school, a crazed killer picks off the students one by one.

Released at the tail end of the slasher craze, *Deadly Lessons* may be the small screen slasher that follows the most tropes of the subgenre (1979's *She's Dressed to Kill* may qualify as well, but that's another story). Most of the elements—minus the two biggies: violence and nudity—are here and ready to set the stage for a decent stalk and slash flick. We've got an all girls' school set out in desolation and brimming with a group of vivacious but privileged young women, a couple of cute male employees, a priggish headmistress (played by Donna Reed, no less), and a gaggle of red herrings. Unfortunately, despite a game cast and a script that wants to hit the right beats, *Deadly Lessons* is convoluted and, worst of all, a bit boring.

Director William Wiard brought so much flair to *This House Possessed* and *Kicks* but drops the ball on this telefilm. Aside from a great score by Ian Freebairn-Smith, *Deadly Lessons* is missing Wiard's slicker savvy, leaving audiences with a rather dry version of a slasher film. What saves the whole affair from becoming a total loss is the bevy of soon-to-be famous faces (and voices!) that permeate the production. Ally Sheedy, Bill Paxton and the future Bart Simpson (Nancy Cartwright) are featured in important roles, with Sheedy managing to be both likeable and unpleasant at the same time. Other familiar faces include Rick Rossovich, Renée Jones, Krista Errickson, Ellen Geer and Deena Freeman (trivia: Freeman and Cartwright appeared together in the 1981 pilot *In Trouble*). Fourth billed Final Girl Diane Franklin is plucky and adorable, and despite limited character development, she is easy to root for. Larry Wilcox is also good as the gorgeous but serious cop who is intent on solving the murders.

Playing more like a nighttime soap (which is not a knock), *Deadly Lessons* gives its older characters the meatier, albeit melodramatic, material. Headmistress Ward's affair with the equestrian coach (David Ackroyd) tangles itself up with insecurities and jealousies, leading to a plot twist that explains the killer's motives, and allows ice-cold Ward a chance to not be a total bitch. If only the rest of the telefilm played on that sort of juicy overwrought tension…

Donna Reed came out of a four-year absence to make *Deadly Lessons*. Unfortunately, the actress was unhappy with the film and basically called it a quickie that had no interest in producing anything good (granted, she claimed to have an equally unhappy time working on the nighttime soap *Dallas* from 1984–85). But her turn as the puritanical headmistress will certainly surprise fans of *The Donna Reed Show*.

Deadly Lessons ran against the telefilm *Living Proof: The Hank Williams*

Jr. Story, which came in at #19 in the Nielsen for the week, while this small screen slasher didn't make a show in the top twenty. However, while *Deadly Lessons* seems lost thanks to little or no airplay in the 2000s, it remains a much sought after curiosity for slasher completests. [Amanda Reyes]

DEATH OF A SALESMAN

Director: Volker Schlondorff
Starring: Dustin Hoffman, Charles Durning, Kate Reid, Stephen Lang, John Malkovich
Airdate: September 15, 1985   Network: CBS

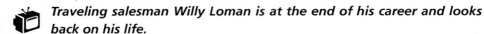 ***Traveling salesman Willy Loman is at the end of his career and looks back on his life.***

Dustin Hoffman has specialized in playing anxious, desperate and harassed characters in films like *The Graduate* (1967), *Midnight Cowboy* (1969) and *Straw Dogs* (1971), men who are—or feel—marginalized in society, and so the part of Willy Loman in Arthur Miller's classic play *Death of a Salesman* is a perfect match for his persona. While Willy is defiant against the world, he is gradually revealed as a weak, pitiable figure who has been worn down by a lifetime of disappointment. The opening scene, with Willy driving a car at night, encapsulates the character's place in society: he seems cut off from everything, with other cars heard sounding their horns and passing him by, giving the impression that he's already being left behind by the world around him.

This opening scene, like the rest of the film, is staged entirely on sets. While this is evident in the driving scene, a striking crane shot in the Loman house early on in the film pulls back and up *through* the ceiling, leaving no

This promo for the small screen slasher *Deadly Lessons* even mimics its theatrical inspiration in the ad campaign.

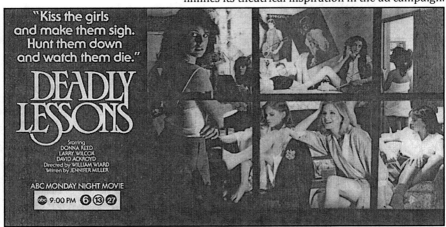

doubt of the artifice. This stylized approach is deliberately heightened in the set design and staging of scenes, which lends the film an oddly unreal feel, often seeming like an embodiment of Willy's fractured mind, where the past frequently intrudes on the present. The film is drained of color and plunged into shadow for a number of Willy's scenes, with the muted palette feeling almost black and white in places. In a number of scenes, the camera positions Willy as a diminished figure in the frame, most evident in a meeting with his boss, Howard (Jon Polito).

Director Volker Schlondorff and his crew—including cinematographer Michael Ballhaus (later a regular collaborator with Martin Scorsese) and composer Alex North—use striking settings, color, music, editing, and lighting and camera techniques to turn the play into a boldly cinematic piece of television. Additionally, the film features a stellar cast. As well as Hoffman, there's John Malkovich as Willy's indecisive son Biff, whose conflict with Willy powers much of the drama, Stephen Lang as Willy's other son, the carefree Happy, Charles Durning as a friendly neighbor, and Kate Reid as Willy's wife Linda, who conveys both support for Willy but also a subtle weariness about her circumstances, with Willy frequently dismissive of her in front of others. Nevertheless, she is also pragmatic, feeling that their simple life is actually rich enough, even if Willy fails to see it.

The UK DVD of *Death of a Salesman* by IN2FILM includes the film plus a candid, revealing feature-length documentary, *Private Conversations: On the Set of Death of a Salesman* (1985), which sheds light on the production process and stands as a memorable piece of filmmaking in its own right. The documentary also shows how this version of *Death of a Salesman* resulted in one of the most striking and unusual interpretations of a stage play ever created for television, a production that's big in ambition and outstanding in execution. [Martyn Bamber]

THE DEMON MURDER CASE

Director: William Hale
Starring: Kevin Bacon, Liane Langland, Cloris Leachman, Eddie Albert
Airdate: March 6, 1983   Network: NBC

Terrorized by a demon, an overwhelmed family asks an exorcist to rid their child of the devil inside.

Despite its alternate title, *The Rhode Island Murders*, this is based on an actual case of the "devil made me do it" murder that occurred in Connecticut, and opens with a written warning explaining that the following feature is a partially accurate re-enactment of a terrible episode of demonic possession that struck a suburban family via its young ward, Brian.

Normally a nice kid, Brian (Charles Fields) flips out one day for no reason and starts hovering around his bedroom talking in a raspy voice (supplied by Harvey Fierstein). A fine mess of bad manners and stained pajamas, he punches his parents and himself, and is soon reduced to just two actions: blowing raspberries and pulling a seizure face. Luckily, evil child specialist Andy Griffith (*Fatal Vision*) is only a phone call away, and it's not long before he and many others are waving their arms and loudly invoking God to rid the child of the evil entity.

Also on hand is nosy reporter Cloris Leachman (*Beer Fest*), who wants to expose the event and publicize the story to boost her own profile, while back at the house, perplexed Liane Langland (*The Squeeze*), Joyce Van Patten (*The Haunted*) and Kevin Bacon (*Super*) take turns shouting "You must fight Satan! You must!" into Brian's little blank face.

Most fondly remembered for its quite awful psychic battles between a near volcanic Eddie Albert (*The Girl From Mars*) and the badly dubbed, utterly useless Brian, you'll be happy to hear that midway through, the movie jumps lanes and takes a soft, unwanted left into a prolonged courtroom murder trial cul-de-sac—a location where Satan himself is called as a witness.

Good for a drunken giggle but not much else. It's loosely knit, a bit cracked and best watched on a double-bill with the far better *Exorcist* rip-off, *Seytan* (1974). [DF Dresden]

DON'T GO TO SLEEP

Director: Richard Lang
Starring: Dennis Weaver, Valerie Harper, Ruth Gordon, Robin Ignico
Airdate: December 10, 1982   Network: ABC

A suburban family is haunted by the ghost of their dead daughter.

Don't Go to Sleep (1982) unofficially marked the end of an era in terms of scary made for TV movies. Although nearly a dozen more such films were made for all three major networks until the end of 1983, *Don't Go To Sleep* was memorable for having a truly frightening ending.

Phillip and Laura (Weaver and Harper), along with their (roughly) twelve-year-old children Mary and Kevin (Ignico and Oliver Robins), move into a new house after Phillip secures a lucrative job. Laura's mother, Bernice (the incomparable Gordon), moves in against her son-in-law's wishes, but he acquiesces under pressure from Laura. Bernice, a smoker who lies about kicking the habit, is a firecracker with a will of her own.

Their first few nights in the house are plagued by crazy events. Mary's four-poster bed is engulfed in flames; strange noises abound; and a creepy, groveling voice emanates from under her bed. Perhaps they should have paid more attention to the house number: 13666. The nocturnal shenanigans force Mary to sleep above her brother in a bunk bed. However, their typically adversarial relationship is further strained when Kevin makes scary sounds on his tape recorder and plays them back to her in the middle of the night.

We come to learn that a third child of theirs, Jennifer (Kristin Cumming), died in an accident. The family struggles to keep it together in their new home, but a key conversation between Phillip and Bernice attempts to lay blame on both of them for Jennifer's death. Bernice lets it be known that Jennifer was her favorite, so she harbors a great deal of guilt.

Jennifer appears to Mary who carries on several conversations with her, which only occurs when Mary is alone. A series of deliberately planned events leads to the death of several family members, the outcome of which has dark consequences for those remaining alive.

Dennis Weaver and Valerie Harper are admirable as the parents, though I wish that they acted a little more like people who lost a daughter and are grappling with it. Oliver Robins is good as Kevin, the antagonistic brother who has more moxie than his character Robbie Freeling did in *Poltergeist* (1982). Robin Ignico is also good as the precocious Mary, who puts her psychiatrist (Robert Webber) in his place.

The film's ending is scary and unexpected, and is one of the most memorable aspects of the film overall. Having not seen the film since the age of fourteen, I wondered what my reaction would be twenty-eight years hence, hesitant that time might have diminished the film's impact. While some sequences seem a tad like plot devices to my older and (hopefully wiser) eyes, I was delighted that my reaction to the denouement was unchanged. [Todd Garbarini]

ESCAPE FROM SOBIBOR

Director: Jack Gold
Starring: Alan Arkin, Joanna Pacula, Rutger Hauer, Hartmut Becker, Jack Shepherd
Airdate: April 12, 1987   Network: CBS

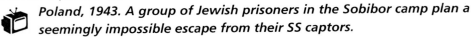
Poland, 1943. A group of Jewish prisoners in the Sobibor camp plan a seemingly impossible escape from their SS captors.

After an opening voiceover and images explaining the Nazi Second World War camps and introducing Sobibor on a map, the credit scene is deceptive. Things seem benign: people are seen working outside a house; they tend the garden and paint the exterior, all accompanied by classical music. As the credits end, we pan up a pole to reveal a flag adorned with a swastika: this is Sobibor prison camp. When a train brings new arrivals to the camp, classical music plays again, the SS captors presenting the illusion of civility and culture to cover up their horrifying intentions.

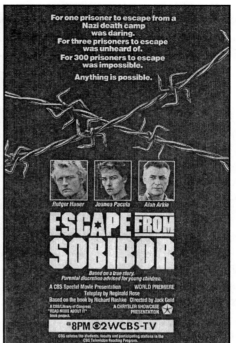

Above: Ad for *The Demon Murder Case*.
Right: Promotional imagery for *Escape from Sobibor*.

These early moments introduce key characters and show how Sobibor operates, as well as demonstrating the savagery of the sadistic SS who rule the camp. Soon, the terrible secret of the camp—now familiar to viewers—is revealed: the numerous people who were led away to the showers after arriving by train will not be coming back. They have been killed. Sobibor is not a labor camp; it is a death camp. This is suggested earlier on in a nighttime scene, where a glowing light is visible in the distance. Later, though, when a young boy is summoned to where the showers are located to run an errand, the full horror is shown: a dehumanized mass of people, stripped of their clothes and possessions, is forced into the showers and then their screams are heard.

Although much of the violence in *Escape from Sobibor* is implied, it is no less impactful. A failed escape attempt results in the execution of the thirteen prisoners who tried to flee, along with thirteen people they are forced to select to be killed with them. This is the turning point for other prisoners who have thought of escape, including Leon Feldhendler (played by Alan Arkin, conveying a calm authority in the midst of the misery around him). After this incident, Leon comes to the conclusion that all the prisoners must escape.

Although Leon and other prisoners know the workings of the camp, the arrival of Aleksandr 'Sasha' Pechersky (Hauer), a Russian Jewish Lieutenant, along with some of his fellow soldiers, is the catalyst that turns the plan for everybody to escape into a reality. Sasha's presence (aided by Hauer's screen charisma) convinces Leon that Polish civilians and Russian soldiers must work together to break free from Sobibor.

The remainder of the film sees the implementation of the plan, which is far from smooth. Among the complications, a manufactured love affair between Sasha and Luka (Pacula), designed to act as cover, blossoms into an unexpected relationship, while the civilians must face the horrifying fact that killing their SS adversaries is the only way to ensure their plan succeeds. While *Escape from Sobibor* is moving and shocking, it's also inspirational in its depiction of the prisoners overcoming a sadistic enemy and triumphing over seemingly insurmountable odds; a gripping true story of courage and determination. [Martyn Bamber]

THE EWOK ADVENTURE

Director: John Korty
Starring: Eric Walker, Aubree Miller, Warwick Davis, Fionnula Flanagan
Airdate: November 25, 1984   Network: ABC

 Award winning children's film revives the adorable Ewoks from <u>Return of the Jedi</u> in this small screen adventure tale.

Crash landing on the forest moon of Endor, human siblings Mace and Cindel are discovered and gently revived back to health by Ewoks—pint-sized furry aliens that have their own mysterious ways and wisdom. Meanwhile, the parents of the two kids, having gone out searching for them, are stolen away by a Gorax—a giant monster that has decided to lock them up in a cage suspended deep within his lair.

Lost in this strange and magical world, where danger lurks just around the bend, it's up to the kids to rescue their parents. But if they are to have any hope of success, they must learn to trust the Ewoks, enlisting their help and setting off on a journey that sees them battling foes and forging friendships along the way.

Nowhere near as bad as the *Star Wars Holiday Special*, George Lucas' second attempt at adapting his creation for the small screen is a much more focused production that provides fans of the previous year's *Return of the Jedi* (1983) with a further helping of that movie's unlikely heroes.

Joining them are fresh faces Eric Walker (as teenager Mace) and Aubree Miller (as four-year-old Cindel), both quite watchable, if understandably limited in their performances given that their chief interaction is with small people in costumes speaking a fictional language. It appears that the casting of these two unknowns was quite deliberate—Walker bears more than a passing resemblance to Mark Hamill, whilst Miller looks like she could very well be Drew Barrymore's twin sister at that time. Facial similarities with the aforementioned notwithstanding, their involvement in the two Ewok movies pretty much remain the sum of their careers in the industry.

As is to be expected with any Lucas production, the special effects are generally top notch. There are some clunky (compared with today's abundance of CGI) stop-motion sequences, but even these conjure a welcome sense of nostalgia for viewers that appreciate the technical wizardry of pioneers like Ray Harryhausen.

The narrative—which feels suspiciously like John Ford's *The Searchers* (1956) if the roles were reversed—sees the characters shuffling onwards against various backdrops that run the full gamut between exquisitely realized matte paintings to some of the most bafflingly transparent location work imaginable. A little too often does the forest moon of Endor share scenery that's much in common with Earth's own California, but that being said, younger audiences at which the movie is squarely aimed are unlikely to notice or care.

One's own investment in the film is understandably predicated on how much one cares about the Ewoks themselves; their introduction in *Jedi* divided fans of the series much the same way that the character of Jar Jar Binks would in the prequels over a decade later. But on the strength of this outing, and removed from the lofty expectations of the precious mythology, it's hard to be cynical about the tiny bears and their Native Indian-inspired rituals. Yes, they may be an excuse to sell more action figures, but on-screen, they're just too harmless to hate.

It's a decent kids adventure film that still holds up rather well, sprinkled as it is with subtle moral messages interspersed with a number of exciting moments for which the term "scenes of mild peril" must surely have been invented for. [Kevin Hilton]

FALLEN ANGEL
Director: Robert Michael Lewis
Starring: Dana Hill, Melinda Dillon, Richard Masur, Ronny Cox
Airdate: February 24, 1981   Network: CBS

When twelve-year-old Jennifer joins a local girls' softball team, she falls into the clutches of pedophile and smut-peddler Howie.

If IMDb reviews are to be believed, *Fallen Angel* was shown to classrooms of American children in the early eighties as a rather hard-hitting warning about the ever-present "stranger danger." Opening with a shot of a young girl crouched on a bed holding a stuffed toy and surrounded by professional lighting equipment, cameras, and a number of unseemly middle aged men, one imagines they didn't forget it in a hurry.

The film focuses on Jennifer (Hill) who, instead of being excited about her imminent transition to high school, is afflicted with a painful shyness and passionate hatred of her widowed mother's (Dillon) new boyfriend, Frank (Cox). After another row with her mother, Jennifer finds herself at Ron's Video Arcade—permanently populated by teenagers on roller skates—where she meets Howie (Masur). Howie is a talent scout of a singular kind, seeking underage girls for pornographic films. He also coaches the girls' softball team (inexplicably advertised by handwritten posters announcing "Girls!! Girls!! Pony tail practice") and Jennifer is quickly recruited into its ranks after Howie brazenly snaps her picture outside the Video Arcade for his casting catalog. It's all downhill from there, with Jennifer coerced into nude photo shoots and lured to sets where kids pop pills before going home to their apartments paid for by the filmmakers.

However well intended the film may have been in its aim to educate children about the perils of strange men who tell twelve-year-old girls that they look like Farrah Fawcett, *Fallen Angel* does rely on some rather stereotypical representations of its key characters. Howie is the quintessential pedophile, hanging around video arcades with a camera, plying girls with ice cream, and buying Jennifer a puppy. The limits of credibility are stretched more than once: Howie takes Jennifer to the edge of a park lake for her photo shoots ("Let's slide the skirt up a little"), snapping away as disinterested rowers glide past in the background, and later photographs her passionately kissing another "child star" while sitting on the swings in a busy playground. Jennifer's mother fits neatly into the inattentive (and thus culpable) mother category, working nights as a waitress to make ends meet and moving her boyfriend into the family home.

That said, the film is genuinely unsettling. Hill's portrayal of Jennifer as she tearfully undresses for a photo shoot makes clear why she won a Young Artist Award for the film (she was actually much older than she looks in the film, being seventeen at the time; childhood diabetes caused her to look younger than her years, a point capitalized on in many of her roles). Perhaps surprisingly, the end of the film sees Howie presented as an individual in need of help, as opposed to a more simplistic evil "monster." The onus still rests with the rest of us, however, as a doom-laden voiceover laments the state of modern society: "… And into this void walks the pedophile, the child lover". [Jennifer Wallis]

Far-fetched but topical issues are broached in a shocking ad for *Fallen Angel*.

FANTASIES

Director: William Wiard
Starring: Suzanne Pleshette, Barry Newman, Robert Vaughn, Lenora May
Airdate: January 18, 1982   Network: ABC

 A nighttime soap opera becomes the setting for several murders when an obsessed fan stalks the cast and crew.

Fantasies was conceived by writer-producer David Levinson as a commentary on the effect of television violence on impressionable minds. The story was inspired by the then-recent court cases of Ronnie Zamora, a teenager who claimed television violence led him to commit murder, and the rape of a nine-year-old that was allegedly triggered by the infamous broom handle assault from *Born Innocent*. Levinson packages his ideas in a well-acted thriller that cleverly meshes the soap opera and horror genres with real (and reel) life, although the end result is a film that works more as entertainment than critique.

"Middleton, USA" is the name of the successful nighttime soap in *Fantasies*, and the cast is comprised heavily of real-life daytime players. They work for Carla Webber (Suzanne Pleshette looking divine), who may have been modeled after Gloria Monty, *General Hospital*'s driven and notoriously strong willed producer. Pleshette is fantastic as the ambitious divorcee who fights to keep "Middleton" on the air, despite the rash of murders. Carla can come across as aggressive, but she's also funny and sometimes vulnerable. Mostly, she is completely independent and that seems to be what terrifies the killer most. However, the real stars of the film are the daytime actors who appear in both major and minor roles. Using luminaries from the soap world adds an air of authenticity to the film, and they are great fun to watch. Stuart Damon, who is most famous for playing Alan Quatermaine on *General Hospital* is wonderfully menacing.

The stalk and kill sequences mirror the slasher genre (minus the more visceral violence) while mixing in common melodrama allusions, such as romance, betrayal and intrigue. Combining the soap opera and horror genres is not particularly farfetched. Indeed, they share similar qualities, such as a strong suspension of disbelief. It's just as unlikely that the unstoppable killing machine Michael Myers actually stalks the streets of Haddonfield as it is that there is an underground city named Eterna beneath the palatial estate of Llanfair. If you know both of these references, this movie is right up your alley.

Fantasies was the second of three telefilms that featured the team of Levinson and director Wiard. The duo, who also made *This House Possessed* (1981) and *Kicks* (1985), were masters of the slick, suspenseful made for TV movie, and *Fantasies* rests nicely alongside the small screen genre films from this era. Unwittingly, *Fantasies* has also become a time capsule, capturing the intense fervor of soap fandom. In the last few years, and much like the victims in *Fantasies*, all but a few of the daytime dramas have been laid to rest. This film lovingly recalls those glorious days of love (and death) in the afternoon, and, in the Movie of the Week. [Amanda Reyes]

HOTLINE

Director: Jerry Jameson
Starring: Lynda Carter, Granville Van Dusen, Steve Forrest, Monte Markham
Airdate: October 16, 1982   Network: CBS

 A struggling bartender volunteers at a local psychiatric hotline and begins receiving calls from a vicious killer.

Released in October 1982 to capitalize on the Halloween season, *Hotline* was also televised right at the peak of the slasher craze. It apes many of the genre's main elements, although it obviously had to play down the more exploitable situations. Despite the lack of gore, *Hotline* manages to summon up a nice amount of suspense, especially with the creepy phone calls and a cat and mouse chase at the airport. It also makes good use of its Pacific Coast Highway locales, with long and winding roads that lead to Carter's small ocean side town. And the wood paneled interiors are oh-so-eighties! Those warm tones tend to belie the outrageous final scenes when the killer is revealed. (Hint: it's a doozy!)

Originally titled *Reachout*, *Hotline* was one of Lynda Carter's many efforts to escape her *Wonder Woman* persona through television movies. Starting in 1980, the actress made four TV movies back to back and this is the best of the bunch. She attempts to become an everywoman as the mixologist with too much on her plate (she's a bartender, a hotline assistant *and* a student!). Lynda is quite good in the part, although it's difficult to disassociate her from her sexy red, white and blue superhero uniform. The rest of the cast is also recognizable and wonderful, with a special nod going to Steve Forrest who plays the airhead Hollywood stud to perfection (he would roll out a similar performance in the fabulously trashy 1985 miniseries *Hollywood Wives*).

"Phone terror" à la *Black Christmas* (1974) and *When a Stranger Calls* (1979) is an interesting device that many TV horror films of this era made good use of. It was perfect for the small screen because it created a venue for tension and suspense, while also permitting filmmakers to skip the gory visual effects that were so popular on the big screen. *When Michael Calls* (1972), *Secret Night Caller* (1975), *Someone's Watching Me!* (1978), *Are You in the House Alone?* (1978) and *Hotline* all feature the creepy phone caller, a milieu not as readily used today thanks to the advent of the cell phone (although the *Scream* films make the best of it).

Hotline enjoyed a VHS release and it remains a bit of cult item, most likely because the horror elements allowed younger audiences to enjoy something reminiscent of a slasher without having to sneak into a theater. That sense of nostalgia has carried over, making *Hotline* one of the better remembered horror telefilms of the early eighties. [Amanda Reyes]

I, DESIRE

Director: John Llewellyn Moxey
Starring: David Naughton, Dorian Harewood, Brad Dourif, Marilyn Jones
Airdate: November 15, 1982   Network: ABC

A female vampire poses as a Hollywood hooker to feed from wayward men; a coroner who has learned of her secret tries to convince others. David Naughton is probably best known for fighting a losing battle against lycanthropy in the horror classic *An American Werewolf in London*. Rarely is he given credit for his hard won victory against a seductive female vampire on television later the same year (interestingly enough, in both tales Naughton's characters share his own name, David). In *I, Desire* he plays a law student making ends meet as a coroner's assistant who begins to suspect something supernatural is afoot when corpses show up at his workplace drained of blood. As the bodies pile up, he's ahead of the police in learning that a powerful female vampire is posing as a Hollywood Boulevard prostitute and singling out men who stray from their marriages as dinner. Soon his fascination with the murders makes him a suspect in the eyes of the police and a perverted obsessive in the eyes of his wholesome girlfriend. It seems the only person taking his suspicions seriously is a shifty eyed ex-priest wonderfully played to the maniacal-hilt by the always-reliable Brad Dourif.

What differentiates *I, Desire* from your garden-variety vampire story is the clever way in which it presents David's growing interest in his nemesis as an allegory for his difficulties adjusting to a committed relationship. When the story begins, David's girlfriend Cheryl (Jones) has just moved into his apartment so they can cohabitate. Several hints are dropped that things have shifted between the two from Cheryl wondering if now they'll stop kissing when they meet to David wondering why the heck she randomly reorganized everything in the kitchen. Driving around town, David is constantly craning his neck to stare with infatuation at hookers and although we know he's on the up and up unraveling a mystery, Cheryl only sees a wolf in sheep's clothing dissatisfied with domesticity. Matters escalate to the boiling point when curious David attempts to interview a lady of the evening and offers to pay for her time; he's arrested for soliciting a prostitute and it requires Cheryl to pay his bail. He explains his actions but you don't need to be a couples therapist to recognize that having to spring your partner from the slammer for such a thing rarely strengthens romantic ties. When a well-played twist finally reveals the identity of the vampire named "Desire," we learn that she has no power over David if he is a "righteous" man unwilling to forsake his commitment to Cheryl.

I, Desire is directed by John Llewellyn Moxey, a TV veteran responsible for what's easily one of the greatest television vampire movies, *The Night Stalker*. This is a worthy companion piece updated with neon eighties splashes including a bluesy saxophone score. Its only real substantial flaws are a disappointing blink and you'll miss it demise for its well-established evil

Lynda Carter tracks down a crank calling psycho in *Hotline*.

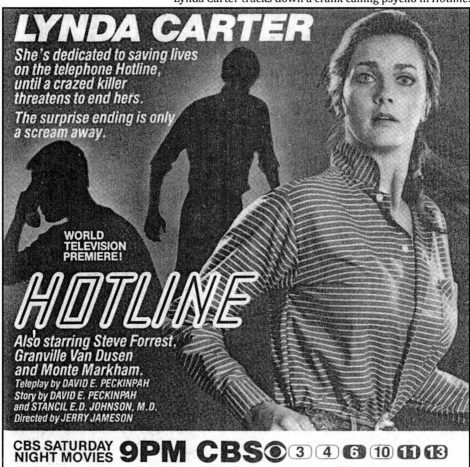

seductress and the poorly chosen canned bobcat growl clumsily pasted over her attacks. Overall, though, this is a surprising, thoughtful and engaging effort that is unquestionably worth sinking your teeth into. [Lance Vaughan]

THE INCREDIBLE HULK RETURNS

Director: Nicholas Corea
Starring: Bill Bixby, Lou Ferrigno, Jack Colvin, Steve Levitt, Eric Kramer.
Airdate: May 22, 1988   Network: NBC

 David Banner has managed to control his monstrous alter ego, the Hulk, for two years when troubled Dr. Donald Blake arrives on the scene.
The Incredible Hulk Returns catches up with our old, tortured friend Dr. David Banner (Bixby) six years after CBS unceremoniously cancelled the TV series in 1982. He's over on NBC now, and it seems time has been pretty kind to him. He's shacked up in a beach house with a WASP-y squeeze half his age, has neat, blow-dried hair, and has found fulfilling work leading a new gamma radiation project at a prestigious research institute. What's more, his afterhours work with the lab's Gamma Transponder is close to curing him of those anger management problems that used to turn him into a raging monster on a regular basis. Good for him, I say.

Of course, we don't expect Banner's sense of calm to last for long, but that's all part of the fun. Sadly though, *The Incredible Hulk Returns* quickly reveals its true colors, and green isn't one of them. It turns out the movie is not really an attempt to rejuvenate a well-loved show, but a "backdoor pilot" for another Marvel character, Thor (Kramer). Actually it's two characters, as Thor needs the hapless Dr. Donald Blake (Levitt) to summon him up (in the original comic strips they were one and the same, like Banner and the Hulk). Anyway, Blake shows up desperate for Banner's help just after the first commercial break and things go steeply downhill from there.

It seems the only way Bixby (whose company co-produced) could get the Hulk back on TV was to hire him out as a platform for another would-be superhero series. The formula would be sadly repeated for the next feature-length Hulk installment—*The Trial of the Incredible Hulk* (NBC, 1989), which tried to foist Marvel's Daredevil on us—but none of the piloted characters graduated to their own shows. (For that we can be thankful.) Kramer gamely plays the arrogant Thor for laughs, but he soon becomes tiresome and grates against Bixby's rock-solid sincerity and the raw power of Lou Ferrigno's Hulk.

Never mind, it's almost worth putting up with this Viking chump just to be back, even for a few minutes, in the company of Bixby, Ferrigno and the irrepressible Jack Colvin (in his last appearance as newspaperman McGee, still on Banner's trail and still not liking him when he's angry). The

American public broadly agreed; *The Incredible Hulk Returns* garnered surprisingly good ratings, paving the way for two more reunion TVMs (the aforementioned *Trial* and *The Death of the Incredible Hulk* [1990]). But the guiding hand of original series' creator-producer Kenneth Johnson is missing and it shows. [Julian Upton]

I SAW WHAT YOU DID

Director: Fred Walton
Starring: Shawnee Smith, Tammy Lauren, Robert Carradine, David Carradine
Airdate: May 20, 1988   Network: CBS

 In this update of a 1965 William Castle thriller, two teen girls (with a younger sister in tow) find themselves in danger after a prank call.

Teens Kim Fielding (Smith) and Lisa Harris (Lauren) are, on the surface, not very much alike. Responsible Kim knows all the answers in class, while unruly Lisa knows all the best ways to meet up with her boyfriend without her mother's knowledge. When Kim invites Lisa over to keep her company while her father's out for the evening, Lisa accepts but only for the opportunity to have a clandestine rendezvous with her forbidden beau.

The girls' contrasting personalities make the evening together at Kim's remote home awkward at first, but, with some help from Kim's precocious younger sister Julia (Cameron), they find common ground in a mutual attraction to phone related mischief. The girls egg each other on and their phone pranks become more brazen until Kim dials the ultimate wrong number and connects with Adrian Lancer (Robert Carradine), a dangerous psychopath who has just finished killing the girlfriend who spurned him. "I know what you did and I know who you are!" Kim tells him, unaware she's making herself his next target. Complicating matters further, the misguided teens pursue Adrian, mistaking him for suitable dating material.

Much of *I Saw What You Did*'s suspense is earned by the audience knowing more than the likeable protagonists and the fact that Carradine's Lancer genuinely does come off as mentally ill. Director Fred Walton is a perfect fit for this material having previously helmed the classic jeopardy-by-phone thriller *When a Stranger Calls* (1979). There is an impressive sleek and shadowy noir feel to many scenes and cinematographer Woody Omens was rightfully awarded an Emmy for his efforts. Most impressive, though, is the attention paid to the teen's believable relationship. We get to know the girls fairly well and learn as they do that they are not as different as once thought. Kim eventually proves herself to be far from docile and Lisa's latent reliability saves the day.

Comparing the manners and morals of the time in this late-eighties, made

Left: Stan Lee joins the gang in a promo still for *The Incredible Hulk Returns*. Above: David Naughton, vampire hunter, at your service in *I, Desire*.

for television offering with that of its mid-sixties theatrical film predecessor—William Castle's *I Know What You Did* (1965)—is an added entertainment in and of itself (each based on a 1964 novel by Ursula Curtiss entitled *Out of the Dark*). In some ways, both resemble cautionary educational films meant to scare the young away from reckless behavior. Naturally, it was the girls' prank calls that lead them into trouble here but there's a larger lesson to be learned about not judging a book by its cover. Just as the girls misread unhinged Adrian as harmless, based on his appearance, it turns out that an unkempt vagabond who they instinctively fear comes to their aid in the dramatic, fiery conclusion. The tale's forced final jolt is cheaper than it deserves but for the most part, *I Saw What You Did* is mischievous fun and well worth seeking out. [Lance Vaughan]

KICKS

Director: William Wiard
Starring: Anthony Geary, Shelley Hack, Susan Ruttan, Tom Mason
Airdate: March 11, 1985   Network: ABC

 An adrenaline junkie gets more than she bargained for when her thrill seeking lover makes her the prey in a game of cat and mouse.

ABC's 1984/85 season was one known for ratings so low it grabbed newspaper headlines. Not long before, it had been a network to contend with, but quickly lost its position with new programming that was simply not capturing an audience. In the hopes of finding a quick fix, ABC attempted to revive their popular Movie of the Week programming and put several small screen films into production. The slick thriller *Kicks* was part of a package designed to resuscitate the fledgling network (along with a remake of *The Bad Seed*, and an intriguing and strange sci-fi TVM titled *Starcrossed*, among others), and it employed daytime superstar Anthony Geary, who was bringing millions of fans to the network daily on its wildly popular soap opera *General Hospital*.

Shelley Hack, probably best known for replacing Kate Jackson in the fourth season of *Charlie's Angels*, followed up her jiggle-TV past working mostly in made for TV movies (while also appearing in cult-y theatrical films such as *King of Comedy*, *Troll* and *The Stepfather*), and manages to prove that she may have been unfairly maligned as the "Unpopular Angel." She holds her own here against Geary, who had already brought home a Daytime Emmy for his work on *General Hospital*. Despite the critical disdain for the daytime genre, there is no denying that Geary is a formidable talent. He either lifts Hack's performance, or maybe she just needed to step outside of Spelling's iconic detective series to find her strength, but both actors are in fine form, and their intense performances lend credence to the outrageous story.

Known in foreign markets as *Destination Alcatraz*, *Kicks* also benefits from screenwriter David Levinson's deadpan dialog and Wiard's crisp, sometimes dreamy, direction. While the film lacks a sense of humor, it is wild in its extravagance, and becomes a metaphor for finding the ultimate high in a world where everything is at your fingertips (a problem I'm sure most of us would like to be burdened with).

Shot around Los Angeles and San Francisco, *Kicks* is all about the beautiful and/or rich and bored who need to constantly up their endorphins by executing potentially dangerous acts on a daily basis. Emblematic of the excessiveness of the eighties, this telefilm goes all out in its efforts to make the treacherous look glamorous. High-speed chases in expensive cars, jewelry heists and even exotic cobras add to the flavor of this straight-faced actioner, and to fairly satisfying results. [Amanda Reyes]

L.A. TAKEDOWN

Director: Michael Mann
Starring: Scott Plank, Michael Rooker, Ely Pouget, Vincent Guastaferro
Airdate: August 27, 1987   Network: NBC

After a daring daylight robbery in Los Angeles, a meticulous crook and obsessed investigating cop become embroiled in a battle of attrition.

L.A. Takedown is a notable television movie in that it represents a kind of dry run for Michael Mann's later crime epic, *Heat* (1995). *L.A. Takedown* also shares some of the stylistic traits that have come to typify the director's films, from the general (cops and criminals being two sides of the same coin) to the specific (a shower sex scene later used for the movie version of *Miami Vice* in 2006), as well as featuring a soundtrack that mixes moody 1980s rock songs and a synthesizer score.

Despite Mann creating a cinematic feel in the *Miami Vice* TV show (1984–90), the small screen world of *L.A. Takedown* feels like it's restricting his vision, and a comparison with *Heat* makes this clear. The larger canvas of the cinema screen allows the director to broaden his story with multiple locations and an extended running time, giving greater depth to numerous supporting characters, and the use of pauses in the action help establish mood. While there is nuance and subtlety in *Heat*, Mann also deals with archetypes, creating an almost mythic battle between the order of law and the chaos of criminality, interestingly represented in both versions by a cop who is flamboyant and a criminal who is restrained. It is better served on the big screen in *Heat*, becoming a clash between titans, both in terms of the larger than life characters of cop and criminal, and the iconic movie star presence of Al Pacino and Robert DeNiro who essay these respective roles.

A number of famous moments from *Heat* appear in *L.A. Takedown*, including the opening robbery, the bank heist and the coffee shop encounter between cop and criminal. Surprisingly, the latter scene feels less contrived in *L.A. Takedown*. In *Heat*, Pacino's cop pulls over DeNiro's criminal in his car and asks if he wants a cup of coffee, whereas *L.A. Takedown* has the two characters coincidentally meeting each other and reaching for their holstered guns in a tense standoff. The subsequent coffee shop conversation in *L.A. Takedown* feels like a naturally unfolding moment, rather than two acting heavyweights being maneuvered into a location in order to share their—admittedly iconic—first scene together. In terms of performances, Scott Plank's version of cop Vincent Hanna is a little flat, with none of Pacino's charisma and fireworks, while Alex McArthur's crook doesn't match the focus and intensity that DeNiro brought to the part.

While *L.A. Takedown* lacks the epic scope and star power of *Heat*, it nevertheless offers viewers an intriguing opportunity to see how a film idea can develop. Most of the time, the early version of a story has its rough edges confined to the page, with numerous revisions done before filming. *L.A. Takedown*, whatever its limitations, is a rare example of a first draft in film form, offering a fascinating glimpse into Mann's creative process and artistic evolution. [Martyn Bamber]

THE MIDNIGHT HOUR

Director: Jack Bender
Starring: Lee Montgomery, Shari Belafonte, Peter DeLuise, LeVar Burton
Airdate: November 1, 1985   Network: ABC

 A group of teens unwittingly unleash a slew of supernatural entities upon their hometown.

Phil Grenville (Montgomery; whose TV movie pedigree includes playing the title character in a memorable segment of the 1977 Dan Curtis anthology, *Dead of Night*) is your average American teen sporting an unrequited crush on Mary (DeDee Pfeiffer). The two, along with pals Melissa (Belafonte), Vinnie (Burton) and Mitch (DeLuise), break into a museum to swipe some costumes for a Halloween party at a spooky old house. These aren't just any costumes, though, they're artifacts from a time long ago when their quaint little town of Pitchford Cove was the setting for many a nasty witch hunt. The most infamous of these witch hunts involved Phil's ancestor hanging Melissa's great-great-great-great-grandmother. The kids throw the stolen garments into an old trunk that also happens to hide a cursed scroll; when read aloud by Melissa in a graveyard, the scroll invokes a menagerie of hellish demons, including Melissa's vengeful relative, assorted zombies and vampires, at least one rampaging werewolf, and a pretty and rightfully confused fifties era pony-tailed cheerleader named Sandy (Jonna Lee).

Featuring an eclectic soundtrack—everything from Creedence Clearwater Revival's Bad Moon Rising to The Smiths' How Soon is Now?, not to mention an original song entitled Get Dead sung by Sheri Belafonte—and boasting occasional radio voiceovers from Wolfman Jack himself, *The Midnight Hour* is not shy about putting its Halloween party atmosphere front and center. Although I'd guess its foremost inspiration to be Michael Jackson's seminal music video *Thriller*, this candy sack is so full of assorted goodies that it's hard to fit into any one box. Every time you open the door for this slicker-than-usual production, it's wearing an entirely different mask. Viewers are treated to wholesome small-town nostalgia, over-the-top sight gags, *Afterschool Special* drunk dad drama, fifties style monster movie mayhem (will cops ever believe teenagers?), eighties style ensemble casting, a fish-out-of-water love story, a random musical number, a surreal nightmare car cruise along main street accompanied by the howl of an undead opera singer, and Dick Van Patten as a demented dentist with vampire fangs. Who'd want to trade in any of that haul?

At least one thing about *The Midnight Hour* is thoroughly consistent, and that is an unwavering dedication to the holiday it's celebrating. There's nary a shot that does not include a Halloween decoration, a floating autumn leaf or a billowing cloud of well-lit smoke (there's even a bit of an Easter egg for TV movie buffs as a theater marquee gives director Jack Bender's other 1985 effort *Deadly Messages* top billing). Overall, I'd say it's next to impossible not to get swept up in the giddy carnival-like atmosphere or get a bit of a contact high from its rambunctious Halloween house party. This is frothy fun that shouldn't be missed, will leave you with a few choice songs stuck in your head, and a winking reminder that the excitement of the season is not exclusive to any one generation. [Lance Vaughan]

MIDNIGHT OFFERINGS

Director: Rod Holcomb
Starring: Melissa Sue Anderson, Mary Beth McDonough, Patrick Cassidy
Airdate: February 27, 1981   Network: ABC

When high school domination is at stake, a teenage witch goes to battle with the new girl in town, who possesses her own special powers.

Witches owned the airwaves this Friday night in February 1981. On ABC, *Midnight Offerings* presented the bewitching casting of Mary Beth McDonough (of *The Waltons*) and Melissa Sue Anderson (of *Little House on the Prairie*) as good witch and bad witch. On that same night, CBS offered a similar good vs. evil battle in the classic *The Wizard of Oz*. Not only was the competitively themed timing clever but so was the casting of *Midnight Offerings*, as the stars of two wholesome period pieces went toe to toe in an exciting and fun teen thriller, one that also featured the likes of Patrick Cassidy, Cathryn Damon, Gordon Jump and Marion Ross.

Frequent Stephen J. Cannell collaborator, Juanita Bartlett, wrote the script (Cannell was one of her producers) that pits good teenage witch against bad. Anderson, who would soon be making her slasher debut in *Happy Birthday to Me* is glorious as Vivian, the terrifying bad girl who will do *anything* to keep her mitts on David (Cassidy), including blowing up a teacher's car (with the teacher still in it!) if she has to. McDonough does not fare quite as well, but what starts off as a wooden performance relaxes itself throughout the film. Still, she's hardly a match for crazy Vivian and her black cat, and this is one battle where all bets are on evil winning!

Girl-friendly small screen witch flicks were not an uncommon staple in the seventies, and movies like *The Initiation of Sarah* and *The Spell* exploited the metaphor of witchcraft to symbolize the young outcast who uses their power when the "normal" world just won't let them in. *Midnight Offerings* utilizes a more tongue-in-cheek approach in handling the issues of the early eighties teen, and these problems are touched on only lightly, as real-life concerns serve simply as a backdrop to some fairly decent sorcery showdowns.

Like many small screen horror flicks from this era, *Midnight Offerings* does not offer much in the way of fancy special effects, but the snappy dialog and Anderson's inspired performance move the film along at a brisk pace. And, it never takes itself too seriously, even allowing the put-upon good girl McDonough a few quips, before she has to take on the bitchiest witch in the west.

Finally, if we're going to explore the metaphor of young girls and witchcraft, this TVM does a credible job of showing the pros and cons of youthful empowerment and agency. All that, *and* a cameo by Vanna White as a cheerleader? Good times for all! [Amanda Reyes]

MOM, THE WOLFMAN AND ME

Director: Edmond A. Levy
Starring: Patty Duke, Danielle Brisebois, David Birney, Keenan Wynn, Viveca Lindfors
Airdate: October 20, 1980   Network: Syndicated

 A busy single mother ignores her lonely heart until she meets a man with a beard and a wolfhound.

A charmless romantic muffin, there's sadly no hirsute matricide nor any sign of lycanthropy in this gooey pile of inactive daytime love tat starring Patty Duke (*Love Finds A Home*) as a single mother/photographer *not* in search of true love and a possible stepfather for her talkative, pushy daughter Danielle Brisebois (*As Good As It Gets*). Too busy to cook, independent to the max and preoccupied snapping covers for elite New York magazines, Duke ignores her family and is unaware of the loving glances shot her way by goofy admirer John Lithgow (*Raising Caine*), a man who wants to marry her and make her love again—a topic Duke's father Keenan Wynn (*Hysterical*) is keen to discuss during many hospital visits.

Eventually, while photographing a set that requires the presence of an Irish wolfhound dog, Duke notices the dog's relaxed owner David Birney (*Night Fall*) also has a lot of fur, and is also single and hungry for love. So, she christens him "The Wolfman" and sits back while he and buffoon Lithgow try to romance, delight and woo her into a Sunday afternoon coma—a place you'll soon find yourself residing unless you're kept awake by the ugly interior design, awful beards, rotten jumpers, growing pains and much talked about feelings.

Produced by Time-Life Television and based on a soft novel of the same name by Norma Klein (*Young Love, First Love*), the small, brash and demanding Brisebois grew up to dodge hot lead with Angie Dickenson in Jim Wynorski's *Big Bad Mama II* (1987), while Lithgow (who roller skates in a park in this) went on to fame with TV series *3rd Rock From The Sun*

(1996–2001); although, he'll always be regaled in my household for the phone-book/hammer fight in the barely remembered, brilliantly scripted *Ricochet* (1991). [DF Dresden]

THE NIGHT THE BRIDGE FELL DOWN

Director: George Fenady
Starring: James MacArthur, Desi Arnaz Jr., Char Fontane, Leslie Nielsen
Airdate: February 28, 1983   Network: NBC

 After an earthquake destroys a bridge, a crazed gunman defies police and holds the bewildered survivors hostage.

Having possibly grown bored by the predictability of his own well-worn disaster plots, Irwin Allen hired four writers (Alvin Boretz, Arthur Weiss, Michael Robert David and Ray Goldstone) to spice up his jaded formula, and all they could come up with was this—a slight re-working of the disaster/gunman combination of Allen's near identical and far funnier *Cave In!* (1979).

Spanning the Ohio River, the Madison Bridge is the setting for this Warner Bros. Television production starring bridge inspector James MacArthur (*Hang 'Em High*), a man who is sure the structure is one flood or big wind away from collapse. He wants the bridge closed down and repaired, but city boss Philip Baker Hall (*Zodiac*) won't allow it because likely he's just seen *Jaws* and that's what Mayor Murray Hamilton did when told about the shark.

Before long, there's an earthquake, a partial collapse and a multi-car pileup involving police and fleeing criminal Desi Arnaz Jr. (*Billy Two-Hats*), an armed psycho who ends up holding the survivors hostage on a teetering section of bridge cut off from both banks.

While Desi fires wild and a cop bleeds out in the backseat of a car, Leslie Nielson (*Nuts*) worries about his tiny, sick infant (hilarious) and Eve Plumb (*The Brady Girls Get Married*) and Barbara Rush (*Harry Black*) look on doe-eyed as the emergency services, the cops and the air force (possibly) back up MacArthur's heroic attempts to resolve the situation and save the day.

Far from spectacular and not that much fun, you'll dig it best if you like crappy models, sirens, electrical fires, cut-price peril, shaky cam and the chair rescue scene from Allen's *The Towering Inferno* (1974). [DF Dresden]

NO PLACE TO HIDE

Director: John Llewellyn Moxey
Starring: Kathleen Beller, Mariette Hartley, Keir Dullea, Gary Graham
Airdate: March 4, 1981   Network: CBS

 A mysterious man stalks a young artist, either in an effort to kill her or drive her crazy.

The hauntingly beautiful Kathleen Beller starred in a few TV movies in the seventies and eighties, but may best be remembered for two: *Are You in the House Alone* (1978) and this, *No Place to Hide*. While so many small screen movies linger in some sort of telefilm limbo, both *Alone* and *Hide* enjoyed VHS releases, and *Alone* still finds play on streaming sites like Netflix, and, more recently, found its way to DVD. *Place* remains a bit of a rarity, however, and that's too bad because it is a slick and twisty popcorn thriller that still manages to entertain.

The is-she-crazy-or-isn't-she storyline is not particularly unique and *Hide*'s screenwriter, Hammer Films legend Jimmy Sangster, used it to great effect in his earlier TVM *A Taste of Evil* (1971). The prolific John Llewellyn Moxey directed both *Evil* and *Hide*, and, indeed, the two telefilms are similar in approach and tone (although *Evil* is far more gothic). Obviously, this is a tried and true technique for both screenwriter and director, but they one-upped themselves with *Hide* (which was adapted from an unpublished story by Harriet Steinberg), because their film is brimming with twists and turns that might not always be a wholly unpredictable venture but still throw a few curves and manage to hold viewer's interest throughout.

Relying on traditional (i.e. restrained) scare tactics, the maybe-killer in *Hide* is at times reminiscent of the predator in the 1980 slasher *Prom Night*, a killer wearing a similar ski mask who also had a signature whispering tagline before he dispatched each victim. Here the killer hisses "Soon Amy. Soon," and in an early scene, he chases Beller though the school halls, much like the killer does with one of his victims in *Prom Night*. But after *Hide* finds its footing in familiar slasher territory, it veers from horror into thriller before settling back to more organic scares with its twist (and twisted) ending.

Aside from Moxey's confident direction, the film also features strong performances. Beller's doe eyes and small stature make her look like she built the mold for the damsel in distress and that compelling beauty draws you in. In an interview with the Associated Press, Beller, who was twenty-five at the time but still looked like a teenager, remarked that this was the first film that allowed her to portray an adult character. It isn't much of a break though, and the original script probably saw Amy as a teen anyway, given the very high school like location of the above referenced chase scene.

Mariette Hartley balances out Beller's anguished presence with a severe hairstyle and uber-sophisticated wardrobe. One may chuckle when she puts on her "grubbies," which feature a perfectly pressed pair of slacks (granted, she did let her hair down)! She's a distant character—rich and aloof—but Hartley's conflicted portrayal gives her depth and adds the right amount of intrigue to the part.

Hide's production company, Metromedia Producers Corp., dabbled heavily in television, but primarily in episodic fare. They did produce a few noteworthy telefilms, including *She Waits* (1972), *Go Ask Alice* (1973) and this fine little film that deserves a wider audience. [Amanda Reyes]

THE PEOPLE ACROSS THE LAKE

Director: Arthur Allan Seidelman
Starring: Valerie Harper, Gerald McRaney, Barry Corbin, Tammy Lauren
Airdate: October 3, 1988   Network: NBC

An upwardly mobile family exchanges dangerous city life for a quiet small town, only to uncover a terrible secret and a few random bodies. In *The People Across the Lake*, Valerie Harper is in comfortable mom mode as the city-phobic head of a family that decides to move to a lakefront house in northern New York to get away from it all. Of course, we viewers know there's something up, not just because we're watching an ominously-titled TV movie, but because we've seen the opening scene in which an unseen man stalks and kills a woman among the greenery, then takes her body to the middle of the lake and, er, avoids dumping it in. We realize that it's just a matter of time before our most nuclear of nuclear families (The younger son is cheery! The older teenage daughter is bratty! The dad is played by Gerald McRaney!) is going to be involved in a heap of mysterious goings-on.

"Heap" is kind of the operative word here, because *The People Across the Lake* is a strange, unwieldy movie. The opening scene pegs it as some sort of a horror film, then it moves into being a light domestic drama as we see the family make the decision to move out of the city, then it becomes a mystery as dad stumbles across a body (while skinny dipping!) that disappears and nobody will believe him. At first, it looks as though dad is going to be the lead, but it's Harper's mom that ends up taking the initiative to investigate even after everyone else in the family is bored with everything. The killer is eventually revealed to the audience, and *that* character takes central focus, gleefully chewing scenery in a *Psycho*-like twist that borders on camp, and then, finally, the whole film becomes *Straw Dogs* as the family tries to fend off… well, that would be telling, and I'm not going to spoil it for you.

As much of a scattered film as *The People Across the Lake* is, it's never dull—you certainly can't call it "predictable," even if it's essentially just cribbing moments from other films. Seidelman's direction is solid—an insanely prolific filmmaker, he's an expert at shooting sequences with a sense of menace even when limited by the television medium.

As much as the film has a central figure, the protagonist is Harper, for whom the part feels like a natural fit. She manages the rare feat of being a mother figure that comes off as both realistic yet perfectly in tune with the bizarre plotting of the film, adamant without being bitchy (even when dealing with her actively irritating daughter), and interested in the mystery without delving into obsession. She's more akin to a woman who's trying to find a place in this business without losing her sense of "mom" identity.

Granted, it's doubtful that the script has taken any of these things into consideration, but it does allow for some nice moments of absurdist character development, such as the couple's nonchalant reaction to a pair of stereotypical country folk berating them for investigating after handing them fried fish(!). *The People Across the Lake* certainly isn't the best TV movie Harper headlined, but it gives her a rare chance to act as an aggressive character in a more suspense-based setting. It would make an ideal bottom half of a double-bill with *Don't Go to Sleep*, and serves as a reminder of how talented an actress she can be even outside a comedy setting. [Paul Freitag-Fey]

PROTOTYPE

Director: David Greene
Starring: Christopher Plummer, David Morse, Frances Sternhagen, James Sutorius
Airdate: December 7, 1983   Network: CBS

 When the military seeks to reprogram a very humanlike robot for war, the "humanoid's" creator takes him on the run.

The *Frankenstein* tale (and formula) has enchanted audiences since Mary Shelley unleashed her darkest demons in 1818. *Prototype* plays on several of Shelly's tropes, while placing a more positive spin on the father/son relationship. The film makes several overt nods to the novel and the 1931 film, most notably during the heartbreaking finale.

Christopher Plummer plays Dr. Carl Forrester, a man haunted by his childless existence. The audience is never told why Michael (played with exquisite heartbreak by David Morse) was created, but he becomes a military pawn, as well as the son Dr. Forrester has been desperately searching for. Michael serves as the catalyst for a major manhunt, but *Prototype* isn't about a search and destroy mission, it is instead an intimate look at blind ambition, missed opportunities and unconditional love.

The screenwriting and producing duo Richard Levinson and William Link are probably best known for their creation of America's favorite disheveled detective, *Columbo*. The popular team was, in fact, behind many wonderful television movies and programs, moving effortlessly from popcorn entertainment (*Rehearsal for Murder*) to striking and important commentaries (*That Certain Summer*). *Prototype* uses the entertainment angle to create an intriguing and somewhat distressing comment on our technologically driven society. Levinson and Link set out to make a very human story about an inhuman situation. Military warfare and cyborgs are hefty plot points, but the writers concentrate on the ways people learn about themselves through interaction with others.

Director David Greene was a Levinson and Link go-to guy and he puts the film (set around Christmas, subtly commenting on Forrester's desire to play God—with Michael fulfilling the Jesus role) in wonderfully familiar and somewhat idyllic locations (aside from the laboratory). It is devoid of special effects and manages to make the viewer see Michael as both human and a robot. Morse, with his overly skinny frame, is physically perfect for the part, and one wonders if his shirt were removed whether only cool metal would be revealed. He becomes a Frankenstein's Monster for our times; an experiment gone awry, a lost young man in a world where technology separates him from human contact. In today's social media culture, Michael remains a relevant reminder of our desire for love and our inability to communicate that need.

Although it didn't receive much fanfare, Trinity Home Entertainment released *Prototype* on DVD in 2004. Featuring the tagline "The future is not friendly," the grossly misleading cover art makes the film look like a bad B-movie. It is unfortunate that so few made for TV movies get a shot on the home video market, and this presentation by Trinity only manages to make matters worse by pushing a product that does not exist. *Prototype* is a thoughtful antidote to the sci-fi movies that prefer big guns and no brains. There is certainly room for it in the genre, and if one can get past the misrepresentative advertising, this film is guaranteed to offer some food for thought. Highly recommended. [Amanda Reyes]

THE RAPE OF RICHARD BECK

Director: Karen Arthur
Starring: Richard Crenna, Meredith Baxter, Pat Hingle, Frances Lee McCain
Airdate: May 27, 1985   Network: ABC

Richard Beck re-examines his own chauvinistic attitude toward sexual assault when he becomes a victim.

Richard Crenna (*Wait Until Dark, First Blood*) stars as a cocky divorced cop in a long line of alpha males. Unapologetically confrontational, self-assured and frequently pontificating from his made-up "Beck's Standard Manual of Police Procedure," he happily scours the streets looking for criminals to bust even when he's off duty. Beck sees himself as a rule-breaking rogue in the Popeye Doyle mold, but his lack of empathy for victims of sexual assault becomes apparent when he offhandedly refers to rape as a "mickey mouse" crime while letting a rapist walk in exchange for a tip on a murder case. As punishment for this "trade," Beck is temporarily reassigned to the Sex Crimes unit, which provides no end of jeers from his co-workers—especially since the job requires him to be surrounded by "uppity women" like rape crisis hotline volunteer and activist, Meredith Baxter (fellow eighties TV mom Joanna Kerns also makes an appearance as Beck's neighbor and sometime lover). But Beck will soon find these jeers turn mean when he is playing "cowboy" off duty and follows some potential drug dealers into Seattle's famous underground city only to become a victim of sexual violence himself.

The film does not contain a graphic depiction of rape, but we see belt buckles being undone and the subsequent discovery of Beck beaten, bloodied and hysterical. His humiliation is compounded by the fact that he has to suffer the traumatic aftermath of being prodded and interrogated by his peers—in scenes mirroring those that female assault victims have to endure every day—whose own constructed masculinity requires them to reason that Beck must be a closet homosexual. His own boss asserts that Beck was "asking for it" by going into the underground without backup. Even his father—the retired cop from whom he probably got all his macho bad habits—is ashamed that his son would "let" the assailants rape him and "take his gun" (the latter becomes the go-to analogy for all the men afraid to use the word "rape").

One of the great things about the film is that the humorous tone of the first half works; the audience easily aligns with Richard Beck. Even his misogynistic humor—he describes coaxing a naked rape victim out of a public phone booth with the same sort of punchy narrative detachment one would use in telling an off-color joke—doesn't come off as foreshadowing; the director allows Beck's character to work on his own terms. This is especially poignant considering the film was directed by a woman, Karen Arthur—a prolific, award winning TV director whose few feature films include indie psychodrama oddity *The Mafu Cage* (1978). Crenna's performance here— for which he won an Emmy—is superb; he transforms brilliantly from cocksure cop to quivering mess, and his subsequent development as a more empathetic person never seems forced (of course, as one contemporary review pointed out, the fact that Beck is a "better person" after being raped was in itself problematic[2]).

Equally acclaimed and controversial, the film was the first television depiction of the rape of a man by other men (only two months later, the sitcom *Too Close for Comfort* would release its controversial episode 'For

2 Jon Anderson, TV Critic, *Chicago Tribune*, May 27, 1985.

Every Man, There's Two Women' in which the character Monroe gets raped by two large ladies). But its creators were no strangers to tough material; it was written and exec-produced by James Hirsch (who had co-written the previous year's herpes TV movie *Intimate Agony*) and produced by Robert Papazian who not only started out with some solid exploitation credits (*Coffy*, *Dillinger*) but also produced the highest rated TV movie of all time, *The Day After* (1983). The film was later released on home video under the title *Deadly Justice*, branded as a generic cop movie with all references to rape removed from the promotional copy. [Kier-La Janisse]

THE RETURN OF THE SIX MILLION DOLLAR MAN AND THE BIONIC WOMAN

Director: Ray Austin
Starring: Lee Majors, Lindsay Wagner, Richard Anderson, Martin E. Brooks
Airdate: May 17, 1987   Network: NBC

 Steve Austin is reunited with the Bionic Woman and his estranged son, Michael. But a terrible accident sees history repeating itself.

This big-haired, eighties sequel to two of the most successful TV shows of the 1970s sees Steve Austin (Majors) long since retired from his role as a secret agent at the high tech Office of Scientific Intelligence (OSI). Steve now spends his time deep-sea fishing (and, by the look of it, eating everything he catches). When called upon by Oscar Goldman (Anderson, whose wig also seems to have put on weight) to tackle a dangerous new terrorist group, Steve turns down his former boss, insisting he wants to forget his OSI past. So Goldman arranges an "accidental" meeting between Steve and his former bionic belle Jaime Sommers (Wagner) and the romantic memories come flooding back, courtesy of some Vaseline-smeared footage from the seventies. But Steve still won't commit to the new mission—that is until fate steps in.

While the handling of Steve and Jaime's relationship is hamfisted (director Ray Austin was always more at home with stunts than human emotion), Majors and Wagner manage to inject some feeling into their characters. Majors' chunkier physique and beaten-down demeanor actually work well for his portrayal of a wistful, bruised, middle aged man whose action-hero days are behind him. And although she's now under half a can of hairspray and a yard of shoulder padding, Wagner's dynamic allure is undimmed.

The plot takes an interesting turn when it echoes Steve's dilemma over the original "bionicization" of Jaime. This time he has to call on the OSI— still under the medical supervision of Dr. Rudy Wells (Brooks)—to "rebuild" his trainee pilot son, Michael (Tom Schanley), when the young man sustains horrific injuries in a plane crash. But this is where the backdoor pilot nature of the enterprise becomes clear—it's all a big pitch for a *Son of the Six Million Dollar Man* TV series. Austin *fils* is transformed into a bionic man for a more advanced era, with improved skills and functions such as a laser-equipped eye. But while Schanley is agreeable enough as a "microchip off the old block," thankfully his presence doesn't displace the Majors/Wagner focus too much.

No new series was forthcoming, but two more reunion TV movies rolled off the production line: 1989's *Bionic Showdown*, in which Steve and Jaime mentor a new bionic woman (a pre-stardom Sandra Bullock), and 1994's *Bionic Ever After?*, where Steve and Jaime tie the knot (but can it last?).

Trivia buffs might be interested to spot Bryan *Breaking Bad* Cranston in an early role as a fresh-faced doctor, as well as Lee Majors' real-life son Lee Majors II, offering some comic relief as a bumbling OSI lawyer (playing Michael would have been a stretch for the grinning, bouffanted Majors II.) Also adding weight to the cast, and looking more like Bela Lugosi here than when he actually played him seven years later, is the saturnine Martin Landau. [Julian Upton]

REVENGE OF THE STEPFORD WIVES

Director: Robert Fuest
Starring: Sharon Gless, Julie Kavner, Arthur Hill and Don Johnson
Airdate: October 12, 1980   Network: NBC

The town of Stepford is perhaps the most blissful residency in the country. TV personality Kaye Foster wants to know why.

Not just a rare find, but a rare thing—a sequel that gets it right! This is a follow-up that actually evolves the story rather than merely retreading it for the small screen, and it's a creative decision made all the more admirable for being done so well. In fact, it's arguably a better, more assuredly paced venture than the original, which suffered from teasing out the reveal of Stepford's perfect mystery beyond breaking point. Since the twist has already been revealed—at least to the audience, though not to the protagonists—the tone is less on suspense and far more on action. The movie also deals with the long term effects of the small town's eerily unnatural domestic bliss and the moral implications that the menfolk wrestle with and the decisions that some of them, regrettably, have already made.

Gless, as Kaye Foster, is less of a star than the previous film's Katherine Ross, but she does assert her character with far more gusto, and is easily a more engaging heroine. Although the rest of the film's female population may be drones, the town is nevertheless brought to life by the introduction of several familiar character actors that provide a richness, and even a

A trio of ads promoting the TV sequels to the *The Stepford Wives*.

credibility, to the more absurd details of the plot.

Of course, it's not without its faults, opening as it does with perhaps the most lethargic bumper-to-bumper car chase ever committed to film, so much so that when it climaxes in slow motion, the effect is almost imperceptible! And similar to the original, it loses its way at the halfway mark. A brilliantly whimsical and lush piece of string music that serves to re-enforce the 1950s Rockwellian-nightmare subject matter, ends up playing for so long that it becomes jarringly distracting from the events on-screen. But thankfully, as the film reaches its climax, the director re-asserts control, as do the merry wives of Stepford themselves, when, as the title suggests, they regain their power, though in a nice twist, not necessarily their humanity!

Not a classic of any kind, but a far more entertaining film than its big screen predecessor and worth watching for a couple of early spirited performances from a young Don Johnson, as well as Julie Kavner as his subservient bride, long before *The Simpsons* would cement her as perhaps the most archetypical TV housewife of all time. [Kevin Hilton]

SHATTERED INNOCENCE

Director: Sandor Stern
Starring: Jonna Lee, Melinda Dillon, John Pleshette, Nadine Van der Velde
Airdate: March 9, 1988   Network: CBS

 A film based on the true story of Shauna Grant, a small-town girl drawn into the world of adult movies with tragic consequences.

Shauna Grant, star of a string of adult movies in the 1980s, has become a cause célèbre of the anti-pornography camp since her suicide at the age of twenty. Having left her family home in Minnesota, she had traveled to Los Angeles in search of work and excitement, and quickly found herself immersed in nude modeling, progressing to hardcore pornography. Increasingly dependent on cocaine, she retired from the business within a year, but struggled to cope with her addiction and relationship with her coke-dealer boyfriend; she shot herself in March 1984.

Grant's is a tragic and complex story, though perhaps less complex if you're of the opinion that pornography ruins all the lives it touches—unfortunately, this is the simplistic stance that *Shattered Innocence* takes in its dramatization of Grant's life. Names are changed—Shauna Grant becomes Lara Dawn—but the basic bones of the story are all there. In L.A., Shauna/Lara answers a small ad requesting models, arriving at the office of agency owner Lou. Swayed by the promise of $200 a day, she quickly agrees to semi-nude modeling, which predictably turns into fully nude shots. Upon her family discovering what she's doing, she is defiant, going to stay with fellow model and actress Nora Jett (and what a porn star name that is).

The remainder of the film documents Lara's descent into a seedy underworld populated by sleazy blokes in bad suits, wild parties, and indiscriminate drug use. Despite the clichés, it's on the whole quite engaging: Jonna Lee, as Lara, is well cast as a loveable but immature small-town girl, and the rest of the cast are interesting enough to keep the viewer's attention even through several rather *too* contrived scenes (a row of women gaze into a bathroom mirror, not adjusting their makeup but wiping white powder from their nostrils).

Looking further into the Shauna Grant story, though, the bias of *Shattered Innocence* comes to the fore (for this, I recommend viewing the PBS documentary, *Death of a Porn Queen*). Those elements of Grant's life that might have ruined the film's "porn will kill you" message have been omitted; there is no reference to Grant's earlier (pre-film career) suicide attempt, for example. Contrasting *Shattered Innocence* and the PBS documentary, there is quite a role reversal: in the former, our sympathy is with the parents while Lara is presented as naïve and childish; in the latter, however, it is the parents who come across as blinkered and uncaring. There is no subtlety in *Shattered Innocence*—the final scene sees Lara's mother crying "Who did this to you?" as Lara lies unconscious in a hospital bed—and this is what grates most about the film. In mythologizing Grant, *Shattered Innocence* succeeds in making her as much of a puppet as the adult film industry it tries to accuse. [Jennifer Wallis]

SOMETHING ABOUT AMELIA

Director: Randa Haines
Starring: Roxana Zal, Ted Danson, Glenn Close, Lane Smith
Airdate: January 9, 1984   Network: ABC

A thirteen-year-old girl claims that her father is abusing her. Mother and sister struggle to come to terms with the revelation.

It's hard to think of a more difficult topic to handle in a film than incest, and this tale of a father abusing his teenage daughter could easily have gone badly wrong. Luckily, *Something About Amelia* is a carefully crafted and, on the whole, sensitively presented story, aided by some above-average casting.

Roxana Zal is quietly brilliant as Amelia, clearly struggling with the material at hand and injecting just the right amount of emotional authenticity into the role. The scene in her teacher's office is a heart stopper, as she finally, reluctantly, volunteers that her father has been "messing around" with her. Ted Danson, as said father Steven, also deals well with the subject matter, conveying a subtle air of menace as his overprotectiveness is gradually revealed to be something altogether more sinister. Faced with the prospect of Amelia attending her first school dance with a date, he sulks that this interferes with their usual father/daughter bowling night, telling Amelia, "No one could like you better than I do, princess." *Cheers* it is not.

Following Amelia's disclosure, the film is meticulous in its attention to the details of the legal system, with police coldly explaining the procedures to follow, and social workers gently questioning Amelia about the events of the last few years. Glenn Close, as Amelia's mother Gail, is engaging to watch, at first disbelieving before gradually accepting the truth of her daughter's story. Neither she nor Steven are presented particularly sympathetically. She demands to know how Amelia could have "let it happen"; he seems to have no explanation for his actions, and in one presumably meaningful but under-articulated scene we see him slumped on a motel room floor watching an old Shirley Temple movie. It's in this respect that the film falls down somewhat, with Steven's motivations never fully explored. There is a rather bizarre underlying suggestion that his abuse of Amelia is a result of problems with his marriage. Early on in the film, Gail notes that they haven't slept together in four weeks, while he shows a distinct lack of enthusiasm for the subject, and the two bicker about each other's drinking and smoking habits.

This suggestion, that the abuse has occurred due to an unsatisfactory marriage, makes the film's lack of resolution even more infuriating. In the final scenes, Steven, Gail and Amelia are reunited in a therapist's office—an uncomfortable idea, but one that was famously employed by California's Giarretto Institute in the 1970s. Although the end credits highlight that this is just one of many approaches to incest, the emphasis on the couple's marriage above Amelia's experience leaves the viewer with more than a few questions about the practicalities of the American legal system. [Jennifer Wallis]

STARFLIGHT: THE PLANE THAT COULDN'T LAND

Director: Jerry Jameson
Starring: Lee Majors, Hal Linden, Lauren Hutton, Ray Milland
Airdate: February 27, 1983   Network: ABC

Disaster strikes the Starflight, the first hypersonic passenger jet, on its inaugural flight through the stratosphere from Los Angeles to Sydney. Released theatrically in several countries outside of the US (where it was retitled *Starflight One*, also the title given on its later American home video release), *Starflight: The Plane that Couldn't Land* melds the popular disaster movie genre of the 1970s (in particular, the series of *Airport* films based on the novel of that name by Arthur Hailey) with the renewed interest in space exploration—triggered by the successful launch of the first space shuttle in April 1981—and its potential as a future mode of express intercontinental travel.

Taking a break from his role in the hit television series *The Fall Guy*, Lee Majors, the former Bionic Man, toplines *Starflight* as Captain Cody Briggs, pilot of Starflight One, and, as is typical of these films, a married man who is taking some personal problems onboard with him, chief among which is an affair he is having with the attractive media representative of the aviation company that has built the space-age jetliner. Appearing alongside Majors is the usual mix of familiar television faces, attractive young newcomers and aging Hollywood stars, including Hal Linden (as the designer of Starflight One), Lauren Hutton, a pre-*Growing Pains* Kirk Cameron, Tess Harper and a pretty frail-looking Ray Milland (in one of his last performances before his death in 1986). Even a deceased body—that of the Australian ambassador—gets to hitch a ride on Starflight One's inaugural flight, much to the consternation of first officer Del, who recalls the bad luck which struck the last time he flew a plane with a corpse on board.

Director Jerry Jameson was no stranger to the disaster movie, having previously helmed *Airport '77* (1977), the TV movie *A Fire in the Sky* (1978) and *Raise the Titanic* (1980). Unlike its title vehicle, *Starflight* never reaches exceptional heights, but Jameson's familiarity with the genre, along with his prolific background in episodic television, helps keep the film and its preposterous events reasonably entertaining. Budgets were kept to a minimum thanks to the use of stock footage of the space shuttle Columbia launching and landing, and shots of an old Apollo Saturn V rocket on the launch pad (doubling for the Australian rocket containing the communications satellite). The Australia angle to the film is kind of amusing (at least for me, being an Australian), and was probably thrown in to take advantage of the growing interest that Americans were showing toward things Australian at the time (thanks to the success of Olivia Newton John's Physical and Men at Work's Down Under).

Executive produced by the Fonz himself, Henry Winkler, and featuring a nice score by Lalo Schifrin and special model effects by *Star Wars* and *Battlestar Galactica* veteran John Dykstra, *Starflight: The Plane that Couldn't Land* represents one of the dying gasps in that cycle of disaster cinema that had started a decade earlier with the likes of *Airport* (1970), *The Poseidon Adventure* (1972) and *Earthquake* (1974). The subsequent tragic destructions of the space shuttles Challenger (in 1986) and Columbia (in 2003) give the film a bit more resonance than it would have had when it first aired, especially since the Columbia is the shuttle featured in it. [John Harrison]

THE STEPFORD CHILDREN

Director: Alan J. Levi
Starring: Barbara Eden, Don Murray, Tammy Lauren and Randall Batinkoff
Airdate: March 15, 1987   Network: NBC

 A loving father relocates his family to Stepford, the cherished town of his own upbringing, but with disastrous results.

A seemingly safe and idyllic community, Stepford appears to be the perfect environment in which to curb a son and daughter's rebellious ways. But when ordinary disciplinary action fails to correct their bad attitude, the menfolk of the town have no choice but to employ more cruel and unusual methods to keep their juvenile delinquents under control.

Not half as much fun as its immediate predecessor, *The Revenge of the Stepford Wives*, and stripped of the underlying mystery and suspense that buoyed the original toward its revelation ending, this offers no new take and no new twists on the now familiar plot.

Barbara Eden stars as the mother of the family. As a veteran of the small screen, she is far too professional to break the fourth wall, but that being said, she looks throughout like an actress somewhat frustrated at how far beneath her this material really is. And she's right to look that way. None of her co-stars fare much better either, but Tammy Lauren (who would later flirt with leading lady success in the Wes Craven produced horror movie *Wishmaster*) does prove slightly memorable as the tearaway teen with the biggest eighties hair imaginable!

Directed with pace, but without flair, and readily acknowledging the fact that the audience (thanks to the previous entries) is in on what is happening, the mood of this one is far too complacent with its tired narrative to adequately pass itself off as a thriller in the truest sense. Although one might argue that the central idea of "fixing" disobedient kids as opposed to housewives is at least inspired enough to justify its running time and, therefore, its addition to the franchise.

Fans of the series will no doubt abhor or welcome the detail that there is a little more exposure given to the process the victims undergo in order to be changed into their subservient counterparts; the fact that they are kids naturally means that they do not meet quite the same ill-fated end as the adults in the previous films. It's a tonal compromise that would make perfect sense if it were not for the fact that its execution is very confusing. It's quite unclear (and strangely more distressing) not knowing whether the human originals are simply abducted and imprisoned—as is at first shown—or are in fact, stolen and scientifically cloned, which is also offered as a possibility.

Otherwise, predictable and without purpose, this excursion to Stepford is one jaunt too many, and although it does try to ratchet up the excitement in the final act, it remains a no-thrills ride that leaves one impatiently waiting for the credits to roll while asking in a whiney manner—well suited to the brats in the film—"Are we there, yet? Are we there, yet?" [Kevin Hilton]

THIS HOUSE POSSESSED

Director: William Wiard
Starring: Parker Stevenson, Lisa Eilbacher, Shelley Smith, Joan Bennett
Airdate: February 6, 1981   Network: ABC

A convalescing pop star and his nurse discover their dream home is less than perfect when it starts disposing of visitors.

There are actually two love triangles in *Possessed*. The most prominent one is the one where the house violently fights against Gary's charms for Shelia's affection. The second love triangle is more traditional and features Shelia in a battle for Gary with a supermodel named Tanya (Smith in a spirited

Tantalizing *TV Guide* ad for the enigmatic ghost story *This House Possessed*.

performance), a woman who wears tacky stoles, pops pills and uses words like "schlep." She, like the infatuated house, is a big brick wall to break through. Neither will take no for answer, and her persistence is so strong (bordering on annoying) that even the house spits her out for the bad taste she leaves behind.

Originally titled *American Gothic*, *This House Possessed* remains perched on the ledge of preposterous, but also has a lot going for it, and is surprisingly brutal. Victims are crushed in cars, boiled in pools and showered in blood. The whole set-up remains a mystery—why the house chooses Gary (Stevenson) as a potential love interest for Sheila (Eilbacher) is never answered. And, because the house seems to be the extremely jealous type, the fact that it would even entertain this bizarre love triangle is all the more perplexing.

Possessed takes place in an ultramodern dwelling that comes complete with monitors that follow the protagonists while also allowing for long shots or close ups (ah, the eighties!). The actual house resides near San Diego in a place called Rancho Santa Fe, and was designed by noted architect Fred Briggs. The California Country design gives this telefilm an air of class, and more importantly, atmosphere.

Adding to the ambience is the moody soundtrack composed by the prolific and iconic Billy Goldenberg, who also scored TVMs like *Fear No Evil* and *The Legend of Lizzie Borden*. However, the atmospheric soundtrack tends to play second fiddle against the crazy cool lyrics of Gary's superb pop tunes, which are penned by Carol Connors (*Rocky*). Choruses that cheer "Sensitive, you're not / It's a joke / Your sensitivity" are charmingly delivered by Stevenson, who had not considered singing until he was offered the part in *Possessed*. (Note: he's not so bad at it.) He belts out the tunes with a lot of heart, and fulfills all of the adornments needed for a leading romantic interest, which makes him a fine foe in this tale of man vs. house.

Producer/writer Levinson teamed up with accomplished TV director William Wiard for three interesting made for TV movies. They worked together on this haunted house tale, a small screen slasher titled *Fantasies* (1982), and the thriller *Kicks* (1985). The duo showcased an attractive knack for stylish settings and confounding tales of dread, and while their films might leave a few questions behind, they are undeniably entertaining, slick and fun. *Possessed* relies heavily on a suspension of disbelief, but if the viewer is willing to shut their brain off for a while, it is a tremendously enjoyable place to spend an hour and a half. [Amanda Reyes]

He makes you laugh about his dad's drinking.

That's his act.

His brother gets drunk. His sister takes pills. They're a family who've grown up... under the influence.

ANDY GRIFFITH

Under the Influence

Written by Joyce Rebeta-Burditt
Directed by Thomas Carter

CBS SUNDAY NIGHT MOVIES
WORLD PREMIERE

A CBS/Library of Congress "READ MORE ABOUT IT" book project.

9PM CBS 6,7

Andy Griffith hits the bottle in *Under the Influence.*

UNDER THE INFLUENCE

Director: Thomas Carter
Starring: Andy Griffith, Season Hubley, Paul Provenza, Keanu Reeves
Airdate: September 28, 1986   Network: CBS

 A family tries to cope with an alcoholic father.

Alongside AIDS, cancer, cocaine addiction, spousal abuse, kidnapped children and toddlers trapped down disused mine shafts and wells, alcoholism is a much maligned human condition poked at and utilized as a hot topic by lazy TV screenwriters commissioned to fill ninety sensational minutes of airtime.

Here, we have a serious and sappy cocktail of booze, beatings and standup comedy courtesy of gin-soaked Andy Griffith (*The Strangers in 7A*) as a pissed up father who destroys himself and his family while viewing them through the blurry end of an empty bottle.

Andy shouts, drinks in church, drives drunk and gets arrested, much to the ire of pill-popping, co-dependent wife Joyce Van Patten (*The Haunted*) and disappointed children, young dipso Keanu Reeves (*Dracula*), suicidal Season Hubley (*Kiss the Sky*), artist Dana Anderson (*The Karate Kid*) and comedian Paul Provenza (*The Shot*)—who all reluctantly tolerate and help the sozzled bollox hide his embarrassing secret from the outside world.

Instead of working when he's supposed to, Andy warms a bar stool and fails to notice the damage his scotch-infused hobby is causing to his loved ones and himself, until it all ends horribly with an exploded liver, sirens, a slapped face and a bullet riddled grave.

Told in "comedic" flashbacks by number one son Provenza (who uses his father's vodka-fuelled exploits in his nightclub act), it's a CBS production that is hard to recommend to anyone other than curious winos or hardcore Keanu lovers. [DF Dresden]

VICTIMS FOR VICTIMS: THE THERESA SALDANA STORY

Director: Karen Arthur
Starring: Theresa Saldana, Adrian Zmed, Lelia Goldoni, Lawrence Pressman
Airdate: November 12, 1984   Network: NBC

 A dramatization of real-life events, actress Theresa Saldana recreates the attempt on her life and subsequent recovery.

In March 1982, actress Theresa Saldana was attacked and stabbed multiple times by drifter Arthur Jackson, who had come to Hollywood from Scotland for the sole purpose of killing Saldana after seeing her in a film. Having recently starred in Martin Scorsese's *Raging Bull* (1980), Saldana and her agent were caught off-guard by Jackson, who obtained the actress' home address by posing as one of Scorsese's assistants.

Victims for Victims is a faithful account of the attack and its immediate aftermath, made all the more effective by Saldana playing herself. The stabbing occurs within the first fifteen minutes, and the unexpected nature of the incident—taking place in the middle of a residential street in broad daylight—conveys well the inexplicability of Jackson's behavior. As neighbors gather and ambulances and police cars arrive, we learn that Jackson expressed disappointment upon hearing he had not killed Saldana—apparently obeying the voices of angels, he had planned to kill her and receive the death penalty, imagining the two of them united in Heaven. The scene is graphic, depicting Jackson coldly and determinedly plunging the knife into Saldana's chest; the following scenes continue in much the same way, as Saldana's husband and neighbors struggle to stop the bleeding, paramedics arrive, and she is treated in the hospital.

Throughout all of this, viewers have to constantly remind themselves that Saldana is playing herself; flashbacks are alluded to throughout the film, so that the boundaries between fact and fiction, actress and non-actress, are consistently blurred. There is no doubt that the screams of anguish and sobs of pain uttered by Saldana are horrendously heartfelt—her reactions to surgical interventions, for example ("It's gonna hurt but it'll help you breathe."). The bulk of the film charts her struggle to recuperate, and the strain put on her relationship with her husband, part of which is attributed to the spiraling financial costs of her treatment.

The practicalities of Saldana's care rather abruptly become the focus toward the end of the film, with none-too-subtle railing against a system that is unable to pay the medical bills of victims of crime, but can house and feed their assailants in jail indefinitely. It is at this point that Saldana teams up with two female friends to form the Victims for Victims support group, drawing attention to the problem of both stalking and victim support as

Jackson's trial draws to a close. (Jackson was found guilty and sentenced to twelve years, later extended when he began to send Saldana death threats. He ended his days in a British institution for the criminally insane.)

Victims for Victims makes for compelling if uncomfortable viewing; as part of Saldana's own coming-to-terms with her ordeal, it is less a film than a therapeutic venture. It's difficult not to feel a certain degree of voyeurism while watching it, but equally difficult to look away from Saldana's riveting performance. [Jennifer Wallis]

REVIEWS
1990–1999

While trends had been set over the last couple of decades, the nineties definitely had a vibe all their own. Audiences from this period reveled in true crime thrillers, goofy exploitation and celebrity biographies.

Original network telefilms were dwindling but cable picked up the slack, sometimes sticking with the more traditional devices, but often exploiting their ability to show and say more. Epic fare came to HBO, while the more conventional telefilms found a home on channels like USA or Lifetime. In fact, "Television for Women" became a bit of a powerhouse, although much of their programming from this era was carefully cherry-picked from some of the more salacious network TVMs (along with a selection of USA Originals). And, within this new thoroughfare, a more contemporary group of TV movie queens emerged. Actresses like Meredith Baxter, Tori Spelling and Kellie Martin became Lifetime darlings as the channel re-aired (*and re-aired… and re-aired…*) the actresses' most memorable network output. We can thank Lifetime for making *Mother, May I Sleep with Danger* part of our post-nineties pop culture lexicon. Take that as you will.

Sure, the product might be slightly questionable, but it was also downright entertaining. And, unlike the bulk of made for television films that aired in the sixties, seventies and eighties, many of these titles are accessible to a public hungry for women in peril, devious doctors and tell all tales!

CO-ED CALL GIRL

Director: Michael Rhodes
Starring: Tori Spelling, Susan Blakely, Scott Plank, Barry Watson
Airdate: February 6, 1996   Network: CBS

A naïve pre-med student, enticed into high-priced prostitution, finds herself in deep trouble after she shoots her pimp in the head.

Despite the ludicrous premise of *Co-ed Call Girl*, the events of the telefilm are surprisingly (very) loosely based on a real case involving a young woman named Elizabeth Dugan who shot her pimp, Robert Staudinger. The real story manages to be a tad more salacious (*Weekly World News* reported that Dugan's nickname was "Psycho"), but this Tori Spelling potboiler throws all of its sympathies onto the protagonist, and does a great job of making a tawdry true crime tale fun. Yes, fun.

Dugan came from a wealthy family and was attracted to life as a call girl because she enjoyed the excitement. However, in this sanitized TV version, Joanna (Spelling) is a scrimping and scraping pre-med student who turns to prostitution both for the money and because she longs to be loved, or at least the object of desire. Joanna's trek into the call girl world is played out with wide eyes, no sense of logic, and unabashed innocence (i.e. this girl has no control over her horrible circumstances). But what starts off as somewhat innocent (Joanna is assured that she doesn't have to sleep with a client unless she wants to), turns ugly when she's made into a cheap Sunset Boulevard tart who feels her only escape is to shoot her pimp in the head! Too bad for her that he lives, and the last third of the film explores why she is guilty but innocent. Before you know it, her whoremongering employer (Plank in a wonderfully sexy and menacing turn) is treated as the criminal. Ah, justice.

Spelling was on a roll in 1996, starring in three made for TV movies. Including *Co-ed Call Girl*, the platinum blonde actress also appeared in *Deadly Pursuits* and *Mother, May I Sleep with Danger*. *Co-ed Call Girl* is the best of the three, thanks to the ludicrous story, energetic pacing and unintentional humor. This made for TV movie is nineties melodrama at its best, featuring bronze lip-liner, big hair, lines like "You only do what your girlfriends do for free," and a smarmy pimp who ogles Joanna with lust in his eyes—after she's shot him! There's nothing here that can't be criticized and trashed, but would anyone who sat down to see something called *Co-ed Call Girl* ever take it that seriously? For pure campy entertainment value, this daffy telefilm hits all the right notes.

Co-ed Call Girl was part of a rather schizoid network lineup for the February sweeps. Other escapist fare such as *If Looks Could Kill* (which aired directly opposite this TVM) were shown along with highly respected productions such as *The Boys Next Door* and *A Brother's Promise: The Dan Jansen Story*. Of course, this TVM garnered some bad press but, like, *Mother May I Sleep with Danger*, went on to a second life on Lifetime Television. And we are better off for it. [Amanda Reyes]

THE DEATH OF THE INCREDIBLE HULK

Director: Bill Bixby
Starring: Bill Bixby, Lou Ferrigno, Philip Sterling, Elizabeth Gracen.
Airdate: February 18, 1990   Network: NBC

 David Banner is working as a janitor at a science institute to gain access to research he believes will rid him of the Hulk. But terrorists intervene.

This third TV movie revival of the classic series starts off far more promisingly than the previous two installments (*Return of* and *Trial of*).

Bixby's David Banner, now calling himself David Bellamy[1], is holding down another job at a state-of-the-art science institute. This time though he's not employed as a researcher. Masquerading as a simpleton, he's scrubbing floors and cleaning toilets as the janitor, forever tugging his forelock as senior staffers walk past patting him on the head and throwing him the odd dog biscuit. At night he's the phantom of the opera, creeping around the deserted institute, not composing music but surreptitiously catching up on (and contributing to) research that's being carried out by eminent scientist, Dr. Ronald Pratt (Sterling). Banner believes Pratt's study holds the key to curing him.

When a struggling Dr. Pratt leaves for the day with a half-finished formula etched on the blackboard, Banner sneaks in and completes it. (Yes, it's *Good Will Hunting*, seven years early.) After Pratt blows the janitor's cover, a meeting of minds follows and he and Banner become friends, vowing to work together to get to the bottom of the latter's problem.

So far, so much better than the last couple of *Hulk* TVMs.

Of course, something has to come and ruin it, and it arrives in the shape of beautiful spy Jasmin (Gracen), who's working for some nefarious Russians (or maybe they're Middle Eastern, whichever race was the most menacing to conservative Americans at the time) and who's been tasked with stealing Dr. Pratt's research.

This is where *Death of the Incredible Hulk* goes off the boil. But at least Bixby enjoys himself. Banner and Jasmin, having turned against her paymasters, go on the run and fall in love. Hiding out from the baddies in an idyllic woodlands cabin, Banner gets Jasmin to take her top off while he treats her wounds. Before you know it they're getting down to the series' only sex scene. (Note that Bixby directed this installment himself.)

Elsewhere, there's the usual shenanigans: sub-James Bond action with screeching cars, Banner getting beaten up and thrown into some cardboard boxes, everyone getting tied up, etc. Obviously the Hulk makes a welcome appearance at these moments, but there isn't even the scantest of build-up to the transformation. (He comes too quickly, if you will.) And something odd has happened to Lou Ferrigno's Hulk wig; he looks like a giant green Bee Gee.

The Death of the Incredible Hulk pans out like a below-average, over-padded series episode. At least we get the closure (the clue's in the title)

---

1 This is enough in itself to warrant an amused snort from British viewers of a certain age. Britain's David Bellamy was an eccentric TV naturalist with a speech impediment that was once part of every amateur impressionist's repertoire.

Left: Tori Spelling and her lip liner star in *Co-ed Call Girl*.
Above: Perry King can't believe that tiny Tracey Gold is *The Face of Evil*, but she'll prove it.

so sorely missing from the TV series. Even this is perfunctory, but Bixby's sad death from cancer three years later now lends it extra poignancy. [Julian Upton]

FACE OF EVIL

Director: Mary Lambert
Starring: Tracey Gold, Perry King, Shawnee Smith
Airdate: April 9, 1996   Network: CBS

 Attempting to escape her fiancé, a disturbed woman kills a college bound student and assumes her identity.

I have seen the face of evil and it is… Tracey Gold.

No joke.

In *Face of Evil* the waifish actress plays the maniacal, cold blooded Darcy Palmer, a girl on the run and someone who will do anything to get what she wants. If that means putting acid in someone's eye drops, so be it! Early on it becomes obvious that Darcy has an ugly and empty core, and perhaps that would seem like tough stuff for such a campy thriller, but Gold is up to the task of making the psycho roommate scenario fresh and interesting.

Through the opening murder, and simply because she just doesn't seem quite right, Darcy is mapped as a no-frills stereotyped psychopath from the start. However, Gregory Goodell's script has a few sly moments, taking lengths to keep Darcy's duplicity not just on target (this ninety-pound darling always comes across as menacing), but extremely fun to watch as well. At one point, Darcy goes as far as to bash in her own fingers to hide the fact that she's not a violinist!

Like Darcy, the other characters are built on the same typical psycho killer thriller traits that we've come to know and either love or revile. There's Smith as the wallflower, and King, the rich, sensitive love interest. No one sees much in the way of development (although Smith does toughen up for a great good vs. evil smackdown at the end), but Gold is too fabulous as the roommate from hell, and she elevates the treachery and chaos to the next level. *Face of Evil* manages to endure because the actors take the madcap premise and run with it. It's so much fun that the viewer may not realize (or maybe they just won't care) that they have seen it all before.

Face of Evil was met with mixed critical reception, but the film has stood the test of time, finding a new audience on Lifetime and DVD. Director Mary Lambert, probably best known for directing *Pet Sematary*, has enjoyed a fascinating career that has taken her from music videos (she directed Madonna's infamous cross burning video, Like A Prayer) into all sorts of other mediums including video games. She's only dabbled in the made for television genre, but this telefilm and the USA Original *My Stepson, My Lover* were made a year apart, making this era of her work something of interest. She brings a strong sense of humor and her music video background adds style to the proceedings (the lovely University of Utah stands in for a back east campus located in New Hampshire). In the end, *The Face of Evil* seeks only to entertain, and delivers on that promise in abundance.

But lesson learned: If you see a tiny Tracey Gold walking down a dark alley one night—go the other way. You have been warned. [Amanda Reyes]

THE FACE ON THE MILK CARTON

Director: Waris Hussein
Starring: Kellie Martin, Sharon Lawrence, Edward Herrmann, Jill Clayburgh
Airdate: May 24, 1995   Network: CBS

A teenager suspects she was kidnapped as a toddler, and embarks on a quest to discover her true identity.

I've often wondered if those appeals for missing children on milk cartons ever yield any results. Well, at least in TV movieland, they do. Sixteen-year-old Janie (Martin) spots the photo of a pudding-basined moppet on the side of a carton and (it could only happen in a movie) immediately suspects that she could be that beaming cherub. Now, her parents' evasiveness over her birth certificate and her flaming red hair all makes sense. Did they kidnap her all those years ago?

The plot, based on a book by Caroline B. Cooney is, truth be told, a little convoluted. The couple Janie thought of as her parents are actually her grandparents *and* she was kidnapped! Well, once you've got that straight, *The Face on the Milk Carton* is actually a professionally made, well-acted piece of fluff. You can have fun with the sight of Janie's birth family, with their slightly unconvincing auburn mops and aching sincerity. They are so, so nice, I was half expecting things to go all *Rosemary's Baby*—what a TV movie *that* would be! Will Janie (or Jenny as she's now called) be able to fit in with her new family? Why is her carrot-topped brother so obnoxious? Speaking from experience: how can a family of redheads venture out in broad daylight to play football without withering under the sun's rays? The answer to all but one of these questions is given in due course.

Because the film isn't based on a true story, the storyline has free rein to stray into the realms of improbability or melodrama once or twice. Reunited with her daughter after thirteen years and facing the thought of losing them again, this mother invokes the Old Testament story of Solomon and the two mothers. But who cares, it gives Primetime Emmy Award Nominee Sharon Lawrence a beautifully overwrought scene.

The acting is what makes this film worthwhile. The "Star Name" is probably *ER*'s Kellie Martin, but she's ably supported by a slew of TV and film veterans, most notably *All My Children*'s Richard Masur, who delivers a delicate, sensitive performance despite looking like the eighties British wrestler Giant Haystacks (remember him, grapple fans?).

Films like this are never going to change the world, but when you find an example as well put together as this one, the inevitable bittersweet ending can even move an old cynic like me. [Rich Flannagan]

A FRIEND TO DIE FOR

Director: William A. Graham
Starring: Kellie Martin, Tori Spelling, Terry O'Quinn, Valerie Harper
Airdate: September 26, 1994   Network: NBC

"Fact-based" account of a shy schoolgirl whose obsession with becoming popular leads to murder.

Angela Delvecchio (Martin) is an everyday teenager with high ambitions. She's scholarly and respected, but what she really wants to be is popular, so she sets about ingratiating herself with the coolest clique in her school, The Larks. The Larks are dominated by cheerleader Stacy Lockwood (Tori Spelling), publicly adored by her friends, but privately loathed by some of them on account of her undue popularity and bitchiness; she personifies the lifestyle that Angela desires.

On their way to a party one evening, Angela's attempt to befriend Stacy fails terribly. Incensed and in fear of humiliation, Angela stabs Stacy to death. In the days and weeks following the incident, the town is in turmoil; grief becomes gossip, fingers are pointed in the wrong direction and the police struggle for evidence that confirms their chief suspect. All the while Angela rises to the social strata she's always dreamed of, but confronted with her guilt and facing mounting pressure from the authorities, her perfect life soon descends into a nightmare.

A Friend to Die For is a fascinating study, being among that small number of TV movies it seems everyone has seen, and moreover, remembers with a modicum of nostalgia. But conversely, few people are likely to recollect it without their memory first being jogged by its punchy alternate title *Death of a Cheerleader* (this aka was used in foreign markets and in the US video and rerun releases).

Presented here is a kind of David and Goliath story, with teenagers as the protagonists and social acceptance as the stakes. On one hand, it's a tale as old as the hills, yet it also addresses contemporary cultural concerns about bullying, peer pressure and the fight to fit in. And, for these reasons, one can assume that it resonated not just with young adults, but with their parents, too.

Tori Spelling, rises to the occasion as the doomed cheerleader, gamely playing up to her public image (as it was back then) of the *It* girl that everyone loves to hate, and her exit from the movie halfway through leaves the film noticeably less engaging as a result.

Credit should also be given to Kellie Martin; thoroughly convincing as the social climber with a slightly unhinged glint in her eye, but it must be said, she plays it irritatingly whiney when the script demands that she emote the desperate, needy side of her character's personality. But these are small quibbles for what is otherwise a strong, noteworthy performance.

In regards to the supporting cast, Terry O'Quinn (*Lost*), who has spent far too much of his career being the best thing about generally lackluster productions, repeats this feat here, whilst Valerie Harper (*Rhoda*) is shamefully underused in a hardly visible guest role as Angela's stoic and devoutly religious mother.

Considering it was one of the highest rated TV movies of the 1994/95 season, it should really have been a far more polished production on a technical level. The depiction of the various high school cliques are mind numbingly clichéd and the film drags too long in the second half, dangerously misdirecting its empathy on Angela to the point that a reasonable perspective on her crime, and, unforgivably, sympathy for her victim is all but lost.

The film is easily available on DVD, and for those concerned, the real-life Anegla Delvecchio—Bernadette Protti—was released from prison two years before this film's release, having killed her classmate Kirsten Costas in 1984. [Kevin Hilton]

FRIENDS 'TIL THE END

Director: Jack Bender
Starring: Shannen Doherty, Jennifer Blanc, Jason London, John Livingston
Airdate: January 20, 1997   Network: NBC

 A disturbed would be singer attempts to assume the life of a girl who has the world at her feet.

Friends 'Til the End is a time capsule that captures that era when grunge rock went totally commercial. The movie's band, Dead Pink (!), is something like Veruca Salt Lite or the Cranberries (not a surprising comparison since the Cranberries supplied some of their music to the soundtrack), and features Doherty brazenly providing her own vocals. I use the word "brazenly" with all due respect, of course. Because, while the music itself is pleasantly diverting, Doherty's monotone vocals leave just a little to be desired. But don't you worry, because she and co-star Jennifer Blanc (probably best known for playing the infamous "wheelchair girl" in an episode of *Saved by the Bell*) are otherwise wonderful in this college set riff on *Single White Female*.

In this, the first of three telefilms that Shannen Doherty would lead in 1997, she attempts to escape her notorious bad girl image by playing Heather, a sweet natured sorority girl who just happens to be in the coolest band at her college. Unfortunately, despite the group only enjoying a moderate amount of local fame, their success also comes with a dangerously infatuated "fan" named Zanne (Blanc), who is really looking to avenge losing out on a childhood talent pageant to Heather. Obsession, sex and murder all play out in extremely innocuous ways as Zanne systematically destroys everything Heather has built up for herself during her arguably enviable years at college. No man, sexy dress or music video is safe from this strange girl, who, at the end of the film, finds herself curled up on the backstage floor as Heather belts out a tune called Mental Pollution (Does Anybody Hear Me). If that's not a metaphor for waking up in the post-college world, I don't know what is.

Essentially a retelling of *All About Eve* (1950), except with Doc Martens, Doherty is good as the unflappable victim, and makes for an interesting princess in a grunge rock inspired fairy tale, where, no matter what happens, there will always be a man waiting in the wings (and a handy ballad to help win the Battle of the Bands competition). The conflict between Heather and Zanne is fun, if restrained, and it is somewhat curious that by the end of the film no one knows that she has elevated her act from man stealing to murder!

Largely forgotten about until VH1 picked up *Friends 'Til the End* as part of their Movies that Rock series, it is nothing more than late nineties small screen fluff. But I'd be lying if I didn't say it is an enjoyable way to kill ninety minutes. The airy pop music, nineties fashion and two talented actresses make this film a fun endeavor. [Amanda Reyes]

THE GIRL NEXT DOOR

Director: David Greene
Starring: Tracey Gold, Sharon Gless, Tom Irwin, Michael Dorn
Airdate: October 20, 1998   Network: CBS

 This is the tale of a fragile young woman coerced into committing murder in the name of love—or so she believes.

Tracey Gold has played the victim, the predator, and the hero… you name it. Her baby faced, but world-weary appearance allows her to take on all kinds of melodramatic roles, and although I prefer when she goes a bit psycho, she's pretty fun at playing other characters too. Unfortunately, in *The Girl Next Door* she's about as weak as a wet paper bag, barely finding any real strength at the end. She plays Annie Nolan, a sweet but naïve girl in a bad relationship. A kindly cop named Craig Mitchell (Irwin) appears in her life (but not coincidentally). He's older, nice and cute, and he finds it rather easy to woo Annie. She soon discovers that Craig is married, but she buys every line he feeds her. He promises he's in a loveless marriage, but also that he can't leave because his wife will take the kids. Somehow Craig talks Annie into killing his spouse, and, as luck would have it, she is pretty good at it (*finally* she's good at something!). After the murder she moves into Craig's life in a more public way, but the guilt eats away at her and after some time Annie starts to suspect that she'll end up as Dead Wife #2.

Written by Mel Frohman, *The Girl Next Door* is told mostly through flashbacks as Annie recounts her tale to Dr. Gayle Bennett (Gless). The cops are brought in, but since Craig is one of the boys in blue, Annie is reluctant to involve him too much in her confession. It's common in this sort of domestic thriller for the woman to grow into a stronger person (and, admittedly, in one minor respect she does), but there's not much of a development here, and in the end it's all kind of a letdown.

The Girl Next Door would end up being director David Greene's last film. Greene had a flair for this kind of material, having directed many incredible thrillers such as *A Vacation in Hell* and *Rehearsal for Murder,* among others. He was also behind some wonderful dramas as well (*Friendly Fire, Roots,* etc.), and perhaps that's why we end up with such an uneven film here. *The*

Girl Next Door can't decide whether it wants to be a thriller or a drama and ends up stuck in that gray area in between. It would have worked better as an out and out thriller because the premise is solid, but needs more guts to completely engage its audience. Of course, it does feature tiny Tracey in a ski mask packing heat, so not all is lost. [Amanda Reyes]

THE HAUNTED

Director: Robert Mandel
Starring: Sally Kirkland, Jeffrey DeMunn, Diane Baker, Stephen Markle
Airdate: May 6, 1991   Network: FOX

 A religious middle class family battles against demonic forces in this supposedly true tale of good vs. evil.

Shortly following a move into a duplex building in a quiet neighborhood for Jack and Janet Smurl (DeMunn and Kirkland), Janet begins to experience strange occurrences. Although skeptical at first, Jack also begins to fall prey to the sinister presence that is plaguing their new home. Desperate to be rid of whatever demons are lingering, they seek help, but having been dismissed by their church, their remaining hope lies with supernatural investigators Ed and Lorraine Warren (Markle and Baker), who confirm their worst fears—the haunting is real, malicious, and worst of all, maybe unstoppable.

This is a popular and revisited TV movie of the early nineties, being the kind of material that some found scary on first viewing, only to later find that it wasn't so frightening after all. Is it worthy of its small cult following? No, not really. But that's not to say it isn't worth a viewing. There are some interesting sequences—DeMunn's character being raped by a lunatic apparition will linger in the mind awhile—but for the most part, the haunting scenes are disappointingly generic and tame.

Embracing the limitations (lower budget, low intensity scares) of the medium for which it is intended, the movie wisely attempts to introduce elements of external drama to complement the building's interior terror plotline. These include Janet's ostracization from her local church, and also the suggestion that the distress the Smurl family is suffering may actually be the result of unaddressed marriage problems, rather than supernatural forces. However, the handling of these subplots and various teases toward more profound subject matter is clumsy and forced, and as a result, they feel like unwelcome distractions for the lightweight by-the-numbers bump in the night ghost story that lies at the film's center.

Sally Kirkland, in a Golden Globe nominated performance (which may be praise too far, but still…), is believable in the lead role and certainly deserves fair credit for the carrying and selling all the predictably daft and clichéd spooky shenanigans going on around her. Whereas everyone else (it's actually a very small cast) look as if they're simply there to collect a paycheck. This is a shame, since the film, based on so-called true events, introduces us to real-life demonologists Ed and Lorraine Warren—a remarkably fascinating duo in real-life, but whose characters here are bland and one-dimensional.

Hardly a hidden gem, *The Haunted* seems terribly dated, being neither as dark and dirty as the genuinely scary TV movies of the seventies, nor as shamelessly sleazy as some of its contemporaries. It takes itself far too seriously for a film that has little aspiration to shock or enlighten audiences on its theme of supernatural phenomena, but rather, it seems content to do just enough to meet its one-watch-and-then-forget-about-it mandate; which—thanks chiefly to its sensational subject matter and Kirkland's earnest performance—it manages to do. But only just. [Kevin Hilton]

IN THE DEEP WOODS

Director: Charles Correll
Starring: Anthony Perkins, Rosanna Arquette, Will Patton, D.W. Moffett
Airdate: October 26, 1992   Network: NBC

 After her friend is murdered, a woman finds a long list of suspects— a list that includes someone with whom she is in love.

Made for television movies are often reliant on clichés, but the best of them utilize these clichés as a form of shorthand, quickly establishing the archetypal characters that we know and love with the minimum of plot— you can get the idea of an internal family relationship within about ten minutes after the title card, because we've known these people in so many films before that a few lines of dialog is all we need.

This shorthand extends to casting as well, very much apparent in *In the Deep Woods*, the final film of *Psycho* star Anthony Perkins, airing a month after his death in 1992. Norman Bates may have made Perkins a household name, but it was a performance so iconic that his presence in any film made his character a suspicious one even before he said a word. (This may have inadvertently turned *Mahogany* [1975] into an edge-of-your-seat thriller.) Casting Perkins as a man who may or may not be responsible for a series of murders? That's just a gimme, and one that resulted in a vast bulk of Perkins' roles in the eighties.

It helps that *In the Deep Woods* is a solid thriller with plenty of twists beyond mere gimmick casting. Perky Rosanna Arquette stars as Joanna Warren, a successful children's book author whose friend is the latest victim of the Deep Woods Killer, who murders well-regarded women and places their cigarette-burned bodies in the woods. This unfortunate occurrence happens just as Joanna is starting a relationship with wealthy businessman Frank (Moffett), much against the warnings of Frank's co-worker and Joanna's brother, Tommy (Christopher Rydell). Her schedule is so busy that police investigator Will Patton can barely work his way in.

Anthony Perkins plays Paul Miller, who claims to be a detective investigating the case at the behest of the family of one of the victims, though his story changes and Joanna becomes increasingly suspicious about the odd character following her. Miller isn't, of course, the only potential killer in the midst, but the fact that he's Anthony Perkins is a great red herring. Like the casting of Leonard Nimoy in a "he's-so-alien-he-can't-possibly-be-alien" role in 1978's *Invasion of the Body Snatchers*, Perkins' Miller is *so* suspicious that he's simultaneously not suspicious at all and potentially the most lethal person on-screen.

It's par for the course for the film, handled with flair by prolific TV director Charles Correll, with enough twists and turns to cover a half-dozen television movies. Based on a book by Nicholas Conde, *In the Deep Woods* feels as though it could have been a miniseries: several reliable performers (including a pre-*Sabrina* Beth Broderick, a pre-*Office* Amy Ryan and *Friday the 13th: The Final Chapter*'s Kimberly Beck) are given relatively short shrift and a couple of plot threads suddenly vanishing into the ether. The results may be a little uneven, but *In the Deep Woods* is never dull and moves in some unexpected directions, making it a perfectly good little thriller for a low key weekend evening. [Paul Freitag-Fey]

LETHAL VOWS

Director: Paul Schneider
Starring: John Ritter, Marg Helgenberger, Megan Gallagher, Lawrence Dane
Airdate: October 13, 1999   Network: CBS

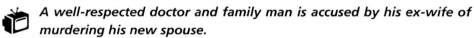 ***A well-respected doctor and family man is accused by his ex-wife of murdering his new spouse.***

It is inevitable that John Ritter will forever be associated with his *Three's Company* alter ego, Jack Tripper, clumsily walking into walls or dancing with a potted plant on his head. But after his long and successful run with the sitcom, Ritter sought out roles that would allow him to shed his comedic persona and play it down, dirty and mean. He was good at it too. One of his most frightening roles came in a *Buffy the Vampire Slayer* episode titled "Ted," where he played a menacing cyborg that terrorized Buffy's family. Ritter also chose several interesting telefilms that allowed him to showcase different sides of his talent, and one film in which he becomes the man to hate: *Lethal Vows*.

Based on the true story of Dr. Rick Overton, it's an odd case of a successful sociopath who thought he could get away with anything, including murder (for a more in-depth look at the story, read *Final Affair* by Frank McAdams and Tim Carney). Here, Overton's name is changed to Dr. David Farris, and Ritter plays him with a calculated cool. His co-star, Marg Helgenberger completely immerses herself in the role of Ellen, playing an extremely timid woman trying to find the strength to prove that not only is she right about the state of her deteriorating health but also that her respected ex-husband is a murderer. (A bit off topic, but her wardrobe is so frumpy that it almost upstages her. At one point she is wearing a long flowing dress… with sneakers! The nineties were tough on everyone.) She and the rest of the cast are uniformly great, but this is definitely Ritter's movie. His poker-faced performance is dark and ugly. If *Lethal Vows* portrays the real killer correctly, he was a total egomaniac who thought nothing of human life, only of status.

CBS released *Lethal Vows* in 1999, toward the end of a decade famous for its disease-of-the-week and true crime television films. The filmmakers do a nifty job of combining both genres and *Lethal Vows* has since become a mainstay on Lifetime, which has given audiences a second chance to catch Ritter taking on more serious fare. Yes, Ritter will be remembered best for his ability to make people laugh, but he also showed us that we should fear him in *Lethal Vows*. Now that's a legacy. [Amanda Reyes]

MIRACLE ON I-880

Director: Robert Iscove
Starring: Ruben Blades, Len Cariou, David Morse, Sandy Duncan
Airdate: February 22, 1993   Network: NBC

 After an earthquake collapses a busy California highway, emergency services race against time to save the injured.

Produced by Columbia Pictures Television and helmed by the director of *Roller Revolution* (1980), here's a functional retelling of true events that took place in San Francisco on October 17, 1989.

If you can't recall, a massive earthquake struck the area, cracking roads, damaging buildings, collapsing bridges and destroying the lives of Oakland residents played here by Ruben Blades (*Spin*), Len Cariou (*Drying Up the Streets*), Sandy Duncan (*Survivor*) and the fantastically named Sabrina Wiener (*Bad Blood*).

Predominantly an inoffensive tale of courage, human resolve, faith and determination in the face of terrible circumstances, you'll only have a brief introduction to a list of cookie-cut characters before the quake strikes hard, shaking the support legs of Interstate 880—collapsing the double deck highway into a lethal concrete sandwich that has cars, trucks and people for a filling.

On call and hoping to get everyone out alive or dead, complete or not, are doctors David Morse (*Hurt Locker*) and Jerry Wasserman (*I, Robot*), a heroic duo who amputate a child's leg and do their best to treat those trapped under and inside the two tier debris.

Beefed up with decent, but brief, disaster SFX and the inclusion of actual news footage of the genuine calamity, the padded out running time is dotted with daring rescue scenes that will have you rooting for the injured and squashed, although, if you do decide to watch it, be prepared to endure the non-stop, ever so needy music of Lawrence Shragge. [DF Dresden]

MOTHER, MAY I SLEEP WITH DANGER?

Director: Jorge Montesi
Starring: Tori Spelling, Ivan Sergei, Lisa Banes, Lochlyn Munro
Airdate: September 30, 1996   Network: NBC

A too-trusting co-ed courts trouble when she gets involved with a charming killer.

Like the actresses Kellie Martin and Tracey Gold, Tori Spelling created a niche for herself in the made for television movies of the 1990s. These actresses who appeared in TVMs with such sensational titles as *Co-ed Call Girl* and *The Face of Fear* found a second life on Lifetime (and are often confused as Lifetime Originals), and they enjoy a ridiculous amount of play on the channel that calls itself Television for Women (or as a good friend of mine clarifies, "It's not so much television for women as much as it is television *not* for men"), and because of its outrageous title, *Mother, May I Sleep with Danger* ranks among the most recognized films in Lifetime's canon. This was just one of three Spelling telefilms to come out in 1996, but despite its reputation, it ranks at the bottom of the list.

Spelling, following in her father, Aaron Spelling's lifelong desire to create fun, escapist television, was at the forefront of diverting programming in the nineties. With a few exceptions, she played capricious, but likeable characters who found themselves in sticky situations (she used her wide eyed stares and goofy giggles to great melodramatic effect). Here, the protagonist's problems lie in a charming psycho (Sergei) who is obsessed with Spelling because of her resemblance to a girl he once loved but had to murder when she wanted to dump him. Spelling's character sort of *has* to be stupid to even fall for the handsome but dangerous stranger because he's obviously disturbed. This is all well and good, but the film derails itself when

Clockwise from top: Main title for *The Face on the Milk Carton*; John Ritter pledges *Lethal Vows* to Marg Helgenberger; and Jennifer Blanc promises to be *Friends 'til the End* with Shannen Doherty... whether she likes it or not.

Spelling takes a 180-degree turn out of nowhere. Moving from puppy dog love to "he's keeping me a prisoner" in about ten seconds, she quickly hooks up with a new guy to see a grunge-lite band called Rimes with Oranges (you gotta love the nineties!), and then the not-great stalking scenes ensue.

The transition is awkward and the ending is completely predictable. Granted, it's not like there is a huge amount of original women in peril thrillers out there, but whatever was likeable about Spelling to begin with is overshadowed by the realization that she is not only dumb, but her about-face turnaround is forced.

What of her mother, though? While she is prominent in the film, her importance is almost an afterthought. It's as though someone wrote the movie, thought of the title and then squeezed in the mother to make it fit. Lisa Banes is good in the part, but ultimately Spelling saves her own day, leaving her mother's detective footwork feeling superfluous. Also, the tension between mother and daughter is played down throughout the film and their "bond" over finally getting rid of Sergei doesn't serve a purpose. And what of Spelling's character's eating disorder and the fact that she is a long distance runner? Both of these interesting traits have disappeared by the end of the film.

I am a fan of Tori's small screen work, but the more appropriate title of this film should be *Mother, May I Sleep with Boredom*? There, I said it. See *Co-ed Call Girl* instead. [Amanda Reyes]

OBSESSED

Director: Jonathan Sanger
Starring: Shannen Doherty, William Devane, Clare Carey, Lois Chiles
Airdate: September 27, 1992   Network: ABC

A cautionary tale about leading on the wrong woman.

Shannen Doherty, in the midst of her infamous turn as the sometimes sweet but wildly emotional Brenda Walsh on the hit nighttime melodrama *Beverly Hills, 90210*, lands a role that allows her to drop the sweet and speed straight ahead to the emotional part (add psychotic to that list as well). Her character's May–December romance with the handsome Devane is an instant glimpse into the horrors of the Daddy Complex, but Doherty's deadpan delivery only heightens the *Fatal Attraction* rip-off, which, for the most part, delivers.

Lorie (Doherty) is a girl racked with emotional problems, and even at the start of the film it is obvious that there is something not quite right about the flirty young girl. Things quickly turn sour, but Ed (Devane), who considers himself a very nice guy, thinks he's helping Lorie out by going along with the love charade for as long as he can, most likely because he's too chicken to dump her (the obvious benefit being that he can have unlimited sex with the gorgeous twenty-something). While this movie is clearly in Ed's corner, he is not blameless. His daughter Andie (Carey) points out that his fraudulence is only doing Lorie a disservice (and that's an understatement!). Of course, he's not setting boats on fire, slitting his wrists or pulling guns on people, but the fact that his behavior is noted as its own form of toxic makes this telethriller a little more likeable and intriguing.

Despite the limitations placed upon the small screen, television has never shied away from creating its own version of the erotic thriller—TV-PG style. For fans of the saucier stuff (*Basic Instinct*, *Night Eyes*, et al.), these telefilms are sure to disappoint, but for those who weren't old enough to watch sex and death in a darkened theater, or have access to late night pay cable, these TVMs often hit an enjoyable note. Although, even by television standards, *Obsessed* is fairly light—and it is *really* light in comparison to Doherty's notorious sex thriller *Blindfold: Acts of Obsession* (which premiered on Showtime in 1994), and her 1993 *Playboy* debut—but this soft imitation makes the most of Doherty, and captures the actress when she and her *90210* counterpart were both loved and hated by fans, but—like she hopes Ed realizes—never ignored.

Doherty appeared in a lot of decent TVMs throughout the nineties (and beyond), and there is something so right about her work in these types of straight-faced thrillers. However, in her later work she eschewed the bad girl roles in favor of playing the damsel in distress. More's the pity, because when Doherty goes from zero to sixty on the insanity scale, she is an absolute blast to watch. [Amanda Reyes]

THE ONLY WAY OUT

Director: Rod Hardy
Starring: John Ritter, Henry Winkler, Stephanie Faracy, Julianne Phillips
Airdate: December 19, 1993   Network: ABC

 A woman who finds herself in an abusive relationship turns to her ex-husband for help, leading to calamitous consequences.

Funny guys John Ritter and Henry Winkler opted for a change of pace when they took this very-nineties thriller that features Winkler as a truly terrifying sociopath and Ritter as his weak victim. Originally titled *Grounds for Murder*, *The Only Way Out* was co-produced by Ritter's company Adam Productions. He and Winkler had been searching for a project to work on together, and Ritter was as surprised as anyone that their collaboration wound up being a domestic thriller.

Not unlike theatrical releases of this era (*Pacific Heights* instantly comes to mind), *The Only Way Out* is structured to play on very real fears using a somewhat over-the-top method. It's obvious from the start that Winkler is a few bricks short of a full load, yet he ensnares pretty blonde Lynn (Stephanie Faracy, another actor known mostly for comedy). And while it may be easy for the audience to roll their eyes and say they would never find themselves in a similar situation, we also know that Lynn is carrying a lot of responsibility as Ritter's ex. She's now a single mom with three kids trying to get a degree in college. Who wouldn't want a cute and funny guy helping out around the house? He plays up his strange but somewhat charming sense of humor throughout the film, and he also slowly confesses to a tortured past, invoking Lynn's motherly compassion. What Ritter shakes his head at, she sees almost as a wounded dog, and someone she can take care of.

Ritter is never less likeable than Winkler who instantly smarms the audience, but he's spineless when it comes to confronting his ex's abuser (less so when he faces off with Lynn, which may show the type of man she's attracted to). It's not until he's backed into a corner that he can really stand up for himself, and even then, he overreacts and creates a new problem for himself. The dark ending comes as a surprise.

The Only Way Out was met with mixed reviews, although most critics were pleased with both actors, and they especially took a shine to Winkler who is amiable and terrifying at different points in the film. In an interview to promote the telethriller, Ritter stated that this was the third project to come to the duo. The first two were much lighter—a comedy called *The Sob Sisters* that never went into production, and the dramedy *The Boys* (1991), which was based on the true story of *Columbo*'s co-creators, Richard Levinson and William Link (the parts eventually went to James Woods and John Lithgow). Ritter also said that both actors auditioned for the part of bad guy Tony, and it is obvious that the best man won. Ritter is great at playing menacing, as noted in *Lethal Vows* (1999), but Winkler really sheds his Fonzie skin and brings a sort of deliberate madness that makes him seem all too real.

Less slick than its theatrical counterparts, *The Only Way Out* is still woefully underrated and deserves a wider audience. [Amanda Reyes]

PROJECT: ALF

Director: Dick Lowry
Starring: Miguel Ferrer, William O'Leary, Jensen Daggett, Martin Sheen
Airdate: February 17, 1996   Network: ABC

Picking up where the series ALF left off, the wisecracking alien finds himself captured by the US government.

The most shocking thing about *Project: ALF*, the 1996 feature made six years after the ending of the *ALF* television series, isn't that the Tanner Family, the band of generic sitcom archetypes that served as a foil to the fuzzy Melmacian's antics, is nowhere to be seen. (If the behind-the-scenes gossip is to be believed, the actors didn't care much for being second fiddle to a wisecracking puppet either.) The most shocking thing is that *My Favorite Martian* star Ray Walston appears as a hotel clerk, and despite several interactions with ALF, there is no reference made to the actor's most noteworthy alien-centric series.

This is particularly odd because *Project: ALF* is exactly the sort of movie that loves its quick-witted cultural references. Written by *ALF* writers Tom Patchett and Paul Fusco, *Project: ALF* provides references to such timely material as Marion Berry, Jeffrey Katzenberg leaving Disney, "Don't Ask, Don't Tell," and Carl Sagan's pronunciation of the word "Uranus," and it's to the credit of the performers and director Dick Lowry that even the nods to things that might go right over the heads of anyone under the age of thirty still seem funny.

The film picks up shortly after the series left off. *ALF* is in the hands of the military, and has made quite a life for himself, becoming friends with the troops and starting a gambling ring in his giant suite. Sure, there's the occasional scientific testing (featuring cameos from Ed Begley, Jr., Charles Robinson and *Mama's Family*'s Beverly Archer), but overall, he's got things under control, so he has to be drugged when well-meaning Captain Mulligan (O'Leary) and Major Hill (Daggett) sneak him off base.

This deception needs to be done, however, because *ALF*'s life is in danger due to a personal vendetta against aliens harbored by Colonel Milfoil, played by Martin Sheen three years shy of *The West Wing*. Milfoil wants ALF destroyed, and Mulligan, Hill and ALF do their best to make their way to safety in their form of a former alien expert and creator of passive-aggressive robots Dexter Moyers. This may not be such a good idea, as Moyers is played by Miguel Ferrer, the man who delivers the best-unamused face in film.

Intervening years have turned *ALF* from a spewer of punchlines to a punchline itself, the embodiment of all things ridiculous and eighties, so it's easy to forget that *ALF* was actually a fairly funny, quick-witted show when it wasn't bogged down in sitcom minutia, and that wit is much more evident here in a feature form without a laugh track. The character of *ALF* is at his best when everyone else around him is frustrated by his antics, and his gags are meant to be smirked at, not to be met with forced laughter—a fact alluded to in the film with a bit of a meta-gag as ALF mimics the condescending laughter his jokes are greeted by.

Sure, plenty of the gags don't work, but Lowry's direction ensures that even a dud doesn't have much impact on the pace. The same can't really be said for the "will-they-or-won't-they" subplot involving Mulligan and Hill, but every time ALF is actually on-screen, *Project: ALF* delivers. For once, the change in format from sitcom to feature actually benefits the writing, and *Project: ALF* is a rare case in which the delayed postscript to a television series actually surpasses the series upon which it sprung. [Paul Freitag-Fey]

QUICKSILVER HIGHWAY

Director: Mick Garris
Starring: Christopher Lloyd, Matt Frewer, Raphael Sbarge and Missy Crider
Airdate: May 13, 1997   Network: FOX

 On an open stretch of deserted highway, Aaron Quicksilver regales those who enter his curiosity store with macabre tales.

An unremarkable and half-assed attempt to unite contemporary horror fiction's two heavyweights, Stephen King and Clive Barker, this compendium movie (unambitiously comprised of just two short stories) disappoints from the outset by having selected examples of their weakest works for adaptation.

The first tale, 'Chattery Teeth,' taken from King's collection *Nightmares and Dreamscapes*, is about a family man who stops by a gas station in the desert and impulse buys a strange novelty toy for his son's birthday—an oversized pair of metal teeth—only to then immediately pick up a dangerous hitchhiker who is able to outwit the man, but not his fiendish new possession.

As any of his constant readers know, King's work largely falls into two categories, very good or very bad, and this is an example of the latter. A possessed inanimate object that avenges at his master's bidding? Come on, this is a retread of *Christine*, and, being set against the backdrop of a vicious hitchhiker story, it's suffice to say that this isn't the master of imagination firing on all cylinders.

Hokey plot elements aside, the hammed-up performances do nothing to endear this instantly forgettable slice of low rate chills that are otherwise best reserved for kiddie-friendly shows like *Are You Afraid of the Dark* and *Eerie, Indiana*. Honorable mentions however go out to Veronica Cartwright; excellent in a small role as the gas station owner, and to the glistening set of teeth themselves—a neat looking prop woefully underused in a tired tale that lacks bite.

The second story is derived from Barker's 'The Body Politic,' and is about a doctor whose own hands turn against him, and, once severed from his body, begin a revolution of their own. The tongue-in-cheek handling of the material better suits this tale than the previous one, and although it's every bit as maudlin, and even as unoriginal as the King yarn, it does boast some relatively fun—if terribly dated—special effects, as an ever growing population of dismembered hands unite for an ill-fated uprising.

Director Mick Garris is used to adapting horror for the small screen, with mixed results, but this is surely the worst of them. The production seems under-budgeted, the screenplay disturbingly unpolished and the acting unforgivably irritating, especially by the usually solid (if rarely impressive) Lloyd; he is given the unenviable task of being the central character in the pointless wraparound that given the film's title—ironically perhaps (but that's doubtful)—goes nowhere.

All things considered, *Quicksilver Highway* is not worth the detour—even for the most discerning fans of horror anthologies. [Kevin Hilton]

REAR WINDOW

Director: Jeff Bleckner
Starring: Christopher Reeve, Daryl Hannah, Robert Forster, Ruben Santiago-Hudson
Airdate: November 22, 1998   Network: ABC

Paralyzed Jason Kemp passes time looking out of his apartment window and becomes convinced that one neighbor is a murderer.

First things first: this new version of *Rear Window* is inevitably going to be compared to the classic 1954 film directed by Alfred Hitchcock, which starred James Stewart and Grace Kelly. Interestingly, this adaptation, written by Eric Overmyer and Larry Gross, is credited as being based on the original short story by Cornell Woolrich, with no mention of the Hitchcock film. While this new version lacks the thematic depth, quirky humor and unique style of Hitchcock's original, it is still of interest if viewers can put aside their preconceptions.

Undoubtedly, the chief reason many will watch this version is to see the late Christopher Reeve playing a role that reflected his real-life circumstances. Reeve was always a dignified and strong presence, as shown in his most famous role of Superman, and that quality is evident in his role here as architect Jason Kemp, whose life is devastated by a car accident, but who is determined to overcome adversity. Early on, the viewer is shown how vulnerable Jason is when a "pop off" occurs, with a tiny tube popping out of his breathing apparatus. Not only does this moment show how helpless Jason can be when his lifesaving equipment doesn't function, it also sets up his vulnerability later in the film.

Soon, Jason is settling into his spacious apartment, with parts of his home controlled by his voice, as he operates a wheelchair—and later a video camera—by breathing through a pipe. When Claudia (Daryl Hannah), a work colleague, enters the picture, she offers Jason the possibility of both a personal relationship and an eager assistant in his sleuthing. While Claudia's presence mirrors Grace Kelly's role in the original film, this update also offers Jason a range of equipment to help him in his detective work. The use of computers and video cameras adds another dimension to the story, with the technology becoming an extension of Jason's character, helping him out in many ways, but also putting him in danger when he uses it to spy.

Visually, the film rarely evokes Hitchcock's original. Maybe this was a conscious—and perhaps wise—directorial decision by helmer Jeff Bleckner, as any shot even vaguely resembling something by the Master of Suspense may draw unfavorable comparisons and detract from the new story being told. Still, like the original, the scenes with Jason spying on his neighbors are memorable, with one highlight being a woman across the way lighting a cigarette in the dark, looking at Jason, then blowing out the match, creating a ghostly, unsettling image.

Ultimately, this updated film is not Alfred Hitchcock's *Rear Window*, but Christopher Reeve's *Rear Window*. Watching the film in 2014, it represents a testament to Reeve's own life, taking a familiar premise and molding it to fit his personal circumstances. The film is also a moving tribute to a man that embodied an iconic superhero and became a symbol of real-life heroism.[2]

[Martyn Bamber]

THE STEPFORD HUSBANDS

Director: Fred Walton
Starring: Donna Mills, Michael Ontkean, Cindy Williams and Louise Fletcher
Airdate: May 14, 1996   Network: CBS

 An unhappily married couple moves to the idyllic Stepford, whose townswomen harbor a secret that has terrifying consequences.

The fourth entry in the original *Stepford* cycle disappointingly ends the series with a whimper. Arriving nearly ten years after the previous chapter, it's hard to understand the reasoning behind yet another jaunt to Stepford, and although the switch in gender from wives to husbands has some interesting potential, none of it is explored and even less (especially for those who appreciate continuity in their franchise) is explained.

A relatively starry cast of female veterans familiar from both big screen and small have little to do but reel off hamfisted dialog and knock into each other as mindless exposition turns into badly staged action and back again until events reach a conclusion that is neither satisfying nor logical.

The horror and satirical elements that were integral to the narrative in the original, and then double charged in the sequel, were severely watered down in the third movie, and are all but nonexistent in this episode. As a result, the plot unwinds with the sapped enthusiasm of a standup comic setting up jokes that the audience already knows the punch line to. It's a sad demise to what could have been a return to greatness.

At the helm of this wasted opportunity is director Fred Walton, a journeyman in the made for TV thriller—but certainly no hack—responsible for some truly exceptional output that includes the original theatrical release *When a Stranger Calls* (1979), its belated small screen sequel *When a Stranger Calls Back* (1993) and the daft but fairly enjoyable *Trapped* (1989).

At the time of writing, *The Stepford Husbands* remains his last foray behind the camera, leading one to presume (perhaps wrongly) that the movie was as joyless to make as it is to watch.

All things considered, the *Stepford* saga remains a fun and unjustly neglected curiosity for fans of the original movie. Classics they ain't, and oftentimes their low budget reveals their limitations, but for followers of

2 For further reading, visit Christopher Reeve Homepage, www.chrisreevehomepage.com/m-rearwindow.html. Accessed Aug 4, 2014.

such things, it's all part of their charm. Viewed back to back (which isn't necessarily advisory), it's a terribly uneven series of films—and fashions! But for the most part, is still vastly more enjoyable than the 2004 mega budget remake that served only to make the *Stepford* title mud in Hollywood, and quite possibly the reason why these titles remain so hard to find on current formats. [Kevin Hilton]

TWILIGHT ZONE: ROD SERLING'S LOST CLASSICS

Director: Robert Markowitz
Starring: James Earl Jones, Amy Irving, Gary Cole, Patrick Bergin, Jack Palance
Airdate: May 19, 1994   Network: CBS

Two new stories from __The Twilight Zone__. In one, a woman sees her life on the big screen, in the other a doctor makes a death defying discovery.
These two new stories by Rod Serling, creator of the classic original anthology *Twilight Zone* TV series (1959–64), were produced between the two revivals of the show in the eighties (1985–89) and the noughties (2002–03). While not as gripping, moving or surprising as many tales from the classic era of the show when Serling was involved, these two resurrected stories are still fascinating examples of how *The Twilight Zone* can be updated for viewers, as well as being items of historical interest, representing hitherto unseen examples of Serling's work.

The first story, 'The Theater,' is a teleplay by Richard Matheson (writer of many classic *Twilight Zone* episodes), based on a story by Serling. Both Amy Irving and Gary Cole are strong leads, but the intriguing premise feels underdeveloped and consequently there is not much for the actors to work with. 'The Theater' is the shorter of the two tales, and while many original episodes benefitted from being thirty minutes or less, this seems too short to fully explore its central idea. Perhaps a longer running time and an expansion of the core theme, that of someone's life passing them by and experiencing more from films than they do in their own life, would have been more effective. The ethereal, almost otherworldly setting of the movie theatre is spooky, but it feels too isolated from the rest of the locations depicted in the story, which are more realistic.

'Where the Dead Are,' written by Serling, is the stronger story, with the expressive lighting and eerie feel seeming less self-conscious and distracting in the period setting of 1800s Boston. Patrick Bergin stars as the obsessed professor has an intensity that suits the role, while Jack Palance embodies a strong willed character of a doctor who is nevertheless exhausted by the knowledge of what he has done. Palance's doctor has found a way to extend life, which initially is interpreted as a blessing but is actually a curse; both for him and for the people he apparently saved.

Intriguingly, both stories share common threads; those of living one's life to the full and of the inability to cheat death. While the absence of Serling's iconic on-screen introductions and voiceovers is keenly felt, James Earl Jones has a natural authoritative presence and memorable voice as the host. Both stories feel like morality tales from a bygone era, like many of the episodes from the original series. This is not a criticism, though; just an observation that this type of storytelling, and its presentation in an anthology format, is a rarity on contemporary television. While there seem to be rumors of a new *The Twilight Zone* film every so often, the format could still work on the small screen. Perhaps a series of TV movies, with a new creative team honoring Serling's intentions, could follow the example of this pair of stories and update the show for a new generation.[3] [Martyn Bamber]

TWISTED DESIRE

Director: Craig R. Baxley
Starring: Melissa Joan Hart, Jeremy Jordan, Daniel Baldwin, Meadow Sisto
Airdate: May 13, 1996   Network: NBC

A teenage girl convinces her boyfriend to murder her parents.

Jennifer Stanton (Hart) is a spoiled teenager with a domineering father and a submissive mother. Bound by what she perceives to be unfair curfews and prudish behavior, she struggles to keep up with the in-crowd at her school, and as a consequence, is dumped by her boyfriend. Hopelessly distraught, she secretly begins to defy her parents, lying about her whereabouts and her out of school activities. Her increasingly reckless behavior leads to a chance meeting with Nick (Jordan)—a local ex-criminal—and the two begin a romantic relationship that is brought suddenly to a halt when they are found sleeping together in her parents' bed. Outraged, her father forbids them from seeing each other. However, this decision has devastating consequences, for at Jennifer's bidding, Nick murders her parents in cold blood. But as one problem is solved, new threats to their happiness emerge, and suddenly it seems that young Jennifer is far more cunning than her friends, lovers and even the police, could possibly imagine.

Easily watchable but just as easily forgettable, the only unpredictable element in this rigidly by-the-numbers made for TV true-life thriller is just how stupid everyone is. The setup, murder and the aftermath are so mind numbingly simplistic that one wonders how the real world perpetrators

3 For further reading, visit *The Twilight Zone Archives*, www.twilightzone.org/index2.html. Accessed Aug 4, 2014.

of the crime never stopped and said to themselves, "Wait! This feels too much like something I've seen on daytime TV." In fact, like the horror movie *Scream* released the same year, so familiar are the sequence of events and dramatic twists and turns that it'd be nice to believe that the movie isn't plainly run of the mill, but is actually more clever and subtly self-referencing. But I don't think that's the case.

Melissa Joan Hart, playing against type as the bad girl, is underwhelming, being too bratty to earn our sympathies as the innocent teen in the first act, and then later on, simply isn't vampy enough to convince as the poisonous femme fatale that the rest of the film's narrative demands.

Jeremy Jordan on the other hand is affecting as the loner from the wrong side of the tracks. His is a portrait of a rebel—not so much without a cause, but without a clue or even one iota of commonsense to see the lurking trouble so obviously in wait. But in the end, his characterization is letdown by clumsy writing that tries to make the audience forget that this person killed two innocent people and, instead, begs for us to see him as some sort of lovelorn dupe.

In regards to the technical talent, there are some pretty impressive hands on deck. Most notable is the writing team of Carey and Chad Hayes, the brothers behind recent big screen fare such as *House of Wax* (2005), *Whiteout* (2009) and their most successful effort to date (and also based on a true story), *The Conjuring* (2013). Furthermore, one time stuntman turned director Craig R. Baxley boasts a very strong résumé himself, his earliest efforts including such cult favorites as *Action Jackson* (1988), *Dark Angel* (1990), and *Stone Cold* (1991). However, he has primarily settled into working on small screen projects.

It's an engaging story, worthy of a TV movie and worthy of your time, but having said that, it's a little too daft a little too often, and given the pedigree of those involved, should really be better. [Kevin Hilton]

APPENDIX: CABLE AND THE 2000S.

The last network telefilm of the nineties was something called *Miracle on the 17th Green*. Keeping in line with television's now-vast TVM history, this Christmas-y CBS special starred Robert Urich, an actor who appeared in over two dozen small screen films. *Miracle* is also an adaptation, presenting another strong commonality in the small screen film; and, it attempted to pluck a few heartstrings by incorporating a few well-worn tropes of the holidays. Aren't TVMs all about familiarity?

As the new millennium dawned, TV movies of all sorts continued to find their way into our living rooms, although the bulk of the genre moved into cable, where less restrictions allow filmmakers to throw in an extra curse word or tantalize with a little more skin. And while the networks trudge on, the telefilm presence on free TV has sadly dwindled.

There were some notable exceptions to this rule, and a lot of the old school B-movie fun could be found on CBS around the mid-2000s when they attempted to re-energize the Movie of the Week brand with a couple of over-the-top entries. In 2005, *Locusts* featured Lucy Lawless battling a swarm of nasty buggers, and *Spring Break Shark Attack* let lots of horrible CGI chomp away at a young, nubile cast (and it was awesome). The disaster miniseries found a nice resurgence in *10.5* (2004), *Category 7: The End of the World* (2005), and *Meteor* (2009). Heck, even *The Poseidon Adventure* rocked the high seas once again in an all-star miniseries that aired on NBC in 2005.

While cheap effects and larger than life scenarios fought for Nielsen ratings, cable channels were picking up steam. Although Lifetime had been airing original telefilms since the nineties, television for women really came into its own with a ridiculous amount of by-the-numbers productions that might not be terribly creative, but definitely pleased audiences who love these types of thrillers (myself included). The SyFy channel also enjoyed an amazing number of premieres and built a niche for itself that continues to bring in viewers.

However, it's pay cable that tends to receive all the kudos. Huge, cinematic productions like *Angels in America* (2003) and, more recently, *The Normal Heart* (2014) are critically acclaimed epics. What makes them different is that they are allotted much bigger budgets, can step outside of the FCC's ongoing list of sanctions, concentrating on creativity. Yet, despite the constant uphill battle the networks face with viewership, every so often they take a risk. In 2014 NBC tried their hand at a four-hour remake of *Rosemary's Baby*.

This appendix is a simple alphabetical hodgepodge of post-2000 and made for cable titles with no theme or system, but is meant to represent the wide array of telefilms that still exist, in some form, to this day. That's a good feeling.

12 ANGRY MEN

Director: William Friedkin
Starring: George C. Scott, Ossie Davis, James Gandolfini, Hume Cronyn
Airdate: August 17, 1997   Network: Showtime

In this remake, a jury convenes to decide the fate of a young man.

A young man on trial is accused of murdering his father. Possibly facing the death penalty, his life is in the hands of twelve jurors who retire to a closed room on a stiflingly hot day to deliberate a verdict. The decision must be unanimous, and almost is, but for one man who's procrastinations and suppositions will push the other eleven to the limits of their patience, and will force them to question the nature of everything they believe—not just about the case—but themselves.

Arguably one of the most popular dramatic plays of the twentieth century, one of the great virtues of writer Reginald Rose's masterpiece is that given the brilliance of the dialog and the simplicity of its one room setting, it's almost impossible to screw up. Still, it is with great relief that although this adaptation never threatens to eclipse the much beloved 1957 cinema version (which ironically disappointed at the box office but found its audience through subsequent airings on television), this made for TV movie remains an accomplished and worthwhile production in its own right and proudly does justice to the source material, which Rose himself modernized, without tampering.

Like the original, it boasts an impressive cast that combines veteran actors alongside contemporary talent. Big names such as Jack Lemmon, Armin Mueller-Stahl and Edward James Olmos all provide solid performances and a pre-*Sopranos* James Gandolfini notably shines. But, it's George C. Scott in an award winning role as the angriest juror, struggling to conceal his personal regrets behind a veil of prejudice, that steals the show, providing much of the simmering intensity—ever threatening to explode—that helps keep the near two-hour pace feeling lean and mean. Perhaps the real crime most worthy of discussion is precisely how under-appreciated this movie is for being a genuine late-career highlight for director William Friedkin. His brilliant craftsmanship here being far better utilized than much of his work of the past two decades, and at its best, he is able to evoke the dramatic tension between human relations that made his celebrated output in the seventies so compelling.

It's a bona fide rare gem. Rare that it should exist at all (dialog heavy remakes of box office under-achievers, however beloved, are fairly uncommon); rare that it should be as good as it is; and finally, rare to see a cast of this caliber and diversity (who would ever expect to see Tony Danza and Hume Cronyn share a screen?!) come together without the reliance of inflated budgets and silly CGI set-pieces. It's better than that. It's a classy production starring a wealth of big screen names in the twilight of their careers but still in fine form and with their talents unwithered, or, in other words, perfect television. [Kevin Hilton]

AN AMISH MURDER

Director: Stephen Gyllenhaal
Starring: Neve Campbell, Christian Campbell, C. Thomas Howell, Katy Grabstas
Airdate: January 6, 2013   Network: Lifetime

Returning to her hometown, a young police officer is faced with finding the man who is killing young women in the community.

A small Amish community lives under the shadow of terror. A killer is preying on the town's young women, and the clues disturbingly echo the trademarks of a murderer that was brought to justice sixteen years previously. Into this otherwise peaceful community arrives Detective Kate Burkholder (Campbell), a native of the town, who, as a child, was forced to flee the local way of life and thus moved to the big city. Estranged as an outsider and hunting a killer as deceptive as he is lethal, Kate must try to put old demons to rest and confront the dark secrets of her own past in order to solve both the case and the crises of her own identity.

Awarded some modest hype and interest upon its premiere and produced as a standalone movie that, if successful, would have served as a backdoor pilot to a series, it's easy to see why this looked so promising a prospect, and yet, couldn't help but miss the mark so flagrantly.

The cast is ably led (but sadly, not quite commanded enough) by Neve Campbell, who has always appeared more comfortable on the big screen than the medium that launched her career. However, this is not the case for eighties-teen-heartthrob-turned-'Where are they now?' column regular C. Thomas Howell, who steals the show in a small but crucial role as Kate's law enforcement colleague who may, or may not, have his own personal demons to keep in check.

The wintry setting, the sense of isolation and the fascinating Amish way of life are all executed well by journeyman director Stephen Gyllenhaal (father of acting siblings Jake and Maggie), but what the movie fails to do is ratchet up any sense of suspense, instead misplacing the focus too heavily on insinuating Kate's romantic interests past and present, thus becoming all too touchy-feely for a movie that's very title suggests something more grisly and unusual.

In short, pretensions to repeating the winning formula of Peter Weir's *Witness* soon give way to the limitations of making family entertainment for the masses, revealing instead an underwhelming mix of *Father Dowling Mysteries* and *Midsomer Murders*, that is a serviceable distraction, but a huge disappointment considering what could have been, especially given the tantalizing subject matter and Hollywood caliber cast. A shame. [Kevin Hilton]

THE BIRDS II: LAND'S END

Director: Rick Rosenthal (as Alan Smithee)
Starring: Brad Johnson, Chelsea Field, James Naughton, Tippi Hedren
Airdate: March 19, 1994   Network: Showtime

 A family relocate to a quaint seaside town, only to find their newfound peace disrupted by a series of inexplicable bird attacks.

Sequels to Hitchcock movies are rare. Popular ones, rarer still. Of the very few that exist, *The Birds II* is easily the most despised, which is all the more impressive, since most people have never heard of it and few have actually suffered through its running time.

So, is it as bad as all that? Well, yes and no. On a technical level, it's a stinker from start to finish. The dialog is woeful, the characters and the situations are embarrassingly clichéd and it seems to lack any discernible attempt at direction whatsoever (with Rosenthal insisting on the Director's Guild pseudonym of Alan Smithee in an effort to distance himself from the finished product entirely). But having said all that, it does have some merits.

It's fast paced, surprisingly grisly and has capable enough lead turns by Brad Johnson and Chelsea Field as the terror-struck couple. They are ably supported by James Naughton, who is particularly good as a photographer trying to open up the cracks in their less than idyllic marriage, and there's even a welcome cameo role for the original's heroine, Tippi Hedren, who in a frustratingly nonsensical move does not reprise her most famous character, but instead, plays someone new.

Released a year after the world had experienced the thrills of *Jurassic Park* (1993), it's impossible to believe that the studio realistically believed that a flock of seagulls causing havoc would make the same impact as they had thirty years earlier. And, as such, it's hard not to feel sorry for those involved as they try in earnest to make the best of a bad job.

Hard to find and perhaps not worth the effort, but one for the curious Hitchcock fan, if only to put at the very bottom of their pecking order! [Kevin Hilton]

THE BLING RING

Director: Michael Lembeck
Starring: Austin Butler, Yin Chang, Tom Irwin, Sebastian Sozzi
Airdate: September 26, 2011   Network: Lifetime

 A group of privileged teens literally attempt to break into the world of the rich and famous by plundering their property.

Zack Garvey (Butler) is a new kid in school. Socially awkward, his only wish is to be popular and to gain acceptance for the first time in his life. However, his path takes a twisted turn when he falls in with the wrong crowd, who begin to employ both his smarts and his inside information to break into the homes of celebrities in order to get rich and experience a taste of the high life for themselves. Flush from the success of their bounties, their notoriety bumps them up the social ladder. But as their escapades become more frequent, the risks begin to increase and very soon "The Bling Ring" find themselves knee-deep in trouble as the authorities begin to close in on their illicit, and suddenly very famous, after school activities.

A true story that occurred in the Hollywood Hills and made headlines throughout 2008 and 2009, was then quickly adapted into this TV movie in 2011, and revisited again on the big screen in 2013, *The Bling Ring* is that curious little story that seems to demand far more of the spotlight than it deserves. As such, it's difficult to balance objectively the merits of the film with the details of the real-life drama that inspired it.

On the surface, this is a tale about a motley crew of would-be yuppie teens, stealing from yuppie celebrities and then... actually, that's pretty much it. No doubt there is a deeper statement begging to be made about how thin the line is now drawn between infamy and celebrity, but sadly this theme isn't explored, merely hinted at. The result is that we get a glimpse at a sort of purse snatching *Breakfast Club*, or selfish Robin Hoods in designer shades, if you will. But somehow, one feels it's a lost opportunity to elaborate on what might best be described as the "franchised dis-enfranchised"; the kind of fashion-slaved youths that first appeared in the eighties in the written works of Bret Easton Ellis, and, frighteningly, seem to be reaching a zenith in today's popular culture.

As for the production, there's nothing wrong with the performances here; in fact, the young cast that make up the disparate gang of thieves all provide solid turns, which is commendable, given that none of the characters are particularly likeable. If anything, the fact that they appear to be over privileged brats to begin with, only serves to make their inevitable downfall all the more satisfying, although this was probably not the filmmakers' intention. The chief narrative fault is actually in the rendering of the adult characters. The audience is invited to see things from the point of view of both the parents and the police as they attempt to apprehend the criminals. But, somehow, the portrayals feel too extreme, that is to say, extremely stupid or extremely annoying. And not much in between. They're simply sounding boards for the young protagonists to rage against. In the end, you want the teens to get caught, but not by the bumbling idiots that we are told (via the bland wraparound narrative device) are eventually going to get them.

Ironically, it's like watching a ninety-minute episode of MTV's *Cribs* just after the house has been burgled. There's still the attractive people and everything looks fancy, but there's really nothing to see here, and finally, you wonder what the point of it all was in the first place. [Kevin Hilton]

CAST A DEADLY SPELL

Director: Martin Campbell
Starring: Fred Ward, David Warner, Julianne Moore, Clancy Brown
Airdate: 9/9/1991   Network: HBO

An alternate 1940s Los Angeles. The practice of magic is commonplace, but detective Harry Philip Lovecraft prefers to keep things real.
Hired by the wealthy and mysterious Amos Hackshaw to locate and retrieve a highly valuable tome called the *Necronomicon*, Detective Lovecraft soon finds himself engaged in a deadly power struggle being waged in the criminal underworld of the city. Now all he has to do is stay alive, follow the clues, trust no one and stop the forces of an ancient evil from engulfing Earth.

A cult favorite for audiences attracted by in-joke references and classic Hollywood noir, HBO's *Cast a Deadly Spell* is an affectionate tongue-in-cheek celebration of two of its most beloved artistic industries—cinema and pulp fiction—combining the two and stirring the pot to produce a harmless commentary on the self-indulging, back-biting, superstitious and just plain strange folk that populate L.A.

It's the kind of jokey high concept movie that Hollywood loves to throw serious money at, but by doing so, usually end up ruining by forcing the filmmakers to compromise the wild abandon of their vision in favor of more linear storytelling; thankfully, that doesn't happen here. In fact, if there is to be a chief criticism (though with a film as playful as this—any feels curmudgeonly), it would be that its outpouring of ideas sadly dilute the narrative, and proceedings become a one-note satire, putting it a stone's throw from the status of a hidden gem that fans claim it to be.

Fred Ward leads the star-studded cast, playing the part of the Bogart-archetype gumshoe to perfection. David Warner and Clancy Brown provide good foil as the larger than life villains and Julianne Moore oozes sex appeal in one of her earliest roles as the de rigueur femme fatale and Lovecraft's old flame.

In a rare case (at least for TV movies) of there being equally distinguished talent behind the camera as in front of it, producer Gale Anne Hurd (*The Terminator*, *Aliens*) and director Martin Campbell (*The Mask of Zorro*, *Casino Royale*) prove themselves one hell of a creative team, effortlessly bringing writer Joseph Dougherty's eclectic vision to life without rendering it an incomprehensible screwball mess. Admittedly, the film lacks any real substance, but it's a modest price to pay for a good kick of entertainment.

How this madcap production was commissioned is anyone's guess, but one can fairly surmise it was a labor of love for those involved. In purely stylistic terms, it arguably owes much to the work of B-movie maestro Don Coscarelli (*Phantasm*, *The Beastmaster*) as it seamlessly weaves horror, comedy, science fiction, monsters, magic, and above all, sentimentalized history as a platform for the absurd.

Produced at the beginning of the nineties, just before the CGI boom that arrived with *Terminator 2* and *Jurassic Park*, the special effects are surprisingly acceptable, with just the right mix of excellent puppetry and models interspersed with digital work, that, though flawed by today's standards, fit the bogus schlock period setting to such a degree it almost feels intended.

It doesn't live up to the fanboy hype, but it is good fun and was deservedly rewarded a sequel—*Witch Hunt*—in 1994. [Kevin Hilton]

CITIZEN X

Director: Chris Gerolmo
Starring: Stephen Rea, Donald Sutherland, Max von Sydow, Jeffrey DeMunn
Airdate: February 25, 1995   Network: HBO

A true-life story detailing the horrific crimes of serial killer Andrei Chikatilo, and the attempt by the authorities to track him down.

Although the Home Box Office network is known for creating acclaimed, violent episodic dramas like *The Sopranos* (1999–2007) and *The Wire* (2002–08), they have also produced a number of television movies that are equally unflinching in exploring potentially contentious subjects. One such film is *Citizen X*, which focuses on a prominent serial killer case in Soviet

Russia from the 1980s and 1990s.

Citizen X begins with credits over a shot of some woods, followed by a tractor driver finding a dead body in a field. The corpse is brought to forensics expert Viktor Burakov (Stephen Rea), who immediately orders the police to search for clues around the field, which reveals multiple dead bodies. Burakov concludes that these bodies are the work of a serial killer and, after meeting a committee of officials, he is made a detective and put in charge of the "killer department" by Colonel Fetisov (Donald Sutherland) to investigate these murders.

The killer is revealed to viewers early on as a seemingly mild-mannered man named Andrei Chikatilo (Jeffrey DeMunn), whose meekness conceals a deeply disturbed mind. He is first shown meeting a girl at a train station, walking with her in the woods and quickly killing her. After this shocking act, Chikatilo is then seen coming home to his wife and children. However, in contrast to Burakov's happy domestic life, which gives the detective welcome relief from the grim case and his obstructive superiors, Chikatilo is bullied and humiliated at work, and finds no solace with his family.

While the film shows some incidents from the point of view of Chikatilo, the focus is mainly on the work of Burakov and Fetisov. Burakov's investigations are frequently undermined by administrative intransigence, with particularly fierce resistance from committee member Bondarchuk (Joss Ackland). While Burakov tries vainly to fight a system that hinders his efforts, Fetisov successfully operates in the system, because he understands the workings of the bureaucratic machine. As the investigation continues over many years, Burakov and Fetisov are aided in their work by a psychiatrist, Dr. Alexandr Bukhanovsky (Max von Sydow), who writes a report on the killer, dubbing him "Citizen X."

The film's style is restrained for the most part, with scenes playing out with the minimum of stylistic flourishes, yet there are some expressive visual and aural touches. Early on, the focus is on Burakov's hands as he examines various corpses and dictates his observations soberly into a microphone, the scene concluding with a reveal of his tear-stained face. Later, the sound of a screeching train, a mode of transportation that ties Chikatilo to his crimes, plays over a montage of Burakov's investigation.

Citizen X appeared in an era that popularized (and arguably glamorized) cinematic serial killers, most famously with Anthony Hopkins' portrayal of Dr. Hannibal Lector in *The Silence of the Lambs* (1991). However, *Citizen X* takes a more restrained tone toward its subject matter, resulting in a somber examination of a serial killer investigation, and showing the impact these crimes have on the investigators. [Martyn Bamber]

CLEAR HISTORY

Director: Greg Mottola
Starring: Larry David, Bill Hader, Phillip Baker Hall, Jon Hamm
Airdate: August 10, 2013   Network: HBO

 An ex-Marketing Executive is out for revenge when his old boss moves into the neighborhood.

Nathan Flomm (David) is a Marketing Executive and co-investor in a car company that is on the brink of revolutionizing the automobile. Finding himself intensely dissatisfied with the branding of the new product, he voluntarily resigns. However, by doing so, he makes the biggest mistake of his life. The new model car is a colossal success and Flomm's self-termination from the company makes national headlines. He leaves his career and reputation in tatters, changes his identity and starts a brand new life, settling quietly in Martha's Vineyard, Massachusetts.

Years later, after having found some peace on the island living in obscurity under the name of Rolly DaVore, his tranquil life is again disturbed by the appearance of his previous boss, Will Haney (Hamm). Will is now a multimillionaire who has decided to move into the neighborhood, thus re-instigating Flomm's sense of injustice, leading him to employ his friends in a scheme of revenge that soon begins to get ever more elaborate, and completely out of control.

Larry David, taking a page from Woody Allen's book, leads the kind of ridiculously all-star cast that's borderline show-off; and again, like Allen, wisely decides to write and perform his own character, keeping it close to audience expectations after his long running stint as television's most popular social agitator. The result is a mixed bag. While it never fails to entertain, it sadly lacks cohesion, feeling like (as it may well be) a sort of collection of left over lines and set-pieces from *Curb Your Enthusiasm*, or even a "thank you" gift to the fans of his hit series—a noble idea, but not wholly necessary.

The tried-and-tested formula from the TV show guarantees plenty of laughs (with David up to his familiar philosophizing about life's many frustrations), but delivers absolutely no surprises. Audiences expecting— and not unreasonably—to see the bar raised by David and his collaborators for a movie outing (albeit made for television), may find themselves a little disappointed that the underdog they love to champion is running out of new tricks, and recycling his old ones with almost embarrassing predictability.

The disproportionately (in terms of the material that some of them are provided) glitzy support cast includes other big names from the small screen, including Bill Hader (*Saturday Night Live*) and Danny McBride (*Eastbound and Down*). In addition, the already very talented ensemble is augmented by cinema stars such as Kate Hudson and Eva Mendes, who are just fine except for the fact that they are perhaps all too noticeably big fish in a small pond, with little to do but show up every now and then, clearly enthusiastic and pleased to be attached to the project, but ultimately surplus to requirements.

Conversely, the same certainly can't be said for Michael Keaton, ever impressive and almost unrecognizable in his get-up as a small-town yokel who is quick to befriend our misguided hero in his crusade for payback. It's a show stealing performance that generously doesn't steal the show—a wildman role that in a less generous actor's hands could easily demand too much attention. But Keaton—a veteran and professional, well versed in drama and comedy—proves brilliantly Stanislavski's observation that there really are no small parts.

Wholly unnecessary, but funny enough to justify the effort, Larry David fans would be remiss to pass it up. Yet, much as it pains me to say it, they'd be wise to curb their expectations. [Kevin Hilton]

GAME CHANGE

Director: Jay Roach
Starring: Julianne Moore, Woody Harrelson, Ed Harris, Peter MacNicol
Airdate: March 10, 2012   Network: HBO

 The story of how Sarah Palin might not have been the right choice to run for Vice-President in 2008.

It's the 2008 US Presidential elections and Republican candidate John McCain is seeking a viable running mate to improve his bid for the White House. At the eleventh hour, McCain's staff locates and approves Sarah Palin—the Governor of Alaska, and quite possibly the perfect woman for the job. At first look, her personality and her credentials check all the right boxes, but thrust into the lion's den of national politics and media scrutiny, it slowly begins to unravel that they may have made a huge mistake; and one that threatens not only to ruin their hopes for the Presidency, but also, the reputations of everyone involved in the campaign.

First off, it has to be said that movies based on public figures—especially living ones—are rarely satisfying, and examples in recent years have frequently disappointed. Screen depictions of famous subjects have a tendency to either over-sentimentalize the well-revered (as in Michael Mann's *Ali*) or seem produced with the aim of taking cheap-shots at easy targets (Oliver Stone's *W.*); which is why it's so refreshing to find that HBO's *Game Change* gets the tone just right.

In a movie set against the backdrop of political agendas and its focus on one that self-destructed so very publicly, writer Danny Strong (having previously penned *Recount* for the same network, a film that dealt with the aftermath of the 2000 election) has wisely approached the narrative with the utmost respect, not just for the audience, but more importantly, the characters of the subjects he's dramatizing. The result is that we are treated to an insider's (although understandably some details are particularly fictitious) view of the debacle that is altogether different from how the media had the rest of the world perceive it.

As is standard for HBO movies, the cast is comprised of actual A-list talent, not simply A-list names. Julianne Moore and Ed Harris give superlative portrayals of Palin and McCain respectively, and received Golden Globes for their efforts, whilst Woody Harrelson (also nominated in a supporting role) has rarely been better.

Arguably, Moore's performance is the most impressive, effortlessly uniting the disparate strands that we know of Sarah Palin the public figure and creating a character of depth and complexity, that, thankfully, could not be further removed from the ditzy caricature the viewer might reasonably expect. Had the latter been played, it might well have been amusing for a while, but the former is an infinitely braver choice and is executed to perfection, urgently reminding us that, yes, Palin may have been a weak choice as Vice-President, but by no means was she a weak woman. Whilst McCain, here presented as the serene eye of the storm, is equally well serviced by Harris in a suitably restrained performance that is just as memorable, albeit in a quieter, subtler way.

In the hands of lesser talents, *Game Change* could quite easily have excelled as a monotone political comedy that simply regurgitated the known facts of the true-life farce, but this is a far more ambitious production that is effective on several levels. It's humorous but does not use comedy as a device. It finger-points how the tactical misjudgments were made, without mockingly pointing its finger.

Apparently Palin and McCain denounced the movie, although reportedly, neither of them actually saw it; which is a shame, because considering how good it is, that's one mistake too many. [Kevin Hilton]

MAGIC BEYOND WORDS: THE J.K. ROWLING STORY

Director: Paul A. Kaufman
Starring: Poppy Montgomery, Emily Holmes, Janet Kidder and Andy Maton
Airdate: July 18, 2011   Network: Lifetime

Biopic based on the popular author J.K. Rowling, and her rise to fame.
In 1997 the first *Harry Potter* novel was published. Its unprecedented success would soon make its female author a household name and one of the

richest women in the UK. But long before the immense fame and fortune, there was the tumultuous and bittersweet journey of how Joanne Rowling grew up—facing hardships and setbacks along the way—from being a young girl with a dream of being a writer, to becoming a single mother, whose series of books about a boy wizard would inspire both children and adults the world over.

It had to happen sometime. And so it did; timed very neatly with the theatrical release of the final big screen *Harry Potter* epic, so too arrived this small screen celebration (it's too shamelessly laudatory to be considered a balanced biopic) of the woman that penned the phenomenon.

Probably of zero interest to children, this is squarely aimed at the older generation of fans and readers, an equally sizeable audience that look up to the achievements of Rowling in much the same way that the kids look up to Harry; that is to say, eyes wide with wonder. In fairness, there is perhaps a reasonably fascinating story to be told about how Rowling—fleeing an abusive relationship to raise a child by herself while living on welfare—was able to find the energies to summon forth one of the most beloved characters of recent literature. But this isn't it.

Informed from the outset that this is "An Unauthorized Biography," the sole objective of *Magic Beyond Words* seems merely to dramatize every character-building moment in her life, with nothing in between, in such a preposterously hamfisted way that in the end, for all its efforts at presenting Rowling as a hardworking, humble woman that went from rags to riches, does nothing so much as put her on a pedestal of Mandela-like proportions. Indeed, this could just as easily have been called, "Rowling: Long Walk to Publication." Of course, given that she is the main subject, generous amounts of flattery are to be expected, but martyrdom of this kind is cringeworthy.

Doing the best she can with the risibly stilted dialog is Australian actress Poppy Montgomery. Her task of carrying the picture—which she just about does—is hampered by the fact that no attempt whatsoever has been made to flesh out any of the supporting roles, and so it seems that everyone that Rowling ever encountered on her journey to success is either a help or a hindrance. Had she really been surrounded by such one-dimensional people, a fanciful imagination would be a necessity.

Dismissible by most and not nearly weighty enough to interest serious fans of the author, the episodic nature of how events in Rowling's life are presented does at least lend momentum to an otherwise unwatchable and pandering biopic—one that, despite its best efforts to prove otherwise, somehow feels as invented and contrived as one of Rowling's own books.
[Kevin Hilton]

ROADRACERS

Director: Robert Rodriguez
Starring: David Arquette, John Hawkes, Salma Hayek, William Sadler
Airdate: July 22, 1994   Network: Showtime

 Small-town rebel Dude Delaney is caught between his love for rock'n'roll, girlfriend Donna, the corrupt sheriff and his thuggish son.

"Imagine a movie like *Grease* or *Happy Days*, but where everyone dies at the end."[1]—That's how Robert Rodriguez originally pitched his episode of the 'Rebel Highway' series to the producers. Made for the Showtime channel in 1994, this series of ten low budget films aimed to remake American International Pictures' fifties' B-movies, spiced up for the nineties. It was created and produced by Debra Hill and Lou Arkoff, son of AIP producer Samuel Z. Arkoff, who had worked on the original movies. The directors involved included Joe Dante, William Friedkin and John Milius. When Wes Craven dropped out, Rodriguez was asked to direct *Roadracers*, but as everyone agreed that the 1959 original was dismal, he wrote a new story and only kept the title (which also happened with other films in the series).

Made between the low budget *El Mariachi* (1992) and the much bigger *Desperado* (1995), *Roadracers* gave Rodriguez his first taste of 35mm film and professional crews—the size and cost of which horrified him. Applying his lean and mean filmmaking style to a heavy, old school TV production set-up, Rodriguez shook it all up to deliver a fun, witty fifties' teen drama throwback full of youthful energy.

Written fast and furiously with Rodriguez's rock'n'roller friend Tommy Nix on a road trip down to Mexico, the film clearly riffs off *Rebel Without a Cause* (1955). David Arquette is Dude Delaney, the town's rebel picked on by the sheriff and embroiled in a feud with his son, Teddy Leather (Jason Wiles). But sexy girlfriend Donna (Salma Hayek in her first American role) wants him to join a band so they can get out of town. Great support comes from John Hawkes as the goofy best friend obsessed with *Invasion of the Body Snatchers* (1956).

The film has all the conventional elements of a fifties teen B-movie—the rival gangs, the girls, the drag race, the rumble—but it has lots of fun with them. Fetishistic about the cars, the greased hair, the leather jackets and the music of the period, it is also irreverently inventive. The rumble in the ice rink is the most hilarious example of this, and one of the most memorable scenes in the film: as the DJ plays Hasil Adkins's brilliantly inappropriate No More Hot Dogs (a song in which the Boone County hillbilly fantasizes about

---

1 Robert Rodriguez, *Roadracers: The Making of a Degenerate Hot Rod Flick*, p.3.

decapitating his girlfriend) for "couples' dance," Dude uses his hair grease as an incongruous weapon to spectacularly shake off Teddy's gang on the ice.

The excellent soundtrack also includes Charlie Feathers' Stutterin' Cindy, Gene Vincent's Race With The Devil, which Rodriguez said inspired the film, and Rumble by Link Wray, another key figure for the director, who hoped that his film would help "turn people back onto the legendary guitarist."[2] Together with his hyperkinetic editing style, Rodriguez's genuine love for fifties rock'n'roll is what gives his "rockabilly opera" an authentically raw energy amid all the pastiche.[3] [Virginie Sélavy]

SPRING BREAK SHARK ATTACK

Director: Paul Shapiro
Starring: Shannon Lucio, Riley Smith, Justin Baldoni, Brian Brown, Kathy Baker
Airdate: March 20, 2005   Network: CBS

 Spring break. Killer sharks. Just when you thought it was safe to turn on your TV...

This no brain entry into the animal (or fish as it were) gone amok genre, which surprisingly popped up on network television in the mid-2000s, contains many of the elements needed to make a decent campy horror flick: pretty girls in bikinis ... bad acting ... even worse dialog ... superfluous subplots ... a semi-name actor putting in (one) good day's work ... lots of sharks chowing down on teenagers ...

And, my friends, it was heaven.

After a boatload of women—who look like precursors to *The Real Housewives of Beverly Hills* (and who must surely be sending up *Desperate Housewives*, which this telefilm ran against)—end up on the bad side of a shark fin, our hero, Danielle (Lucio), is seen lying to her father about where she'll be during Spring Break before she boldly heads for the white sands of Florida, where she plans to expand her horizons and her legs. After she meets up with her friends, she quickly becomes the object of affection for two men: the pretty hunky but ultra-sleazy J.T. (Baldoni), and the Luke Perry wannabe, Shane (Smith). After a bit of heavy partying Danielle decides love will find a way, but she may not have the time as she soon discovers a school of tiger sharks are chowing away at the baked to perfection teens. I thought only Hammerheads swam in schools... But never you mind, because it's the more the merrier during this *Spring Break Shark Attack*.

CBS, a network whose most famous later telefilm output came via the highly regarded Hallmark Hall of Fame series, took a 180 degree turn in

2 Ibid, p.24.
3 Ibid, p.3.

2005 and gave their audiences a bit of a shock when they decided to chase ratings with B-movie magic. *Shark Attack* was just one of three CBS Movies of the Week that year that were relying on salacious premises and hip actors to attract a new crowd (the other two films were the middling *Locusts* with Lucy Lawless and *Category 6*). And they did a good job, too! Three more original TVMs appeared during the next season.

Riffing on fodder that would have been more appropriate on the Sci-Fi/SyFy Channel, it seems rather odd that this movie made its way all the way up the small screen food chain to a major network—and a network that primarily caters to an older audience. How it ended up there is anyone's guess but there was something so comforting about curling up to a throwback to the original Movie of the Week. Sure, this flick could never live up to the legendary TVMs of yesteryear, such as *Trilogy of Terror* or even *Shark Kill*, but it is heartwarming to see a network put down some change for a fun little horror movie. And, trust me, this was made on spare change. The very sparse special effects look like they were financed on the leftover CGI money from *CSI*. Yes, the special effects could have been much better, but they are perfectly at home among the tanned bait. [Amanda Reyes]

WHEN A STRANGER CALLS BACK

Director: Fred Walton
Starring: Carol Cane, Charles Durning, Jill Schoelen
Airdate: April 4, 1993   Network: Showtime

A stalker victimizes a teenage babysitter. She escapes, but he remains unapprehended. Years later she fears that he has returned.

When a Stranger Calls Back remains that rarest of things, especially in the horror genre—a sequel that may actually be better than the original. And yet, because of its TV movie standing, it's rarely seen.

This follow-up to 1979's *When a Stranger Calls* (which incidentally deserves its place alongside—and for my money even above—the George C Scott chiller *The Changeling* [1980] as one of the scariest movies that no one cares to mention) is a much more finely tuned thriller than its predecessor, whose modest reputation was based primarily on it's terrifying (and often imitated with lesser results) opening sequence.

Unsurprisingly, this movie opens with the same set-up that made the original so effective, and yet, it still holds up. The soft focus, cheaper lighting that is evident in most television movies (particularly from the late eighties and early nineties) means that we feel we are in a slightly warmer environment than the original film, whose look was dark, gritty and a whole lot less stylized. It is now more perhaps like our own homes.

The rest of the movie plays like a much more gripping version of a good *Murder, She Wrote* episode. That may put people off, but in this case it's intended as a compliment. The original film was accused by critics of tending, not so much to lose the plot, but to reveal that there simply wasn't one after the stellar opening sequence was over and done with. Here, it's as if director Fred Walton (returning again as writer/director) was particularly wary not to repeat the same mistake and invests a lot more in the second and third acts of the picture. He achieves this by bringing back the first movie's two leads (the ever impressive Carol Kane and the routinely excellent Charles Durning) and this time gives them something to do.

Whereas the opening sequence of the movie is rooted purely in the horror genre, the majority of it plays out like a Thomas Harris thriller, sans the gore. This is, of course, unsurprising, given the Oscar winning success of *Silence of the Lambs* (1991) just two years previously; its buzz still going strong when this movie was put into production.

At any rate, it would seem that the small screen is the best home for this particular *Stranger.* It's high time that audiences forget the nonsense of the big budget Hollywood remake of the original, re-discover this gem, and welcome the stranger back properly. [Kevin Hilton]

WITCH HUNT

Director: Paul Schrader
Starring: Dennis Hopper, Eric Bogosian, Penelope Ann Miller, Julian Sands
Airdate: December 10, 1994   Network: HBO

 H. Phillip Lovecraft returns as a private investigator in this cosmic tale of black magic mystery.

In this sequel to the cult favorite *Cast a Deadly Spell*, Dennis Hopper assumes the role of private eye H. Phillip Lovecraft, this time investigating the mysterious death of a Hollywood film executive at the hands of magic-wielding murderers.

Less fondly remembered than its 1991 predecessor and sorely missing the always underrated Fred Ward in the lead, it would be easy to dismiss *Witch Hunt* in advance as a cynically produced obligatory sequel-come-rehash that has been shipped out with the added attraction of a star name. But thankfully that's not the case. Not entirely, anyway.

Whilst one could certainly argue that Ward was a better fit in the lead than Hopper (who seems fairly befuddled throughout) and that the previous movie had a supporting cast better equipped in handling the genre-bending subject matter, this follow-up adventure is in many ways a more focused production, jettisoning the screwball elements of the first and replacing the madcap approach with a breezier pace that's more in step with the kind of fifties noir films it's emulating.

The movie's subplot concerning the government's attempts to discover and purge all practitioners of magic, riffs effectively on the infamous McCarthy witch hunts that particularly caused a stir throughout Hollywood, and by virtue of this obvious but appropriate subtext, there's a welcome attempt at gravitas to counterbalance the comic book nonsense that the first film was only too satisfied to revel in.

The best and most interesting thing about *Witch Hunt* is its direction. Paul Schrader, probably still best known for writing *Taxi Driver* despite earning his own journeyman status as a filmmaker of similarly gritty projects, is surprisingly assured at delivering what is essentially a straight-up genre film—in the fantasy mold, no less. As such, it remains the most out of kilter work on his filmography, and is worth your attention for that fact alone. As it transpires, it's actually one of his more fully realized efforts and, contrary to his other works (which tend to engage rather than entertain), is actually a lot of fun.

The special effects that were everywhere in the first film, return in this one; no doubt cutting edge when first released, they now look as crude as Ray Harryhausen's early ventures with stop-motion, but given the otherworldly premise and setting, the hokeyness—though certainly unintended—almost feels apt.

A fine sequel and companion piece to the original that should please fans of both Lovecraft mythology and retro cool. Thin on plot but full of energy, Schrader's confident direction results in a thoroughly enjoyable, if not especially noteworthy, slice of small screen entertainment, that, just like its predecessor, still awaits a DVD release. Shame. [Kevin Hilton]

SELECT
BIBLIOGRAPHY

Jon Anderson, TV Critic, *Chicago Tribune* (May 27, 1985).

Richard B. Armstrong & Mary Willems Armstrong, *Encyclopedia of Film Themes, Settings and Series*. Jefferson: McFarland, 2001.

M. Bevacqua, *Rape on the Public Agenda: Feminism and the Politics of Sexual Assault*. Boston: Northeastern University Press, 2000.

G. Edgerton, "High Concept Small Screen: Reperceiving the Industrial and Stylistic Origins of the American Made-for-TV Movie," *Journal of Popular Film and Television* 19 (1991).

J. Feuer, *Seeing through the Eighties: Television and Reaganism*. Durham, NC: Duke University Press, 1995.

I. Hacking, "The Making and Molding of Child Abuse," *Critical Inquiry* 17 (1991).

A. Heller-Nicholas, *Rape-Revenge Films: A Critical Study*. London: McFarland, 2011.

S. Hilgartner & C.L. Bosk, "The Rise and Fall of Social Problems: A Public Arenas Model," *American Journal of Sociology* 94 (1988).

P. Hutchings, "'I'm the Girl He Wants to Kill': The 'Women in Peril' Thriller in 1970s British Film and Television,'" *Visual Culture in Britain* 10 (2009).

Billy Ingram, "A Short History of the Movie of the Week," *TV Party*, www.tvparty. com/vaultmov.html (accessed Mar 25, 2016).

Paula Krebs, "Burning Bed Prompts Floods of Calls," *Off Our Backs* (Nov 1984). Pub: off our backs, inc. www.jstor.org/stable/25775203 (accessed Jan 1, 2013).

Alvin H. Marill, *Movies Made for Television: The Telefeature and the Mini-Series 1964–1979*. Westport: Arlington House, 1980.

Ron Miller, "Nominations made for 10 worst TV 'reunion' programs," *Bangor Daily News* (Apr 11, 1991).

Alan W. Petrucelli, "Original Cast to Reprise Their Roles in 'Return to Mayberry,'" *Herald-Journal* (Apr 6, 1986).

J. Read, *The New Avengers: Feminism, Femininity and the Rape-Revenge Cycle*. Manchester: Manchester University Press, 2000.

Robert Rodriguez, *Roadracers: The Making of a Degenerate Hot Rod Flick*. London: Faber & Faber, 1998.

L.J. Schulze, "Getting Physical: Text/Context/Reading and the Made-for-Television Movie," *Cinema Journal* 25 (1986).

Kerry Segrave, *Movies at Home: How Hollywood Came to Television*. Jefferson: McFarland, 1999.

Aaron Spelling. *A Prime Time Life: An Autobiography*. New York: St. Martin's, 1996.

Cobbett S. Steinberg, *TV Facts*. New York City: Facts on File, Inc., 1980.

Jeff Thompson, *The Television Horrors of Dan Curtis: Dark Shadows, The Night Stalker and other Productions, 1966–2006*. Jefferson: McFarland, 2009.

H. Wheatley, *Gothic Television*. Manchester: Manchester University Press, 2006.

A. Young, *The Scene of Violence: Cinema, Crime, Affect*. NY: Routledge-Cavendish, 2010.

CONTRIBUTOR NOTES

Martyn Bamber holds a BA (Hons) in Film and Television from the University of Westminster, London, and an MA in History of Film and Visual Media from Birkbeck, University of London. He has worked in film and television subtitling and translation for over ten years, and has written on film for various websites including *Close-Up Film* and *Senses of Cinema*.

Daniel Budnik's book, *Bleeding Skull!: A 1980s Trash-Horror Odyssey*, was published by Headpress. His second book, due out soon, covers 1980s action films. He co-hosts a podcast on made for TV movies with this book's editor. His writing can be found on the blog *Some Polish American Guy Reviews Things*. He lives in Los Angeles with his beautiful wife and many animals.

Jeff Burr is a noted filmmaker and made for television movie lover. He has directed Vincent Price (*From a Whisper to a Scream*) and Leatherface (*Texas Chainsaw Massacre III*), and he thinks *Bad Ronald* is a good time.

David Ray Carter is the author of *Conspiracy Cinema: Propaganda, politics and paranoia* from Headpress. He began writing about film in 2000. In addition to reviewing several thousand films, he has contributed essays to anthologies on topics as varied as comic books and professional wrestling. He lives in Dallas, Texas.

Jean-Paul Coillard is a long-time music, cinema and books fanatic who lives and works in Paris. Former journalist in the rock, metal and industrial press (*Rage Magazine*, *Elegy*, *Feardrop*), he has written books of fiction and biography (NIN, Rob Zombie, Slayer) and one book dedicated to the cinema of Alejandro Jodorowsky, written alongside the creator of *Santa Sangre* and *Holy Mountain*.

Tom Crites lived and worked back and forth across the US. He was actively involved in independent publishing for over twenty years and contributed much artwork and writing to zines until his untimely death in 2013.

DF Dresden is the owner of many fine Sharkskin suits. Currently residing in Dublin, Ireland, in a house made entirely out of guitars and VHS tapes.

Rich Flannagan has been a writer for several years now, and spends much of his time trying to reconcile his love for the films of Powell and Pressburger with his obsession with Rudy Ray Moore's no-budget Blaxploitation extravaganzas. He is the editor at *Videotape Swapshop*, a site devoted to the crappier side of film.

Paul Freitag-Fey is a freelance film writer whose work has appeared *in Cashiers du Cinemart*, *VideoScope* and *Shock Cinema*, and online at *Daily Grindhouse* and *Bright Lights Film Journal*. When not indulging in cinematic curiosities, he does computer stuff. He lives in a Chicago suburb with his husband, Sid, their dog-like cat Laszlo and their dog-like dog Roscoe.

Lee Gambin is a writer, author and film historian. He writes for *Fangoria*, *Shock Till You Drop*, *Delirium*, Warner Bros. and *Scream Magazine*. He has written the books *Massacred By Mother Nature: Exploring the Natural Horror Film*, *We Can Be Who We Are: Movie Musicals of the 1970s* and the soon-to-be released *The Howling: Studies in the Horror Film*. He runs Melbourne based film society Cinemaniacs and lectures on cinema studies, currently working on a lecture series called "Can You Dig It?: Tortured Young Men in Film from 1976–1986."

Todd Garbarini's love affair with horror began after catching a rerun of an NBC airing of Dan Curtis's *Burnt Offerings* in the summer of 1981. A writer for *CinemaRetro.com* and *HorrorNews.net*, he thrives on spooky made for TV movies from the 1970s, in addition to meeting in person those responsible for the on-screen fright fests that have fuelled his dreams for years.

John Harrison is a freelance writer based in Melbourne, Australia. His book on vintage adult paperbacks, *Hip Pocket Sleaze*, was published by Headpress in 2011. In 2013, he self-published *Blood on the Windscreen*, a booklet which examined the violent and notorious Driver's Education films produced in America between 1959-1975. He is currently working on several fiction and nonfiction projects, including a compendium of his late-90's fanzine *Reel Wild Cinema*!

Kier-La Janisse is a film writer and programmer, Editor-in-Chief of Spectacular Optical Publications, founding director of The Miskatonic Institute of Horror Studies and the Festival Director of Monster Fest in Melbourne, Australia. She is the author of *House of Psychotic Women: An Autobiographical Topography of Female Neurosis in Horror and Exploitation Films* and co-edited the books *KID POWER!* and *Satanic Panic: Pop-Cultural Paranoia in the 1980s*.

Kevin Hilton has been a lifelong fan of film and television. He has a BA Combined Honors degree in Film and Communication and has been a regular guest panelist on Cambridge radio's film review show. He currently lives in Cambridge, England.

David Kerekes is a founder of Headpress. He is co-author of the books *Killing for Culture* (revised and expanded in 2016) and *See No Evil*. He is the author of *Sex Murder Art: The Films of Jörg Buttgereit*, and has written extensively on popular culture. His meditation on family and the Italian Diaspora, *Mezzogiorno*, was published in 2012.

Chris Mikul is a Sydney-based writer and collector of curiosities. His books include *Bizarrism*, a compilation of articles from his long running zine of the same name, *TV Poems, Tales of the Macabre and Ordinary*, *The Cult Files* and *The Eccentropedia*. A second *Bizarrism* book will be published by Headpress in 2016.

Amanda Reyes is a writer who specializes in the beloved made for television movie. Her blog and companion podcast, *Made for TV Mayhem* covers everything from the Movie of the Week to Lifetime. Her other work has appeared on *Film Threat*, *Retro Slashers*, in *Butcher Knives and Body Counts: Essays on the Formula, Frights and Fun of the Slasher Film*, and in the magazine *Sirens of Cinema*.

Thomas Scalzo has written extensively for the film review website *notcoming.com*, focusing primarily on horror and cult films. He is also a co-author of *ShockOctober*, the latest in the ongoing *ShockMarathons* series of film review books dedicated to horror offerings from the 1970s and 1980s. A selection of reviews from this series can be found on *shockmarathons.com*.

Virginie Sélavy is the founder and editor of Electric Sheep, the online magazine for transgressive cinema. She has edited the collection of essays *The End: An Electric Sheep Anthology* and has contributed to *World Directory Cinema: Eastern Europe* and *Film Locations: Cities of the Imagination—London*. Her work has appeared in various publications, including *Sight&Sound*, the *Guardian* and *Frieze*.

Julian Upton has written on US and British film for publications such as *Filmfax*, *Bright Lights* and the *Journal of British Cinema and Television*. He is the author/editor of the Headpress books *Fallen Stars* and *Offbeat: British Cinema's Curiosities, Obscurities and Forgotten Gems*. He lives in Leicestershire, UK.

Lance Vaughan is a lifelong horror fan living in Philadelphia, Pennsylvania. He is co-creator of the website *Kindertrauma*, which focuses on exploring the films, books, and TV shows that scared us as children. His writing can be found in *Butcher Knives & Body Counts: Essays on the Formula, Frights & Fun of the Slasher Film* and *Mad Monster Magazine* and he has been interviewed by *The New York Times*. His hobbies include cat wrangling and reminding people of the things they've tried so very hard to forget.

Jennifer Wallis is a historian of medicine and science at the University of Oxford. She has previously contributed to Headpress titles *Offbeat: British Cinema's Curiosities, Obscurities, and Forgotten Gems* and *Gathering of the Tribe: Music and Heavy Conscious Creation*.

INDEX

Numbers in **bold** refer to films that are reviewed in full.

3rd Rock From The Sun 263
9½ Weeks 173
10.5 308
12 Angry Men **309**
21 Hours at Munich 213, 234
200 Motels 184
2001: A Space Odyssey 62

Accused, The 28n
Aces High 174
Action Jackson 307
Act of Violence 11
After Hours 222
Afterschool Special 108, 202, 261
Against Their Will: Women in Prison 66
Airplane! 175
Airport 175, 275, 276
Airport '77 155, 276
Alexander: The Other Side of Dawn 128
ALF 300
Alfred Hitchcock Hour, The 221
Alfred Hitchcock Presents 54
Ali 317
Aliens 144, 145, 314
All About Eve 290
All My Children 33, 288
All the Kind Strangers 67
All the Lonely People 52
All the President's Men 185
Amazing Stories 81
American Gothic 279. See also: This House Possessed
American Graffiti 124
American Idol 123
Amerika 225
Amityville: the Evil Escapes **226**
An American Werewolf in London 254
An Amish Murder **310**
Andromeda Strain, The 122
Andy Griffith Show Reunion: Back to Mayberry 74
Andy Griffith Show, The 10, 74
An Early Frost 70
Angels From Hell 127
Angels in America 308
A Nightmare on Elm Street 34
Animal House 140

Ants 22. See also: It Happened At Lakewood Manor
Apollo 13 124
Apple's Way 192
Arachnophobia 23
Are You Afraid of the Dark 302
Are You in the House Alone? **108**, 253, 265
Arizona Ripper, The 233. See also: Bridge Across Time
Armageddon 144
Arnold 114
As Good As Dead 39
As Good As It Gets 263
Assassin, The 50
Assault on Precinct 13 139
Assault on the Wayne **109**
Atlanta Child Murders, The 96
Atomic Dog 39
Attack of the Phantoms 170. See also: KISS Meets the Phantom of the Park
At the Earth's Core 97
Avengers, The 62
Awakening of Candra, The 30

Baby Monitor: Sound of Fear 41
Bad Blood 295
Badlands 212
Bad Ronald 8, 41, **110**, 125, 133
Bad Seed, The 20, 44, 172, **227**, 259
Baffled! **111**
Bag of Bones 77, 90
Bait, The 25, 28, 30
Bait, The **112**
Baltar's Escape 51
Banana Splits, The 191
Barnaby Jones 126
Baron Blood 223
Basic Instinct 298
Bates Motel **228**
Batman 59, 60, 151, 169
Bat People, The 155
Battlestar Galactica 50, 51, 276
Baxter 110
Baywatch 127
Beach Red 146
Beastmaster, The 314
Beasts Are On The Streets, The

21, 24
Beasts, The 191
Beauty and the Beast: A Concert on Ice 208
Bedeviled 142
Beer Fest 245
Bees, The 22
Beginning of the End 19, 222
Bermuda Depths, The 170, **113**
Best Little Girl In The World, The **229**
Beverly Hillbillies, The 67, 158
Beverly Hills, 90210 74, 298, 299
Beverly Hills Madam 70
Bewitched 10, 14, 15, 171
Big Bad Mama II 263
Big Doll House, The 63, 115
Big Driver 77
Bigfoot 201. See also: Snowbeast
Billy Two-Hats 264
Bionic Ever After? 271
Bionic Showdown 271
Birds II, The: Land's End 23, **311**
Birds of Prey 62, 223
Birds, The 19, 23
Black Christmas 136, 253
Black Dynamite 121
Black Gunn 119, 132
Black Noon **114**
Blackout 144
Black Widow Murders, The: The Blanche Taylor Moore Story 11
Blade 121
Bladerunner 238
Blindfold: Acts of Obsession 298
Blind Rage 198
Bling Ring, The **312**
Blood 223
Blood Link 111
Blood Song 141
Blue Knight, The 92
Body Language 39
Bonanza: The Next Generation 71
Born Innocent 43, 65, **115**, 129, 252
Born Losers, The 109
Bowery Blitzkrieg 141

Boys Next Door, The 284
Boys of St. Vincent, The 44, 47
Boys, The 300
Boy Who Drank Too Much,
  The 192, **231**
Brady Bunch, The 10, 128,
  184, 196, 201
Brady Girls Get Married, The
  264
Brainstorm 164
Breach of Conduct 39
Breakfast Club, The 312
Breaking Bad 271
Bride of the Reanimator 146
Bridge Across Time **232**
Bridge, The 151
Bring Me The Head Of
  Alfredo Garcia 206
Broken Silence 47n
Brotherhood Of The Bell, The
  117
Brother's Promise, A: The Dan
  Jansen Story 284
Bubba Ho-Tep 139
Buffy the Vampire Slayer 146,
  294
Bug 150
Bunny's Tale, A 30
Buried Alive 39, 40
Buried Alive II 39
Burning Bed, The **233**
By Dawn's Early Light 58, 106

Caddyshack II 198
Caged Heat 63, 115
Cage Without a Key 65
Caine Mutiny, The 109
Cake Eaters 141
California Kid, The 17
Call Me Anna 174
Call To Danger **118**
Capricorn One 118
Captain America 131
Carrie 133, 161, 206, 207
Case of Rape, A 11, 28, 30n,
  31, 107, 108, **120**
Case of the Baltimore Girls,
  The 52
Case of the Hillside Stranglers,
  The **235**
Casino Royale 314
Cast a Deadly Spell **313**, 323
Cat Creature, The 21
Category 6 322
Category 7: The End of the
  World 308
Cat People, The 21
Cat's Eye 87
Cave In! **237**, 264
Chained Heat 115
Changeling, The 322
Chariots of the Gods 145

Charlie's Angels 10, 68, 138,
  192, 193, 234, 259
Cheers 97, 274
Chevy Chase Show, The 208
Chevy Mystery Show, The 189
Child of Rage 44
Children of the Corn 90
Child's Play 81
Chiller 35
Chill Factor, The 123. See also:
  A Cold Night's Death
China Syndrome, The 221
Chinatown 151, 174
Chinese Typewriter, The 147
CHiPs 118, 147
CHiPs '99 73
Chisum 114
Chopping Mall 150
Christine 302
Chrome Soldiers 39
Circumstances Unknown 39
Citizen X **314**
City Beneath the Sea 145
City of the Living Dead 140
Clear History **316**
Climate for Murder, A 50. See
  also: Epitaph for a Swinger
Climax! 110
Cloning of Clifford Swimmer,
  The **121**
Clonus Horror, The 118
Cocoon 153. See also: Hawaii
  Five-0
Co-ed Call Girl **283**, 296, 298
Coffy 270
Cold Night's Death, A **121**
Columbo 107, 177, 178, 189,
  190, 267, 300
Coming Home 235
Commander USA's Groovy
  Movies 37
Commish, The 127
Companion, The 39
Concorde... Airport '79, The
  175
Condor **238**
Conjuring, The 307
Con, The 41
Conversation, The 118
Coogan's Bluff 200
Cool Breeze 112
Cool Hand Luke 174
Cotton Candy **123**
Countdown to Looking Glass
  58
Countdown to Terror 52
Crawlspace 110
Creepshow 79, 90
Cribs 313
Crowhaven Farm 6, 114, 115,
  125, 133
Crow, The 240

Cruise Into Terror **126**
Cruising 141
Crying Child, The 39
Cry Panic 126
Cry Rape 28
CSI: Crime Scene Investigation
  101, 322
Curb Your Enthusiasm 316
Curse of Dracula, The 49
Curse of the Black Widow 15
Curse, The 168
Cutter's Trail 131
Cylons Landed, The 52

Dallas 242
DA: Murder One, The 100
Danger Doberman 218. See
  also: Trapped
Dangerous Pursuit 39
Dark Angel 307
Darkman 240
Darkman II 240
Dark Night of the Scarecrow
  217, 225, **239**
Darkroom 54
Dark Secret of Harvest Home,
  The **92**
Dark Shadows 8
Daughter of the Mind **127**
Daughter of the Streets 43n
Dawn: Portrait of a Teenage
  Runaway 107, **128**
Day After, The 106, 225, **240**,
  270
Daydreamer, The 170
Day of the Animals 21, 22
Day of the Dolphin 174
Day of the Triffids 222
Days of Rage 50
Dead Air 39
Dead and Buried 187
Dead End 238
Dead in the Water 39, 41
Deadly Desire 41
Deadly Game 39, 41
Deadly Justice 270
Deadly Lessons 225, **241**
Deadly Messages 262
Deadly Pursuits 284
Deadly Relations 39
Deadly Silence, A 155
Dead of Night 211, 261
Dead Witness to a Killing 50
Death Car on the Freeway
  129
Death Chain 50
Death Follows a Psycho 52
Death of a Cheerleader 289.
  See also: Friend to Die For, A
Death of a Porn Queen 273
Death of a Salesman **243**
Death of Me Yet, The **130**

Death of Ocean View Park,
The **132**
Death of Richie, The 125, **133**
Death of the Incredible Hulk,
The 257, **284**
Death Squad, The 176
Deep Impact 144
Deep, The 113
Defenders, The 59
Deliberate Stranger, The 236
Deliverance 50, 240
Deliver Us From Evil 163
Demon Cop 145
Demon Murder Case, The **244**
Desperado 320
Desperate Hours, The 109
Desperate Housewives 321
Desperate Lives 108
Desperation 77
Destination Alcatraz 259. See
also: Kicks
Devil Dog: Hound of Hell 20,
24, **134**
Devil Rides Out, The 206
Devil Thumbs A Ride, The 156
Diagnosis Murder 127, 191
Diary of a Teenage Hitchhiker
43, 108
Dick Tracy 134
Dillinger 270
Dirty Dozen, The 223
Disaster on the Coastliner 17
Doberman Patrol 218. See
also: Trapped
Dobie Gillis 72
Dolls 90
Doll Squad, The 119, 145
Donna Reed Show, The 242
Don't Be Afraid of the Dark 8,
110, **135**
Don't Go to Sleep 225, **245**,
267
Don't Look Now 161
Don't Say a Word 39
Don't Talk to Strangers, 39
Don't Touch My Daughter 45
Double Indemnity 41
Double Jeopardy 155
Do You Know the Muffin
Man? 46, 47
Do You Remember Love 234
Dracula 8, 280
Dracula '79 49
Dracula's Dog 134
Dragnet 70, 71
Dr. Cook's Garden 11
Dressed To Kill 188
Dr. Franken 109
Dr. Giggles 240
Drive Like Lightning 41
Dr. No 176
Dr. Strange 60, 61, 62

Drying Up the Streets 295
Duel 6, 6n, 8, 17, **136**, 181,
197, 209
Dukes of Hazzard, The 69
Duplicates 39
Dying Room Only 209
Dying to Remember 39
Dynasty 39, 192
Dynasty: The Making of a
Guilty Pleasure 74

Earthquake 276
Eastbound and Down 316
Easy Rider 215
Ebony, Ivory and Jade **137**
Eerie, Indiana 302
Eight is Enough 32, 73, 225
Elephant in the Room 52
El Mariachi 320
Elvis **138**
Empire of the Ants 22, 189
Enter the Dragon 176
Enter the Ninja 175
Epitaph for a Swinger 50
ER 288
Escape **139**, 141
Escape from Bogen County 68
Escape from Sobibor **246**
Every Mother's Worst Fear 48
Evil Roy Slade 198
Evil Stalks This House 54, 55
Ewok Adventure, The **248**
Executioner's Song, The 155
Exorcist, The 20, 115, 117,
182, 187, 188, 210, 245
Experiment in Terra 51
Express to Terror 8
Eye Creatures, The 223

Face in the Crowd, A 10
Face of Evil **286**
Face of Fear, The **141**, 296
Face on the Milk Carton, The
287
Failure to Communicate 53
Fallen Angel **249**
Fall Guy, The 275
Fame 133
Fantasies 225, **252**, 279
Fantasy Island 232
Fatal Attraction 298
Fatal Encounter 238
Fatal Vision **95**, 245
Father Dowling Mysteries 311
Father Knows Best 70
Fat Tuesday 53
Fear No Evil 117, **142**, 279
Feast 119
Feminist and the Fuzz, The
107
Fer-de-Lance 16
Fifth Missile, The 134

Fire! **143**
Fire in Space 51, 52
Fire in the Sky, A **143**, 276
First Blood 268
Five Desperate Women 15
Flash, The 59
Flood! 132, 143, **144**
Flowers in the Attic 41
Food of the Gods 19
Forces of Evil 144
Forgotten, The 37, 39
Fort Apache The Bronx 155
Four Past Midnight 76, 81
Frankenstein's Daughter 109
Friday the 13th Part VI 86
Friday the 13th: The Final
Chapter 294
Friendly Fire 291
Friends 'Til the End **290**
Friend to Die For, A **288**
Fright Night 76, 81
Frogs 19, 238
Frogs for Snakes 145
From Russia With Love 134
Frosty the Snowman 113
Fugitive, The 16
Fuller House 74
Full House 74
Full Metal Jacket 219
Fury, The 221

Galactica 1980 50, 51, 52
Galactica Discovers Earth 52
Galaxy Of Terror 200
Galyon 143
Gambler, The 216
Gamblers, The 211
Game Change **317**
Gargoyles 134, **145**
Gay Deceivers, The 127
General Hospital 53, 252, 259
Gentle Savage 224
Georgia Peaches, The 69
Get Christie Love! 127
Ghost and Mrs. Muir, The 125
Ghost Rider 109
Ghoulies III: Ghoulies Go to
College 231
Gidget's Summer Reunion 71
Gilligan's Island 71, 158
Girl From Mars, The 245
Girl in the Empty Grave, The
146
Girl Most Likely To…, The
147, 213
Girl Next Door, The **291**
Glove, The 109, 163
Go Ask Alice 43, 146, **149**,
266
Godfather, The 52
Godfather, The (miniseries).
See: Godfather, The

God Is My Co-Pilot 238
Golden Cage, The 229
Golden Gate Murders, The
   150
Golden Girl 144
Golden Girls, The 15, 208
Golden Years 77, **78**
Goliath Awaits **96**
Good Against Evil 142
Goodnight, My Love **151**
Good, the Bad and the
   Priceless, The 53
Good Will Hunting 285
Goonies, The 191
Graduate, The 243
Graduation Day 126
Gramps 188
Grand Theft Auto 123
Grease 129, 147, 188, 320
Great Escape, The 206
Green Acres 67
Griff 52
Grifters, The 38
Grizzly 19, 200
Grounds for Murder 299. *See
   also:* Only Way Out, The
Growing Pains 275
Guilty Conscience 177
Gunsmoke 225
Guyana: Crime of the Century
   98
Guyana Tragedy: The Story of
   Jim Jones **98**, 216

Halloween 136, 188, 203
Handgun 120
Hand of God, The 51
Hanged Man, The 111
Hang 'Em High 264
Hanging by a Thread 199
Happy Birthday to Me 262
Happy Days 32, 49, 176, 201,
   320
Harness, The 238
Harold and Maude 228
Harpy 140
Harry Black 264
Harry O 16, 117, 199
Harry Potter 319
Hart to Hart 73
Haunted, The 280, **292**
Haunting of Hill House, The
   77
Haunting of Sarah Hardy,
   The 38
Haunts of the Very Rich 11, 15
Have Gun—Will Travel 152
Hawaii Five-O 141, **152**, 160
Healers, The 222
Heartbreak Hotel 139
Heat 260
Heatwave! **154**

Hebrew Hammer 211
Hefner Unauthorized 41
Hell's Bloody Devils 174
Hell to Pay 126
Helter Skelter **100**, 119
Herbie Goes Bananas 156
Here Comes Peter Cottontail
   170
Heroes 101
Hey, I'm Alive **155**
Hider in the House 41
High Desert Kill 38, 39
High Rollers 53
Highway to Heaven 188
Hills Have Eyes, The 32, 34
Hillside Strangler, The 236
His Bodyguard 39
Hitcher, The 156
Hitch Hike 156
Hitchhike! **155**
Hit Lady 199
Hobbit, The 113
Hog Wild 119
Hollow Point 176
Hollywood Detective, The 38
Hollywood Wives 253
Home for the Holidays 9, 9n,
   156
Hondo 114
Honey West 239
Honky 223
Horror At 37,000 Feet **157**,
   175
Hostage Flight 121
Hostages 53
Hotline **253**, 225
Hound of the Baskervilles,
   The **159**
House of Frankenstein **101**
House of Wax 307
House on Greenapple Road
   50
House That Would Not Die,
   The 156
Howie And Rose 112
Howling in the Woods, A 14,
   160, 161
Human Feelings 187
Hunter 232
Hurricane 132
Hurt Locker 296
Hush Little Baby Don't You
   Cry 47n
Hysterical 263

Ice Castles 117
I, Desire 10, **254**
I Dream of Jeannie 14, 72,
   160
I Dream of Jeannie: Fifteen
   Years Later 72
If Looks Could Kill 284

I Know What You Did 258
I'm Dangerous Tonight 38, 39
Impact 144
Inchon 199
Incredible Hulk, The 169
Incredible Hulk Returns, The
   256
Indictment: The McMartin
   Trial 47
Initiation of Sarah, The **161**,
   262
Inmates: A Love Story 66
Inn of the Damned 143
Interview with the Vampire
   84
In the Deep Woods **293**
Intimate Agony 270
In Trouble 242
Intruders 134
Invaders, The **102**, 193
Invasion of Carol Enders, The
   163
Invasion of the Body Snatchers
   294, 320
Invasion U.S.A. 56
Invitation to Hell 33, 34, 35
I, Robot 296
Iron Fist 59
Ironside 127, **164**
I Saw What You Did 225, **257**
Island at the Top of the World
   224
Island Claws 198
Isn't It Shocking? **165**
I Spit on Your Grave 25, 191
IT 75, **79**
It Couldn't Happen to a Nicer
   Guy 30
It Happened At Lakewood
   Manor 22
It Lives Again 144
It's a Wonderful Life 186
It's My Party 145

Jackson County Jail 68, 201
Jade 144
Jagged Edge 211
Jake Spanner, Private Eye 38
Java Tiger, The 53
Jaws 19, 113, 132, 168, 188,
   196, 200, 201, 264
Jaws 2 224
Jaws 3 196
Jealousy Factor, The 50
Jericho Fever 39
Joe Panther 141
Joe Pyne Show, The 118
Juggernaut 53
Jungle Raiders 163
Jurassic Park 145, 311, 314
Justice League of America 62

Kansas City Massacre 18
Karate Kid, The 280
Kaw 174
Kicks 242, 252, **258**, 279
Killdozer 6, 143, **166**
Killer Bees, The 19, 20, 24
Killer On Board **168**
Killer's Delight 164, 238
Killers, The 5n
Killer's Three 127
Kill Point 156
Kindred, The 150
Kingdom Hospital 77
King Kong 19
King of Comedy 259
King of the Pack 67
Kiss Meets the Phantom of
the Park **169**
Kiss the Girls 39
Kiss the Sky 280
Knight Rider 239
Knight Rider 2000 73
Knots Landing 15, 32, 74, 112
Knots Landing: Back to the
Cul-de-Sac 74n
Kojak 72
Kunoichi 53

L.A. Confidential 146
Ladies of the Big House 63
Ladies They Talk About 63
Langoliers, The 76, **80**, 81
Last Ballad, The 52
Last Bride of Salem, The 114
Last Dinosaur, The 113, **170**
Last House on Dead End
Street, The 142
Last House on the Left 32, 33
Last Seduction, The 38
Last Unicorn, The 170
L.A. Takedown **259**
Late, Great Planet Earth, The
58
Laverne and Shirley 49, 74
Law and Order 101
Legend of Bigfoot, The 201
Legend of Hell House, The
193
Legend of Lizzie Borden, The
11, 14, **171**, 279
Legmen 53
Lenny 185
Lethal Vows **294**, 300
Let's Scare Jessica to Death
231
Liar, Liar: Between Father and
Daughter 44, 45n, 47
Like Normal People **172**
Lipstick 120
Little Darlings 128
Little Girl Who Lives Down the
Lane, The 110, 212

Little House on the Prairie
262
Live and Let Die 168
Living Legends 51
Living Proof: The Hank
Williams Jr. Story 242
Locusts 322
Logan's Run 183, 233
Long Patrol, The 51
Look What Happened to
Rosemary's Baby **174**
Lost 289
Lost Boys, The 84
Lost Warrior, The 51
Love Boat, The 147, 191
Love Finds A Home 263
Love Me Deadly 223
Love Me Tender 139
Loves of Dracula, The 49
Luke Cage 59

M.A.D.D: Mothers Against
Drunk Driving 126
Mad Monster Party? 170
Mafu Cage, The 269
Magic Beyond Words: The J.K.
Rowling Story **318**
Magnificent Warriors, The 52
Mahogany 293
Malpertius 111
Maltese Falcon, The 151
Mama's Family 301
Man Called Horse, A 203
Maniac Cop 121
Mannix 117, 127, 191
Man Trap 150
Manufactured Man, The 50
Man Who Haunted Himself,
The 121
Man with Nine Lives 51
Marathon Man 118, 185
Marilyn: The Untold Story 155
Marvin Purvis, G-Man 18
Mary Tyler Moore Show, The
74
M*A*S*H 214, 240
Mask of Fu Manchu, The 22
Mask of Zorro, The 314
Master Ninja, The 53. See
also: Master, The
Master, The 53
Maternal Instincts 41
Matlock 211
Maverick 71
Max 53
Mayday at 40,000 Feet! **174**
Mazes and Monsters 108, 223
McCloud 17
McMillan and Wife 107
Medium Cool 192
Melvin Purvis G-MAN 8
Men of the Dragon **176**

Meteor 144
Miami Vice 239, 260
Midnight Cowboy 243
Midnight Express 141
Midnight Hour, The **261**
Midnight Offerings **262**
Midsomer Murders 311
Mike Hammer 239
Miles, the Angel 187. See
also: Human Feelings
Miracle on I-880 **295**
Miracle on the 17th Green
308
Missile 58
Mission: Impossible 119, 160,
239
Mod Squad, The 127, 215
Mommie Dearest 188
Mom, the Wolfman and Me
263
Mongrel 134
Monkees, The 127
Monolith 206
Monster Dog 134
Monsters 54
Monster Squad, The 102
Moon of the Wolf 68
Moonshine County Express
198
Mortuary 22
Mother, May I Sleep with
Danger 283, 284, **296**
Mountain Justice 67
Mr. Ben 111
Mr. Majestyk 198
Ms.45 25
Munsters, The 225
Murder 101 39, 40
Murder by Natural Causes
177
Murder By Proxy 50
Murder in Peyton Place 71
Murder on the Rising Star 51
Murder, She Wrote 126, 323
My Antonia 41
My Favorite Martian 300
My Giant 222
My Kidnapper, My Love 212
My Stepson, My Lover 41, 287
Mysterious Island of Beautiful
Women 8
Mysterious Monsters, The 145
Mystery Science Theater 3000
53
My Sweet Charlie 177

Naked City 125
Naked Prey, The 146
Nanny, The 93
Nashville Beat 145
NBC Follies 186
Near Dark 84

Nevada Smith 200
New Jack City 168
New Leave it To Beaver, The 72
Nick Fury: Agent of SHIELD 60, 61, 62
Night and the City 141
Night Drive 182. See also: Night Terror
Night Eyes 298
Night Fall 263
Night Flight 37
Night Gallery 127
Night Games 156
Nightmare in Badham County 10, 64, 65, 67, 69
Nightmare on Elm Street, A 90
Nightmares and Dreamscapes 77
Night of the Comet 121
Night of the Grizzly 201
Night of the Lepus 19
Night Shift 86
Night Stalker, The 7, 8, 9, 16, 156, **178**, 180, 181, 183, 209, 220, 255
Night Strangler, The 16, **180**, 183, 220
Night Terror **181**
Night the Bridge Fell Down, The 237, **264**
Night Tide 135
No Blade of Grass 57
No Child of Mine 143
No Place to Hide 10, 156, **264**
Norliss Tapes, The 158, **182**
Normal Heart, The 308
North and South 92
Nurse 190
Nurses on the Line: the Crash of Flight 7 175
Nuts 264

Obsessed **298**
Octopussy 57, 106
Odd Couple, The 186, 203
Office Space 96
Office, The 294
O Lucky Man 111
Omega Man, The 120
Omen, The 20, 21, 191, 210
Once is Not Enough 50. See also: Double Jeopardy
One Dark Night 86
One Day at a Time 74
One False Move 38
One Step Beyond 110
Only Way Out, The **299**
Other Victim, The 31
Our Town 82
Outer Limits, The 200

Outfoxed: Rupert Murdoch's War on Journalism 235
Out of Annie's Past 41
Out of Darkness 96
Outside Chance 68
Over the Hill Gang, The 9

Pacific Heights 299
Pack, The 19
Panic Button 132
Panic on the 5:22 127
Parallax View, The 118
Parasomnia 141
Past Midnight 40
Peking Encounter 132
Penny's Old Boyfriend 55
People Across the Lake, The **266**
People vs. Inez Garcia, The 27
Perfect Bride, The 41
Perfect Crime 41
Perfect Daughter, The 41
Perfect Strangers 81
Perils of Pauline, The 49
Perry Mason 70, 73, 165, 225
Petrified Forest, The 38
Petrocelli 201
Pets 168
Pet Sematary 90, 287
Petticoat Junction 67
Phantasm 314
Phantom Empire, The 49
Phantom Of The Paradise 211
Phase IV 22
Pieces 22, 176
Pin 222
Piranha 211
Place to Call Home, A 53
Planet of the Apes 110, 117, 171
Play it Again, Sam 151
Point, The **184**
Poltergeist 90, 226, 246
Poor Devil **186**
Poseidon Adventure, The 276, 308
Possessed, The **187**
Postman Always Rings Twice, The 42
Pray for the Wildcats 10, 11, 17, 150, **188**
Praying Mantis 39
Predator 145
Prelude To A Kiss 168
Premature Burial 176
Prescription: Murder **189**. See also: Columbo 177
Prime Target 188
Profiler 146
Prognosis Homicide 50
Project: ALF **300**
Prom Night 265

Prophecy 200n
Prototype **267**
Psychic Killer 145
Psycho 156, 195, 200, 228, 266, 293
Psycho 2 81, 143
Psycho IV: The Beginning 87

Quantum Leap 239
Queen Kong 206
Quicksilver Highway **301**

Raging Bull 281
Raise the Titanic 276
Raising Caine 263
Raising Dead 140
Rambo III 56
Rampage: The Hillside Strangler Murders 236
Ransom for a Dead Man 190. See also: Columbo
Rape and Marriage: The Rideout Case 28, 29, 31
Rape of Richard Beck, The 30, 31, **268**
Rape Victims, The 27
Rats, The 24
Rawhead Rex 144
Reachout 253. See also: Hotline
Real Housewives of Beverly Hills, The 321
Rear Window 203, **302**
Rebel Without a Cause 320
Recount 318
Red Dawn 56, 106
Rehearsal for Murder 177, 267, 291
Repulsion 206
Return of Marcus Welby M.D., The 71
Return of Perry Mason, The 225
Return of Starbuck, The 51
Return of the Beverly Hillbillies 71
Return of the Incredible Hulk, The 285
Return of the Jedi 248, 249
Return of the Mod Squad 224
Return of the Six Million Dollar Man and the Bionic Woman 72, **270**
Return, The 184. See also: Norliss Tapes, The
Return to Mayberry 70, 73, 225
Revenge for a Rape 27, **190**
Revenge of the Stepford Wives, The **271**, 276
Rhoda 289
Rhode Island Murders, The

244. See also: Demon Murder Case, The
Ricochet 264
Ride Beyond Vengeance 114
Rifleman, The 158
Ritual of Evil 143
Rivals 110
Roadracers **320**
Road Warrior, The 57, 241
Roar 22
Rockabilly Baby 211
Rock-A-Bye Baby 223
Rock 'n' Roll High School 124
Rock 'n' Roll Mom 156
Rocky 279
Rocky IV 56
Rollercoaster 132
Roller Revolution 295
Rolling Man 17
Romance Theatre 54
Roots 291
Rosemary's Baby 23, 95, 174, 210, 288, 309
Rose Red 77, 77n
Route 66 72
Ruckus 126
Rudolph, the Red-Nosed Reindeer 113, 170
Runaway Father 143
Runaway Jury 39

Sabrina, the Teenage Witch 294
Salem's Lot 75, 77, **82**
Santa Claus is Coming to Town 170
Sarah T.--- Portrait of a Teenage Alcoholic **191**, 232
Satan's School for Girls 107, **192**
Satan's Triangle 8, **193**
Saturday Night Live 316
Savage Bees, The 23
Savages 10, 63
Saved by the Bell 290
Scooby Doo Where Are You! 193, 229
Scorpion 200
Scream 102, 254, 307
Screaming Woman, The 11
Scream of the Wolf 8
Scream, Pretty Peggy **195**
Searchers, The 249
Seconds 121, 222
Secret Empire, The 49
Secret Night Caller, The 11, **196**, 253
See How They Run 5, 107
Sensitive, Passionate Man, A 16
Seven in Darkness 9, 9n, **197**
Shaft 216

Shark Kill 8, 322
Shattered Innocence **273**
Shattered Silence 221. See also: When Michael Calls
Shattered Trust 45
Shazam 207
She Devils in Chains 138. See also: Ebony, Ivory and Jade
Sheriff, The 28, 29
She's Dressed to Kill **198**, 242
She Waits 266
Shield, The 101
Shining, The 76, 77, **84**, 86
Shogun 55
Shootist, The 126
Shrunken Heads 132
Silence of the Lambs, The 315, 323
Silent Witness 28, 28n
Simon, King of the Witches 127, 142
Simpsons, The 272
Single White Female 290
Sisters 146
Six Million Dollar Man, The 168, 201
Skyway to Death 199
Sleepwalkers 87
Sliver 203
Smash-Up on Interstate 5 10
Smile Jenny, You're Dead 16, **199**
Snapdragon 41
Snowbeast **200**
Snow Kill 39
Sob Sisters, The 300
Sole Survivor 17
Someone I Touched **201**
Someone's Killing the World's Greatest Models 199. See also: Dressed To Kill
Someone's Watching Me! **202**, 253
Something about Amelia 44, **274**
Something Evil **204**
Sometimes They Come Back 77, **86**
Son of the Six Million Dollar Man 270
Sopranos, The 309, 314
Sorry, Wrong Number 39
Special Bulletin 58, 106
Specter On The Bridge, The 150. See also: Golden Gate Murders, The
Spectre 145, **205**
Speed Trap 112, 145
Spell, The **206**, 262
Spies Like Us 56, 57
Spin 295
Split Second for an Epitaph

165
Spring Break Shark Attack 308, **321**
Spy Hard 205
Squeeze, The 245
Sssss 198
Stand, The 76, 85, **87**
Starcrossed 259
Starflight One 275. See also: Starflight: The Plane that Couldn't Land
Starflight: The Plane that Couldn't Land **275**
Star Trek 111, 201, 213
Star Wars 50, 187, 200, 207, 208
Star Wars Holiday Special **207**, 248
State of the Union 53
Statutory Theft 55
Stella Dallas 41
St. Elmo's Fire 53
Stepfather, The 259
Stepford Children, The **276**
Stepford Husbands, The 112, **304**
Stepford Wives, The 305
Still the Beaver 70, 72
Stingray 223
Stone Cold 307
Stonestreet: Who Killed the Centerfold Model 14
Stop at Nothing 44, 45, 47
Stop Susan Williams 49
Storm of the Century 77, **89**
Strange and Deadly Occurrence, The 10
Strange Possession of Mrs. Oliver, The 13, **208**
Stranger in Our House 32, 33, 34, 68
Strangers in 7A, The 10, 280
Stranger Within, The 14, **210**
Straw Dogs 185, 243, 266
Streetcar Named Desire, A 110
Street Killing **211**
Streets of San Francisco 126
Striptease 112
Studio One 118
Substitute, The 39
Such Dust as Dreams are Made Of 199. See also: Harry O
Suicide's Wife, The 206
Summer of Fear 32, 33, 35
Summer of Fear 68. See also: Stranger in Our House
Sunset Blvd. 19
Superman: The Movie 169
Super Password 138
Supertrain 8

Surf Ninjas 238
Surviving 108
Survivor 295
Suspiria 193
Swarm, The 22
Sweet Hostage 17, 148, **212**
Sweet, Sweet Rachel 15
Swinging Barmaids 176

Tails You Live, Heads You're
   Dead 39, 42
Take the Celestra 51
Tales from the Crypt 81
Tales from the Darkside 54, 75
Tales of the Haunted 54
Tall, Dark and Deadly 42
Tapeheads 130
Tarantulas: The Deadly Cargo
   19, 23
Targets 153
Taste of Evil, A 265
Taxi Driver 324
Teenage Mutant Ninja Turtles
   185
Tenth Level, The **213**
Terminator 2 314
Terminator, The 145, 314
Terror Among Us 176
Terror at London Bridge 233
   See also: Bridge Across Time
Terror at the Wax Museum
   114
Terror in the Sky 175
Terror on the 40th Floor 144,
   190
Terror on the Beach 17
Testament 106
That Certain Summer 17, 107,
   177, 267
Them! 19
Then Came Bronson **214**
Thief **215**
Thing, The 122
Thirteen Women 22
This Gun for Hire 39
This House Possessed 225,
   242, 252, **277**
Thorn Birds, The 92
Threads 57, 58, 106, 241
Three's Company 294
Thriller 54, 261
Till Dad Do Us Part 55
Time after Time 232
Time for Timer 185
Time Machine, The 201
Tingler, The 201
Titan, The 50
To Catch a Killer 236
To Kill a Clown 111
Tommyknockers, The 76, **90**
Too Close for Comfort 269
Too Scared to Scream 190

Top Gun 56
Touch of Evil 131
Tour of Duty 146
Towering Inferno, The 143,
   264
Trailmakers, The 223
Trapped **217**, 304
Trap, The 174
Trial of the Incredible Hulk,
   The 256, 257, 285
Tribes **218**
Trilogy of Terror 6, 8, 13, 163,
   211, **219**, 322
Troll 259
TRON 231
Trucks 77
Turbulence 176
Turnabout 55
Turn Back The Clock 238
Twilight Zone, The 35, 36, 54,
   75, 76, 81, 158, 210, 305, 306
Twilight Zone: Rod Serling's
   Lost Classics **305**
Twin Peaks 78
Twins 223
Twisted Desire **306**
Two-Minute Warning 175

Uncanny, The 126
Under the Dome 77
Under The Influence **279**
Unspeakable Acts 47n
Up All Night 37

V 104
Vacation in Hell, A 8, 16, 291
Vampira 206
Vampire 12
Victims for Victims: The
   Theresa Saldana Story **281**
Violation of Sarah McDavid,
   The 29
Visions 140, 143
Viva Knievel 176
Voyage 40
Voyage Into Evil 126. *See also:*
   Voyage Into Evil
Voyage of the Damned 112

W. 317
Wacky World of Mother
   Goose, The 170
Wagon Train 239
Wait Until Dark 268
Waltons, The 73, 262
WarGames 57, 106
Warlords of the Deep 97
Web of Deceit 39, 168
Weekend of Terror 8
West Wing, The 301
What A Carve Up! 111
Whatever Happened to Baby

Jane? 195
When a Stranger Calls 253,
   257, 304
When a Stranger Calls Back
   304, **322**
When Danger Follows You
   Home 41
When Michael Calls **221**, 253
When She Says No 28
When the Shouting Dies 50
Where Have All The People
   Gone? **222**
Where's the Money, Noreen?
   41
While Justice Sleeps 45, 45n
White Lie 39
Whiteout 307
Who's the Boss 172
Why My Daughter? 43n
Wicker Man, The 93
Wild Bill 188
Wild Orchid 173
Wild Women **223**
Willard 19
Willow B: Women In Prison
   176
Winds of War 8
Winter Kill 211
Wire, The 314
Wishmaster 277
Witches, The 93
Witch Hunt 314, **323**
Witness 311
Wizard of Oz, The 165, 262
Women in Chains 66
Women's Prison 66
Wonder Woman 169, 201,
   253
World of Dracula 49
World War III 57, **105**, 225
Worst Crime, The 50
Wrecking Crew, The 119

Xanadu 235
X-Files, The 16, 74, 183, 184

Year Without a Santa Claus,
   The 170
Yellowbeard 150
Yin And Yang Of Mr. Go, The
   176
You'll Never See Me Again
   223
Young Frankenstein 202
Young Lords, The 51
Young Love, First Love 108

Zodiac 264
Z.P.G. 58

A HEADPRESS BOOK
First published by Headpress in 2016

[email] headoffice@headpress.com

ARE YOU IN THE HOUSE ALONE?
A TV Movie Compendium 1964–1999

Text copyright © Amanda Reyes & individual contributors
This volume copyright © Headpress 2016
Cover design: Mark Critchell <mark.critchell@googlemail.com>
Book design & layout: Ganymede Foley
Headpress diaspora: Thomas McGrath, Caleb, David, Giuseppe

Publisher note: The reviews of Night Terror and Trapped by Thomas Scalzo contained here
originally appeared on Not Coming to a Theater Near You (NotComing.com).
The publisher would like to thank Gary Ramsay and Julian Upton for the germ of the idea
that became this book.

The moral rights of the authors have been asserted.

A CIP catalogue record for this book is available from the British Library

978-1-909394-44-5   ISBN PAPERBACK
978-1-909394-45-2   ISBN EBOOK
HARDBACK   NO-ISBN

1 HEAD PRESS Est 1991

WWW.WORLDHEADPRESS.COM
the gospel according to unpopular culture
Special editions of this and other books are available exclusively from Headpress

CPSIA information can be obtained
at www.ICGtesting.com
Printed in the USA
FFOW01n0846170617
36702FF

9 781909 394445